Lloyd J. Ogilvie General Editor

THE
PREACHER'S
COMMENTARY

GALATIANS, EPHESIANS, PHILIPPIANS,
COLOSSIANS, PHILEMON

Maxie D. Dunnam

THOMAS NELSON PUBLISHERS
Nashville

The Preacher's Commentary Series, Volume 31: *Galatians, Ephesians, Philippians, Colossians, Philemon.* Copyright © 1982 by Word, Inc.

Published in Nashville, Tennessee, by Thomas Nelson, Inc.

Library of Congress Cataloging in Publication Data

The preacher's commentary (formerly The communicator's commentary).

  Includes bibliographical references.
  Contents: v. 31. Galatians, Ephesians, Philippians, Colossians,
  Philemon/Maxie D. Dunnam
  1.Bible. N.T.—Commentaries—Collected works.
I. Ogilvie, Lloyd John. II. Maxie D. Dunnam.

BS2341.2.C65   225.7'7   81–71764
ISBN 0-7852-4806-4   AACR2

HB 07.01.2021

Printed in the United States of America

CONTENTS

EDITOR'S PREFACE

God has called all of His people to be communicators. Everyone who is in Christ is called into ministry. As ministers of "the manifold grace of God," all of us—clergy and laity—are commissioned with the challenge to communicate our faith to individuals and groups, classes and congregations.

The Bible, God's Word, is the objective basis of the truth of His love and power that we seek to communicate. In response to the urgent, expressed needs of pastors, teachers, Bible study leaders, church school teachers, small group enablers, and individual Christians, the Preacher's Commentary is offered as a penetrating search of the Scriptures to enable vital personal and practical communication of the abundant life.

Many current commentaries and Bible study guides provide only some aspects of a communicator's needs. Some offer in-depth scholarship but no application to daily life. Others are so popular in approach that biblical roots are left unexplained. Few offer compelling illustrations that open windows for the reader to see the exciting application for today's struggles. And most of all, seldom have the expositors given the valuable outlines of passages so needed to help the preacher or teacher in his or her busy life to prepare for communicating the Word to congregations or classes.

This Preacher's Commentary series brings all of these elements together. The authors are scholar-preachers and teachers outstanding in their ability to make the Scriptures come alive for individuals and groups. They are noted for bringing together excellence in biblical scholarship, knowledge of the original Greek and Hebrew, sensitivity to people's needs, vivid illustrative material from biblical, classical, and contemporary sources, and lucid communication by the use of clear outlines of thought. Each has been selected to contribute to this series because of his Spirit-empowered ability to help people live in the skins of biblical characters and provide a "you-are-there" intensity to the drama of events of the Bible which have so much to say about our relationships and responsibilities today.

The design for the Preacher's Commentary gives the reader an overall outline of each book of the Bible. Following the introduction, which reveals the author's approach and salient background on the book, each chapter of the commentary provides the Scripture to be exposited. The New King James Bible has been chosen for the Preacher's Commentary because it combines with integrity the beauty of language, underlying Greek textual basis, and thought-flow of the 1611 King James Version, while replacing obsolete verb forms and other archaisms with their everyday contemporary counterparts for greater readability. Reverence for God is preserved in the capitalization of all pronouns referring to the Father, Son, or Holy Spirit. Readers who are more comfortable with another translation can readily find the parallel passage by means of the chapter and verse reference at the end of each passage being exposited. The paragraphs of exposition combine fresh insights to the Scripture, application, rich illustrative material, and innovative ways of utilizing the vibrant truth for his or her own life and for the challenge of communicating it with vigor and vitality.

It has been gratifying to me as Editor of this series to receive enthusiastic progress reports from each contributor. As they worked, all were gripped with new truths from the Scripture—God-given insights into passages, previously not written in the literature of biblical explanation. A prime objective of this series is for each user to find the same awareness: that God speaks with newness through the Scriptures when we approach them with a ready mind and a willingness to communicate what He has given; that God delights to give communicators of His Word "I-never-saw-that-in-that-verse-before" intellectual insights so that our listeners and readers can have "I-never-realized-all-that-was-in-that-verse" spiritual experiences.

The thrust of the commentary series unequivocally affirms that God speaks through the Scriptures today to engender faith, enable adventuresome living of the abundant life, and establish the basis of obedient discipleship. The Bible, the unique Word of God, is unlimited in its resource for Christians in communicating our hope to others. It is our weapon in the battle for truth, the guide for ministry, and the irresistible force for introducing others to God. In the New Testament we meet the divine Lord and Savior whom we seek to communicate to others. What He said and did as God with us has been faithfully recorded under the inspiration of the Spirit of God. The cosmic implications of the Gospels are lived out in Acts and spelled out in the Epistles. They have stood the test of time because the eternal Communicator, God Himself, communicates through them to those who would be communicators of grace. His essential nature is exposed, the plan of salvation is explained, and the gospel for all of life, now and for eternity, is proclaimed.

A biblically rooted communication of the gospel holds in unity and oneness what divergent movements have wrought asunder. This commentary series courageously presents personal faith, caring for individuals, and social responsibility as essential, inseparable dimensions of biblical Christianity. It seeks to present the quadrilateral gospel in its fullness which calls us to unreserved commitment to Christ, unrestricted self-esteem in His grace, unqualified love for others in personal evangelism, and undying efforts to work for justice and righteousness in a sick and suffering world.

A growing renaissance in the church today is being led by clergy and laity who are biblically rooted, Christ-centered, and Holy Spirit-empowered. They have dared to listen to people's most urgent questions and deepest needs and then to God as He speaks through the Bible. Biblical preaching is the secret of growing churches. Bible study classes and small groups are equipping the laity for ministry in the world. Dynamic Christians are finding that daily study of God's Word allows the Spirit to do in them what He wishes to communicate through them to others. These days are the most exciting time since Pentecost. The Preacher's Commentary is offered to be a primary resource of new life for this renaissance.

This volume of expositions on some of the most crucial of Paul's epistles was written by a world leader in prayer and spiritual renaissance. Maxie Dunnam is a man in Christ, an exciting expositor of the Word, a Christian statesman, and a faithful churchman. As the Executive Director of Upper Room, the daily Bible study and devotional guide, he expressed his commitment to providing materials and programs for individual and church renewal. The impact of his leadership provided contemporary Christianity with a recall to the basics of Bible study, prayer, witness, and discipleship. His commitment to the local congregation has been expressed through ministries in churches in Georgia, Mississippi, California, and Tennessee. Since 1994 he has been training others for ministry as president of Asbury Theological Seminary in Wilmore, Kentucky.

Dr. Dunnam's expositional style is rich in contemporary illustrative material, and he has the rare gift of parabalizing from the drama of daily life. He is personal without being sentimental and prophetic without being negative. In touch with his own humanity and the central issues gripping our time of history, Dr. Dunnam is a biblical expositor whose messages are rooted in ultimate truth for urgent needs of people. The warmth of his gracious personality becomes a vehicle for inclusive and impelling communication.

In this volume on Galatians, Ephesians, Philippians, Colossians, and Philemon, you will find solid scholarship blended with word pictures and helpful illustrations. His admiration for Paul as a man and apostle shines through. The dynamic faith and life of the apostle and the issues and conflicts he faced as a world missionary are applied with remarkable clarity to the challenges and opportunities we face today. Paul's love for the church thunders through the expositions and the implications for the church today are carefully spelled out. It is obvious immediately that the author of these expositions has done his homework in the scholarship of the ages on Pauline literature and then has allowed the Spirit to infuse fresh truth and insight for our enrichment. The outline of each book will provide practical help for teachers, preachers, and leaders of small group discussion. Dr. Dunnam's commitment to understand what Paul was saying and why is extremely helpful. His illustrations will provide a model for our efforts to look for and use metaphors and parables from our own experience.

I am indebted to Maxie Dunnam for this volume in the Preacher's Commentary because he is a communicator of excellence who is in touch with what our Lord is doing in the church in America and is faithfully living out the discipline of study and exposition. He will help you live in Paul's skin, think with him, and grow in an adventuresome life in Christ.

—LLOYD J. OGILVIE

INTRODUCTION TO GALATIANS

Theme and Contemporary Relevance

Galatians is the Magna Charta of evangelical Christianity. It is Paul's great declaration of religious freedom—a freedom that involves independence from men and dependence on God.

The overarching theme of this epistle is grace—God's grace alone by which we are saved. By grace God frees us from the law, liberates us from legalism and the rigidity of rules, and gives us a Spirit-filled life of joy, meaning, and ministry. Accepting Christ by faith, we are not only justified, we become new beings in Him. We enter a new realm of power—the Spirit. And Christ lives in us. Our lives reflect His life as He is "formed" in us. We produce the fruit of the Spirit which is the expression of Christ in us.

The letter is set in the context of conflict and controversy against which the theme stands out as in flashing neon lights. The intensity and clarity of it is captured in Paul's closing words. He has been dictating his letter to a scribe. But now, as though he does not trust anyone to put it as plainly as he wants it to be, or to make sure that no one will mistake that this is the most powerful conviction of his life, he takes the pen and writes boldly: *"For in Christ Jesus neither circumcision nor uncircumcision avails anything, but a new creation"* (6:15).

The church is always in need of hearing the message of Galatians. No matter what we have experienced, it is our nature recurringly to fall into a system of merit, and to think in terms of achievement and reward. But here, flowing spontaneously from his head, yet deeply from his heart, Paul expresses the life-transforming, world-changing affirmation of justification by grace through faith. We are at the mercy of God's grace, and that mercy encompasses all our sins.

The Occasion, Character, and Purpose of Galatians

There is no question that Paul wrote Galatians. The letter is highly personal, devoting fully one-third of its content to the story of his faith-development, spiritual pilgrimage, and ministry.

Even in the other two-thirds, the faith he is proclaiming is personal and rooted in his own experience of Him *"who loved me and gave Himself for me"* (Gal. 2:20).

The letter swirls in controversy. Following Paul's preaching in Galatia, both the truth of the gospel and Paul's right to preach it were being challenged. Paul's need to respond occasioned in him a vigor and sharpness of mind, a passion of soul. But even when his anger erupted in outrage, his human tenderness and loving concern shone through.

Paul had preached in Galatia at least once, maybe twice. His universal gospel of redemption through faith in the death of Christ had been heard with extraordinary openness and enthusiasm. Though he had been stricken by what must have been a repulsive physical illness before arriving there, the Galatians had received him as if he were an angel, and with extreme gratitude accepted the new life he shared.

While there were some Jews among them, most of them were Gentiles who had never known the true God. Babes in the faith and vulnerable to any teaching, these new Gentile Christians found the going difficult when later they were confronted by a message different from that which Paul had brought them.

This "new" message came from the Judaizers, a party in the church, who, though Christian, accepted Christianity as the fulfillment of the Jewish hope and tenaciously held that God's holy people must be a part of Israel. Their social, cultural, and religious mindset meant a despising of the Gentiles; yet their new faith in Christ would not allow them to think that God could not or would not save the Gentiles. Performing some fancy mental and practical footwork, they declared that, to experience salvation, the Galatian Christians must also be initiated into Israel by the rite of circumcision. Even more, like all true Israelites, they must accept the obligations of the Jewish law.

For Paul nothing could have been further from the truth; salvation was a matter of grace, entirely and completely.

But this was not the total controversy with the Judaizers. What right had Paul, who was not one of the Twelve nor accredited by the Jerusalem church, to admit Gentiles to the church on baptism alone without circumcision? Even more serious, he was preaching a revolutionary gospel of grace that exploded the self-righteous legalism of the law and was bringing a whole new order of things. The Jews, who couldn't break with the rigid system, found it much easier to oppress the new movement by discrediting the person behind it.

When the news reached Paul that his Galatian converts were responding to the Judaizers, he was heartsick. Hoping to offset the Judaizers' claims and answer their accusations, he fired off this letter, in which, like the gushing of a mountain stream, erratic thoughts interrupt one another, then reappear. Throughout, there is the feel of a dauntless Paul talking personally to his hearers, directly from his mind and heart.

Destination and Date

Authorship and unity are unquestioned, but exact destination and date are not. This is really one problem, because if we could be certain about one, we could be certain about the other.

Confusion arises in determining what geographical area Paul means by Galatia. In its earliest use, Galatia referred to the region in the heart of Asia Minor settled by people from Gaul (including the cities of Pessinus, Ancyra, and Tavium), which had the status of a kingdom until 25 B.C. At that time, this kingdom came under the Roman provincial system and was only a part of a larger area comprising the Roman province of Galatia. (The province included as well parts of Phrygia, Pisidia, and Lacaonia, with the southern cities of Antioch, Iconium, Lystra, and Derbe.) The so-called North Galatia hypothesis concerning the letter's destination assumes Paul was writing to churches apparently founded in his second missionary journey in the earlier smaller area; the South Galatia hypothesis, to churches founded during his first missionary journey in the Roman province.

The problem of date depends heavily upon the Book of Acts for its solution. The Galatian letter had to have been written later than the latest event recorded in it, and Paul mentions having made two visits to Jerusalem. There has been some acceptance—unjustified, I feel—of the hypothesis that Paul's second visit to Jerusalem was for the Jerusalem Council (see Acts 15), which probably took place in A.D. 48, thus dating the epistle after that event.

While there are questions in both hypotheses, the South Galatia one seems to be the better and a date earlier than 48 seems likely. The two most supportive streams of data for this have to do with when and where Paul established churches, and the content of the letter itself in relation to what happened at the Jerusalem Council.

The first argument has it that Paul organized churches in the *original* Galatia on his second missionary journey and visited them again. Acts 16:6 (KJV, NIV) does say Paul and his companion went "throughout Phrygia and the region of Galatia"; yet there is no convincing evidence that he established churches in Galatia. Also, "the region of Galatia" may refer to only the western part bordering Phrygia.

Perhaps more important, Luke, contrary to his usual custom, doesn't mention any cities in either Acts 16:6–8 or 18:23. In the latter he says Paul strengthened "all the disciples." Elsewhere Luke refers to Paul's activity as strengthening the *churches*. Galatians is addressed to churches, not individual disciples. Luke's failure to mention churches is pretty good evidence that none were there.

What about Paul's *second* visit to Jerusalem? This is difficult to harmonize with the Jerusalem Council of Acts 15, since Paul describes his *second* visit (Gal. 2:1–10) as a private time with the Jerusalem leaders. Acts 15 reports a formal conference that set down agreements and decrees to be shared with all the churches concerned. If a formal agreement about the matter under debate had been made with Paul on his second visit, the Judaizers would have been using it, and Paul surely would have responded.

Concerning the question of Jewish and Gentile Christians eating together, it is natural to assume that the episode related in Galatians 2:11ff. came after the visit of 2:1–10. How could that difficulty have developed if this visit was in fact the Jerusalem Council which had discussed and settled the table-fellowship question?

For me George S. Duncan's reconstruction of the chronology of developments seems more convincing.[1] Paul and Barnabas had been working among the Gentiles at Antioch for approximately a year (Acts 11:26) before the visit of Acts 11:30/Galatians 2:1. One of its purposes was to take a relief offering, but Paul also felt divine guidance for the trip since it gave him the opportunity of sharing with the apostles in Jerusalem the growth of the church among the Gentiles.

Still unknown to most members of the church, Paul was also under lingering suspicion because of what he had been and had done to the church. Nevertheless he knew that the general question of *on what terms Gentiles should be accepted into the Christian fellowship* had to be dealt with.

There was no formal conference, but the Spirit worked. The Jerusalem leaders acknowledged the genuineness of his apostleship and endorsed his work among the Gentiles. Duncan concludes that Galatians 2:1–10 represents quite an early stage in the development of events and preceded the controversy addressed by the Jerusalem Council (Acts 15).

Returning to Antioch, Paul *continued* in table-fellowship with Gentile members of the church, acting out his conviction that if Gentiles were to be admitted to the fellowship, then within the fellowship Jews and Gentiles were one. Barnabas and other Jewish Christians did likewise, and when Peter visited Antioch, he too joined in. Emissaries from James in Jerusalem came to Antioch and challenged the practice, but Paul weathered that storm, taking decisive action to save a split of the Fellowship in Antioch and preserve unity.

But clearly a more ominous storm was brewing which would eventuate in the calling of the Jerusalem Council. In the meantime, before that happened, Paul and Barnabas initiated a great missionary crusade throughout South Galatia, preaching the gospel and winning many converts. Then, as previously described, the Judaizers moved in and began to persuade the new converts to accept the Jewish law. This was the situation that evoked Paul's letter, perhaps from Antioch, where Acts says he spent a lot of time on his return. New converts are usually open to whatever is presented to them for developing their experience and perfecting their faith. Paul need not have been there long for enough time to have passed for the trouble to reach alarming proportions. Paul could not go to them personally, so he wrote his letter, probably from Antioch and probably just before the Jerusalem Council in A.D. 48.

NOTE

1. George S. Duncan, *The Epistle of Paul to the Galatians,* The Moffatt New Testament Commentary (New York: Harper and Brothers, 1934), pp. xxvi ff.

An Outline of Galatians

I. The Man and His Message: 1:1–24
   A. Paul's Greeting: 1:1–5
   B. Paul's Disappointment: 1:6–10
   C. Paul's Commission as an Apostle: 1:11–17
   D. Paul's Establishment of His Cause: 1:18–24
II. Paul Stakes His Claim: 2:1–21
   A. Clarifying and Defending the Gospel: 2:1–5
   B. The Gospel's Relevance to All: 2:6–10
   C. Inconsistency and Conflict: 2:11–14
   D. The Futility of the Law for Salvation: 2:15–16
   E. All in Grace: 2:17–21
III. Justification by Faith: 3:1–29
   A. Jesus Christ: Crucified and Risen: 3:1–5
   B. Abraham: The Prototype of the True Believer: 3:6–9
   C. Redeemed from the Curse by the Cross: 3:10–14
   D. The Changeless Promise: 3:15–18
   E. The Law: Our Custodian: 3:19–25
   F. Baptized into Christ: 3:26–29
IV. Sons and Heirs of God: 4:1–31
   A. Not a Servant But a Son: 4:1–7
   B. Substituting Gods for God: 4:8–10
   C. The Power of the Person and the Personal: 4:11–20
   D. Two Covenants: 4:21–31
V. Practical Implications of the Gospel: 5:1–26
   A. Participation and Anticipation in Christ's Freedom: 5:1–6
   B. Another Personal Appeal: 5:7–12
   C. Responsible Freedom: 5:13–15
   D. Walking in the Spirit: 5:16–26
VI. The Shared Life of the People of God: 6:1–18
   A. Bearing and Sharing Burdens: 6:1–6
   B. The Law of the Harvest: 6:7–10
   C. Glory Only in the Cross: 6:11–15
   D. A Blessing and a Plea: 6:16–18

CHAPTER ONE—THE MAN AND HIS MESSAGE

GALATIANS 1:1–24

Scripture Outline

Paul's Greeting (1:1–5)

Paul's Disappointment (1:6–10)

Paul's Commission as an Apostle (1:11–17)

Paul's Establishment of His Cause (1:18–24)

PAUL'S GREETING

1:1 Paul, an apostle (not from men nor through man, but through Jesus Christ and God the Father who raised Him from the dead), **2** and all the brethren who are with me,

To the churches of Galatia:

3 Grace to you and peace from God the Father and our Lord Jesus Christ, **4** who gave Himself for our sins, that He might deliver us from this present evil age, according to the will of our God and Father, **5** to whom be glory forever and ever. Amen.

—Galatians 1:1–5

Paul's Identification: An Apostle of Jesus Christ

In his introduction to the Galatians, Paul addresses an obvious source of conflict and opposition. Some were saying to the Galatians that Paul was not really an apostle, therefore they need not pay him too much attention. True, he was not one of the original twelve. True, he had been a savage persecutor of the church. True, he had no official appointment from the hierarchy of the church. But Paul does not even seek to answer those arguments. Rather, in the style common to such a formal letter, he states his case by affirmation—his own knowledge of who he was: "I am an *apostle* of Jesus Christ. My apostleship came neither of men or by men, but from Jesus Christ, and God the Father, who raised Him from the dead."

Two things stand out about Paul's affirmation. (1) He was certain that God had spoken to him. This gave him a confidence that often verged on arrogance. Is there not a thin line here? When we are confident of God's call to us and His will for us, we stand and act with a kind of carefree abandon that challenges the powers of the world.

I was a young pastor in Mississippi at the time of the Civil Rights revolution in the late fifties and early sixties. At the height of the turmoil, when public schools were being threatened and blacks were being turned away from white churches, with three other young ministers I drafted a "born-of-conviction" statement about the issues facing us. Twenty-four other ministers joined us in signing and issuing it publicly. My congregation knew what my convictions were, but for some strange reason they could not tolerate such a public stance on my part.

I remember with pain and joy the occasion when the officials of the church called a meeting to confront me and to "settle this issue once and for all." I was as frightened as I have ever been. But in a marvelously surprising way there was healing and reconciliation as I was given the guidance and strength to make the case for my apostleship and to plead for the freedom of the pulpit. One leader, who was unmoved, kept pressing: "What can we expect of you in the future?" I was surprised by my calmness because this was one of the wealthiest and most powerful men in the church, one who had been among my dearest friends, and was one of the strongest in his opposition to my stand. I was equally surprised at my response:

"You can expect me to be consistent in my understanding of and stand for justice and human rights as I have shared those with you tonight."

"How can you be so arrogant?" he shouted, as he stormed out of the room. Sometimes I know I am arrogant and I guard against that, praying for humility. However, that is the only time I have been openly accused of arrogance, and I felt none at all. I felt a freedom, though, that made me bold to speak. I was certain of who I was and what God's Word and will was for my life and our church. I was certain God had spoken to me, and was speaking through me.

(2) There is another striking feature in Paul's affirmation. Confident of who he was—an apostle not of or by men, but of and by

Jesus Christ—he received the strength to toil and suffer, to persist and endure, because he knew his task had been given him by God.

Paul's favorite designation for himself, the Greek word *apostolos,* comes from the verb *apostellein,* which means "to dispatch" or "to send out." In his letters to the Romans, the Corinthians, the Ephesians, and to Timothy, he used this title in his greeting: *"An Apostle of Jesus Christ."* For Paul this meant at least three things. One, he belonged to Jesus Christ. Two, he was dispatched by, sent out by Jesus Christ; his commission was from his Lord. Three, his power was not his own, but came from Christ. Should it be any less with any Christian than with Paul?

Paul's Greeting

After identifying himself, Paul gives his introductory greeting: *"Grace* [be] *to you."* This key word, *"grace,"* appears over and over again in Paul's writing. In Galatians, Paul's *freedom* letter, he is calling these new Christians to retain the freedom given them by Christ. This freedom is the result of God's grace which delivers us from the legalism and rigidity of the law and looses us for a Spirit-filled life of joy and fulfillment.

Grace, from the Greek work *charis,* has many facets. From it we derive "charismatic." It has to do with *gift*—gifts we have received but have not earned and do not deserve. The gifts come out of the sheer, unreserved, extravagant generosity of the ever-giving God.

Charis/grace has in it all the love of God, the unmerited, unmeasurable, unlimited self-giving mercy of God. Even in his greeting Paul expresses this core of the gospel. God's grace reaches its ultimate dimension in the giving of His Son. The Son, in turn, "gave Himself for our sins, that He might deliver us."

This is grace—God's love expressed in Jesus Christ. This love gives and suffers and finally conquers and delivers.

There is a sense of beauty and charm in the word "grace." Paul is wishing that for the Galatians. How we have confused and perverted its meaning. The western world spends billions of dollars seeking to be beautiful and charming, and calls the jet set, the Christian Dior, Pierre Cardin clan, "the beautiful people." In the grace Paul wishes for the Galatians, however, there is a beauty and a charm that transcends outward appearance.

Malcolm Muggeridge's book about Mother Teresa of Calcutta is titled *Something Beautiful For God.* The beauty and charm about Mother Teresa's simple goodness and self-giving service to the poorest of the poor in Calcutta captured this hard, cynical, agnostic broadcaster and led to his conversion to Christ. This is the way he wrote of her:

> I ran away and stayed away: Mother Teresa moved in and stayed. That was the difference. She, a nun, rather slightly built, with a few rupees in her pocket; not particularly clever, or particularly gifted in the arts of persuasion. Just with this Christian love shining about her; in her heart and on her lips. Just prepared to follow her Lord, and in accordance with his instructions regard every derelict left to die in the streets as him; to hear in the cry of every abandoned child, even in the tiny squawk of the discarded foetus, the cry of the Bethlehem child; to recognize in every leper's stumps the hands which once touched sightless eyes and made them see, rested on distracted heads and made them calm, brought back health to sick flesh and twisted limbs. As for my expatiations on Bengal's wretched social conditions—I regret to say that I doubt whether, in any divine accounting, they will equal one single quizzical half smile bestowed by Mother Teresa on a street urchin who happened to catch her eye.

I suppose there is goodness without charm. And I know there is much charm without goodness. But when those unite—goodness and charm—grace is at work and that is sheer beauty—"something beautiful for God."

Paul continues: *"And peace from God the Father."*

In Greek the word translated "peace" is *eirēnē;* the Hebrew is *shalom.* In the Bible, peace means far more than the absence of conflict or trouble. In fact, peace *(eirēnē/shalom)* is often ours in the midst of conflict and trouble. The peace God gives is independent of outward circumstances.

PAUL'S DISAPPOINTMENT

6 I marvel that you are turning away so soon from Him who called you in the grace of Christ, to a different gospel, 7 which is not another; but there are some who trouble you and want to pervert the gospel of Christ. 8 But even if we, or an angel from heaven, preach any other gospel to you than what we have preached to you, let him be accursed. 9 As we

have said before, so now I say again, if anyone preaches any other gospel to you than what you have received, let him be accursed.

10 For do I now persuade men, or God? Or do I seek to please men? For if I still pleased men, I would not be a bond-servant of Christ.

—Galatians 1:6–10

Paul's was the explosive gospel of free grace. He had experienced it and it had turned his life around, and this is what he shared. Because of his own pilgrimage away from the dead-end of an arduous self-effort at salvation by keeping the law and seeking to be righteous, Paul was absolutely convinced that a person can do nothing to gain favor with God. He had been on that road for a long time and he knew its frustration and futility. In his Philippian letter he called himself a Pharisee of the Pharisees; in keeping the law, blameless, "though I might also have confidence in the flesh. If anyone else thinks he may have confidence in the flesh, I more so: circumcised the eighth day, of the stock of Israel, of the tribe of Benjamin, a Hebrew of the Hebrews; concerning the law, a Pharisee; concerning zeal, persecuting the church; concerning the righteousness which is in the law, blameless. But what things were gain to me, these I have counted loss for Christ" (Phil. 3:4–7).

Fervent self-righteousness had sent Paul to Damascus to root out and persecute the Christians. God turned him around and now he knew: no one can ever earn the love of God. God's love is gift. All we can do is fling ourselves on the love and mercy of God in faith. And miracle of miracles!—we are accepted, loved, and given life.

The Galatians had experienced the grace of Christ and had tasted the glorious freedom that comes when in faith we trust our lives to Christ. Little time had passed, but here they were, back where they had been, as slaves of a lifeless system that could only end in despair, for no one can keep the law perfectly, and no one can save himself. Paul was amazed.

Yet, we fall into the same snare over and over again. Do we find it constitutionally impossible to trust our salvation to God's grace? It seems so. We get delivered from "the law," discover the joyous liberty that can be ours as we trust ourselves in faith to the Lord's keeping and guidance. But then, egotists that we are, so enamored of our own ability and power, so engulfed in the self-sufficiency of our technological secular culture, we believe we must *do something* to save ourselves. We take on another system, another "law," becoming slaves again. It may be the law of proper liturgy and worship, or correct doctrine, or church polity and order. But it is still law, and grace is superseded by our system. I know a group of people now who have developed an order of elders who are given oversight of the community. Anyone who questions this order is ostracized. I visit churches in whose worship I would never dare lift my hands in praise, and others where I would feel condemned if I prayed a written prayer. In one, the congregation is a slave to form; in the other, they are slaves to formlessness.

Paul was singleminded in pressing his point. If the Galatians followed the distorted gospel being preached to them they would leave this sphere of grace and reenter the domain of law. In such preaching there is no gospel, no good news. Paul was vehement. "But even if we, or an angel from heaven, should preach to you a gospel contrary to that which we preached to you, let him be accursed" (v. 8, RSV). Paul becomes more explicit in the expression of his anger in Galatians 5:12. But even here as he begins his letter, he can't restrain himself. Anyone who would pervert, water down, minimize, abuse, or corrupt the gospel of God's grace, freely given, requiring no law, involving only a response of faith, is to be accursed.

Paul would make no pretension at being religiously tolerant, if being tolerant means that it doesn't really matter what persons believe so long as they believe. How naive and glib we often are: "What persons believe is their business—a private matter. We don't need to be too concerned about theology or doctrine. Being brotherly is what matters, living by the Golden Rule, doing good, refraining from harmful activity—that's what counts. And if you are sincere, you'll be led to the right truth and in the right path."

"Hogwash!" Paul would say. "What you believe eventually determines how you live. You can't encrust the gospel of grace with a system of law. To do so diminishes the sovereignty of God and puts salvation back in the hands of humans to be earned by merit." Whatever the case, Paul warned against a gospel that was not centered in one gift—the grace of Christ—and in one event— the Christ event in which Crucifixion and Resurrection could not be separated. He could have pleased the Jews by preaching law observance, and the pagans by making the death of Christ a mere sacrificial transaction that placed no obligation upon the follower. But from the moment he became a Christian Paul knew nothing else but Jesus crucified. This freed him from the law, but it called him to be crucified with Christ. The only way to prove he was pleasing to God rather than men was to keep the scandal of the Cross at the heart of his preaching and take the consequences of the Cross to the heart of his living.

PAUL'S COMMISSION AS AN APOSTLE

[11] But I make known to you, brethren, that the gospel which was preached by me is not according to man. [12] For I neither received it from man, nor was I taught it, but it came through the revelation of Jesus Christ.

[13] For you have heard of my former conduct in Judaism, how I persecuted the church of God beyond measure and tried to destroy it. [14] And I advanced in Judaism beyond many of my contemporaries in my own nation, being more exceedingly zealous for the traditions of my fathers.

[15] But when it pleased God, who separated me from my mother's womb and called me through His grace, [16] to reveal His Son in me, that I might preach Him among the Gentiles, I did not immediately confer with flesh and blood, [17] nor did I go up to Jerusalem to those who were apostles before me; but I went to Arabia, and returned again to Damascus.

—Galatians 1:11–17

A key to understanding Paul's letters is his conviction that it is not he who legitimates his gospel ("It is true because I say it; it is mine"), but it is the gospel that legitimates Paul ("I am an apostle because the gospel is true"). Paul did not separate the experience of coming to faith from knowing himself to be called by God to be an apostle to the Gentiles. His conversion and his call coincided (vv. 15–16).

Can we identify with that? Can we locate religious experiences in which the presence of God not only changed us, confronted us, challenged us, but out of which also came a call? The truth is that *in our acceptance of the revelation of Christ as our forgiving Savior is also the call to be His servants.* That call can be as explicit for us as Paul's call to be an apostle to the Gentiles. We dare not forget the call!

Paul's assertive conviction that his gospel rested on no human foundation has meaning in every generation. It "is not man's gospel. For I did not receive it from man, nor was I taught it, but it came through a revelation of Jesus Christ" (vv. 11–12). His experience was an act of God's grace, not the result of an extended religious quest; in fact, he had been quite convinced and settled in his religion— extremely *"zealous for the traditions of my fathers"* (v. 14). This led to this violent persecution of the church. The Damascus Road experience was a divine intervention to rescue him from self-destruction. Since it was such a break-in upon an unsuspecting, unseeking person, Paul could only see his coming to faith as an act of God.

Sometimes Paul's theology has been regarded as simply an explication of his experience. If you leave out the word "simply," the truth is there. Paul never grounds his theological arguments in his conversion experience. Rarely does he refer to his religious experiences (1 Cor. 9:1; 2 Cor. 12:1–10; Gal. 1:12–17; 2:2). Nor does he say that his theology was revealed to him. What he says is that his gospel is the revelation of Christ to him. Thus the big point for us is that the spiritual apprehension of Jesus cannot be conveyed by tradition alone. Through his Spirit, Jesus became the eternal contemporary of every generation. Though Paul did not see him "in the flesh," nor can we, we can have the spiritual affinity that Paul had. Even for the original disciples, time, space, and physical sight were not in themselves the essential factors of relationship. Had they not experienced a mystical companionship after the Crucifixion and Resurrection, they could not have understood the message and ministry of Jesus. And certainly without that mystical companionship, they could not have continued the message and ministry.

Paul did not hesitate to use the pronoun "I." He was talking about the earthquake impact Christ had made upon his life, completely changing his existence. Everything that followed was enlightened by the luminous revelation by God of his Son to Paul. Revelation was not the gift of a body of information, or a systematic knowledge about God. Rather, it was an act of self-revealing. God came to Paul in the person of Jesus Christ, entered Paul's life and took command. For that reason Paul was so brazen in his insistence that no human being was the ultimate source, not even the intermediary of his gospel.

Paul does not hesitate to share his own sin and failure in order to show the power of God. The law had been his life, to the extent that he had become an arch-persecutor of the church. Now what a change! From a passionate intensity to earn God's favor and approval he had moved to a humble faith to take whatever God offered. From an arrogant glorying in what he could do for God and for himself, he had been overcome with an awestricken glory in what God had done for him. When a person's life is turned upside down, when a person's values are reversed as though to turn from daylight to dark, there must be an explanation. For Paul, it was the direct intervention of God. And this is what God can do with any life.

As Paul reflected upon all that had happened, he felt that God had set him apart for a special task even before he was born (v. 15). This conviction is rooted in the marvelous Old Testament prophets in whom Paul was so thoroughly grounded. Life is not just an eddy of a purposeless stream; it is a part of God's mainstream. "Before I formed thee in the belly I knew thee; and before thou camest forth out of the womb I sanctified thee, and I ordained thee a prophet unto the nations" (Jer. 1:5).

Two truths emerge here. One, God had a plan for Paul—as He does for every person, for you, *for me.* Paul saw the intervention of God in his life not as an unpremeditated happening but as a part of the eternal plan of God. He may have recalled the conviction of the psalmist: "For thou didst form my inward parts, thou didst knit me together in my mother's womb." (Ps. 139:13, RSV).

As indicated earlier, Paul associates his call with his conversion; it may even appear that the two coincided. We should not allow this to diminish the possibility that God's call is often addressed to persons long before they are spiritually sensitive enough to hear the call, or prepared to answer it. (See Is. 49:1–4 and Rom. 8:28–30.) But the time comes, in the fulfillment of His purpose, when God acts in power *"to reveal His Son in me"* (v. 16).

The initiative is still with God, and we can make no claim or take no credit for spiritual insight. It is grace—all grace. Such a revelation, so wonderful and unexpected, has a purpose behind it. Thus a second truth.

Paul knew that he was chosen for a task—*"that I might preach him among the Gentiles"*—not for honor and glory, but to bring honor and glory to God, through service. As I write this China has just begun to open to the United States after having been closed for thirty years. I know some individuals and some missionary organizations who have long been preparing for Christian service in China, should they be permitted such an opportunity. They feel called to a specific task and are equipping themselves for it. The call of Christ is a call to service.

PAUL'S ESTABLISHMENT OF HIS CAUSE

[18] Then after three years I went up to Jerusalem to see Peter, and remained with him fifteen days. [19] But I saw none

of the other apostles except James, the Lord's brother. [20] (Now concerning the things which I write to you, indeed, before God, I do not lie.)

[21] Afterward I went into the regions of Syria and Cilicia. [22] And I was unknown by face to the churches of Judea which were in Christ. [23] But they were hearing only, "He who formerly persecuted us now preaches the faith which he once tried to destroy." [24] And they glorified God in me.

—*Galatians 1:18–24*

Paul's religious experience was so direct, so overwhelming, so clear that he knew his first business was with God, not with man. Also, because the authority of his apostleship was being questioned, he asserted his independence of human authority. "*. . . I did not immediately confer with flesh and blood, nor did I go up to Jerusalem to those who were apostles before me . . .*" (vv. 16–17).

This section of the letter sketches a three-year period to show the Galatians that Paul's apostleship is firmly rooted in God's revelation and call, and that he was dependent upon God alone for his message and for the power to be an apostle. In the movement of Paul during this early part of his ministry there are some challenging directions for us.

Paul's Journey to Arabia

What impelled Paul to go to Arabia? Was he frightened? Was he threatened by his enraged Jewish brethren? Was persecution a possibility? Did he go to preach? Or was it to seek communion with God?

It is only from this letter that we know Paul went to Arabia. He doesn't tell us why he went or how long he stayed. It is reasonable to conjecture that however clearly the call of God had come, Paul felt a need for reflection and preparation to enter into his apostleship. Separating himself from human contact, he left the city and its distractions and sought the quietness of the desert. He needed to be alone, *to be sure of himself*—to confirm that this was no flash-in-the-pan experience, no emotional upheaval without deep meaning. A time for extended prayer, meditation, and reflection was even more imperative because of his former security and self-confidence in his Judaism. What was happening to him could not be a mere addition to his old religion. This was new wine that would require a new wineskin.

Not only did he need to be sure of himself, he needed *to be sure of God.* To take the time to face ourselves and to face God is essential for all, but evaded by most. We often symbolize being alone with ourselves and with God, in order to face ourselves and God openly and honestly, as spending time in the desert. Whether we experience the desert as a geophysical fact is not important. That we experience it as the reality of being alone with ourselves and God—questing, clarifying, testing, committing, and cleansing—is absolutely necessary.

Paul's Return to Damascus

After Arabia, Paul returned to Damascus. It is implied, though not definitely stated, that it was from Damascus that he had gone away to Arabia, and not until three years later did he go to Jerusalem (v. 18).

What courage this required! Paul had been on a mission of destruction to wipe out the Christians in Damascus when he met Christ and his life was turned around. Without doubt, the people in Damascus knew this. They knew who Paul was, and of his vehement and violent opposition to the Christ movement. It was to that very place that Paul returned from Arabia, a new man with a new message. He would be facing the ultimate test of one's faith and experience: to reveal our lives and share our witness in these areas where we have been most desperately wrong, where our sins have been most glaringly known. For many of us testing comes not at a distance but very near—in our homes, in our places of work and social involvement, among those who know us at our worst.

Paul's Visit to Jerusalem

Then Paul went to Jerusalem, in a sense taking his life into his own hands. His former friends, the Jews, knew him now as a turncoat, a renegade. If they were as vehement in their commitment to Moses and the Law as Paul had been, they would be as violent in their opposition to Paul as he had been against Christians before he met Christ. *Paul had to face his past.* Not only the Jews in Jerusalem, but the Christians as well could be a threat. As his former victims, they might well ostracize him. How could they trust his assertion of being a changed man?

The primary reason for his return to Jerusalem was to visit with Peter. Paul is careful how he talks about his Jerusalem visit. His detractors sought to use that in their efforts to discredit him by confirming his subjection to the Jerusalem "authorities." So

Paul takes pains to say he did not go to Jerusalem until three years after his conversion, and he stayed only fifteen days. During those two weeks, he saw just one person other than Peter—James, the Lord's brother.

Seeing James was perhaps incidental; seeing Peter was primary. This was a natural desire on Paul's part, to see "the rock," the one who had emerged as the spokesman, the leader of the apostles, the one who had been with Jesus in the flesh. During his first three years of new life in Christ, Paul had deliberately stayed away from the apostles, until his revelation and gospel were confirmed. Although his experience and the content of his preaching did not require the confirmation of the "authorities" in Jerusalem, Paul wanted it for the unity needed in presenting the gospel to a pagan world. It would become increasingly clear that Paul's principle of grace for all necessitated a vision of the church as the one body of Christ.

This vision is no less crucial for our day. Different structure, varied polity and organizational patterns may be necessary in the pluralism of world culture, but these multiple outward expressions of the church must never be deterrents to the expression of universal grace, salvation available to all, and the church as the body of Christ, the extension of his Incarnation in the world.

The Regions of Syria and Cilicia

After his visit in Jerusalem, Paul went *"into the regions of Syria and Cilicia."* The Book of Acts tells us that, on leaving Jerusalem, Paul went to Tarsus, the chief city of Cilicia, and that later Barnabas took him from Tarsus to superintend the missionary work in Antioch, in Syria. It must have been difficult for Paul to go to Tarsus, the city where he had been born and had gone to school. No doubt, friends of his growing-up years were still around. In Nazareth they said sneeringly of Jesus, "Is this not the carpenter's son?" "A prophet is without honor in his own country," Jesus had said. Paul was willing to risk the ridicule, the difficulties, the hardships, even persecution to take the gospel into inhospitable places.

The Key to Paul's Thought

The closing verses of this first chapter provide a key to an understanding of Paul's ardent commitment, his freedom, and his total commitment to the centrality of Christ. A prepositional phrase is the key to his thought: *"in Christ."* Whereas normally this phrase designates the experience of an individual, here Paul uses it in relation to the church—*"the churches of Judea which were in Christ."* This mystical quality of the fellowship makes the church more than a human institution. When the fellowship is in and with Christ, the church is the body of Christ, a divine institution against which the gates of hell cannot prevail.

We, like Paul, are to stand *as* Christ before others, to become *as* Christ to others in order that they might see *in* us what the Christ way is. Paul knew, as we must learn, that before the Judean churches could glorify God in Paul, Paul first had to glorify God in himself. The only way he (and we) could do that was by living among them as Christ had lived. In that sense every Christian is to be *as* Christ. To the degree that we are as Christ, to that degree God can be glorified *in* us.

CHAPTER TWO—PAUL STAKES HIS CLAIM
GALATIANS 2:1–21

Scripture Outline

Clarifying and Defending the Gospel (2:1–5)

The Gospel's Relevance to All (2:6–10)

Inconsistency and Conflict (2:11–14)

The Futility of the Law for Salvation (2:15–16)

All in Grace (2:17–21)

Paul sought to prove the independence of his gospel. In this chapter he seeks to clarify the fact that this independence is not sectarian or self-seeking. He defends his gospel as *the faith in God's grace which is sufficient for all,* Jew and Gentile alike.

Still asserting his independence of the Jerusalem apostles, Paul tells of his second visit to Jerusalem. He conferred with the leaders of the church, and out of that relationship his mission of preaching to the Gentiles was confirmed.

Paul designates this visit to Jerusalem as being *fourteen* years later than his first.

This was not an easy visit for Paul. His inner being is in turmoil. Even as he wrote, his worry and agitation are visible in the broken and disjointed sentences.

He was totally committed in his mission to the Gentiles. His passion to share the Good News with the non-Jew was like an intense fire, everlastingly burning in his breast. He struggled not to say too little lest he compromise his commitment. Nor did he want to say too much, lest it might appear that he was at variance with, and antagonistic to, the leaders of the church.

CLARIFYING AND DEFENDING THE GOSPEL

2:1 Then after fourteen years I went up again to Jerusalem with Barnabas, and also took Titus with me. [2] And I went up by revelation, and communicated to them that gospel which I preach among the Gentiles, but privately to those who were of reputation, lest by any means I might run, or had run, in vain. [3] Yet not even Titus who was with me, being a Greek, was compelled to be circumcised. [4] And this occurred because of false brethren secretly brought in (who came in by stealth to spy out our liberty which we have in Christ Jesus, that they might bring us into bondage), [5] to whom we did not yield submission even for an hour, that the truth of the gospel might continue with you.

—Galatians 2:1-5

The Ongoing Tension between Revelation and Reason

In verse 2 we have an expression of the ongoing tension within the Christian life: *revelation* and *reason*. Often we play the two against each other. To experience the two in tension is creative; to see them as opposites is misunderstanding and stifling.

Paul *was led* to go to Jerusalem; he *"went up by revelation."* The word used here for revelation has the same meaning as in verse 12 of the first chapter: . . . *it came through the revelation of Jesus Christ."* Now the reference is to a disclosure of divine will in regard to a specific matter, while in 1:12 it is a revelation of Jesus Christ giving Paul his gospel.

Paul does not say how the revelation came, whether directly from Spirit, or through some other person. Nor does he specify whether this was a specific revelation uniquely related to this visit or ongoing guidance—the indwelling Christ in his life moving him with conviction. In either sense, the truth is relevant to our lives. *We can be led,* and we can claim that leading.

Sometimes, God speaks to us directly, Spirit to spirit, to meet a particular need in our lives, or to provide specific guidance. We should guard against always associating this experience with the dramatic. The revelation doesn't have to come directly. It can come through another who speaks the right word at the right time. In that word, things can come together and bring clarity for our confusion and we can know ourselves led. And of course revelation—leading—comes through Scripture. Immersing ourselves in the Word, we are led to passages for particular needs. Or, the cumulative power and inspiration that comes from disciplined reading of Scripture builds up within our minds and hearts to provide a residual stream of guidance and strength.

Paul went by revelation to Jerusalem, but he responded to reason—our God-given capacity to think through and decide. He wanted to communicate with the Christian leaders *"lest by any means I might run, or had run, in vain."*

Reason and revelation were working together, though at times in tension. Paul had no doubt about the truth of the gospel he was preaching; he was certain of his revelation. His dis-ease came from his reasoned belief that the disapproval of his work by the leading apostles would render him ineffectual. Certainly it could seriously interfere with and hinder his mission.

It was a matter of utmost importance to Paul not only to prevent the forcing of the Jewish law upon Gentiles, but also to maintain the unity of the church, avoiding division into Jewish and Gentile branches. Paul carried that tension within him, and his conduct throughout his notable career demonstrated his commitment to that unity. (See 1 Cor. 16:1–3; 2 Cor. 8 and 9; Eph. 4:12–15; Rom. 15:25–32.) Following his reason, Paul was willing to divert energy and time from his work of preaching to the Gentiles to raise money for the poor, personally to carry that offering to Jerusalem, and to consult with the apostles there to divert division.

The Importance of Structures and Relationships

Still another lesson is implied in this passage. *Structures and relationships are important.* As strong-willed and independent as Paul was, he gave authority due respect. He may have gone his own way, but he did so in the context of structure and relationship. Even though he differed from the leaders in Jerusalem he went and talked with them, kept communication open, and recognized authority and structure.

How many schisms in local churches and even national church bodies could have been averted if this lesson had been learned. In the rural community of Mississippi where I grew up there are two churches of the same denomination within a half mile of each other. No one remembers exactly what happened, but years ago the original congregation from which they came split over some minor point of doctrine. Some think it was over an issue of conduct—whether women could cut and curl their hair. Now in both congregations women cut and curl their hair, and no one can describe any significant doctrinal differences in the two churches.

33

How many cleavages have come in Christian communities by the refusal to work at relationship, to value structure and order? What heartbreak and dissension have come to churches by the insistence that a particular revelation was final and could not be contaminated by reason. We too easily forget that personal commitment and interpersonal communication are allies, not enemies, and that individual determination does not preclude courtesy and respect to the opinions and convictions of others.

The Open Door to Fellowship

The way into the Christian life and fellowship must be an open door through which one can move freely and joyously, not an impenetrable maze of superficialities and artificial barriers. This is the heart of Paul's argument with the Galatians. The argument here (vv. 3–5) moves from general philosophical discussion to concrete reality in a person. Titus, a Greek, who had no cultural kinship to Abraham, accompanied Paul to Jerusalem. Jewish Christians sought to compel Titus to be circumcised according to Jewish law. Verse 4 seems to be parenthetical, even an afterthought, but it is important. Paul says this divisive put-down of Titus would not have occurred had not *"false brethren . . . who came in by stealth to spy"* brought testimony against the *"liberty which we have in Christ Jesus."*

It is a grave moment when we presume to judge others. Any judgment we make must always be accompanied by fear and trembling, in awareness of the admonition that we are not to judge unless we are willing to submit to the same tests we have applied to another.

The *"false brethren"* were *"secretly brought in"*; they sneaked in. This is foreign to a Christian style of relationship.

The Christian style is open. Deliberate effort is made to be trusting, not suspicious; to be constructive, not condemning in judgment; to interpret people up, not down; to be less tolerant of our own sins than those of others; to be above board in handling disagreement; to have genuine dialogue that values the other, not critical debate that is destructive of the other.

Paul resisted the pressure and *"did not yield submission even for an hour."* The nature of the pressure was subtle, but powerful, and indicates an area of concern common to most of us. The Scripture implies three parties to the question of Titus' circumcision. First, there were Paul and Barnabas, whose conviction was that Gentile Christians should be received into the Christian fellowship without circumcision. The second party were the *"false brethren"* who slipped in—who ardently contended that Gentile Christians *must* be circumcised. Then there was the third party, among whom evidently were the pillar leaders with whom Paul had privately consulted (v. 2). These seemed supportive of Paul, having no strong conviction that circumcision should be required. Paul says later in verses 7–9 that they confirmed him in his position and in his preaching to the Gentiles.

Here comes the rub. The Scripture implies that Paul never had personal contact with the second party. They are mentioned as persons for whose sake, not by whom, the insistence of Titus' circumcision was being made. It must have been the third party, those who did not regard circumcision as necessary, who sought to compel it. What was happening now comes clear. The third party was acting *expediently,* insisting on the circumcision of Titus as a concession to the second party. While the third party agreed with Paul and not with the second party, still they felt that the feelings and convictions, however misguided, merited consideration, even concession.

No pressure is more subtle and thus weighty: Let's do this for the sake of others, for conciliation. There is nothing wrong with conciliation *per se,* but conciliation at the price of an important conviction erodes our spiritual power, our credibility, and the integrity of our witness.

Paul was aware of the implications. Even though the third party may have been seeking conciliation, the circumcision of Titus could have been a precedent. If the third party was urging the circumcision of Titus not on principle, but for expediency, the same reasons could be used to convince Paul that all Gentile converts should be circumcised. This was too important a matter to compromise, no matter how powerful the pressure, and Paul stood firm.

Let it be said again: expediency is not intrinsically wrong; conciliation is often an honorable path. The question is what is being sacrificed for expediency's sake. Paul says he did not yield—*"that the truth of the gospel might continue with you."* Had Paul yielded and his opponents prevailed, the Gentiles would have been robbed of the gospel's truth and left with a perverted, false gospel. That was too big a price for expedient conciliation.

THE GOSPEL IS RELEVANT TO ALL

[6] But from those who seemed to be something—whatever they were, it makes no difference to me; God shows personal favoritism to no man—for those who seemed to be something

35

added nothing to me. [7] But on the contrary, when they saw that the gospel for the uncircumcised had been committed to me, as the gospel for the circumcised was to Peter [8] (for He who worked effectively in Peter for the apostleship to the circumcised also worked effectively in me toward the Gentiles), [9] and when James, Cephas, and John, who seemed to be pillars, perceived the grace that had been given to me, they gave me and Barnabas the right hand of fellowship, that we should go to the Gentiles and they to the circumcised. [10] They desired only that we should remember the poor, the very thing which I also was eager to do.

—*Galatians 2:6–10*

The Value of Persons

In the economy of the kingdom of God all persons are of equal value.

Paul affirms this in a rather erratic, disjointed way in verse 6. In the original Greek, the sentence that begins here is ninety-five words long, strung together with relative pronouns and tumbling participles. It is a typical example of Paul's headlong style. He started out simply to say that James, Peter, and John had no problem with his gospel, that they found nothing lacking in it. Recognizing the quality of his apostleship, they sealed that by giving him and Barnabas the "right hand of fellowship." But as Paul began to dictate this, a big thought flashed in his mind and he pursued it: God plays no favorites.

The Relevance of the Gospel

The gospel is relevant to all. It can and should be made indigenous to every racial, cultural, and national setting.

The outcome of Paul's visit (vv. 7–10) was recognition that Paul's ministry with the uncircumcised and Peter's with the circumcised were equally needed and effective. The leaders of the Jerusalem church—James, John, and Peter—perceived the grace of the Lord Jesus working in Paul and Barnabas among the Gentiles, and they affirmed them in that by *"the right hand of fellowship."* The bottom line of that conference report was that Paul and Barnabas should go to the Gentiles, the uncircumcised; and James, John, and Peter to the Jews, the circumcised.

Beyond the circumcision/uncircumcision question is the fact that within Christianity there is a place for different expressions of the faith—expressions indigenous to the unique cultural, educational, social, economic, racial, and national identities of people. The World Christian Mission has not always been sensitive to this, and our history has too much evidence of the destruction of rich cultural heritage and custom in the name of Christianity. United States Southern colonial architecture set down in India does not pay proper respect to the richness of India's cultural tradition. But that is a surface symbol of a deeper issue—the issue of respect, appreciation, and acceptance for the customs and traditions of people that are not in conflict with the Christian faith and its moral and ethical demands.

Another issue here is the question of evangelism. We know the gospel is not limited to a particular class or category of people, and that the body of Christ is the welcome point and the meeting place of persons in all stations. It is precisely this same conviction that makes it necessary in our complex cultural situations, for the church to "fit" the people she seeks to reach culturally. In our evangelistic efforts there must be an absence of class intimidation or cultural imperialism. We must work at providing music, worship and preaching style, hymns—even architecture—to which those we are seeking to reach will subjectively and spontaneously respond.

Who reaches out to prospective Christians is very important. Those who have studied growing churches and effective ways of sharing the gospel personally in our modern day have concluded: (a) If the witnesser is a person within the intimate social network of the persons being witnessed to (a relative, friend, colleague, etc.) and is a transparently credible Christian who has some influence with them, then the chances of positive response are generally the greatest. (b) If the witnesser comes from outside the persons' social network but is a member of their "homogeneous units," the chances of a positive response are next greatest. (c) If the witnesser is an especially credible Christian, is gifted in cross-cultural communication, appears to love them, wants the best for them, is willing to take risks to reach them, and is willing to contact the same persons a number of times—then positive response to the messenger and the message is also possible from many receptive persons in a target population, but probably not all.[1]

An evangelistic strategy reflecting these principles recognizes that any community is composed of groups of people who have some characteristics in common and who feel that they belong and can communicate because of those characteristics. There are adequate data to support the position that "people are more likely to respond to the appeal of a congregation whose members are perceived to be like them culturally, among whom they feel comfortable and accepted and with whom they can communicate easily."[2]

To the degree that such a strategy refuses to recognize that the gospel breaks down all barriers, it is suspect. But, to the degree that it recognizes that there are significant linguistic, ethnic, and cultural distinctions in which people comfortably move, and therefore the gospel is to be shared as effectively as possible in such settings, such strategy is thoroughly Christian and responsive to the great commission of Christ to go into all the world and preach the gospel.

The Importance of Sharing

The early Christians knew that "man does not live by bread alone," but they also recognized that he does not live without bread. Along with the agreement that the gospel to the uncircumcised was committed to Paul and to the circumcised committed to Peter went the request that Paul and Barnabas should continue to remember the poor (v. 10). Paul said this was *"the very thing which I also was eager to do."*

The Galatians knew how earnest Paul was in this matter. During his ministry among them he had urged them to remember the poor (1 Cor. 16:1). He attached great importance to raising funds for the poor (2 Cor. 8–9; Rom. 15:25–28). Two ideas were behind this emphasis: such giving was an expression of gratitude for the love and grace of Christ, and such sharing was a means of knitting the Gentile and Jewish members of the body of Christ together in the Spirit.

Here are pivotal concepts for an understanding of Christian stewardship: gratitude and solidarity. We give because we are grateful, and we give cheerfully. In 2 Corinthians 9, Paul makes a marvelous statement about the spirit of giving as he writes about the offering he is taking for the saints: Be ready to give "as a *matter of bounty,* and not as of coveteousness." "Bounty" literally means "blessing." Such giving is to be done "not grudgingly, or of necessity: For God loves a cheerful giver" (2 Cor. 9:7).

Solidarity is the concept that because we belong to Christ we belong to each other. We are one body, and the needs and concern of one are the concerns of all. There was an added unique dimension to this truth in the early church. The gospel, in Palestine and abroad, found its most receptive hearing among the poor, the underprivileged, the slaves. The early Christian community was often referred to as "the beggars." It was an honorable title for the people whom Jesus called *blessed*. They were materially and spiritually at their wits' end. Then Jesus came and filled their lives with joy and meaning and bound them together in a fellowship so strong that the rich sold their goods to give to the poor. When the Spirit came with power at Pentecost it brought a unity of spirit and purpose—a solidarity that resulted in a glorious period of joyful sharing of all that the community possessed.

Unfortunately that period couldn't last forever. The Second Coming, expectantly awaited, was delayed and resources were exhausted. The unbelieving Jews who controlled the temple treasury were unsympathetic to the Jews who had newly become *Christian*. When they expelled them from the synagogues and denied them relief money from the temple treasury, the need for solidarity was intensified. Christians from other places were kept aware of the needs of Christians in Palestine where resources were limited, poverty rampant, and political strife the normal experience.

In the course of history, the gratitude of Christians moved the sense of solidarity from the bounds of the church to the whole of humanity. To be sure, there is a unique indissoluble bond among Christians, but Christians also feel a tacit bond with all humankind. Thus our missionary enterprise has been characterized by a concern for the plight of the poor, the enslaved, the disenfranchised of every nation. Ministering to physical needs is not separated from spiritual needs. Both flow from Christ's redemptive love as expressed in the lives of his followers.

INCONSISTENCY AND CONFLICT

[11] Now when Peter had come to Antioch, I withstood him to his face, because he was to be blamed; [12] for before certain men came from James, he would eat with the Gentiles; but when they came, he withdrew and separated himself, fearing those who were of the circumcision. [13] And the rest of the Jews also played the hypocrite with him, so that even Barnabas was carried away with their hypocrisy.

[14] But when I saw that they were not straightforward about the truth of the gospel, I said to Peter before them all, "If you, being a Jew, live in the manner of Gentiles and not as the Jews, why do you compel Gentiles to live as Jews?

—*Galatians 2:11–14*

39

It is an affirmation of the divinely inspired quality of Scripture, and of the validity of its message, that disagreement and conflict are not glossed over. These are not super human beings to whom we are looking and listening, but weak persons with the same foibles, failures, and inconsistencies that we know too well. That this weak side of their characters is revealed authenticates their witness.

This passage records one of the most significant incidents in the affirmation of Paul's independence as an apostle. Until this point, his claim of independence has been negatively asserted. He had not inherited his gospel, nor had he been taught, and he had never changed his gospel because of the wishes of alleged superiors. Now he has to take initiative and make a positive assertion of his independence by resisting the position of Peter and publicly remonstrating with him.

Peer Pressure

It is not easy to resist the pressure of our peers, or to go against the cultural structures of the community in which we live. Peter was caught in the crosscurrents of both. He came to Antioch where the majority of Christians were Gentiles. It was natural and unquestioned that he would have complete fellowship with them. They were one in the Spirit, and eating together was a normal expression of their unity. Then came "certain men from James," Jewish Christians, who put on the pressure that there could not be "table fellowship" between Jew and Gentile. So Peter yielded and separated himself from the Gentiles, *"fearing those who were of the circumcision"* (v. 12).

Peter is caught. Bless him! There is a sense in which the weak inconsistency of his relationship to Christ is again revealed. In one moment he had declared his willingness to lay down his life for Christ, had even drawn his sword in defense of his Master and cut off the ear of a man. But when they came to arrest his Lord, within hours, he denied Christ three times before being brought to repentance at the crowing of a rooster by memory of Jesus' word.

Is not the same impulsive courage followed by shrinking timidity illustrated again here? Paul's account doesn't say so, but it would be only consistent with his record that when brought to his senses, Peter would be ashamed and repentant of his denial of Christ in the presence of these Gentile converts.

We must not be too hard on Peter. It was a severe test to which he was exposed, and none of us can say how well we may stand in the fire. The beautiful thing to see is that in this instance, as in his attitude toward Cornelius, Peter's initial response is a readiness for fellowship with Gentiles. At the outset his course of action is dictated by Christian love. His heart carried him farther than his later judgment was prepared to go. Was he guilty then of weak vacillation? Yes, to a degree. But was this willful temporizing? No, not for Peter. What is apparent dishonor is rooted in honor. He simply found himself in the midst of an ordeal with baffling complications and implications, and he did not know what was right or wrong.

Paul, despite his tough language, understood the difficulty of the situation. His anger and anguish has more than a touch of personal appreciation as he adds that his loyal supporter, *"even Barnabas,"* has been carried away.

It is to our spiritual benefit, growth, and maturity, not that we are fickle in our loyalty, wavering in our convictions, but that, like Peter, when our weakness is revealed we acknowledge our betrayal, repent in sorrow, and dedicate ourselves again to be Christ's representatives and servants.

"He was to be blamed" is a gentle translation of the Greek here. Peter *stood condemned.* His fear of the ultraconservative Jews of the circumcision overcame him and led him to betray himself as well as the Gentile Christians. He betrayed the Gentile Christians by refusing table fellowship with them. He betrayed himself by denying his own Spirit-given insight that "God shows no partiality" (Acts 10:34).

Only Peter and Peter's God could know whether, and to what degree, Peter was hypocritical. Paul could not get inside his heart, know his thoughts, feelings, and purposes; only God could. But the inconsistency was so glaring and the cause so great Paul had to storm the gates of his heart and "blame him" to his face.

Here is another indicator of the Christian style. Conflict can be resolved only in *face-to-face* encounter. No positive purpose is ever served by "behind the back" accusation or innuendo. This becomes gossip, which is always counterproductive and often destructive.

Hypocrisy

"Even Barnabas was carried away with their hypocrisy" (v. 13). The KJV renders that "Barnabas also," but that misses the impact of Paul's assertion, *"even Barnabas."* All the New Testament notices of Barnabas reveal an attractive, effective Christian. None are exempt from temptation. All of us are potential victims of the pressures that would deceive, convince, lead astray, diminish our witness. Even

persons *"full of the Holy Spirit and of faith"* such as Barnabas must keep vigilance and pray for divine guidance and perspective.

FUTILITY OF THE LAW FOR SALVATION

15 We who are Jews by nature, and not sinners of the Gentiles, 16 knowing that a man is not justified by the works of the law but by faith in Jesus Christ, even we have believed in Christ Jesus, that we might be justified by faith in Christ and not by the works of the law; for by the works of the law no flesh shall be justified.

—Galatians 2:15–16

Law as a basis for right relationship with God is futile and must be abandoned once and for all (Gal. 2:14–19). Only through faith in Christ Jesus are we justified. Paul had learned this through his own bitter defeat as well as from his observation of others (Rom. 1:16—2:29; 7:4–25).

The heart of the gospel and Paul's immortal expression of it is in verse 16: *A man is not justified by the works of the law but by faith in Jesus Christ.*

In the following verses (16–21), Paul soars to breathless heights. Though he is recalling what he said to Peter at Antioch it soon looks as though Peter is forgotten. By the time he gets to the end, he is so passionately captured by the truth of the gospel he is proclaiming that he even transcends the particular focus of his letter. Paul pours out the passion of his soul and moves to the ultimate height of the powerful work of Christ in his own life: *"I have been crucified with Christ; it is no longer I who live, but Christ lives in me"* (v. 20).

There are three key words in this passage: *law, justified,* and *faith.*

The Jewish Understanding of the Law

Law, as conceived and experienced by Paul and his fellow Jews, was nowhere near our present understanding of it in a twentieth-century state of representative government. The function of modern law is to govern the relations of persons with each other and with institutions. Such law makes no determination of a person's relationship to God. For the Jews the opposite was true. Obedience to the Law rendered one in right relationship to God and made one acceptable to God. Works of the Law were those deeds done in obedience to the Torah, rather than those things done according to one's own will.

42

The object of obedience was to justify oneself in relation to God in order to be accepted by Him. The anguishing turmoil running through Israel's effort at salvation confirms Paul's experience that no effort on the part of persons is ever adequate to make one righteous before God. Psalm 143 gives expression to this anguish: "Hear my prayer, O Lord; give ear to my supplications! In thy faithfulness answer me, in thy righteousness! Enter not into judgment with thy servant; for no man living is righteous before thee" (Ps. 143:1–2, RSV).

Paul had personified the Jew's ardent struggle to be righteous by the law. His strenuous efforts to "get right" with God were always thwarted by the weakness of his sinful human nature. He knew the depressing abyss of failure into which one could fall, doing what he decidedly didn't want to do, and failing to do what he desperately wanted to do (cf. Rom. 7:15–20). He could conclude from the history of his race and from his own futile effort that *"by the works of the law no flesh will be justified."*

Righteousness and Justification

"Justified" is a metaphor from a court of law. The Greek for this comes from a root word meaning "point out" or "show." The English root is "right," coming from the Anglo-Saxon "richt," which means "straight," not crooked. A person is "right" when he conforms to a standard of acceptable character or conduct. The state or quality of this conformity is "righteousness" (rightness), or "justice." In Latin the corresponding terms are *justifico, justus,* and *justiflcatio.* In Hebrew you have the same meaning, so that in the four languages the idea is that of a norm by which persons or things are tested. Thus in Hebrew a person is "righteous" when he does God's will. Likewise, a wall is "righteous" when it conforms to a plumb line.

In modern speech we don't use "righteousness" and "justice" in the same fashion, therefore most of us make no connection between justification and righteousness. But for Paul they are simply different semantic forms of the same idea.

We commonly use "justify" in two ways that will give clarity to its use here. We say a person is seeking to *justify* himself by making excuse for what he has done or said. A typesetter justifies type. In fact, we have electric typewriters that will *justify* the margins of a typewritten page—that is, align all the lines of type at both ends.

This latter usage comes near the meaning of Paul. To justify is to rectify in relation to a norm. To justify is to make *right,* not to make just or fair or equitable.

43

Understanding it thus, Paul can conclude that "if righteousness comes through the law, then Christ died in vain" (v. 21). Get it clear: *righteousness* as it is being used here refers not to a quality of goodness as we may see it, but to a relationship.

Here then is the core of Paul's experience and teaching. It is God who justifies, rectifies. No law could force our unruly nature to comply with God's norm. To follow the judicial metaphor, one has to admit that one is a guilty criminal and throw oneself on the mercy of the judge. Then the unbelievable, radical thing happens. God, the judge, contrary to all expectation, not only acquits the guilty one, but accepts him as a son, makes him with Christ a fellow heir of the kingdom.

We cannot understand Paul, nor can we participate fully in the Christian experience, until we grasp the fact that to be *justified* means that as sinners we are "acquitted," "accepted," "set right with God," "saved" despite our sin.

What then is the "righteousness" of God? His righteousness is his justifying action in relation to persons. Paul stated it in this fashion in his letter to the Romans: "But now the righteousness of God has been manifested apart from the law, although the law and the prophets bear witness to it, the righteousness of God through faith in Jesus Christ for all who believe" (Rom. 3:21–22, RSV). His righteousness, then, is his justification of all—Jew and Gentile alike. His unique nature is that he "justifies the ungodly."

What a strange turn of mind in the Jewish system—a God who justifies the *ungodly*, not the godly! Don't miss the importance of this. If God justified the godly, we could calculate and even control our justification, because we would have an achievement-reward system. Such a system can be manipulated, so justification would really be in our hands. Paul says this can't be so: *"A man is not justified by the works of the law but by faith in Jesus Christ"* (v. 16).

The Meaning of Faith

Thus comes the third key word in this core passage: *faith.* The primary meaning of faith for Paul is *trust,* and thus not a passive grateful reception of God's mercy but rather an active entrustment of oneself upon the mercy and into the hands of God. Faith is a personal decision and commitment. Trust is the best understanding of faith because it is both a verb and a noun. We have trust; we also can trust someone. Faith as a word does not have a verb form. We can't say "I *faith* him." We are justified by faith—trust—in Jesus Christ, that is by entrusting ourselves to him.

Jesus provided us the best illustration of faith which is basically trust. "Whosoever does not receive the kingdom of God as a little child will by no means enter it" (Mark 10:15). A child trusts herself to her mother or father; puts herself, without worry or concern, into their care.

This radical faith (entrusting ourselves to Christ for salvation) saves us from two great pitfalls: one, the pitfall of trying to earn favor with God; and two, the temptation to compare our moral and spiritual achievement with others in order that we may be seen in a different light.

ALL IN GRACE

[17] "But if, while we seek to be justified by Christ, we ourselves also are found sinners, is Christ therefore a minister of sin? Certainly not! [18] For if I build again those things which I destroyed, I make myself a transgressor. [19] For I through the law died to the law that I might live to God. [20] I have been crucified with Christ; it is no longer I who live, but Christ lives in me; and the life which I now live in the flesh I live by faith in the Son of God, who loved me and gave Himself for me. [21] I do not set aside the grace of God; for if righteousness comes through the law, then Christ died in vain."

—Galatians 2:17–21

All in grace, said Paul, and this alarmed the Judaizers. They were afraid that this would become "cheap grace." People may delude themselves into thinking that they could sin willfully and flagrantly, believing that God would accept them by a mere profession of faith (vv. 17–19).

Paul was always having to deal with this form of objection to his understanding of grace (cf. Rom 6–8). In verse 17, he repeats his critics: *"if, while we seek to be justified by Christ, we ourselves also are found sinners, is Christ therefore a minister of sin?"* Indignant, Paul utters a resounding *"Certainly not!"* The freedom that comes through Christ is not a license to sin, but a strength to live in righteousness. Being justified places us under obligation: *"For I through the law died to the law that I might live to God."*

The meaning of this will be considered fully when we come to Paul's word about Christian freedom in Galatians 5 (p. 96 ff.).

Here is Paul's most vivid description of what happened to him on the Road to Damascus and since: *"I have been crucified with Christ; it is no longer I who live, but Christ lives in me"* (v. 20).

I have a friend who is a Benedictine monk. The way we live out our lives is vastly different, but I feel a real kinship, a oneness of spirit, with Brother Sam. One of the most meaningful memories, to which I return often in my mind, is an evening he and I spent alone sharing our Christian journeys. The vivid highlight of that evening was his sharing with me the details of the service when he made his solemn vows of life commitment to the Benedictine community and the monastic life.

He prostrated himself before the altar of the chapel in the very spot where his coffin will be when he dies. Covered in a funeral pall, the death bell that tolls at the earthly parting of a brother sounded the solemn gongs of death. Then there was silence—the silence of death. The silence of the gathered community was broken by the singing of the Colossian word, "For you have died, and your life is hid with Christ in God" (Col. 3:3, KJV). After that powerful word, there was more silence as Brother Sam reflected upon his solemn vow. Then the community broke into singing Psalm 118 which is always a part of the Easter liturgy in the Benedictine community: "I shall not die, but live, and declare the works of the Lord" (v. 18, KJV).

After this resurrection proclamation, the deacon shouted the word from Ephesians: "Awake, you who sleep; arise from the dead, and Christ will give you light" (5:14). Then the bells of the abbey rang loudly and joyfully. Brother Sam stood, the funeral pall fell off, and the robe of the Benedictine order was placed on him. He received the kiss of peace and was welcomed into the community to live a life "hidden in Christ."

This great liturgy of death and resurrection, a symbolic reactment of Paul's experience, is the essence of the Christian affirmation "I have been crucified with Christ. I am now alive in Him."

"I have been crucified with Christ" is the literal translation. The KJV uses the Greek perfect tense: "I am crucified." This brings out the continuing result of our being *in* Christ. The life he now lives in the flesh he lives "by faith in the Son of God, who loved me and gave Himself for me" (v. 20).

Three words capture the dynamic meaning of crucifixion with Christ: *pardon, power, partnership.*

1. Being crucified with Christ brings *pardon.* This pardon means forgiveness from past sin, freedom from the law, but also a passionate urge never to sin again (cf. Rom. 4:24–25; 2 Cor. 5:14–15; Col. 2:12–15, 20, 3:1–4).

46

2. Being crucified with Christ brings *power.* This power comes as we give ourselves to the lordship of Christ. We yield ourselves to Him. Our "I will" becomes dominated by "the mind of Christ," and this is our power (cf. 2 Cor. 10:3–6; Rom. 6:1–11). We do not live out of our own resources but Christ lives in us. His power sustains us.

Let's look at this from the posh side of the tracks, where sports cars and riding lawn mowers, tennis clubs and dancing lessons, are common accouterments. But these accouterments don't provide the satisfaction they promise, or make alienation and emptiness less painful.

We'll call the people in our story Mark and Sue. Their Maryland suburb of Washington, D.C. could be any upper middle- or upper-class section in America. Mark's $145,000-a-year salary, the security of his government job, and the comfort and beauty of their $300,000 home weren't adequate, nor was Sue's degree from one of the most prestigious Ivy League universities, to fill the deep need of their life.

The ultimate sign of the family's crumbling came when one of four boys in the family, a brilliant seventeen-year-old, was stabbed almost to death in a drug brawl. Then, though recovered from the stabbing, he was incarcerated in a youth detention home. When I met them, the young son was still in the detention home, but Mark and Sue were coping beautifully. They told me about their transformation. The son's debacle had driven them to a Marriage Enrichment Weekend.

There they not only met themselves and faced up to the emptiness of their lives, the brokenness of their relationship as husband and wife, and the futility of their life-style; they met Jesus. They surrendered themselves to Him and invited Him to be Lord of their lives.

I don't say that casually. Nor did they. It was obvious to me that Jesus had given them meaning and power, and they were gradually, with love, purpose, and commitment, by the grace and guidance of the indwelling Christ, painstakingly putting their broken marriage and shattered family together again. They are not healed altogether, but they are being healed. They still have problems—one son in detention, three others damaged by the limited relationship—but they are coping and they know joy and meaning.

They have entered a new realm, a new kingdom, and are being given *power* as they give themselves to the lordship of Jesus.

3. Being crucified with Christ means *partnership.* This partnership brings power of the sort we have just discussed, but it also brings

suffering and thus another kind of power (see also Phil. 3:10, Rom. 8:17; Col. 1:24–25). Being crucified with Christ, we enter into His creative suffering to "complete what remains of Christ's affliction" for the sake of His body the church.

Death and resurrection is the rhythm of the Christian life. Baptism marks the death of the old person and the miraculous beginning of a new life under the banner of the resurrection. So Paul declares, "It is no longer I who live, but Christ lives in me."

The power of this transformation is seen in countless lives. Here it is in a young man, well along in his religious pilgrimage, reared in a Christian home, actively committed to the cause of justice and peace, studying for the ordained ministry, but only recently coming alive to the power of "not I but Christ lives in me." In a letter following a few days we had spent together he wrote,

> Hey, we love you. . . . Our life in Christ has really taken off. So many things about our faith have taken wings for us. *Absolution*—incredible—that not only does God wipe the slate clean but he also provides the juice for a completely new start.
>
> One night alone in prayer I took God to task on a few of his promises. I was feeling like I needed to come into close contact with him and I was feeling, I guess, a hole in my spirit. I prayed and asked him to fill my life with whatever I was missing. I asked and waited and asked again and waited for a long time. Then I just said, "Lord, I'll try to be your man. I will let you live in me." Immediately I was filled with a powerful ecstatic joy. Like orgasm in every cell, I said, "Fantastic, God! This is incredible, how about some more?" And more came— my head was buzzing and I felt like I would explode with joy. Then I thanked God and went to sleep.
>
> The following day I was no different on the surface. It was my same life, same realities to deal with, *but I felt great knowing God was in this thing with me.* I have a new set of tools at my disposal and I'm finding that they're needed.

The "new tools" at my friend's disposal was the power that comes from the "not I but Christ lives in me" factor of *being crucified with Christ.*

Being crucified with Christ was an experiential fact for Paul. We must guard against the temptation that has plagued the church almost from the beginning—the temptation to take Paul's crucifixion with Christ as symbolic only, or to equate it with the ritual of baptism that seeks to make being crucified with Christ sacramentally automatic—something done or conferred by the church with intrinsic validity apart from our living it out. Paul's "faith" must never be reduced to bare belief and assent to doctrine. Reading his letters, we can never forget that being crucified with Christ means sharing the way of life that led Jesus to the Cross, living by His purposes and being impelled by His motives.

The crucified-with-Christ style requires sharing in the suffering of Christ in the fashion discussed above. It also means vicariously taking the sin-burdens of others, giving and forgiving in love instead of condemning.

Paul's witness to the Galatians is that we are always faced with a call, a call to which we must respond in our thinking, speaking, acting, and suffering. We are called into *being* by God at creation. We are called into *new being* by God at redemption through Jesus Christ. Our redemption as new beings is not simply a state; it is a pilgrimage, a path that is opened to us by "the pioneer and perfector of our faith." This pilgrimage is ceaselessly characterized by forgetting what lies behind and stretching and straining for what lies ahead—"the prize of our high calling in Christ," *with whom I have been crucified.*

"The life I now live in the flesh" is Paul's reference to his whole self. Paul does not set flesh against spirit, as we tend to. Nor does Paul see flesh (Gk. *sarx*) as identical with body *(sōma).* Nor is flesh, in Paul's usage, the substance of the body as we see it. Rather, like Spirit, flesh is a domain of power, a sphere of influence in which one lives. For Paul, to live *"in the flesh"* was to live as a member of human society in a physical body.

There is a kind of pathos for Paul in this word "flesh" because he is talking about the creatively transient, vulnerable, contingent character of life.

It is important to see clearly that Paul did not equate flesh and sin. The only passage in which it might appear that he did is in Romans 8:3 where the Incarnation is seen as "God. . . sending his own Son in the likeness of sinful flesh . . ." and "condemned sin in the flesh." "Sinful flesh" appears to characterize flesh itself as sinful while "condemned sin in the flesh" distinguishes flesh from sin. The latter is true to Paul's understanding. Sin is linked closely to flesh because flesh is the domain of power where sin operates. Sin, not flesh, is condemned. God came in Christ to enter the

49

domain of power, the flesh, in order that sin might be conquered once and for all. Our predicament is not that we are *in the flesh,* but that we are in sin, that is, living according to, setting our minds on flesh rather than the spirit, as a domain of power.

With this understanding, Paul's affirmation makes sense and is the call for us: "The life I now live in the flesh I live by faith in the Son of God, who loved me and gave Himself for me."

We are *in the flesh* and will be until we die. To be in the flesh is not to be in sin, but to live "according to the flesh" is to be in sin. Spirit is the power-sphere of the new age. Living "by faith in the Son of God" is to live in Spirit, not to have the norms and values of our life shaped by the frail, vulnerable transient nature of flesh, but to be in a new realm, the kingdom of Spirit, where power is ours from the indwelling Christ, and hope is ours because of His Resurrection.

"In the flesh," then, is the counterpart of being "in the Spirit" (Rom. 8:9). "Fleshly" living is to have the mind set on our frail, limited flesh, rather than the Spirit.

Paul now flings the argument back upon his critics: It is you, not I, who have set aside the grace of God. ". . . *If righteousness comes through the law, then Christ died in vain"* (v. 21). You wish to retain the law not as God's grace gift to Israel; you want to keep the law along with God's grace gift in Christ. Why would God give us Christ if He wanted only obedience to law? God desired our love, and the only way He could get it was by showing His love in its most extreme yet complete expression—sending His own Son to die for us. If you believe in Christ, then you are denying His purpose by continuing to seek to be justified by law. You can't have it both ways.

So in these concluding verses of chapter 2 (vv. 15–21), Paul has preached his whole gospel again as he did in 1:1–5. It is the gospel of grace, faith, and freedom—a gospel he will now seek to vindicate in the next section of his letter by appeal to the facts of Christian history and experience.

NOTES

1. George G. Hunter, *The Contagious Congregation* (Nashville: Abingdon, 1979), p. 110.

2. Ibid.

CHAPTER THREE—JUSTIFICATION BY FAITH
GALATIANS 3:1–29

Scripture Outline

Jesus Christ: Crucified and Risen (3:1–5)

Abraham: The Prototype of the True Believer (3:6–9)

Redeemed from the Curse by the Cross (3:10–14)

The Changeless Promise (3:15–18)

The Law: Our Custodian (3:19–25)

Baptized into Christ (3:26–29)

JESUS CHRIST: CRUCIFIED AND RISEN

3:1 O foolish Galatians! Who has bewitched you that you should not obey the truth, before whose eyes Jesus Christ was clearly portrayed among you as crucified? **2** This only I want to learn from you: Did you receive the Spirit by the works of the law, or by the hearing of faith?— **3** Are you so foolish? Having begun in the Spirit, are you now being made perfect by the flesh? **4** Have you suffered so many things in vain—if indeed it was in vain?

5 Therefore He who supplies the Spirit to you and works miracles among you, does He do it by the works of the law, or by the hearing of faith?

—Galatians 3:1–5

It is not by works of the law, but by hearing with faith that we become the recipients of God's grace. The message is clear.

The Posted Message

"O foolish Galatians!" Paul addresses them with fire in his heart and his pen. He can't understand it. *"Who has bewitched*

you . . .?" To capture the burning intensity of this address, J. B. Phillips translated it, "O you dear idiots of Galatia . . . who has been casting a spell over you?" *The New English Bible* has it, "You stupid Galatians! You must have been bewitched." How could you miss it?—you *"before whose eyes Jesus Christ was clearly portrayed among you as crucified"* (v. 1).

During a visit to the Peoples' Republic of China, I was using Barclay's Daily Bible Study of Galatians for my daily devotional reading, and I came to this third chapter the day I entered that country. This verse might not have struck me with such power had I read it in another setting. "You before whose very eyes Jesus Christ was placarded upon His cross."

China is the land of posters, and placards were everywhere. Great crowds gather around the walls where posters are displayed. A primary means of communication, posters have been used to share the message of liberation and revolution for thirty years in this vast land. Not only are posters used for the current propaganda, there are some omnipresent ones. Pictures of Chairman Mao, Premier Hua, Marx, Lenin, and Stalin were in every school we visited, every factory, and in every reception room of every commune. The thinkers, planners, and leaders of the socialist revolution are constantly before the eyes of the people of China.

The Greek word which Barclay translates "placarded" in this verse is *phrographien.* One of the words Paul used for preaching, it meant "post a notice," as on a bulletin board in a public square. This is why it came through to me with such power in China. Barclay reminds us that in New Testament times the word was used to describe what a father did when he proclaimed publicly that he would no longer be responsible for his son's debts.

In the same fashion, but conveying the opposite message, Jesus Christ, *placarded upon His Cross,* has been portrayed among the Galatians. The message posted on the bulletin board of our hearts is not that the Father will no longer be responsible for our debts, but that through the crucified Christ He has paid our debts.

Later we will deal more completely with the images of redemption used by Paul. He and other New Testament writers talked about the way of our salvation in such terms as payment of debt, release from bondage, satisfaction for our sins, reconciliation, the old Adam dying and the New Adam coming to life. Whatever the image, the truth is clear. The central message of the New Testament is that in the Cross Christ has done something for us which we cannot do for ourselves. And through the Cross our "lawless deeds are forgiven," and our "sins are buried away."

Paul struggled for an image, as we do, to communicate the full meaning of the Cross—crucified love that frees us and replaces the binding cords of rigid law. And it is all the grace of God which is received by faith.

This crucified love, Jesus Christ on the Cross, had been portrayed among the Galatians. They had known the deliverance, joy, and freedom that comes through "hearing with faith" this message of redemption. But they were deceived again, on the verge of turning again into the dead-end way of seeking salvation by their own efforts of keeping the law.

As in a picket line, Paul carried high the placard of Christ crucified so that all might see God's love, not His condemnation. Every sermon he preached and every letter he wrote publicly portrayed this central message: the dying and rising Christ.

The Foolishness of the Galatians

The Galatians were *"foolish,"* Paul said. The problem of the Galatians, like ours, was not stupidity, but perception; not a lack of sense, but a lack of faith. In the passive sense, the word translated foolish in this passage means "unthinkable," and in modern Greek it is "unreasonable." This was Paul's charge against them. They were doing the "unthinkable," the "unreasonable." They had known the joy and freedom of God's grace operating in their lives. They were being deceived by the Judaizers, and were surrendering *that* glorious freedom for the stultifying structures of law.

Receiving the Spirit

"Did you receive the Spirit by works of the law," Paul wants to know, "or by hearing with faith?" There are two powerful concepts in verse 2 that are central in Paul's understanding of the gospel: Spirit and "hearing with faith."

1. Paul's view of flesh and Spirit is more commonly misunderstood than anything else he wrote, and the consequences of misunderstanding are serious. In the previous chapter we looked at Paul's understanding of flesh, which is not to be confused with *body.* Now, let us look at his understanding of Spirit.

Spirit was important in the Christian experience for Paul. The eighth chapter of Romans mentions Spirit more than any chapter in the New Testament. Both Corinthian letters are dominated by Paul's effort to clarify the meaning and experience of the Spirit.

Our primary problem in dealing with the Spirit is that we are seeking to understand and communicate publicly what is an intensely personal experience. What we can see, and to some degree describe, are manifestations of the Spirit's work such as healing, or certain behavior such as speaking in tongues which is attributed to the Spirit. Neither the Spirit nor the experience of the Spirit is observable—only the manifestations. Even the person having the experience cannot observe it. So we struggle to talk about the most intimate and sometimes most intense experiences of the divine.

Though in our talking we try to distinguish between human and divine Spirit, in actuality one cannot be isolated experientially from the other. Paul was probably the first Christian theologian who recognized that the more we emphasize the action of the divine Spirit, the more we must emphasize human cooperation with the Spirit.

Four aspects of understanding are enough for us to go on as we seek to comprehend Paul's message: (a) The divine Spirit, he said, was not to be confused with heightened human power. The Spirit was power, *divinely given*, thus called the *Holy* Spirit. (b) Every Christian was a recipient of this power. By definition that is what/who a Christian is—one who has been divinely empowered for the life of the new age.

To be empowered by, filled with, lived in, guided by, clothed with, healed by the Spirit should be the norm of the Christian life, not the exception. Nowhere in the New Testament is there even a hint that the Holy Spirit is a special gift to a chosen few. The gift belongs to all who have been reconciled to God through the crucified Lord.

This is not to deny a unique "baptism of the Spirit." Paul affirms that such a baptism is not a completed experience any more than conversion is a completed experience. Conversion is the beginning of an ongoing process of "little" conversions in which the different dimensions of our characters are converted, changed, and born anew to the Christ-life. So any extra or heightened measure of the Holy Spirit that we receive is the sign given us that every area of our lives can be brought under the guiding, sustaining, changing, healing power of the Holy Spirit.

To refer to persons as "Spirit-filled Christians" should never mean that such persons possess the fullest measure of the Spirit that is possible. Such is never the case. Nor should the designation be used to define a "higher" category of the Christian life, or to identify an elitist group that has "made it." Had Paul used that term, he would have used it in the fashion of Galatians 2:20. He could have as well said, "The life I now live in the flesh I live by faith in the Son of God, filled with the Holy Spirit, so that I no longer live, but Christ lives in me." To be Spirit-filled, for Paul, would be no longer to live under the power of sin in the domain of the flesh, but to live under the power of Christ in the domain of the Spirit.

This does not deny that some persons may receive an extra measure of the Spirit, and particular gifts of the Spirit for ministry. The New Testament and Christian history confirm that particular gifts of the Spirit are given to some and not to others, and some persons do receive an extra measure of the Spirit. Acts 11:27–28 tells of Agabus who had the Spirit's power to prophesy. Acts 21:9–12 tells not only of Agabus again, but also of Philip's four unmarried daughters prophesying. Paul worked miracles in the Spirit (2 Cor. 12:12) and witnessed to visions and ecstatic experiences (1 Cor. 9:1; 14:18; 2 Cor. 12:1–4).

(c) The third aspect of understanding central to Paul was the Spirit as a sign that the new age is already dawning. Receiving the Spirit marked one's participation in the kingdom, which, though not fully present, was on the way and would some day soon burst forth full-blown. Paul used two metaphors for this: *down-payment* (Gk. *arrabon*, 2 Cor. 1:22; 5:5) and *first-fruits* (Gk. *aparche*, Rom. 8:23).

The Revised Standard Version renders *arrabon* as a guarantee, the *New English Bible* as a pledge. Pledge is more accurate because it captures the meaning of "earnest," as used in the King James Version. This is like "earnest money" paid in real estate negotiations, indicating that the buyer will complete the transaction. The *aparche* language comes from the Old Testament law requiring that the first part of the harvest be given to God.

In using these two metaphors, Paul expresses his conviction that the Spirit's presence means the inauguration, not the consummation, of the new age. Christians, gifted with the Spirit, are *in-between people,* living as though the "not yet" kingdom is already here. The present gift of the Spirit points ahead, but provides the confidence and power for living in the flesh without being under the domination of sin.

One aspect of this essential reality to be experienced by all Christians must not be overlooked. *The gift must not be separated from the Giver.* God is sovereign and exercises His sovereignty by giving His gifts. Recipients live as subjects in a kingdom where the risen Christ reigns. Thus Spirit is a power-structure. To be "in the Spirit" and to have the Spirit "dwell in you" are different ways to express the fact that as Christians our domain of power is not the flesh but Spirit.

(d) The fourth aspect of Paul's message concerning the Spirit is his insistence that there is a diversity of gifts. This is called *charismata,* and is derived from *charis,* meaning grace. This is also the source of our adjective "charismatic." The gifts of the Spirit are "begracements," given for the common good of the community. (We will examine this in more detail when we discuss *gifts* and *fruits* of the Spirit in Gal. 5.)

How crucial this understanding is for us! To be "begraced" by the Spirit can never be a matter for boasting. Likewise, not to be "begraced" in a particular way, with a specific gift, should not bring a sense of inferiority. There is genius in Paul's comparison of the community (church) with a body (1 Cor. 12). What a challenge! Christians with less impressive gifts need not cower back self-pityingly, in depression, or with a sense of worthlessness any more than a foot should feel inferior to a hand. The opposite is also true. For Christians with more impressive gifts, to be puffed up, thinking more highly of themselves than they ought to think, is as foolish as an eye saying to a hand, "I have no need of you."

It is in the context of this discussion of the diversity of gifts, and gifts given for the common good of the community, that Paul shared the "hymn of love" (1 Cor. 13). Love is the chief gift which all can have. This gift, along with faith and hope, endures long after the prized gifts of prophecy, tongue-speaking, and knowledge pass away.

2. Along with Spirit, the second concept in verse 2 central to Paul's understanding of the gospel is "hearing with faith." These two concepts are connected. In asking the question in verse 2, and in his comments in verses 4 and 5, Paul is saying that we are "begraced," gifted by the Spirit "by hearing with faith."

For the Galatians, "hearing with faith" was not as vague and as ambiguous as it may be to us. Remember that Paul had been with the Galatians, lived with them, preached to them, taught them formally as well as informally in countless hours of conversation. They knew that Paul was referring to what he discussed in a more systematic way in his Letter to the Romans: "Faith comes from what is heard and what is heard comes by the preaching of Christ" (Rom. 10:17, RSV). Paul is talking here not about the content of faith, or the state of mind of the listener, but of the believing kind of hearing that is open to the gospel, welcomes it, and leads the hearer to yield to Christ and entrust his life to Christ.

To hear the law and the traditions set down by Moses and the fathers carried with it the burden of straining nobly to keep it, and the guilt of inevitable failure. Hearing the gospel creates faith in which the Spirit is received.

With his tenacious argumentative skills, Paul gets the Galatians in the steel vise of their own experience. There could be no middle ground. The Spirit came either by hearing with faith, or by law. The Galatians had only one answer from their experience: the Spirit came by the hearing with faith.

It is everlastingly so, Paul would say. We are "begraced" not according to our merit, our accomplishments, our keeping the law, living the "good" life, obeying the commandments, abiding by the Golden Rule, but by obedient trust.

ABRAHAM: THE PROTOTYPE OF THE TRUE BELIEVER

6 just as Abraham "believed God, and it was accounted to him for righteousness." 7 Therefore know that only those who are of faith are sons of Abraham. 8 And the Scripture, foreseeing that God would justify the Gentiles by faith, preached the gospel to Abraham beforehand, saying, "In you all the nations shall be blessed." 9 So then those who are of faith are blessed with believing Abraham.

—Galatians 3:6–9

Paul has appealed to the Galatians by reminding them of their own experience with Christ. He now turns to Scripture and calls Abraham as witness. He exercises a traditional Jewish practice of taking an application of Scripture to explain a proposition of faith. But the truth he draws from this particular application differs from the understanding of the Jews and the Epistle of James. The Jews and James were convinced that God's justification of Abraham was the well-merited reward for his supreme proof of devotion. Precisely the opposite is true, says Paul. No wonder his insight from the Abraham story was so blasphemous to the Jew. Abraham did not receive a gift that was *due* him, but a gift of grace.

In Romans 4, Paul founded his conviction that God "justifies the ungodly" on the story of Abraham. Abraham was not justified according to his works, but according to his faith: "Abraham believed God, and it was reckoned to him as righteousness. Now to one who works, his wages are not reckoned as a gift but as his due. And to one who does not work but trusts him who justifies the ungodly, his faith is reckoned as righteousness" (Rom. 4:3–5). Paul turned to the story of Abraham, which Jews would know so well, to make his case that Gentile believers were by their faith the sons of Abraham and the recipients of God's righteousness/justification, just as Abraham was.

Even before Paul's day in Judaism, and continuing after Paul in the entire New Testament era, Abraham was seen as *the prototype of the true believer.* He is still that personification of faith.

Paul's logic is watertight. He knew that God pronounced Abraham to be righteous in Genesis 15:6, when Abraham believed the Lord's promise to give him an heir and to number his descendants as the stars in the sky. He was pronounced righteous *because of his faith.* It was not until Genesis 17 that the story of Abraham's circumcision is told. The circumcision was "a sign or seal of the righteousness which he had by faith when he was still uncircumcised."

Using this scriptural knowledge, Paul says, *"Know that only those who are of faith are sons of Abraham"* (Gal. 3:7). Paul develops this argument in Romans 4, asserting that the purpose of Abraham's circumcision was to make him (1) "the father of all who believe without being circumcised and who thus have righteousness reckoned to them" (Rom. 4:11, RSV) and (2) "the father of the circumcised who are not merely circumcised but also follow the example of the faith which our father Abraham had before he was circumcised" (Rom. 4:12, RSV).

Here is a subtle point that the Galatians were sure to get. Abraham is the father of all faithful people—those whose relationship to God is one of trust. Implicit here is the denial that Abraham is the father of all circumcised Jews. He is truly father *only* of those who live by trust—circumcised or not.

So Abraham is a personification of faith. His behavior showed Jew and Christian alike what was meant by faith. The dynamics of faith, lived by Abraham are: (1) response to God's call (Gen. 12:1–4); (2) trust in God's promises (Gen. 15); (3) obedience to God's commands (Gen. 22:2–10).

For Paul, the gospel is not a culmination of what had begun with Abraham; Jesus' death is not just a climactic event in salvation history. Rather, the gospel is the recovery of, the actualization of what God did in response to Abraham's faith. "And the Scripture, foreseeing that God would justify the Gentiles by faith, preached the gospel to Abraham beforehand, saying '*In you all the nations shall be blessed*'" (Gal. 3:8). Thus, all who believed are blessed with Abraham (v. 9). God's dream is not realized in the history of Israel, but in the community of Jews and Gentiles whose faith-trustful obedience is like Abraham's.

REDEEMED FROM THE CURSE BY THE CROSS

[10] For as many as are of the works of the law are under the curse; for it is written, "Cursed is everyone who does not continue in all things which are written in the book of the law, to do them." [11] But that no one is justified by the law in the sight of God is evident, for "the just shall live by faith." [12] Yet the law is not of faith, but "the man who does them shall live by them."

[13] Christ has redeemed us from the curse of the law, having become a curse for us (for it is written, "Cursed is everyone who hangs on a tree"), [14] that the blessing of Abraham might come upon the Gentiles in Christ Jesus, that we might receive the promise of the Spirit through faith.

—*Galatians 3:10–14*

The Curse of Living by the Law

With an unbelievable boldness, almost verging on arrogance, Paul attacked his opponents where they themselves felt invulnerable. Again he uses Scripture with which the Jews would be familiar to make his case on behalf of the gospel. He quotes Deuteronomy 27:26, "Cursed is everyone who does not continue in all things which are written in the books of the law, to do them." One has to read all of Deuteronomy 27 to understand the powerful meaning of this quote. Twelve verses of that chapter begin with the word "cursed," and the response of the people is "Amen." To be cursed was to be condemned to the torments of hell.

The list of those who are cursed include those who "dishonor father or mother," "pervert justice due the sojourners," or one who "has sexual intercourse with his sister, or mother-in-law" or "any kind of beast," "takes a bribe" or "slays his neighbor." The climax of the "cursing" was for those who did not keep every law.

Paul's argument was scathingly plain. "For as many as are of the works of the law are under the curse." If any person is going to base his salvation upon keeping the law, there can be no exception. "Continue in" was a legal term meaning "comply with." All laws must be kept, even the least commandment, and a fatal curse is upon a small or great failure.

There is a very important and intricate point here. The *curse* comes from law misconceived as a way of salvation. It is not the curse of God. Rabbis reasoned that since the Scripture was God's Word, the curse pronounced on the disobedient was God's curse. Paul's response to that (v. 19) was that the law was only a codicil which angels added "by the hand of a mediator"—Moses. The law was not God's way of salvation; thus the curse was not God's but the law's. In God's heart Paul saw a cross, not a curse.

Again Paul was devastating in his logic. He put his opponents in a dead-end alley from which there was no escape. His reasoning moves step by step. One, if you decide to seek God's favor by accepting and abiding by the law, then you must live or die by that decision. You must then live by the law and *"continue in all things which are written in the book of the law, to do them."* Two, it is impossible really to do that. No person has ever succeeded in keeping, obeying, and satisfying all the laws demanded. Three, therefore you are cursed because the Scripture says it is so. The inevitable result of trying to be right with God by being right with law is a curse.

Justification by Faith

It is evident that no one is justified by the law, so Scripture gives us another way. "The just shall live by his faith" (Hab. 2:4). Not only here to the Galatians, but in his letter to the Romans (1:17), Paul quotes Habakkuk, as does the writer to the Hebrews (10:38). Abraham's experience should be enough, but Paul piles up the scriptural evidence, calling on the testimony of one of Israel's prophets. What it means to be "justified"—"reckoned righteous"—is hard for us moderns to get in our minds. The problem is that we do not have an English verb to express both "do right" and "be right" with God, and we do not have a noun that means both "righteousness" and "acceptance with God as righteous." There is no descriptive word in English to say that a person is both "just" and "justified."

This difficulty provides a trap into which we easily fall: that of separating faith from faithfulness, of divorcing justification from righteousness. Augustine's admonition "love God and do as you please" does not give us any excuse for immorality or injustice. This is no license for undisciplined, irresponsible living. Rather, this admonition underscores the inseparable relationships between righteousness imputed by God and the righteousness (right-living) of the person who is *justified* and who *lives* by faith.

Paul's primary goal was to make it absolutely clear that we are justified *only* by our faith; not by merit, nor by good works or moral excellence. This does not discount or exclude, as we will see in chapter 5, the demand for *righteous* living. A righteous person is both just and justified. He lives on the basis of faith which has meaning for life in the present as well as the future.

As indicated above, Paul's metaphor of "justification" has a primary focus on being acquitted at judgment and being admitted into heaven. With the quotation of Habakkuk in this passage, Paul is contrasting the curse of law, which is death, with the eternal salvation of those who live by faith." For that reason, the RSV rendering, "The *righteous* shall live by faith," is the better one. Life in Christ begins at the very moment when one becomes a Christian. Faith-life that begins now cannot be separated from the fruits of the Spirit (Gal. 5), nor can it be separated from the future blessedness of eternal life with God.

Life, the sum and substance of God's blessing to the righteous person, is promised to those who are justified by faith. Having shown that from Scripture, Paul now argues (v. 11) that those who base their claim to justification on legal obedience forfeit the hope of obtaining the blessing of *life*. With a kind of bulldog tenacity, Paul turns the law against the legalists: *"The law is not of faith, but 'the man who does them shall live by them'"* (v. 12, NKJV).

Two things must be observed here. First, Paul was not saying that faith and the observance of law are wholly incompatible. Paul knew many devout Jews who were reliant on the divine promises of God, trusted in His divine mercy, yet made the law of God their delight. The combination of faith and legal observance was characteristic of the Jewish Christians in Galatia. What Paul is saying is that faith and observance of law are incompatible *as grounds of justification.* So, live as rightly as you can, observe the law to the best of your ability, but know that faith is what justifies.

Second, Paul is saying that the law takes no account of faith or any other religious attitude of those who are under its authority. Performance or nonperformance is the issue. If you make law the basis of justification, you will have to live by the condemnation that comes when any iota of the law is not observed. Living by the law for justification means that nonperformance entails loss of *blessing.* Failure to keep the law, if you have made this your hope, brings one under the "curse" which is death.

Christ: A "Curse for Us"

For many readers, verse 13 is one of the most difficult verses in the New Testament. *"Christ has redeemed us from the curse of the law, having become a curse for us (for it is written, 'Cursed is everyone who hangs on a tree')."*

A look at the different expressions in this verse help us in an interpretation of the whole.

1. *"The curse of the law"* refers to what has been talked about in verses 10–12. For those who live under law, disobedience to law involves a curse, eventuating in death. This was dire reality, not metaphor or symbol.

2. *"Christ has redeemed us."* This is Paul's great affirmation of the work of Christ. *Redeemed* means "bought out." The metaphor is that of *payment.* In 1 Corinthians 6:20 and 7:23, Paul says we are "bought" with a price. The word used means (a) "to buy up" or "to secure," and (b) "to redeem, to deliver at cost of some sort to the deliverer." In Paul's day, the meaning could readily be connected with slavery— being bought out of bondage. So, Christ has emancipated us—freed us, delivered us—from enslavement, in this case to "the curse of the law."

3. *"Having become a curse for us"* is the way Christ achieved our deliverance. It is vital to note that this was voluntary action on Jesus' part. He "gave himself for our sins" (Gal. 1:4; 2:20), "the righteous for the unrighteous" (1 Pet. 3:18) that He might deliver us and bring us to God.

It is important to note that this is not a judgment of God upon Jesus. He was not *accursed;* he became "a curse." Jesus became "a curse" in the same sense that "he was made to be sin," though he himself was sinless (2 Cor. 5:21). He voluntarily submitted himself to the curse of the law that that curse might be removed from us. Following the success of the communist revolution in China in 1948, two young men were given the job of destroying Christian chapels. One evening at dusk, after they had devastated a small chapel, they decided to sleep in it that night. As they were lying on the floor there, one of them saw a crucifix so high on the wall they had not been able to reach it. He looked at it steadily for a while, then said to his companion, "Do you see the picture of God nailed to that stick of wood?"

"Yes," the other responded, "but what of it?"

The first answered, "You know, I never saw a God who suffered before."

This is something new—a Savior who voluntarily suffers.

4. Here *"for us"* means "for our sakes," "on our behalf"—not "in our stead." The pronoun "us," in the strict sense of this passage, means Paul and all the sons of Abraham (including the Judaizers who were stirring up the trouble in Galatia) who had come under the law.

5. *"Cursed is everyone who hangs on a tree"* is reference to the law itself (Deut. 21:23). The practice referred to here was grotesque and was not related to death by crucifixion, which was a Roman practice, but the barbarous custom of hanging a criminal's body, after whatever mode of capital punishment had been employed, on a tree and leaving it exposed as a special retribution. So horrible was the curse that Jews would not allow the body of a person condemned in this fashion to remain on the tree overnight because it might defile the land given by God to Israel.

Interestingly, as in our day, proponents and opponents of the gospel appeal to Scripture texts. It was easy to condemn Jesus as "accursed of God" because he hanged on a tree. Paul had been in that camp: this messianic pretender (Jesus) had been hanged on a tree for treason; what blasphemy for people to worship Him as the Son of God. Now Paul uses that "horrible curse" to show the limits to which Christ went to redeem us from the curse.

Having looked at the different expressions in this verse, look now at its meaning as a whole.

Redemption in the Cross

Our redemption is in the Cross. Language defies us as we seek to understand Jesus' mighty act in our behalf. A mere surface reflection upon it leads us to exclaim, "It's too good to be true." Deeper reflection causes us to be dumbstruck. We are without adequate speech to make our response.

As Paul saw it, God's people had come to such a condition under the law, and the curse for those implicated in it had become so real, that God had to intervene. There was no way of deliverance except through the action of Christ who voluntarily put himself under the curse of the law, taking "on their behalf" the curse which was theirs.

1. Seeking to plumb the depths of this, we must not give way to easy statements that fail to grapple with mystery. Nor should we be so

uneasy with mystery that we are driven to establish formuli that are more mechanical than loving; that exist more to satisfy human reason, which sees God as a cosmic judge unbending in His demands, than to acknowledge a righteous loving Father who has His own "laws" of dealing with His children. Those "laws," Jesus said, are seen in the Father welcoming home the prodigal son, and the farm owner paying the same money to those who came to work at different hours of the day.

2. This much is here, but there is more—more than that behind legalism there is a false understanding of God, more than being delivered merely from a false understanding. We cannot comprehend *the more that is here* apart from the gospel of the whole Christ event which Paul preached, and the beliefs which filled the souls of the early Christians, bringing them life, giving them hope, and enabling them to withstand every harsh form of suffering and evil inflicted upon them. These beliefs centered in the fact that the One who died for them was sinless, therefore untouched by the curse of the law. He voluntarily chose to die and was resurrected from the dead and was declared by God to be the Messiah. Not only was He the supreme representative of the people, but of God Himself.

This, then, must not be seen as an isolated utterance, but one expression of the whole of our understanding that we are *delivered* by Christ.

We are delivered by Christ, *"having become a curse for us."*

God alone knows all that He did on the Cross. The best intellects of twenty centuries have not been able to plumb its depth. The experience of faith is that Christ has acted on our behalf, entered into the curse of the law for the Jews; into the curse of guilt, failure, and despair for all who seek to be governed and accepted by rules, regulations, and religious practice; has so deeply identified with our lot that—if we are willing, if we will trust Him— in a way that we will never understand, the mystery of deliverance will take place. Our guilt is borne by Him and His goodness comes to us. His love which He poured out so extravagantly on the Cross is now received by us, and we come alive to His powerful Spirit, loving, forgiving, accepting, renewing, empowering.

3. The fact of the law laying a terrible curse on the person who in death was "hanged on a tree" has been mentioned and discussed briefly. This was evidently important to Paul and influenced his understanding of Jesus' death.

The Law declared man unclean who died in this fashion and outside the divine covenant. Here again is the inherent, irreconcilable conflict of law and gospel. Hebrews 13 beginning with verse 12 picks up on this theme as it talks about Jesus dying *outside* the gate, outside the camp of the people of the covenant. Both Paul and the writer to the Hebrews preach that Jesus not only died a criminal's death, He died apart from consecrated grounds.

In the ancient world temples could be seen everywhere. These temples were considered the residence of the divine spirit. There were also places removed from God, where a religious person might not go. Today in Jerusalem, there are places around the Dome of the Rock where the Temple once stood, to which the Orthodox Jew cannot go, lest he be "cursed" by what he believes has been the desecration of that place. This image of the curse, consecrated and unconsecrated ground, was a part of Paul's view of Jesus' death.

Paul cited the verse from Deuteronomy not solely in reference to hanging on a tree, but all that the Crucifixion represents. Those who stand on the law would have to say that Christ, dying on the Cross, is a sinner. Only a sinner would come to such a death. In that verdict which is manifestly false and monstrous the law condemns itself.

Also, since the righteous Christ died on a cross, it follows that God is not a legalistic judge, but one of love and vicarious suffering, who gives Himself in our behalf.

Another point to be made here is that Jesus' life was not unlike His death. Much of His activity and relationships were on alien ground. He turned from the devoutly religious to sinners and tax-collectors. This was scandalous.

We honor the Cross as the primary symbol of our faith, but in that day it was a scandal of the worst sort. This knowledge gives understanding to what Paul meant in 1 Corinthians 1:23 about the cross being "a stumbling block to Jews and folly to Gentiles." We must never forget this. The brutal clutches of the Cross must never become an ordinary, ungripping symbol. Our salvation cost!

The fact that the Cross was set in a sinful world, that Christ lived and died "outside the camp," means that there is no person or place outside the domain of His powerful suffering love. The Cross shows that God is free to justify the whole world and all persons in it. God's justification does not depend on human readiness, or achievement, or self-attained merit, but on God's grace alone.

The Ingathering of the Gentiles

The powerpacked section of verses 10–13 is really only a transition to verse 14, which hones in on Paul's primary concern: the ingathering of the Gentiles into the people of God.

There are two clauses in this verse. The first contains the core of Paul's thought in this passage—that the purpose of God to accept men by faith was revealed in Jesus Christ, and that through faith in Christ the Gentiles could enter into actual participation of the blessing promised to Abraham.

Paul could have stopped there because he had completed his historical statement, but he added another clause coordinate to the first: *"that we might receive the promise of the Spirit."* These clauses together say two things: (1) By faith like Abraham's, and not by adherence to law, the Gentiles will receive the blessing. (2) The way God fulfills His promise and gives them the blessing is by giving them His Spirit.

Though not to be strictly separated, these phrases also show the double nature of Christ's redemptive work: through faith we are justified and through faith we receive the Spirit. The end of faith is not justification—though that is crucial; the Spirit indwells us, giving us power, providing all sorts of gifts for ministry, and pouring out a rich harvest of fruits to bless those around us.

THE CHANGELESS PROMISE

15 Brethren, I speak in the manner of men: Though it is only a man's covenant, yet if it is confirmed, no one annuls or adds to it. 16 Now to Abraham and his Seed were the promises made. He does not say, "And to seeds," as of many, but as of one, "And to your Seed," who is Christ. 17 And this I say, that the law, which was four hundred and thirty years later, cannot annul the covenant that was confirmed before by God in Christ, that it should make the promise of no effect. 18 For if the inheritance is of the law, it is no longer of promise; but God gave it to Abraham by promise.

—Galatians 3:15–18

The cause for which Paul is pleading is so crucial that he must use his skills of argument and debate to their ultimate. As in verses 1–9, he is turning again to Abraham as his hinge point. He also introduces not only a new argument but a new type of argument. He turns from involved exegesis of scripture to an illustration from contemporary human life: the matter of *covenants,* or *wills,* with which both the Jews and the Gentiles would be familiar.

Adding to the difficulty of this passage is that Paul's audience focus includes Gentiles who probably wouldn't understand his allusions to the Old Testament, the troublemakers, as well as those influenced by the troublemakers. He moves in his address from *"O foolish Galatians"* to *"Brethren."*

It helps us to decipher the intricacies of Paul's argument in a passage like this if we keep in mind that he was trained as a rabbi. What would be clear and convincing to a Jew who was familiar with the rabbis' methods may be vague and difficult for us to follow.

Paul builds his case on two points: (1) the trustworthiness of God, and (2) the fact that Christ is the *seed* of Abraham to which and through which God's promise was made.

The Trustworthiness of God

The whole problem of human life is determined by our relationship or lack of relationship to God. Paul Tillich once said that the secular psychiatrist always starts a therapeutic process that he can never finish. He meant that the root problems of humanity are spiritual. Carl Jung always insisted that our deepest problems are religious problems. An irrefutable fact of nature is that persons are made for fellowship with God. Outside that fellowship we can never know complete fulfillment and meaning.

Our need and efforts at fellowship with God are distorted by our understanding of God. How we see God determines how we seek and what we long for in our relationship with Him. If we are afraid of God, if we see Him as an aloof or grim stranger, if God is primarily an inscrutable judge, how will we find peace and joy and love in the relationship? How can we even pursue the relationship?

Paul says that God, with whom we desperately need fellowship, is trustworthy. He has made a promise to bless us with His Spirit and He will keep His promise. *"Brethren, I speak in the manner of men: Though it is only a man's covenant, yet if it is confirmed, no one annuls or adds to it"* (v. 15). The promise (covenant) was made to Abraham four hundred and thirty years before the law. God's original covenant was based on faith as man's response. The legalist had substituted "by works" for "by faith." This could not be. The law was a codicil (an addition) to God's original covenant. The first covenant to save men by grace had been ratified four hundred years before, and no addition to the covenant could annul the primary will of God.

When we are honest we can identify with the Jews. It is not easy to accept God's loving initiative in our lives. In fact, we are constantly refusing it. We don't want to owe anyone; we want to earn what we get. And we can't accept a God who doesn't operate in the same fashion. Yet the truth is, if we are too proud to be definitely in debt we will never be a Christian. God gives—always. We are the receivers—always. The Jews had the same problem. It was incomprehensible to them that the holy God would deal with them out of grace, in response not to their "works" but to their faith.

Christ, the Seed of Abraham

Verse 16 seems to interrupt and even obstruct Paul's argument. After talking about *"covenant"* in verse 15, he abruptly introduces *"Abraham and his Seed"* in verse 16; then returns to his thought-stream of covenant in verses 17 and 18. This had to be an important diversion because the matter under discussion is so crucial.

In this verse Paul interpreted Jewish history and spiritualized Scripture out of his own experience: *"Now to Abraham and his Seed were the promises made. He does not say, 'And to seeds,' as of many, but as of one, 'And to your Seed,' who is Christ"* (v. 16). Paul is referring to Genesis 13:15ff. and Genesis 17:7ff., and is saying that God's promises to Abraham and his offspring were not really fulfilled till the coming of Christ. He argues that the Scripture uses the singular "Seed" rather than the plural "seeds." Yet, Paul surely knew that neither the Greek nor Hebrew plural of the word in question would have created a different meaning. Paul is interpreting this passage as he contended all Scripture was to be interpreted: in accordance with the revelation of God in Jesus Christ.

The orthodox Jew insisted that the true offspring of Abraham was in Israel. God's demand for righteousness could only be satisfied through strict adherence to God's Holy Law. As already indicated, Paul argued that the law, coming 430 years after the covenant, could not put a limitation on the Promise.

Paul's argument, then, is in the great prophetic tradition of Judaism. Christ was the true *Seed* of Abraham; not the whole of Israel nor the circumcised posterity of Abraham, not the "remnant" who had faithfully kept the law, but Christ; in Him the Promise was fulfilled, and through the Spirit God was extending that Promise. Gentiles, as well as Jews, were freed from the "curse" of the law and were brought into the covenantal relationship.

Paul clinches his argument in verse 18: *"For if the inheritance is of the law, it is no longer of promise; but God gave it to Abraham by promise."*

What, then, is the purpose of the law? That is the next question.

THE LAW: OUR CUSTODIAN

[19] What purpose then does the law serve? It was added because of transgressions, till the Seed should come to whom the promise was made; and it was appointed through angels by the hand of a mediator. [20] Now a mediator does not mediate for one only, but God is one.

[21] Is the law then against the promises of God? Certainly not! For if there had been a law given which could have given life, truly righteousness would have been by the law. [22] But the Scripture has confined all under sin, that the promise by faith in Jesus Christ might be given to those who believe. [23] But before faith came, we were kept under guard by the law, kept for the faith which would afterward be revealed. [24] Therefore the law was our tutor to bring us to Christ, that we might be justified by faith. [25] But after faith has come, we are no longer under a tutor.

—Galatians 3:19–25

Paul met a bold challenge with an even bolder response. He would not be driven into the corner of discounting any value of the law. The law had a place, but that place was not the one being given it by those Paul was addressing. They saw the law as an interim measure, by which *"we were kept under guard . . . and kept for the faith"* (v. 23).

God's primary way of dealing with persons is never a requirement/performance method. It was and is always a promise of blessing in response to faith. Rather than being a reflection of God's will, purposed from eternity, the law was an addition to the central stream of God's purpose. It was designed to function in a special way for a special time. Thus the law was a temporary measure, valid in its intentional purpose only until the coming of Christ.

Locked in the Prison of Sin

"Is the law then against the promises of God? Certainly not!" Paul says. If law *"could have given life, truly righteousness would*

have been by the law" (v. 21). The law serves to bring us face to face with our *transgressions. "The Scripture has confined all under sin"* (v. 22). The image in verse 23, *"kept under guard,"* is stronger than *"confined."* Paul is saying we are locked up in sin, a powerful image with which most of us can identify. It is the overpowering presence of sin that Paul presents autobiographically in Romans 7:21–24.

By *"confined"* or "consigned," Paul means that all persons, without exception, are shut up with no apparent possibility of escape. Though Scripture shows God forever active in His work of redemption, Scripture also shows that sin, too, is at work. Everything and everybody is brought under the inexorable power of sin. And if this is true, without exception, and we are hopeless within ourselves to escape, then this is a stage by which humanity comes to see the promise of God's blessing realized in Jesus Christ. We remain locked in that prison of sin until through faith we experience the deliverance of Jesus Christ.

One of the letters I treasure most comes from a young man with whom I had been counseling. He was tired of running, tired of fighting, tired of going from one frenzy and failure to another. "I've got to find myself," he wrote. "Years ago when I felt like this my parents would get me a doctor, a pill, or a psychiatrist. They would shield me from everything. I didn't grow up with the hard knocks of life—because I didn't have to face them. When the going became rough, I got scared and dropped out. I felt relief when Mom would say, "It's getting bad; I will get a psychiatrist this week." But now I have got to face it. I'm at rock bottom and I'm scared to look up. The answer has to be inside me, or nothing from the outside will help. It is me inside that is lost and has to be found."

Roy was locked up in himself because he was locked up in sin. He was delivered from sin and his destructive self when, in faith, he yielded to the release Christ brings.

The Law of Moses was a good law; Paul didn't dispute that. It was good, though, not for redemptive purposes but to make us aware of our transgressions. By *"transgressions"* Paul means something a bit different from sin. Persons may *sin* in ignorance. To *trangress* is to go against the standards which they have accepted for themselves. The law revealed sin; it did not produce it. The law served to goad persons to see the depth of their impotence and sinfulness as they experienced not only their inability to keep the law, but their regular transgressions of it.

Kept For the Faith

Here is another marvelous symbol: *"kept for the faith"* (v. 23). Paul builds on and elucidates this in verse 24: *". . . the law was our tutor to bring us to Christ that we might be justified by faith."*

"Tutor" (Gk. *paidagogos*) is probably better translated as "attendant," or "custodian," as the RSV has it. In the Greek world the *paidagogos* was a household servant. Our words "pedagogue" and "pedagogy" now mean teacher and the art, profession, or study of teaching. The original *paidagogos*, however, was not a tutor or schoolmaster; he was an attendant to a child from six to sixteen. He accompanied the child to school, protected him from harm, kept him out of mischief, and delivered him safely to the teacher. There was a sense in which he was in charge of the child's moral welfare, keeping him from temptation, though he had nothing to do with the actual teaching of the child in school.

The law served that function, said Paul. It *"kept us for the faith"*; it led us to Christ. How could that happen? The law showed persons how utterly inadequate and incapable they were to keep the law within their own power. This sense of inadequacy and inability led them to Christ, the fulfillment of God's promise to Abraham. After coming to this point of recognition and faith, a person no longer needs the law. He is now dependent on grace.

Paul made a distinction between Christian faith and the faith of Abraham. Abraham's was a "waiting faith." Even so, he was saved by that faith. Christian faith is "fulfilled" in Christ. So, Christ did not bring faith. He became the fulfillment of faith.

Two questions arise: (1) Is there no need for law after we enter the arena of grace? Paul answers: We do need law, but our salvation is not dependent upon keeping the law. The law becomes the code of conduct by which social structures are ordered, and by which we order our lives in relation to others and to God. As it relates to civil law, Paul and especially Peter urged "every soul be subject to the governing authorities" (Rom. 13:1) and to "submit yourselves to every ordinance of man for the Lord's sake" (1 Pet. 2:13). The limits of being subject to law are the points at which the law becomes destructive. There comes the time when "we must obey God rather than men." But when law is not in conflict with God's will then the Christian submits to the law for the good and order of all. (2) What is it that will keep our children for the faith? *The law* can no longer be the *paidagogos* of children of Christian parents. How important it is that sabbath worship, stated times of prayer, sharing the Scripture, rehearsing the mighty acts of God be made in a fashion that will permeate the minds and hearts of children and *keep them* until they claim for themselves the Promise: Christ's death for their sins and His Resurrection for their resurrection to new life.

"God has no grandchildren" is an old saying that expresses a life and death truth. We must all accept for ourselves, directly and personally, the gift of God's grace as His children. The image of law as a schoolmaster must never give the false impression that becoming a Christian is an educational process. Paul does not think of Jesus as teacher, but as Redeemer. We are not Christian by osmosis, but by redemption. The function of the law, or ritual, or discipline—whatever we can afford our children—is to *keep them* until they are *justified by faith*.

BAPTIZED INTO CHRIST

26 For you are all sons of God through faith in Christ Jesus. 27 For as many of you as were baptized into Christ have put on Christ. 28 There is neither Jew nor Greek, there is neither slave nor free, there is neither male nor female; for you are all one in Christ Jesus. 29 And if you are Christ's, then you are Abraham's seed, and heirs according to the promise.

—*Galatians 3:26–29*

I remember my baptism. I was converted in a little Baptist church in rural Mississippi. It was in September. Though the freeze of winter had not come, chill of the air foretold it. But baptism was too important to be put off, and we didn't have an "indoor" heated baptistry. So it was the creek—whose waters were cold even in July, and doubly so in the fall without the burning summer sun—for my baptism.

Even as an early teenager, and even without much biblical training, I knew this was a pivotal moment in life. I didn't understand it, and certainly grasped little of its deep significance. Yet enough was there to impact my life profoundly. The "country" preacher had probably read few, if any, books of theology, but he made my immersion in that cold creek powerful in its symbolism and in its fact. 1 was buried with Christ in that baptism, and raised to a new life in Christ as I emerged from the dark depths of the water. *"For as many of you as were baptized into Christ have put on Christ"* (v. 27).

John Donne (1572–1631) is a difficult but rewarding poet to read. His imagery is all-important, and his poems throb with the reality of a person alive to God, *baptized into Christ.* In a stanza from "Hymn to God my God, in my Sickness," he helps us think of what it means to put on Christ.

> We think that Paradise and Calvary,
>   Christ's cross, and Adam's tree stood in one place;
> Look, Lord, and find both Adams met in me.
>   As the first Adam's sweat surrounds my face,
>   May the last Adam's blood my soul embrace.[1]

In baptism the first Adam puts on the second Adam and a new person comes into being—a person whose sin is washed in "the last Adam's blood."

Verse 27 is the only direct reference Paul makes to baptism in this epistle. Its interjection here underscores its significance for Paul. Circumcision may have made a person an Israelite; baptism made one *Christ's person.* The dynamic of baptism involved a dual movement: the believer moved to God by professing faith in Jesus Christ, God moved to the believer by accepting that faith and giving the believer the Holy Spirit.

Baptism then means at least three things: one, to be immersed in Christ's character; two, to take up His Cross; and, three, to receive the power of His Spirit.

Immersed in Christ's Character

The Old Testament has some beautiful metaphors using the word *clothed:* "clothed with salvation" (2 Chr. 6:41); "clothed with shame" (Job 8:22); "clothed with majesty" (Ps. 93:1); "clothed with strength" (Ps. 93:1); "clothed with righteousness" (Ps. 132:9). Paul uses the same metaphor in Romans 13:12: "Let us cast off the works of darkness, and let us put on the armor of light"; and Ephesians 4:24: "Put on the new man." So in baptism, we *put on Christ;* we are immersed in His character.

Note quickly that this is not a matter of "law," nor the result of our doing. This is a work of grace; not a matter of imitation, but of new birth. There is a resurgence in our day of the phrase "born-again Christian." There may be some value in it—maybe a shock value in the dramatic declaration of an adult who, having been "in the church" all his life, when suddenly made aware of being religious but not Christian, of seeking to *do* right without *being* right, comes to an awareness of his sinful state, repents, confesses, yields his life to Christ in faith, and is justified. Transformed, he begins to live a new life. However, there is a sense in which the phrase "born again Christian" is redundant. To be a Christian *is* to be born again; and to be born again *is* to be a Christian. That's what being a Christian means—to receive a new life that was not mine before, to become a new creature in Christ Jesus.

This immersion into the character of Christ is renewal, rebirth, a work of grace, not self-effortful achievement. Even so, there is an imitation that is needful, and this imitation takes discipline. The patience, gentleness, humility and love of Christ; His wide-openness and sensitivity to people and willingness to risk; His childlike wonder and trust are to be cultivated in our lives.

Take Up His Cross

The call of Jesus was certain and clear: "If any man will come after me, let him deny himself, and take up his cross, and follow me" (Matt. 16:24, KJV). We are baptized into Christ and His style is a cross-style. To take His cross means that we are to take His ministry of servanthood and reconciliation. Here is that style in a person, Chaplain Emil Kapaun, in a prisoner of war camp.

> In his soiled and ragged fatigues, with his scraggly beard and his queer woolen cap, made of the sleeve of an old GI sweater, pulled down over his ears, he looked like any other half-starved prisoner. But there was something in his voice that was different—a dignity, a composure, a serenity that radiated from him like a light. Wherever he stood was holy ground, and the spirit within him—a spirit of reverence and abiding faith—went out to the silent, listening men and gave them hope and courage and a sense of peace. By his very presence, somehow, he could turn a stinking, louse-ridden mud hut, for a little while, into a cathedral.
>
> He did a thousand little things to keep us going. He gathered and washed the foul undergarments of the dead and distributed them to men so weak from dysentery they could not move, and he washed and tended these men as if they were little babies. He traded his watch for a blanket, and cut it up to make warm socks for helpless men whose feet were freezing. All one day, in a freezing wind, with a sharp stick and his bare hands, he cut steps in the steep,

ice-covered path that led down to the stream, so that the men carrying water would not fall. The most dreaded housekeeping chore of all was cleaning the latrines, and men argued bitterly over whose time it was to carry out his loathsome task. And while they argued, he'd slip out quietly and do the job. . . .

On the day they took him away to his death, the Chaplain himself made no protest. He looked around the room at all of us standing there, and smiled.. . . . "Tell them back home that I died a happy death," he said, and smiled again.

As they loaded him on the litter he turned to Lieutenant Nardella, from whose missal he had read the services. He put the little book in Nardella's hand.

"You know the prayers, Ralph," he said. "Keep holding the services. Don't let them make you stop."

Then he turned to me. "Don't take it hard, Mike," he said. "I'm going where I've always wanted to go. And when I get there, I'll say a prayer for all of you."[2]

Chaplain Kapaun lived his baptism as he took up the cross-style of servanthood and reconciliation.

The Power of Spirit

One of the primary experiences of the early church was the coming of the Holy Spirit with baptism. There were occasions when the person baptized did not receive or recognize the Spirit (Acts 8:14–17 and Acts 19:5–6), and there were occasions when the presence and power of the Holy Spirit was experienced before (Acts 10). Even so, the most common experience of the New Testament church and the church of the first three centuries connected baptism for the remission of sin and the reception of the Holy Spirit. The liturgies of many churches at baptism and/or confirmation include this affirmation with the laying on of hands: "The power of the Holy Spirit work within you, that being born of water and the spirit you may be a faithful witness of Jesus Christ."

Unfortunately we do not think much about the power that is the natural gift of all baptized Christians—the power of the Spirit. Even the baptism of Jesus had that accompanying sign of the Holy Spirit:

"And Jesus, when he was baptized, went up straightway out of the water: and, lo, the heavens were opened unto him, and he saw the Spirit of God descending like a dove, and lighting upon him: And lo a voice from heaven, saying, this is my beloved Son, in whom I am well pleased" (Matt. 3:16–17, KJV). What transformation would come to the whole church, what strengthening vitality of fellowship, what power for witness, if we who are baptized would claim our baptism with the spirit!

One in Christ

As mentioned earlier, Paul interjected the matter of baptism into this context because he wanted the Gentile converts to know that there is no reason for them to try to put themselves right by circumcision, by becoming like the Jews. For *"there is neither Jew nor Greek, there is neither slave nor free, there is neither male nor female; for you are all one in Christ Jesus"* (v. 28).

Paul could have added other categories—Catholics, Protestants, professors, mechanics, preachers, domestic workers, whites, blacks—for in Christ all social stations, all cultural labels, all races and nationalities are made of no account in the economy of God. Righteousness, wisdom, authority, religion, achievement matter nothing for salvation. *All become one in Christ Jesus.*

Be clear about this. Our solidarity as humans is not in our innate goodness, not due to the spark of divinity residing in every self. Our solidarity is in our bondage to sin. In this solidarity there is neither Jew nor Greek. God justifies us all on the basis of our trust response, and we become *one in Christ.*

Paul comes back to his previous affirmation: Christ is Abraham's Seed, the fulfillment of God's promise; all who belong to Christ, Gentile as well as Jew, are heirs of that promise.

NOTES

1. John Donne, "Hymn to God my God, in my Sickness," in *Beginning with Poems,* ed. Reuben A. Brower, Anne D. Ferry, David Kalstone (New York: W. W. Norton, 1966), p. 39.

2. Ray "Mike" Dowe, Jr., "The Ordeal of Chaplain Kapaun," *Saturday Evening Post,* January 16, 1954.

Chapter Four—Sons and Heirs of God
Galatians 4:1–31

Scripture Outline

Not a Servant But a Son (4:1–7)

Substituting Gods for God (4:8–10)

The Power of the Person and the Personal (4:11–20)

Two Covenants (4:21–31)

There is no emotion quite like that a child has for a parent when the parent's love is certain and the child's love is reciprocal. There is no feeling comparable to the pride a child feels in belonging to a parent whom he deeply appreciates. Unlike much of our pride, this kind is positive, not destructive.

Rita Snowden, the New Zealander who has inspired hundreds of thousands with over sixty books, told me a story one night in Auckland which captures this childlike emotion of pride and love.

> My friend Rene Watts for years taught music in our home. To our home used to come a small boy, for his music. He came from a home where music, and cultural things in general, were appreciated. He came straight from school—a real boy, often with muddy knees, and his shirt out in a way that his mother wouldn't like. And he had always a great deal to say, to put off the beginning of his lesson.
>
> "We had some time at school today," he began, "and I found a copy of *Who's Who*."
>
> "And I expect you found your grandfather's name in it," said his teacher—the grandfather being a man of letters.

"Yes, I did," said the budding musician, "and I found my father's name in it too."

Then looking down shyly at the floor, he added: "And I was mentioned in it, too, but only in a very small way, of course. It said, 'He had one son.'"

A delightful feeling of family pride, a lovely sense of belonging. Multiply that seventy times seven and you may come close to what Paul is affirming in this chapter.

NOT A SERVANT BUT A SON

4:1 Now I say that the heir, as long as he is a child, does not differ at all from a slave, though he is master of all, **2** but is under guardians and stewards until the time appointed by the father. **3** Even so we, when we were children, were in bondage under the elements of the world. **4** But when the fullness of the time had come, God sent forth His Son, born of a woman, born under the law, **5** to redeem those who were under the law, that we might receive the adoption as sons.

6 And because you are sons, God has sent forth the Spirit of His Son into your hearts, crying out, "Abba, Father!" **7** Therefore you are no longer a slave but a son, and if a son, then an heir of God through Christ.

—Galatians 4:1–7

How much Paul knew about the earthly life of Jesus is unknown. We know he spent time with Peter and some of the other disciples, and undoubtedly the stories Jesus told were a part of the preaching of the apostles. Paul's language in this section suggests an acquaintance with Jesus' sayings and indicates that he must have known Jesus' Parable of the Prodigal Son. Also the spirit of Jesus' teaching is here: a simple childlike trust in relation to God is what justifies us. This kind of trustful dependency and open love enables us to pray as Jesus prayed in the garden, "Abba, Father" (Mark 14:36), because we know the joy of being not a servant but a son.

Before we respond in faith to Christ, still under law, even though we are children of God, *heirs,* we are like slaves. It doesn't matter that we are *"master of all."* We are "under age" and the inheritance is not yet ours.

We don't have to know the precise court system relating to minors, or the inheritance codes with which Paul must have been familiar, to understand this image. A modern situation will serve

78

to illustrate. A parent sets aside $100,000 "in trust" for a child. The money actually belongs to the child, but cannot be possessed and used by the child until the age stipulated in the trust—for instance, eighteen or twenty-one years. Until that time comes, there is no way the child can spend what is already his. In a similar ancient setting, Paul is saying that even though a son is designated his father's heir, so long as he is "under age," he must be treated as fully dependent. In fact, in relation to the inheritance, he is in no better position than a servant.

Paul is emphatic. Even though God has established a great "trust" for us—our justification—we are still as servants until we respond in faith to His promise. Our age of accountability, the time when the "trust" is ours to possess, is no chronological time, but that time when we are moved to say *yes*, to claim the glorious freedom that is ours in Christ Jesus.

Adopted by Grace

Until we become of age we are in bondage. *"Even so we, when we were children, were in bondage under the elements of the world"* (v. 3). *"Elements"* meant a lot of different things in the Greek world: the letters of the alphabet; rudimentary knowledge; that of which the world consisted: water, air, fire, and earth; the constituency of the larger universe: sun, moon, and stars; the spirits, angels, and demons which were believed to inhabit the world. Paul often used this latter meaning. In Romans 8:38, he called them "principalities and powers." In verses 9 and 10 of this chapter he refers again to these elements, so it must be that he is using the term in this latter sense.

We are in bondage to the "elements," to "principalities and powers," to the present evil age, until that bondage is broken by grace and we are adopted as sons.

Every word in this section seems carefully chosen. Certain phrases carry almost the full freight of the gospel.

1. *"In the fullness of time."* This phrase expresses a whole philosophy of history. Paul is proclaiming that God operates in sovereign freedom. The Christ-event is the supreme event of the divine plan, the end toward which God has been moving. The Christ-event is the lens through which Paul sees the salvation intentions of God. God was the beginning and the end. Behind the toiling, sweating, caring Jesus, Paul always sees God. Behind the crucified Son, he always sees God the Father. The love that reigned in the heart of the Eternal is behind

the love that bled and died on the Cross. "God demonstrates His own love toward us, in that . . . Christ died" (Rom. 5:8). So, too, with the risen life of Christ. To share in the life of Christ was to share with God who raised Him (cf. Rom. 8:11). The fullness of time was the fullness of God's time to fulfill His promise to Abraham, and that fulfillment was the total Christ event.

2. *"God sent forth His son, born of a woman"* (v. 4). Paul is not talking about Jesus being sent from the carpenter's shop in Nazareth, but about God sending His Son from His pre-existent state in heaven. In Christology we talk about *pre-existence, existence,* and *post-existence:* Christ's life with the Father prior to His earthly existence as Jesus, His existence as Jesus, and His life following the Crucifixion and Resurrection. These three modes of thinking about Christ's existence were present from the start. These modes existed side by side, and no one in the New Testament seemed to think it important enough to put these three expressions together in any sort of way. So we have different expressions, such as in Acts 2:36 which says Jesus was installed in His messianic office at Resurrection; Mark 1:9–11 which reports that He was anointed Son of God at His baptism; and the Matthew and Luke accounts which say that Jesus was Son of God from the moment of His conception onward. Pervading all these expressions was the conviction that the Son existed with the Father. Though it may be too subtle to see, it is important to note that it was the Son, not Jesus of Nazareth, who existed with the Father. This pre-existing Son *became* Jesus.

Because of common acceptance and understanding, Paul did not need to explain or argue for speaking of this Eternal Reality that manifested itself in time and space. Yet he was careful to underscore the full humanness of this reality that had come in Jesus: *"born of a woman, born under the law."*

Through Christ the Son, who assumed humanity and became one with us, God accomplished His purpose of providing the way for all persons to enter a life of sonship. More about that now as we look at the third powerful expression.

3. *"To redeem those who were under the law, that we might receive the adoption as sons"* (v. 5). Whenever Paul mentions the word "redeem" you can be sure he has a picture of the Cross in his mind. From first to last, and especially in his letter to the Galatians, Paul connects the redemptive work of Christ with His death. The message

is, he *"gave Himself our sins"* (Gal. 1:4); *"He gave Himself for me"* (Gal. 2:20).

In chapter 3 we discussed the cross in the context of a kind of "substitution": *"Christ has redeemed us from the curse of the law, having become a curse for us"* (Gal. 3:13). The image suggested here in chapter 4 is *adoption*.

The movement of God to accomplish our redemption is crystal clear to Paul. The long-looked-for deliverance came in Jesus Christ: (1) Jesus came from God. He did not arise from among men to be the leader, the messianic King, but was the Son of God who had come from God to be the Redeemer. (2) In order to deliver, the Son entered the earthly scene, became Jesus, *born of a woman*. He became flesh, truly man, experiencing all the onslaughts of evil, all the temptations of the flesh, all the weakness of humanity, in order to stand beside us. (3) He became our brother and could offer Himself as our representative. As a son of Abraham, born under the law and even sharing the curse which the law imposed (Gal. 3:11–14), He was able to offer Himself on behalf of His brother Israelites. (4) By His Crucifixion, not only did He ransom those under the law, but became the Deliverer of all persons everywhere. Deliverance was from servitude of every sort—the bondage in which all persons in every age find themselves—into freedom as sons of God: *adoption*.

This idea of adoption is confused if we take it in the sense of "natural" and "adoptive" parents. Paul is using it in a religious sense, and it thus may mean much the same as reconciliation.

McLeod Campbell stated the meaning of this great term *adoption* beautifully and succinctly. "Let us think of Christ as the Son who reveals the Father, that we may know the Father's heart against which we have sinned, that we may see how sin, in making us godless, has made us orphans, and understand that the grace of God, which is at once the remission of past sin and the gift of eternal life, restores to our orphan spirits their Father and to the Father of spirits his lost children."

Sonship Implies More than Status

The designation *"the Spirit of His Son"* (v. 6) is not found elsewhere in the New Testament. Paul does not distinguish sharply between the Spirit of Christ and the Spirit of God, as can be seen in Romans 8:9, where Paul refers to "the Spirit of Christ" immediately after designating the Spirit as the "Spirit of God."

Paul is not trying to make a theological distinction; he is expressing an experiential fact. As in the fullness of time God sent His Son to redeem us, to *adopt* us back as His sons, so now He wants to empower us for a life of free and joyous sonship. Thus, our sonship implies more than status; it means that we share the life of the Father.

If Paul was remembering Jesus' story of the prodigal, the distinction between the elder and the younger son must have come into his mind. Both had the status of sons after the prodigal's return. But the elder had only the status. He did not enter into the life of the Father and would not even share the joy of the welcome-home party. He kept acting like a servant even though the Father wanted him as a son. In fact, that is precisely what the Father would not have—sons who acted like servants. He would not accept the pleas of the prodigal, "Make me a hired servant." No! "Bring the robe and the ring and the shoes. Kill the fatted calf. Let's have a party. My son was dead but is alive, was lost but is found."

It is a joyful day in our lives when we move beyond the status of sonship, when we receive the *Spirit of the Son,* and begin the free and glad life of sharing intimately with the Father.

1. *See what this does to our praying.* We don't come groveling to the Almighty. We don't snivel in self-contempt as beggars who have no right to be there, as wayward derelicts who have to come to the back door for a handout. We come as children of the King, knowing that we are welcome.

Abba, Father describes our relationship, a shared love and fellowship in which the Father pours out all His blessings upon His children. And we pray in that knowledge and with the childlike anticipation of receiving all the Father has for us.

2. *See what this does to our sense of self-worth.* Is there a greater need? William Glasser, who became famous in America as the father of "reality therapy," took a radical position about mental illness. He said there was no such thing. Deviant symptoms that are classified as mental illness are the results of the frustration of two basic needs in life: the need to love and be loved, and the need to feel worthwhile to oneself and others.

How difficult it is for us to accept ourselves; to love and be loved, to feel worthwhile to ourselves and others. It is a time of almost overwhelming grace when we accept the fact that God knows us thoroughly and loves us thoroughly. To know that we are loved and accepted by God frees and empowers us to love ourselves and others and to know that we are worthwhile.

3. *See what this does to our ministry.* All of us are ministers, "servants of the Lord Jesus Christ." But how often that is a burden we bear rather than a joy to celebrate. We do what we do out of our own reservoir of strength, rather than freely and spontaneously.

When we accept and realize (make real) our sonship, we discover that we do not operate alone. Strength comes directly from God, and indirectly, through the shared strength of the Christian community. This strength can work in rhythm with our weakness as we become vulnerable. In our sonship we are vulnerable to God, open and receptive to the incursion of His Spirit. But, in the confidence of being loved and accepted by God, we can be vulnerable to others, open to the claims of our neighbors responding in sensitivity and care. We do not have to pretend, therefore we can risk failure, rebuff, shame, unappreciative response, and negative reaction. Our self-worth is secured in our sonship and we can continue to minister, whatever the response.

SUBSTITUTING GODS FOR GOD

[8] But then, indeed, when you did not know God, you served those which by nature are not gods. [9] But now after you have known God, or rather are known by God, how is it that you turn again to the weak and beggarly elements, to which you desire again to be in bondage? [10] You observe days and months and seasons and years.

—*Galatians 4:8–10*

As we saw in our discussion of verse 3, *elements* meant a lot of different things in the Greek world. Paul used the word to designate the spirit-forces which inhabit the universe and are hostile to God. Paul's letters do not provide instruction about these spirit-forces, as he apparently assumes everybody knew what they were. The variety of expressions used also indicates Paul was not concerned with being precise.

The Devil

However we may think about, define, or describe spirit-forces, we are aware of powers, internal and external, that are fighting against God. The comedian Flip Wilson is famous for the phrase: "The devil made me do it." We may not use those words, but we have had the feeling: some power controlled us and made us act in a way that is not our true nature. "I was not myself," or "She was *beside* herself," we say.

"The-devil-made-me-do-it" idea can never be an excuse for lack of accountability. We are not delivered from responsibility no matter what may influence us. However, we need to recognize that there are evil forces operative in the world, and we must be vigilant against them. The power to overcome these forces belongs to every Christian. In verse 9, Paul refers to *the weak and beggarly elements.* The power of God, expressive in our lives through the indwelling Christ, is superlatively greater than the principalities and powers of "this present darkness." We must never forget this. "Greater is he that is in you than he that is in the world" (1 John 4:4, KJV).

Idolatry

A second lesson is expressed in these verses. We are so desirous of power and so attracted to any promises to control fate that we are tempted to take that power from wherever it is available. Thus we substitute all sorts of gods for God.

How many people in America read their horoscopes daily and are influenced by the word for that day? Maybe more than seek a word from God through Scripture and prayer! How many people, even within the church, think they are more influenced by the sign under which they were born (Cancer, Leo, Aries, etc.) than the sign of the Cross under which is our only salvation?

Paul is consistent in his teaching about idolatry. Accepting a creed, obeying a law, eating a sacrament, keeping an eye on the stars, looking for guidance in a horoscope, trying to compel or cajole the gods of fortune and fate-are all in the same category of substituting lesser gods for God. Paul is astounded at the Galatians as he would be at many of us. *"After you have known God, or rather are known by God, how is it that you turn again to the weak and beggarly elements, to which you desire again to be in bondage?"* (v. 9).

THE POWER OF THE PERSON AND THE PERSONAL

11 I am afraid for you, lest I have labored for you in vain.

12 Brethren, I urge you to become like me, for I became like you. You have not injured me at all. 13 You know that because of physical infirmity I preached the gospel to you at the first. 14 And my trial which was in my flesh you did not

despise or reject, but you received me as an angel of God, even
as Christ Jesus. [15] What then was the blessing you enjoyed?
For I bear you witness that, if possible, you would have
plucked out your own eyes and given them to me. [16] Have I
therefore become your enemy because I tell you the truth?

[17] They zealously court you, but for no good; yes, they
want to exclude you, that you may be zealous for them. [18] But
it is good to be zealous in a good thing always, and not only
when I am present with you. [19] My little children, for whom I
labor in birth again until Christ is formed in you, [20] I would
like to be present with you now and to change my tone; for I
have doubts about you.

—Galatians 4:11–20

Here is one of Paul's tenderest passages. He has been firm in
his confrontation, and still "calls a spade a spade." (*"They zealously court you, but for no good,"* v. 17.) Yet, he pulls back the
curtain of his own inner soul, revealing his anguish and pain, his
personal limitations, his feelings of failure, his overwhelming
sense of appreciation (*"you received me as an angel of God,"* v.
14), his willingness to change, his overarching commitment to
those whom he considered his spiritual children. He pulls out all
the stops in the organ of his soul as he appeals for a response to
himself as a person and to the power of the personal.

The Visible Gospel

The gospel must be seen in the person who seeks to communicate it. *"Brethren, I urge you to become like me"* (v. 12). What
a bold plea. It could be seen as arrogance except that Paul had
been willing to reveal his full humanity. His physical infirmity
must have been serious. While we do not know what the affliction
was, we know that it was chronic, very painful, repulsive, and
humiliating. Paul rejoiced *that* the Galatians did not *"despise"* or
"reject" him (v. 14). The literal translation of those words may be
"spit out." The Galatians did not spit in Paul's presence as people
were accustomed to doing when they wanted to ward off an evil
spirit. This kind of language indicates the extremity of Paul's
affliction and the fact that it must have been repulsive. What Paul
actually says here is, "You did not scorn me and did not spit,
although my physical condition was trying to you."

With those strikes against him in his person, Paul still appeals
through himself: *"Become as me."* It is Paul's ultimate appeal: "If

you will not hear me through who I am and what I have been to you, and you to me, I have no other argument." This is the gospel's ultimate appeal.

The Personal Gospel

And the gospel is always personal. The appeal is from person to person, addressing us in the very intimate corners of our life: where we feel and think, hate and love, decide and compromise, weep and rejoice.

The word of the gospel is always a personal word. The issues of the gospel—heaven and hell, peace and justice, good and evil, estrangement and reconciliation, sin and righteousness—though expansive in their dimensions, are personal in the response they demand and the judgment implicit in them.

Personal must not be mistakenly interpreted as *private* or self-indulging. Jesus addressed some of his sharpest condemnation against those who saw spirituality as self-indulgent religious discipline rather than concern for the poor and suffering. "Woe to you, scribes and Pharasees, hypocrites! For you pay the tithe of mint and anise and cummin, and have neglected the weightier matters of the law: justice and mercy and faith" (Matt. 23:23). He was making it clear that the central concern of religion was not self-indulgent, private introspection, but loving service for others. Christianity brings peace, but it is the peace of Christ's presence in our Gethsemane. Christianity brings strength, but more often than not it is the strength to bear our pain when our thorn in the flesh is not removed. Christianity brings meaning, but usually that meaning comes on the Jericho road when we identify with and lend our hearing ear and helping hand in love to a bleeding stranger.

Our holiness is personal but not private. Our personal holiness must find expression in social holiness. At their Christmas Conference in Baltimore in 1784, the question was asked: "What is the rightful task of Methodists in America?" The answer was unequivocal: "To reform a continent and spread scriptural holiness across the land." The church will always fail when either of those tasks is separated from the other.

Transcending Limitations

Another great lesson here is that limitations do not have to limit. As already indicated, we do not know what Paul's affliction was, whether malaria, epilepsy, eye trouble, migraine, or some other malady. Whatever it was, it was bad. Since in that day sickness was regarded as God's punishment for sins, it would have been natural for the Galatians to treat Paul as if he were a devil, not an angel of God. It must have been that Paul handled his affliction in such a Christlike manner that even his limitation became an asset. *"You received me as an angel of God, even as Christ Jesus"* (v. 14).

What we do with our limitations is not only a measure of our faith, but determines the effectiveness of our ministry and witness. Here it is in the life of a modern saint who refused to be limited by her limitation, as recalled in a sermon by Mark Trotter:

> Lizzie Johnson made thousands of bookmarks. At thirteen Lizzie injured her back in an accident, and she was to spend the rest of her life, twenty-seven more years, flat on her back. Her only view of the world was from a mirror mounted above her head. But she still wanted to do a great thing with her life, so when she heard in those days that you could free an African slave for $40, she made a quilt and tried to sell it for $40. Nobody would buy it. So she turned to making bookmarks, and she raised $1,000 a year for each of the twenty-seven years remaining in her life. She gave every penny of that to projects in this world that go to building up rather than tearing down.
>
> What about the quilt? One day a bishop from India was traveling through Illinois and she gave it to him. He took that quilt with him on his speaking tour around the country, and he told the story of Lizzie Johnson. Then he asked people if they would place an offering for missions in the quilt. He raised $100,000 for missions. You talk about how God creates miracles through modest efforts!
>
> One day after Lizzie Johnson had died, her sister, Alice Johnson, heard that a man named Takuo Matsumoto was coming to Champaign, Illinois, to speak. He was one of the most prominent Japanese Christians after the Second World War. He had been principal of the Methodist Girls' School in Hiroshima during the bombing. In John Hersey's book about tragedy, he is mentioned prominently as one of the heroes of those days.
>
> Alice Johnson remembered that her sister had given money to support the education of a young boy in

Japan named Takuo Matsumoto, and she wondered if this was the same person. She resolved to go to Champaign to hear him speak, but she got sick that day and had to stay home. That night someone told Mr. Matsumoto about her, and he said, "You mean that she is Lizzie Johnson's sister? All that I am I owe to Lizzie Johnson." That night he went to see Alice Johnson, and he went from there to the cemetery to put flowers on the grave of a woman who could not leave her bed, who was weak and helpless, but who stitched up her love in bookmarks and quilts and said, "Thank you, God," by loving others.

Limitations do not have to limit.

Tough but Tender

In the power of the person and the personal, love can be tough and integrity can be preserved.

Paul loved the Galatians. He saw them as his spiritual children. This was no surface bond, no sentimental affection. It was the kind of love that was tender, but tough. Integrity was preserved in the honesty of an open and trusting relationship. Try to feel the depth of that relationship. ". . . *If possible, you would have plucked out your own eyes and given them to me*" (v. 15). What love! And sense the probing honesty. *"Have I therefore become your enemy because I tell you the truth?"* (v. 16).

Paul was risking everything—laying on the line the relationship which had been so supportive and gratifying to him. He had to tell the truth *at* the risk of turning his friends into enemies. *"What then was the blessing you enjoyed?"* (v. 15)? *Blessing* is a beautiful, encompassing word. It describes the sense of total well-being Paul's presence and preaching had brought to the Galatians. Yet they were about to sacrifice that limitless joy of well-being and wholeness for transient satisfaction. Paul couldn't let them do it without boldly making his case and risking their friendship.

Within the Christian community we are always endangered by two pitfalls. One is a Pollyanna tolerance that makes no demands and reaps no harvest—a kind of religion-in-general stance that says, "I believe what I believe, you believe what you believe: Either belief is as good as the other; let's respect a person's rights and not seek to convert." The Christian missionary enterprise and world evangelization responding to Jesus' Great Commission does not allow such Pollyanna tolerance.

The second pitfall is a rigid intolerance that contends, "We have the true gospel. There is no freedom to err. You must believe as we believe, and you cannot propagate a gospel contrary to ours."

Either stance is a threat to the spread of the gospel. What is needed is a true catholicity which holds to the centralities of the faith: God's love for us, clearly demonstrated in the life, death, and Resurrection of Jesus, and salvation which comes alone by grace through faith in Jesus Christ.

Paul was a person of solid convictions. Sometimes his spiritual children regarded him as their enemy. Even so, the Galatians preserved his letter. His tough love, and the integrity of his commitment proved stronger than controversy.

Achieving Real Maturity

Personal Christian maturity comes as Christ is formed in us.

Paul's address in verse 19 is one of the tenderest he ever spoke: *"My little children, for whom I labor in birth again until Christ is formed in you."* With sharpness and clarity Paul states the passion of his life and his vision for a new humanity. This is not only a vibrant expression of concern for a people Paul anguished in love over, it is the epitome of his longing for all people. Phillips' translation of this verse has an even more poignant feeling about it: "Oh, my dear children, I feel the pangs of childbirth all over again till Christ be formed with you."

This is the same longing Paul had for the Christians of Ephesus: that they arrive at real maturity, "to the measure of the stature of the fullness of Christ" (Eph. 4:13). In Colossians the aim of the apostle's preaching and teaching was to "present every man mature in Christ" (1:28). This was no shallow goal, nothing taken lightly, no hit or miss proposition of a casual sermon. "For this I toil, striving with all the energy which he mightily inspires within me" (Col. 1:29 RSV).

Paul's great definition of a Christian was a person *in Christ.* He used that picture over and over again. "If any one is in Christ, he is a new creation" (2 Cor. 5:17, RSV). "And the secret is simply this: Christ in you! Yes, Christ in you bringing with him the hope of all the glorious things to come" (Col. 1:27, Phillips). "For to me to live is Christ, and to die is gain" (Phil. 1:21, KJV). "There is therefore now no condemnation to them which are in Christ Jesus" (Rom. 8:1, KJV).

Paul's most vivid description of his Christian experience was expressed in Galatians 2:20: *"I have been crucified with Christ; it is no longer I who live, but Christ lives in me."*

Almost by common consent, especially in Protestantism, the experience and understanding of justification by faith, or to be more theologically correct, justification *by grace* through faith, is Paul's most unique contribution to the Christian faith and life. This doctrine holds a unique place in the Protestant Reformation. "It was one of those classical moments of intense theological perception, when one word, one dogma, one cry of repentance, one assurance of reconciliation appear to contain in themselves the whole truth of God and the whole duty of man."[2]

As signal and central as justification by grace through faith is to Paul, we do him a grave injustice, and we imperil growth in Christian maturity, if we even hint that this was Paul's complete understanding of salvation. When you take all his writings, Galatians included, as a whole, you discover that the dynamic of his life and thought, the struggle and concern of his whole being, is captured not when he is expounding justification, or arguing with the legalists, or defending his apostleship, or relishing in the ultimate triumph of Christ in glory, or giving practical guidance to the church. He reaches the pinnacle of his feeling and thinking when he proclaims "Christ in you, the hope of glory" (Col. 1:27).

It is crucial that we see the *justifying* and *regenerating* work of Christ together. In justification we are given a new status—the status of sons and heirs. We are reconciled to God. Our acceptance by God has its source not in our achievement, but in God's love. Our righteousness is not that which is from the law, but that which is through faith in Christ, the righteousness which is from God by faith (Phil. 3:9). We are made right with God by the justifying death of Jesus.

This takes care of our estrangement from God, our relationship with God. But sin has not only severed our relationship with God, it has distorted the image of God within us, perverted God's divine intention, God's very life within us. Regeneration, the new birth, is the restoration of the image, the recovery of our identity as children of the Father. Christ being formed in us is the reformation of our lives in God's great design for us, and that great design is the *stature of the fullness of Christ.*

So, along with merciful justification, God in Christ gives us a new birth. We become new creatures in Christ Jesus; *the old has passed away; the new has come.* The new that has come is Christ indwelling us by the power of the Holy Spirit, shaping our lives after the image of Christ.

TWO COVENANTS

21 Tell me, you who desire to be under the law, do you not hear the law? 22 For it is written that Abraham had two sons: the one by a bondwoman, the other by a freewoman. 23 But he who was of the bondwoman was born according to the flesh, and he of the freewoman through promise, 24 which things are symbolic. For these are the two covenants: the one from Mount Sinai which gives birth to bondage, which is Hagar— 25 for this Hagar is Mount Sinai in Arabia, and corresponds to Jerusalem which now is, and is in bondage with her children— 26 but the Jerusalem above is free, which is the mother of us all. 27 For it is written:

"Rejoice, O barren,
You who do not bear!
Break forth and shout,
You who are not in labor!
For the desolate has many more children
Than she who has a husband."

28 Now we, brethren, as Isaac was, are children of promise. 29 But, as he who was born according to the flesh then persecuted him who was born according to the Spirit, even so it is now. 30 Nevertheless what does the Scripture say? *"Cast out the bondwoman and her son, for the son of the bondwoman shall not be heir with the son of the freewoman."* 31 So then, brethren, we are not children of the bondwoman but of the free.

—Galatians 4:21–31

Though allegory was a popular style of teaching among Jewish rabbis, Paul used it very little. He had the highest regard, an almost sacred regard, for the actual history of his people. Therefore when he says in verse 24 that these things *"are an allegory,"* he does not mean that the story is unhistorical, but that there is a religious meaning that goes far beyond the literal account.

To grasp the allegorical meaning, we need to rehearse the story from Genesis 16, 17, and 21. Sarah and Abraham were without children. They were getting old; Sarah far too old to bear children. She did what any wife would have done in that social/cultural context. She had Abraham go to her slave girl, Hagar, in order for Hagar to bear a child for her. Hagar bore a son named Ishmael. Then the unbelievable happened. God came to Sarah and promised her a child. Though apparently impossible, Sarah, then over ninety years old, bore the promised son and he was named Isaac.

Paul emphasizes the point that Ishmael was born of the ordinary human impulses—of the flesh—while Isaac was a result of God's intervention.

Sarah was a free woman and Hagar a slave. Yet, because barrenness was a sore shame for a woman in that time, Hagar seemed to triumph over Sarah. This brought tension and trouble. Sarah later discovered Ishmael "mocking" Isaac, and demanded that both Hagar and Ishmael be cast out of the household, contending that *"the son of the bondwoman shall not be heir with the son of the freewoman"* (v. 30).

An allegory is much more than an illustration. It is a spiritual truth embodied in historical events. Paul, in his new mood of tenderness, uses this bit of significant history to teach a great lesson. No longer on the attack, he pleads with his *"dear children"* to *"hear the law"* and let the law teach them that the true children of Abraham, the true inheritors of the Promise, are not those whose bond of union is the law, but those who have been set spiritually free by the grace of Jesus Christ.

Dramatic contrasts shine through the allegory. Hagar is a slave, Sarah is free. Two covenants flow from them. Hagar represents the covenant of law and corresponds to the present Jerusalem. Sarah represents the covenant of promise and corresponds to the Jerusalem on high.

Paul saw the present (earthly) Jerusalem as the center of a religion of bondage where God was shut up in the Temple. Worship of God had ceased to be spiritual worship and had become scrupulous observance of legal enactments. Those who acknowledge such a religion, whether they in fact trace their ancestry to Ishmael or not, are sons of Hagar. That line continues prolifically until today, for it includes all those who seek salvation apart from the freely given grace of God through Jesus Christ.

Those who acknowledge Christ as Lord, who by faith receive His grace, claim the Jerusalem above. Like Isaac, the believing recipients of grace are the children of promise, whether any trace of Isaac's blood flows through them are not. It is grace, all grace!

The first verse of chapter 5 is the conclusion of Paul's appeal: *"Stand fast therefore in the liberty by which Christ has made us free, and do not be entangled again with a yoke of bondage."* We will look at that specifically in the next chapter. For now it is enough to illustrate Paul's great claim with a picture. It was in the newspaper back in the mid-1950s during the height of the civil rights movement. A black man, who must have been over a hundred years old, was being carried on the shoulders of a group of young men. They were taking him up the steps of a courthouse in a Southern town to register to vote. The caption beneath the picture said he was born a slave.

To a marked degree he had remained a slave, even after the Emancipation Proclamation. Unable to vote, subjected to the rigid discriminatory demands and tests of others, he was kept in subjection. But now he was free and the look on his face showed his joy. He was going to express his freedom, his release from the humiliation of being a second-class citizen, by registering to vote. That man could have understood Paul's word. In fact, he and others like him sang often during those days, "Free at last, free at last! Thank God almighty I'm free at last."

Paul was pleading with the Galatians to accept the freedom that was theirs, and not be reshackled in the bondage of law.

NOTES

1. John McLeod Campbell, *The Nature of Atonement and Its Relation to Remission of Sins and Eternal Life* (New York: Macmillan, 1869; reprint 1978), p. 147.

2. E. C. Hoskyns and F. W. Davey, *The Fourth Gospel*, 2nd ed. rev. (London: Faber and Faber, 1947), p. 5.

CHAPTER FIVE—PRACTICAL IMPLICATIONS OF THE GOSPEL

GALATIANS 5:1–26

Scripture Outline

Participation and Anticipation in Christ's Freedom (5:1–6)

Another Personal Appeal (5:7–12)

Responsible Freedom (5:13–15)

Walking in the Spirit (5:16–26)

Throughout the letter Paul has been making his case: Salvation is the grace-gift of God. We are not worthy of it. We cannot earn it. We are justified (made right) with God by God's grace and our faith-response to that grace. In the Cross Jesus has purchased our pardon, doing for us what we could never do ourselves.

The remainder of his letter enunciates the practical implications of the gospel. Christian liberty is not a license to keep on sinning. To receive salvation is to begin a process of working it out in life. Though the yoke of the law has been removed, the Cross has been accepted, and life becomes a rhythm of death and resurrection. Christian freedom makes us slaves of Christ. The only way to use this freedom is by self-investment in the lives of others for Christ's sake, by ongoing dying to those things to which Christ died, and by the continuous production of the fruit of His Spirit.

So, Paul was very specific in taking one third of his letter—chapters 5 and 6—to elaborate on the practical implications of the gospel.

FOR FREEDOM CHRIST HAS SET US FREE

5:1 Stand fast therefore in the liberty by which Christ has made us free, and do not be entangled again with a yoke of bondage.

—Galatians 5:1

The liberty with which Christ has made us free is the pivotal concept as Paul moves into this practical part of his letter.

This verse, as previously stated, may be best regarded as the exhortation with which Paul closed the argument he began in 4:21, rather than the beginning of this new section. (The chapter-divisions of our Bibles were designed in the twelfth century, and sometimes are a bit misleading.) If we see it as a conclusion of 4:21–31, the last part would read, "We are not children of a slave, but of the free-woman, *by virtue of the freedom for which Christ has set us free.*"

Even so, the verse is a great pivotal one, the essence of which can stand alone, especially in the way the RSV translates and punctuates it: "For freedom Christ has set us free; stand fast therefore, and do not submit again to a yoke of slavery."

This verse, along with Galatians 2:20, captures powerfully and succinctly Paul's message. His theme is grace, God's grace alone by which persons can be saved. Christ is the source of grace, and freedom is the result of it in our lives.

We do well to rehearse the nature of that freedom.

1. It is the freedom of *release.* "*God sent forth His son . . . to redeem those who were under the law*" (Gal. 4:4–5). We will never understand the full impact of this meaning of Christian freedom unless we understand the encompassing nature of sin and evil. Paul knew that sin had not alone affected human nature, reducing us to slaves of our passions, but had also affected the entire universe. The whole "creation groans and labor," he said to the Romans (8:22). God had to do something of cosmic significance. What He did—the gift of Himself in His Son on the Cross—revealed the suffering heart of God. From Adam on, sin has inflicted pain in the heart of God.

Humans, and all creation, are in bondage to sin until God's gift of grace, His crucified Son, is received in faith to release us.

2. *Reconciliation* is another aspect of Christian freedom. Is there a greater bondage than being shut up in oneself, being shut off from another, or being estranged from God? Above all else, Paul sees the

work of Jesus Christ as a work of reconciliation. We were made for friendship and fellowship with God. By disobedience and rebellion we ended up alienated, at enmity with God. Through Christ's death, the lost relationship between persons and God is restored.

3. Not only is Christ's freedom that of release and reconciliation; it is *new vision*. When Jesus preached His opening sermon at Nazareth, He took for His text Isaiah 61:1–2. The casual reader may not note that Jesus inserted into the messianic program in this passage a verse from the Servant Song of Isaiah 42:7, "to open the eyes of the blind." This is of special significance. After healing the man born blind, Jesus said, "For judgment I come into this world, that those who do not see may see, and that those who see may become blind" (John 9:39, RSV). The entrance into the life of Christ, the freedom He brings, belongs with *vision*.

Scripture pictures human beings as spiritual creatures in the unity of a physical body with limited capacity, but with enormous potential for spiritual growth. Unredeemed human nature lives like blind people. The world is dark and the frightening shadow of death dogs our steps and devastates our lives. The gospel is the Good News that light has come. The experience of conversion releases us from the bondage of sin and law and gives us a new vision in which all of life, even the physical universe, looks fresh.

4. Freedom of release and reconciliation and the ensuing new vision, is also *the freedom of belonging: "You are no longer a servant but a son, and if a son, then an heir of God through Christ"* (Gal. 4:7).

Release and reconciliation are the beginning of the journey, not the end. Freedom is not only exit—exit from every form of slavery; it is *entrance—entrance* into a new life of the buoyant freedom of belonging.

We belong to Christ, and because we belong to Him, all belongs to us. We will pursue this theme more as we look at verses 13–15 of this chapter.

PARTICIPATION AND ANTICIPATION

2 Indeed I, Paul, say to you that if you become circumcised, Christ will profit you nothing. 3 And I testify again to every man who becomes circumcised that he is a debtor to keep the whole law. 4 You have become estranged from Christ, you who attempt to be justified by law; you have fallen from grace. 5 For we through the Spirit eagerly wait for the hope of

righteousness by faith. [6] For in Christ Jesus neither circumcision nor uncircumcision avails anything, but faith working through love.

—*Galatians 5:2–6*

Paul thought of salvation in two modes: *participation* and *anticipation*. For him Christ's death and Resurrection are not events which only convey benefits to the believer; they are events in which the believer participates: *"I have been crucified with Christ; it is no longer I who live, but Christ lives in me"* (Gal. 2:20). Anticipation is not the alternative to participation, but the hope that sustains us in our participation, the "not yet" which constantly draws us on.

We can understand verses 2–6 only as we understand these two modes of thinking about salvation.

Circumcision or Christ

Paul primarily thinks in terms of structures or whole: Adam and Christ, law and grace, Spirit and flesh. "Each of these polarities is a structure of existence in which one participates, in which one's existence is defined because the participant is, by definition, 'open' to and governed by the structure. The fact that these structures stand over against one another accounts for the either/or quality of much of Paul's thinking. Paul never understands the self to be autonomous, having the option of whether or not to participate in a structure. Paul's gospel therefore announces that emancipation from one structure is possible because participation in another is available."

So *"if you become circumcised, Christ will profit you nothing"* (v. 2). To be circumcised made one a *"debtor to keep the whole law"* (v. 3). Christ frees from the law. You cannot have circumcision and Christ. It is either law or grace.

Fallen from Grace

Once in grace always in grace, some would insist. But Paul is clear here. *"You have become estranged from Christ, you who attempt to be justified by law; you have fallen from grace"* (v. 4). The KJV is "Christ is become of no effect unto you" and the RSV is "You are severed from Christ."

The issue is not eternal salvation, but *effective relationship with Christ.* This is rooted in Paul's thinking in terms of wholes, structures, and in terms of opposites. On the Damascus Road his vision of Christ so radically changed him that he is forever contrasting what belonged to the old life and what belonged to the new. He "died with Christ" to all the evil powers which were ruling in the present age, and he rose with Christ to live, even in this sin-cursed existence, the new life "in Christ." He was liberated from law. Law and grace are modes of relationship which link us to God. Thus they are spheres of power. This is the same idea we discussed in chapter 2: *"Spirit"* and *"flesh"* are contrasting spheres of power in which we live. And this is what Paul meant in Romans 8:7 "You are not in the spirit."

Paul is saying that we cannot participate (cf. introduction to this chapter) in two conflicting spheres of power. The person who has been baptized into Christ's death must regard himself or herself "dead to sin and alive to God in Christ Jesus" (Rom. 6:11). We cannot have "the law" and "grace." We choose. We cannot be "in sin" and "in Christ" *at* the same time (Rom. 6:2).

Paul knew of course that we do not become sinless even though we may be "freed from sin" (Rom. 6:7). To be *in* grace is not a matter of being sinless; therefore falling from grace is not a question of moving from a life without sin (none of us are there) to a life of sin. To fall from grace is to move from one domain of power to another; to seek salvation in any other way than through Christ; to move out of the realm of participating in His death and Resurrection as the source of our life and hope.

The Perfection of Our Righteousness

"For we through the Spirit eagerly wait for the hope of righteousness by faith (v. 5). Not only do we *participate* in the death and Resurrection of Christ, we *anticipate* the perfecting of our righteousness. By the grace of God, through our faith, we are "accepted as righteous" (justified) here and now. The Spirit gives us the hope that what Christ has begun within us will be completed. In response to our faith the Spirit comes into our hearts to witness to us that our *justification* is the first installment. God accepts us, imputing to us the righteousness of Christ. The hope of *righteousness* assures us of God's pardon, for all we have been, all our failure, and the full realization of the perfection He has promised.

There is another dimension of this rhythm of participation/ anticipation. We live between the "already" and the "not yet." The "already" is the assurance of our justification by Christ. The "not yet" is not an extension of the present, but a future in which we can participate now. The kingdom, though not fully come, is the Christian's already. Our present includes what is underway. We participate in the "not yet" by joining Christ in what He is seeking for us and our world.

Only Christ for Justification

Paul again rises to one of his great heights of vision. He will come back to it again as he closes his letter (6:15), the rallying cry of his gospel: *"For in Christ Jesus neither circumcision nor uncircumcision avails anything, but faith working through love"* (v. 6).

When a person is, through faith, *"in Christ Jesus,"* nothing—absolutely nothing, circumcision or uncircumcision—can add one whit to his standing before God. Before and since the Galatians, there has been, and will forever be, an inveterate tendency in human nature to think in terms of merit. Christianity, at its grandest best, continually negates such notions. Emil Brunner honed in to the heart: "It is just in this way that Christian faith is distinguished from all religion. No religion ever had the courage thus to go to the bitter end of giving man up, as the Christian faith does. All religions make an attempt at the self-justification of man—at least of man as a religious subject. It is exclusively the faith in justification by grace alone which sacrifices not only the rational man, or the moral man, but the religious man as well."[2]

Circumcision or uncircumcision—intellectual, moral or religious merit—counts nothing in the economy of God. In that economy all is grace.

Love: The Present Tense of Faith

What a succinct expression of the interrelation of faith and love: *"faith working through love"* (v. 6). Though I titled this chapter "practical implications of the gospel," never let it be thought Paul's letters can be strictly divided into "doctrinal" and "practical" sections. Though Paul clamorously insisted that there was no salvation in "good works," still works of righteousness, ethical behavior, moral goodness, and holiness of life are essential ingredients, not mere incidental by-products of his faith.

This verse is an integral expression of his religion and the relation of his faith to his ethics. He repeated in varied ways the harmony and mutuality of faith, hope, and love. Hope is made the future tense of faith in verse 5, and love is made the present tense of faith in verse 6.

There are two ways of looking at this—both revealing love and faith inseparably bound together.

Faith activated by love is one way to look at it. Paul's experience, graphically described in Galatians 2:20, supports this understanding. It was God *who loved me and gave Himself for me* that claimed Paul's faith.

Faith acting in love is another way to see it. Phillips translates this phrase, "faith which expresses itself in love," and the NEB says "faith active in love." Later in the chapter (vv. 13–15) Paul distinctly calls for the freedom of faith to issue in love of the brethren.

However we view it, the lessons are clear. When God comes to judge us the question will not be whether we were obedient to the law, whether we are circumcised or uncircumcised, but whether in the revelation of His love expressed ultimately in His crucified Son, we have turned to Him in faith. And when there is a testing of that faith, it will involve not the doctrinal propositions to which we have given intellectual assent, but whether our faith expressed itself in love. Jesus' picture of the final judgment is unforgettably clear: "As you did it to one of the least of these my brethren, you did it to me" (Matt. 25:40 RSV).

ANOTHER PERSONAL APPEAL

[7] You ran well. Who hindered you from obeying the truth? [8] This persuasion does not come from Him who calls you. [9] A little leaven leavens the whole lump. [10] I have confidence in you, in the Lord, that you will have no other mind; but he who troubles you shall bear his judgment, whoever he is.

[11] And I, brethren, if I still preach circumcision, why do I still suffer persecution? Then the offense of the cross has ceased. [12] I could wish that those who trouble you would even cut themselves off!

—*Galatians 5:7–12*

In chapter 4 Paul turned from the lambasting style of a fighter, to the tender wooing and beseeching of a parent. This latter style continues in chapter 5, especially in these verses. As we read this section, we recall Jesus' word to His wavering disciples, "Will you also go away?" (John 6:67, KJV).

Paul speaks now not as a skilled debater, measuring his words and sharpening his logic, to win the case. He speaks "man to man," a friend to friends. He begins with his favorite metaphor, running. *"You ran well. Who hindered you. . . ?"* (v. 7). He expresses confidence in them (v. 10). He is not willing to give them up, because his confidence is *in* the Lord. His faith is in Christ's holding power, so Paul appeals not to himself and his doctrine, not to his authority as an apostle, but to the deep conviction that Christ who has set the Galatians free will keep them.

Verse 11 is an abrupt return to an earlier charge made against him; but again, he is laying his own life on the line: *"If I still preach circumcision, why do I still suffer persecution? Then the offense of the cross has ceased."* It would have been simple and easy for Paul to water down the gospel. But he was not willing. The "wisdom" and "power" of the Cross may appear "foolish" to the Greeks, even scandalous to the Jews, but Paul was not willing to avoid persecution by appeasing his hearers.

Paul was so emotionally involved in this personal appeal, so stirred to his depths, that one of the bitterest and cruelest expressions pours out in verse 12: *"I could wish that those who trouble you would even cut themselves off!"*

Galatia was near Phrygia where people worshiped Cybele. The priests and sometimes other devout worshipers, in frenzied devotion, mutilated themselves by castration. Cybele priests were eunuchs. The Galatians who knew about these priests could not miss his inference. If salvation depended on the merit of a physical operation, circumcision, why not go all the way and castrate yourselves like the heathen priests? Wouldn't this more drastic rite give greater assurance than the Jewish custom?

It is a coarse illustration, but dramatically real to the Galatians. And as always Paul could not stay happy with himself after making such a denunciation. He recovers from his emotional outrage, calling the Galatians "brethren" in verse 13. And in Galatians 6:1 he pleads for treating gently those who are taken in a fault.

RESPONSIBLE FREEDOM

13 For you, brethren, have been called to liberty; only do not *use* liberty as an opportunity for the flesh, but through love serve one another. 14 For all the law is fulfilled in one word, *even* in this: *"You shall love your neighbor as yourself."* 15 But if you bite and devour one another, beware lest you be consumed by one another!

—Galatians 5:13–15

Paul's proclamation of *freedom* is based on his doctrine of *redemption.* The tension between freedom and bondage is always high-pitched in our lives. With a holdover of the slavish spirit, and continually caught in a merit system, we are tempted to perform according to what we think are divine requirements, rather than to live as a son of the Father, and heir of His promise.

On the other hand—and here the tension increases—set free, we take our freedom in our own hands and choose as we will, intent on our liberation. Thus we do not give the Spirit a chance to take possession of our lives and form them *in Christ.*

Thus Paul is compelled to talk about responsible freedom— freedom working itself out in love.

Freedom Is a Birthright

Note first that freedom is a birthright. We are *"called to liberty"* (v. 13). There is a freedom that belongs to all persons because they are human beings.

The Declaration of Independence says that freedom is from God and endows us with certain inalienable rights. The United Nations has made a "declaration of human rights" that expresses a basic ideal of freedom for all people. Tragically, member nations continue to deprive their citizens of the basic freedoms that belong to all humans.

Back of both the U.S. Declaration of Independence and the U.N. "Declaration of Human Rights" is the birthright of dignity for human beings. The way God values each person reaches its dramatic height and depth of expression in the gift of His Son, and the willingness of His son to die for us. Augustine was right: God loves each one of us as though we were the only person to love. What a mindboggling, heart-stirring thought—that Christ would have given Himself, even if I was the only sinner needing salvation.

There is a liberty that is our birthright, but there is also a level of freedom that is uniquely Christian—the internal freedom of the spirit that enables us to live with dignity and meaning even in the midst of suppression and oppression.

I never will forget an evening in 1979 I spent with two Christians, a husband and wife, in a hotel room in Peking. They had not had any Christian literature or Bible for over fifteen years. The Red Guard had searched their homes and had burned their Bibles and books. Corporate worship had been suppressed, while churches were turned into factories, warehouses, schools, etc. The depression in the couple was obvious, but it took only minutes to realize that deep within them there flowed a quiet stream of strength. Their spirits were quickened and light and joy came into their eyes as we shared

Scripture together, sang, and prayed. Tears came freely to their eyes and to ours as they shared their faith with us. I felt as though I were back in the first century. The hotel room became a catacomb for me, and I knew that these two precious people, despite the bondage of their circumstance, had retained the freedom with which Christ had set them free.

Freedom Requires Discipline

The second thing Paul says in this passage is "do not use your freedom as an opportunity for the flesh" (v. 13, RSV). Freedom requires discipline.

The Greek word *aphormi* translated here as *"opportunity"* is sometimes translated "opening," and literally means "a place for jumping off." It was a favorite word of Paul; he alone of New Testament writers used it. Originally the word designated a point from which to launch an attack, hence was used in military parlance to mean a base of operation.

Paul knew that if freedom was interpreted merely as the removal of restraint, sin would seize the opportunity and use the weakness of human nature to launch attack against the Spirit.

Paul has more to say about *the flesh* in the next section of this chapter. Here, however, in the same breath, Paul gives a contrast to using freedom as an opportunity for the flesh: "but by love serve one another" (v. 13, KJV). This contrast characterizes *the flesh as selfish*. While in the next section Paul deals with the deeds of the flesh and fleshly indulgences which flow from lack of restraint, here he is enunciating the fact that Christian freedom accepts a willing servitude.

Freedom Requires Love

That's the third thing Paul says: *The criterion to guide our Christian freedom is love.* It is the love that was defined in the law by God to Moses (Lev. 19:18), and reiterated by Jesus (Mark 12:29–31) and now restated by Paul: *"You shall love your neighbor as yourself"* (v. 14).

"Through love serve one another" (v. 13). This is what Jesus meant when He said we would save our lives by losing them. If we give our life in love to others we will find it. *"But if you bite and devour one another, beware lest you be consumed by one another!"* (v. 15).

Here is the losing and finding of life in a person. Marian Preminger was born in Hungary in 1913, raised in a castle with her aristocratic family, surrounded by maids, tutors, governesses, butlers, and chauffeurs. Her grandmother, who lived with them, insisted that whenever they traveled, they take their own linen, for she believed it was beneath their dignity to sleep between sheets used by common people.

While attending school in Vienna, Marian met a handsome young Viennese doctor. They fell in love, eloped, and married when she was only eighteen. The marriage lasted only a year and she returned to Vienna to begin her life as an actress.

While auditioning for a play, she met the brilliant young German director, Otto Preminger. They fell in love and soon married. They went to America soon thereafter, where he began his career as a movie director. Unfortunately and tragically, Hollywood is a place of dramatic illustrations of people "biting, devouring, and consuming" one another. Marian was caught up in the glamour, lights, and superficial excitement and soon began to live a sordid life. When Preminger discovered it, he divorced her.

She returned to Europe to live the life of a socialite in Paris. In 1948 she learned through the newspaper that Albert Schweitzer, the man she had read about as a little girl, was making one of his periodic visits to Europe and was staying at Günsbach. She phoned his secretary and was given an appointment to see Dr. Schweitzer the next day. When she arrived in Günsbach she discovered he was in the village church playing the organ. She listened and turned the pages of music for him. After a visit he invited her to have dinner at his house. By the end of the day she knew she had discovered what she had been looking for all her life. She was with him every day thereafter during his visit, and when he returned to Africa he invited her to come to Lambarene and work in the hospital.

She did—and she found herself. There in Lambarene, the girl who was born in a castle and raised like a princess, who was accustomed to being waited on with all the luxuries of a spoiled life, became a servant. She changed bandages, bathed babies, fed lepers . . . *and became free.* She wrote her autobiography and called it *All I Ever Wanted Was Everything.* She could not get the "everything" that would satisfy and give meaning until she could give everything. When she died in 1979, the *New York Times* carried her obituary, which included this statement from her: "Albert Schweitzer said there are two classes of people in this world—the helpers, and the non-helpers. I'm a helper."

What an obituary! It is the way we find ourselves—by losing ourselves, and the criterion of Christian freedom is serving one another in love.

WALKING IN THE SPIRIT

16 I say then: Walk in the Spirit, and you shall not fulfill the lust of the flesh. 17 For the flesh lusts against the Spirit, and the Spirit against the flesh; and these are contrary to one another, so that you do not do the things that you wish. 18 But if you are led by the Spirit, you are not under the law.

19 Now the works of the flesh are evident, which are: adultery, fornication, uncleanness, lewdness, 20 idolatry, sorcery, hatred, contentions, jealousies, outbursts of wrath, selfish ambitions, dissensions, heresies, 21 envy, murders, drunkenness, revelries, and the like; of which I tell you beforehand, just as I also told you in time past, that those who practice such things will not inherit the kingdom of God.

22 But the fruit of the Spirit is love, joy, peace, longsuffering, kindness, goodness, faithfulness, 23 gentleness, self-control. Against such there is no law. 24 And those who are Christ's have crucified the flesh with its passions and desires. 25 If we live in the Spirit, let us also walk in the Spirit. 26 Let us not become conceited, provoking one another, envying one another.

—Galatians 5:16–26

It is easy to forget, when we read passages like this, that Paul was writing to Christians, persons who have received the Spirit of God. Paul is aware of the potential relapse into fleshly existence, the ever-present possibility of falling from grace. So as we begin our consideration of this power-packed section it may be helpful to recall the discussion of Spirit and flesh in chapter 2 (see pp. 42ff.). For Paul *flesh* is a reference to our whole selves, not to a part of us that is dirty and distasteful. To live *in the flesh* is to live as a member of human society in a physical body. *Flesh* also denotes a domain of power, a sphere of influence in which one lives.

The miracle of justification and the new birth is that fleshly persons become Spirit-persons. Throughout Christian history, every claim that the Holy Spirit is especially present leads to controversy. But controversy should not cause us to avoid some of the strongest messages of the Bible. These verses (16–26) convey such a strong message.

Not only Paul, but countless Christians witness to the fact that the Holy Spirit can become so real that the Spirit is a far more intimate part of our being than some dimensions of *the flesh*. This is what happened to Paul (Gal. 2:20).

Paul is urging the Galatians to remember that, as Christians, they have received the Spirit and they are to walk in the Spirit. The Spirit is the supreme energizing and regulative force in their lives. If they walk in the Spirit, there is no danger that their Christian liberty will become an *opportunity for the flesh.*

For Paul, the Spirit is more than the manifestation of a super-natural power, more than the giver of dramatic gifts, more than an explosive force erupting in the believer now and then. The Spirit is the daily sustaining, inspiring, and guiding power of the Christian's life. The Spirit is the domain of power, the sphere of influence which replaces *the flesh* as the energy force of our lives.

Flesh or Spirit?

What will we allow to dominate?—that is the question. Flesh or Spirit? So long as we are in the flesh there is going to be a con-flict between flesh and Spirit, and this is what Paul is dealing with. Remember that our very existence is "flesh" insofar as we give our-selves over to the world of the flesh, serve that world, and allow ourselves to be determined by it. That means that we can never withdraw from "the flesh" in our earthly lives, but we do not have to forfeit to the flesh. We can fight against its demonic powers. We can do this by walking in the Spirit.

Verse 17, *"For the flesh lusts against the Spirit, and the Spirit against the flesh; and these are contrary to one another, so that you do not do the things that you wish,"* is an echo of Romans 7:14ff. But more is being said here. In the Romans passage, Paul deals with human psychology—the helplessness of our ideals divorced from the saving power of Christ. "For I do not do what I want, but I do the very thing I hate" (Rom. 7:15, RSV). There is no reference in that passage to the Spirit. Here the power of the Spirit is the dominant note. Paul is not concerned with human psy-chology as such, but about the divine work of sanctification—the Spirit shaping us into the kinds of persons who can overcome and rise above the desires of the flesh.

This verse is not a description of equal forces combatting each other, with the outcome indecisive. The flesh will continue always to assert its desires in opposition to the Spirit; nevertheless the Spirit who indwells every Christian asserts opposition to the flesh. Paul is certain who will emerge triumphant—and we can be cer-tain if we *walk in the Spirit.*

All across the land, growing numbers of Christians have allowed the Spirit to have the center of their lives. They are often called "Spirit-people" or members of the "Spirit-movement." Taking a cue from the experience of the spontaneous visit by the Spirit on Pentecost, they are often called Pentecostals. Because the Spirit brings gifts, *charismata*, they are referred to as "charismatics."

As has always been the case, controversy has accompanied the movement. Congregations have experienced schisms; church leaders have been frightened, and have responded bureaucratically and institutionally, rather than pastorally. In some quarters the movement has produced more heat than light, more ecstasy and enthusiasm than genuine Spirit-energy and ministry. Even so, many (I among them) are convinced that the movement has genuine depth and is a response of God to the spiritual hungers of a materialistic, pleasure-oriented, flesh-surfeited people. People are receiving hope, being spiritually transformed, experiencing reconciliation in relationships, receiving physical and emotional healing. Time will tell whether we are on the verge of another great awakening, but in the meantime some of us are discovering afresh, and some for the first time, that we can *walk in the Spirit,* not only to *not fulfill the lust of the flesh,* but to find a new job and to avail ourselves of power for ministry.

The Struggle Is Ongoing

We should never forget the terrible menace of the flesh. The struggle is not an overnight one. Though we may win the victory in an initial, sincere, and complete commitment of our lives to Christ, the war continues, because we must continue living "in the flesh" and are always exposed to that domain of power. The struggle may be long and indecisive, and for many the flesh will at times achieve supremacy until the believer yields to the Spirit's domination.

So Paul catalogs the works of the flesh. This is not an exhaustive listing but is concrete and personal.

(1) *Adultery.* The KJV translates a text which has this first in Paul's list. That position has special relevance for our day. One of the most destructive sins of our day is adultery. At least one out of four (at certain periods in our modern history, one out of three) marriages ends in divorce. One of the primary causes of the ravaging breakup of homes is adultery. Sex has been pictured as a river. It is a good and a wonderful blessing when kept within its proper channel. The Christian vision is that the God-created channel of sex is one man with one woman in marriage for life. A

river that overflows its banks is a dangerous thing. Adultery is a breaking of the marriage vows and more often than not leads to the breaking of hearts, the breaking of homes, the breaking of persons.

(2) *Fornication.* The Greek word is *porneia* and means primarily sexual intercourse between a man and a woman not married to each other. Adultery is fornication. William Barclay reminds us that the one completely new virtue which Christianity brought into the world was chastity. Into a world where sexual immorality was not only condoned, but regarded as normal, the Christian faith came as a purifying fire. Twentieth-century America has reverted back to the "normality of sexual immorality" and the fire of the Christian faith is desperately needed.

(3) *Uncleanness. Akatharsia* is the Greek word translated "uncleanness" or "impurity." In its positive form *(katharos)* it is an adjective meaning *pure,* so in its negative form it could be used for meal or flour that had not been sifted, a tree that had never been pruned, or for the pus of an unclean wound. The positive form of the word could describe a house that is left clean and in good condition, but the strongest use of *katharos* (pure) was to designate that ceremonial cleanness which entitles a person to approach God.

In the mystery cults and in the Law of Moses, the emphasis on ritual in relation to God was to show physical uncleanness contracted from dead bodies, lepers, tabooed animals, etc. But Paul is concerned about "moral impurity" that soils our lives and separates us from God. Though the word is often associated with sexual vice, its broader meaning includes all that defiles us and detracts us from right relation with God, thus from right living.

(4) *Licentiousness.* Even the sound of the Greek word has a sensuous ring: *alselgeia.* It is translated in the KJV as "lasciviousness" in Mark 7:22, 2 Corinthians 12:21, Ephesians 4:19, 1 Peter 4:3, Jude 1:4, and this Galatians verse. The RSV renders it "licentiousness" in all these instances, while in Romans 13:13 and 2 Peter 2:18 it is translated "wantonness." It has been defined as "readiness for any pleasure." It is often used for lewdness and sensuality, but also applies to unrestrained violence, a calloused, runaway passion for pleasure at any cost, desire and lust that cares nothing for what others think. Has not America (in general) come to that point? If TV and movies reflect what we are looking for, then lewdness, sensuality, and unrestrained violence aptly reveal our runaway passions for pleasure, and our callousness.

(5) *Idolatry.* The Jews regarded idolatry as the root of all other sins. It means not only worship of "graven images," handmade gods, but *allowing anything* to take the place of God. Idolatry is a "work of the flesh" in which we create god in our own image, according to our own desires, constructing our theology to rationalize and justify the way we want to live.

Throughout history the most subtle and dangerous forms of idolatry have been materialism and nationalism. In our day these two idolatries have been the primary forces separating us from God. When the two are intertwined as they presently are in modern America, their capacity to draw us from God is especially enticing and powerful.

(6) *Sorcery.* The KJV translates this "witchcraft." The Greek word, *pharmakeia*, literally means the use of drugs. It is the root word from which *pharmacy* comes. It designated the beneficent use of drugs as a doctor would prescribe them, but, also the *poisoning* of drugs, and came to be especially connected with witchcraft and magic of which the ancient world was full because witches and sorcerers used drugs extensively.

Magic and witchcraft was one of the most dangerous competitors to Judaism and then to early Christianity. It was human nature's effort to control God, to compel God to fit into its plan and do its bidding. What forms of sorcery do we have in our modern day? Anything, including the rising tide of horoscope gazing, that replaces prayer as the normal entree to God belongs to the domain of *flesh*, which is contrary to walking in the Spirit.

Idolatry and sorcery fall into the same category—sins directly against God.

(7) The next series of words through *murders* can profitably be lumped together because they describe sins in human relationship, the sins of self-assertion and pride that destroy community. Since Paul was addressing the church, there was special emphasis on the fellowship of the body which was threatened by *hatred, contention, jealously, outbursts of wrath*, etc. Unity within the church was and is absolutely essential. Paul pleaded more than once that that unity be preserved, that "the peace of God rule in your hearts" (Col. 3:15).

The word translated "heresy" deserves special note. The Greek word was *hairesis* and originally had a good connotation. It came from the root which means "to choose," and was used for any band of people who shared a common belief. Applied to religion, it meant a sect or party.

The application of the word to unorthodox doctrine came much later than the New Testament; therefore the RSV translation "party spirit" best captures what Paul was talking about. The varieties of Christian experience and interpretation were not, and are not today, the problem. The problem is twofold: (a) rival ambition in the church—groups wanting special recognition, and (b) the desire of some to make their own variety of Christian experience the norm of everyone. An example is the insistence by some Pentecostals that "speaking in tongues" is the true sign of the "baptism of the Holy Spirit."

Paul called this "party spirit" childish, and enunciated the unity that binds us together (1 Cor. 3:22–23).

(8) *Envy and murders.* Does it hit you hard that these two are said in the same breath? Lightfoot traces a graduation of intensity in the words of this section of sins of human relationship. *Envyings,* as the KJV has it, a greater breach of love in human relations than any of the others mentioned, and *murder* would be a natural climax for this kind of list. If you find it difficult to put envy and murder together, it will help to recall that in Matthew (27:18) and Mark (15:10) it was *out of envy* that the high priests delivered Christ to Pilate to be crucified.

To envy *(phthoneo)* means to harbor "malice" and "ill will." It is a feeling/action word which Euripides called "the greatest of all diseases among men." It begrudges what another has. In envy one may not want what the other person has, but one does not want the other person to have it. Envy leads not only to jealousy, but to an embittered mind. We are sobered in mind and spirit when we remember that envy and murder, according to Genesis, stood with man's first act of rebellion as the three original sins.

(9) *Drunkenness and rivalry.* These are twin "flesh-works," having kept company with each other from the beginning of civilization. In Paul's day, as in ours, strong drink and rivalry ("carousing," RSV) were socially approved forms of recreation. The difference is that in our day they are far more destructive. Lives maimed or snuffed out in auto accidents caused by drunken drivers rival the devastation of war. Families disrupted and destroyed by drink, needs of children gone unmet because of money spent on alcoholic beverage, are stark evidence of their end.

Paul minces no words in concluding his exhortation about works of the flesh. *"Those who practice such things will not inherit the kingdom of God"* (v. 21).

The Fruit of the Spirit

Over against the works of the flesh, Paul contrasts *"the fruit of the Spirit is love, joy, peace, longsuffering, kindness, goodness, faithfulness, gentleness, self-control"* (vv. 22–23).

How different it is when people live the life of the Spirit. In introducing this catalogue of the character traits of a Christian, Paul uses a singular word, *karpos,* whereas he has talked in the plural about the *works* of the flesh. This leads us to see that the *fruit of the Spirit* is love, and each fruit of the spirit which follows in the list is another expression of love. This distinction between the *works* of flesh and the *fruit* of the Spirit grew out of Paul's experience. His life had been in chaos. His sinful nature in rebellion against God made him at war even with himself, and split his life into fragmentary deeds. Then came the reconciling love of Christ, integrating his life with God and with others and bringing him together inside. It all centered in the unifying love of Christ. Thus, *joy, peace, longsuffering,* etc., were simply love in another form.

Sometimes in Holy Spirit movements (i.e., the current charismatic movement), clear distinction is not made between the meaning and significance of the *fruit* of the Spirit and *gifts* of the Spirit. The NEB translates *karpos* as "harvest," the "harvest of the Spirit." Thus you have the beautiful image of Christ growing within us with the harvest of that growth being all these expressions of the *fruit* of the Spirit.

So it is important to see that spiritual gifts *(charismata)* such as those described in 2 Corinthians 12:8–11 are powers or capacities with which we are endowed by the Spirit for ministry. The tendency in every age is to associate the Spirit's working with extraordinary manifestations of activity and power. In current parlance usually the expression "Spirit-filled Christian" designates a person gifted by God with dramatic and ecstatic expression of the Holy Spirit. We need to keep our signals clear. To be Spirit-filled is the gift that belongs to all Christians. The primary work of the Spirit in our lives is making real the indwelling Christ, sanctifying us, bringing us to real maturity—"to the measure of the stature of the fullness of Christ" (Eph. 4:13, RSV).

The fruit of the Spirit is the outward expression of Christ dwelling within. This fruit grows and is expressed in any person that willingly dies to what Christ died to so that the Spirit may bring him or her to new life in Christ. Powerfully and surely the Spirit works—sometimes dramatically; sometimes slowly, almost imperceptibly—in our lives to repeat the miracle of a new creation in Christ Jesus.

Like the preceding list of evils, Paul's cataloguing of the fruit of the Spirit is not exhaustive. The infinite variety by which the indwelling Christ expresses Himself through our unique personalities defies our description, as the outburst of undisciplined passion is also beyond our limitation to label.

(1) *Love* leads the list—naturally. Love is the summing up not merely of the law, but of all true spiritual life.

We may talk and write endlessly about love, but we never fully describe it, never adequately express it, nor probe the impenetrable depths of its meaning. Albert Camus put it this way: "Love is never strong enough to find the words befitting it."

Paul tried, and rose to eloquent heights in 1 Corinthians 13. Even there all is not said. Jesus did more with pictures: a shepherd braving the wilds for a lost sheep and a father embracing in total acceptance a prodigal son who has finally come home. The ultimate dynamic of love Jesus expressed in these words: *Greater love has no man than this, that a man lay down his life for his friends* (John 15:13, RSV). As was always the case, it was not enough for Jesus to say it; He had to live it and die it. So He did—on the Cross.

That love is a fruit of the Spirit and repeats itself daily in the lives of those who are willing to die to themselves and be raised with Christ.

(2) *Joy.* During a two-month period recently, I worshiped in two settings that were vastly different. One was a Christmas Eve morning worship service in a "main-line" Protestant church. I had looked forward with great anticipation to this celebration of the "coming of the light." Seldom have I experienced such dullness and deadness. Soon thereafter I was in an ecumenical service of those who would be labeled "charismatic." What life! The singing, the excitement, the light on faces, the mutuality of sharing reflected a joy that verified the chorus they sang: "Joy is the banner flying high over the castle of my heart when the King is in residence there."

A person knowing nothing about the church or the Christian faith would find it well nigh impossible to believe that those two congregations professed the same faith, both identifying themselves as Christians. The latter gathering was no superficial expression, no manipulated ecstasy, and, looking at them both, my understanding of joy is verified. Joy is two-faceted in its expression. *It is the gift of the Spirit that becomes a condition of the heart which is confident of its relationship to Christ—a forgiven sinner accepted by God's grace with the living Christ as daily companion.* On the other hand, *joy becomes the expression of celebration which empowers us to be Christian.* Joy makes us strong, produces energy. Those who do not celebrate the joy that is a gift will not generate the joy that is strength overflowing into all other facets of our lives.

Nail this down. Joy cannot be self-created. We might generate surface excitement and rile ourselves up to some heights of emotional ecstasy. But joy is something else, and its only source is obedience. Recall Jesus' words when a woman in the crowd shouted out to Jesus, "Blessed is the womb that bore you, and the breasts which nursed you!" and Jesus responded, "Blessed are those who hear the word of God and keep it!" (Luke 11:27, 28). What about that? It is a more blessed thing to live in obedience than to have been the mother of the Messiah! Joy (blessedness) comes from obedience.

(3) *Peace.* By the time Paul used this word, two streams of meaning had flowed into it: the Greek stream from the word *eirene,* meaning primarily "harmony"; and *shalom,* the Hebrew word which expressed "total well-being."

First off, Paul's *peace* was with God. God was the source of peace. His peace, through Christ, is "shed abroad in our hearts," and His intention is for persons to live in harmony with Him and with each other. Not only did God send His Son to make peace, He calls His followers to preach peace, and be peacemakers. This peace includes right relations with God and justice between persons. It is far more than freedom from strife.

In fact, the peace is past all understanding. Paul continued to be amazed at it. Because of what God had done for him—forgiven his sins; stilled his inner strife; made him a son and an heir, a citizen and a co-laborer in the kingdom—Paul knew that nothing, absolutely nothing in all the universe—past, present, or future—could separate him from the love of God (Rom. 8:38–39).

This was the deep well of spiritual reality that gushed forth as peace for Paul. So Christian peace does not mean freedom from strife or exemption from suffering. Storms may rage on the sea of life, even shipwrecks may happen, but making the harbor is certain. Peace is knowing "you are not alone!" That Christ is with us is the result of His indwelling presence, *the fruit of the Spirit.*

(4) *Longsuffering.* One of the most interesting and illuminating things about this *fruit of the Spirit* is that the word is commonly used in the New Testament to describe the attitude of God and Jesus towards men (Rom. 2:4; 9:22; 1 Tim. 1:18; 1 Pet. 3:20).

This word *makrothymise,* is translated "patience" and "forbearance" as well as "longsuffering." The great church father and preacher Chrysostom said that it is the grace of the man who could revenge himself and who does not.

The word is used generally as patience in regard to people, not to things or events. Certainly we have no difficulty thinking, as was suggested earlier, that patience is another expression of love. In the great Hymn of Love (1 Cor. 13), Paul used the word to illuminate the nature of love: "Love is patient and kind."

How patient God is with us. He suffers long, bears with us in all our sinning and rebellion, all our apathy and unconcern. He does not draw back when we spurn His love.

Forebearing provides another shade of meaning. There is the negative sense, "to refrain or abstain" or "to control oneself," and it also carries the positive meaning of *bearing one up,* carrying one. It is this kind of relationship of forebearing that Paul talks about in Galatians *6:6, "Bear one another's burdens."*

(5) Kindness. This is sometimes translated gentleness. Only slight shades of meaning differentiate these words. This is illustrated in the fact that the KJV uses the word gentleness at this point in the listing while the RSV and the NKJV use "kindness." Then later when the KJV uses meekness the RSV and the NKJV use gentleness. The Greek word is *chrestotes,* quite commonly translated "goodness" and sometimes "gentleness."

Again this verifies the integration of the inner character and the outward expression of our lives as we grow up into the full stature of Christ. We become patient and kind, good and gentle.

The brightest facet on this diamond of kindness is suggested by the fact that old wine is called *chrestos* (mellow), and Christ's yoke is likewise called *chrestos* (Matt. 11:30). The yoke of Christ does not chafe or gall; it fits, it is easy. Does that not suggest a style of relationship, being with another in the way that Christ is with us, making the way of the other easier because we are *yoked* with them?

(6) Goodness. The word Paul uses here, *agathosune,* is a strict biblical word, not used in secular Greek (Rom. 15:14; Eph. 5:9; 2 Thess. 1:11). it is a goodness that is "good for something." French says that Jesus expressed *agathosune* in cleansing the temple and driving out the money-changers. His *goodness* was expressing itself *prophetically,* demanding a change, requiring a response, bringing the fruit of the Spirit to fruition. Continuing this thought, French

says Jesus expressed *chrestotes* in His kindness to the sinning women who anointed His feet. Thus *agathosune/"goodness"* is prophetic; *chrestotes/"kindness"* is pastoral.

We need both: the kind of life that has such integrity in relation to Christ that those around us who are comfortable in their apathy, unconcern, and insensitivity will be *afflicted* by our very presence, and those who are afflicted by the pains and problems of life will be *comforted* by our same presence.

(7) *Faithfulness.* The word here is *pistos,* which means both "faith" and "faithfulness." It was a key word for Paul (see commentary on Gal. 2:16 and Gal. 3:10–14). Faithfulness, or fidelity, which is one meaning of the word, is a fruit of the Spirit, but is possible only because of faith—our trusting response to God in Jesus Christ. Because our faith is in God's *faithfulness* we can be faithful in word and deed and reliable in our discipleship. Our response to God in faith evokes His gift of the Spirit, and the Spirit makes us faithful.

(8) *Gentleness.* The Greek word here, *prautes,* is the most untranslatable of Paul's list. Barclay suggests that it is the adjectival form *praus* that throws most light on its meaning. This is used to describe an animal who has been tamed and brought under control. For the Christian it means submission to the will of God. The third beatitude, "blessed are the meek" (Matt. 5:5), is talking about this kind of person, one who is faithful and submissive to God even in the midst of trial. The meekness, or gentleness, that is blessed by our Lord is not weakness; it is strength. The meek person is the person who knows his or her strength, but submits that strength to Christ in a ministry of love and caring for others. This kind of person Martin Luther described as "the most free lord of all, and subject to none; the most dutiful servant of all, and subject to everyone."

The meek are also *teachable.* Their humility grows out of knowing both their strength and their weakness, thus producing an openness to God and to others for the perfecting of their own lives.

Gentleness also describes the way that those in whom the love of Christ is growing treat others: gently, tenderly, with respect, and consideration. Albert Schweitzer was once asked to name the greatest person in the world. Many would have voted on Schweitzer himself as that person but Schweitzer said, "No one can properly determine the greatest person in the world. The greatest person. . . is some unknown person who at this very moment has gone to help another person in the name and with the loving Spirit of Jesus Christ." Schweitzer was echoing Jesus' word about the least becoming greatest and the meek inheriting the earth.

(9) *Self-control.* The KJV translates this word, *egkrateia,* as temperance. It is that, but more. It has to do with the mastery of the self. This is the Christian's overcoming of the "flesh-works" Paul has already listed. It is used both to refer to an athlete's discipline of his body and to the Christian's refusal to give free reign to impulse and desire.

Paul said that even when things are lawful and not harmful, they should be subjected to three tests: Is it helpful? Is it constructive? Is it to the glory of God? (1 Cor. 10:23, 31). If that principle is true of that which is not harmful and lawful, how much more should we ask those questions of those drives, desires, and impulses which we know play havoc with our physical health, our mental and spiritual well-being, our relationship with others?

The purpose of self-control is that we may be fit for God, fit for ourselves, and fit to be servants of others. No wonder Paul listed it as a fruit of the Spirit. Like all the other expressions, it too flows out of love. It is not a rigid religious practice—discipline for discipline's sake. It is not dull drudgery aimed at exterminating laughter and joy. It is the doorway to true joy, true liberation from the stifling slavery of self-interest and fear. In that sense it is bound to joy, for joy is the keynote of all disciplines aimed at self-control.

The Freedom of the Spirit

Paul closes his *fruit of the Spirit* list with a word that catches us off guard, in fact almost takes our breath away. There is little or no surprise in what he has said thus far. We can nod in agreement. If we fill our lives with "flesh-works," there will be no room for the Spirit.

And, it doesn't take great imagination, knowing what we know about Christ, to distill that marvelous list of expressions of the Spirit of Christ flowing out of us—fruit. No big surprises in that list—knowing Christ and knowing Paul.

But here it comes—the surprise as Paul tosses in that extra line. Against the fruit of the Spirit *there is no law.* Wow! You can throw the book away. Forget about codes to regulate your life. Don't think the list of *fruit* is ever exhausted. When you are *in Christ,* and are moved by the Spirit, the unexpected and the unlisted will come. Gifts and fruits you never thought of will be expressed in you. Freedom is yours, and the Spirit is free, so who can tell how

He may express Himself in you? *Spontaneity is the name of the Christian game.*

Paul concludes by simply reiterating what he has already said, *"And those who are Christ's have crucified the flesh with its passions and desires. If we live in the Spirit, let us also walk in the Spirit. Let us not become conceited, provoking one another, envying one another"* (Gal. 5:24–26).

NOTES

1. Leander E. Keck, *Paul and His Letters* (Philadelphia: Fortress Press, 1979), p. 79.

2. Emil Brunner, *The Word and the World* (London: SCM Press, 1931), pp. 80–81.

CHAPTER SIX—THE SHARED LIFE OF THE PEOPLE OF GOD

GALATIANS 6:1–18

Scripture Outline

Bearing and Sharing Burdens (6:1–6)

The Law of the Harvest (6:7–10)

Glory Only in the Cross (6:11–15)

A Blessing and a Plea (6:16–18)

Here again, chapter divisions do not adequately communicate continuity and content. Verses 24–26 of chapter 5 could easily be a part of this chapter because Paul is talking about how the Spirit governs our lives in our social relationships.

As indicated in our commentary on Galatians 5:13–15, Paul calls us to be servants. This requires more than choosing when, where, and whom we will serve; it is a style of life. We willfully become servants. The constraining force of Christ's love replaces the binding force of law which is no longer operative.

Thus Paul talks about "crucifying the flesh" and "walking in the Spirit."

BEARING AND SHARING BURDENS

6:1 Brethren, if a man is overtaken in any trespass, you who are spiritual restore such a one in a spirit of gentleness, considering yourself lest you also be tempted. 2 Bear one another's burdens, and so fulfill the law of Christ. 3 For if anyone thinks himself to be something, when he is nothing, he deceives himself. 4 But let each one examine his own work, and then he will have rejoicing in himself alone, and not in another. 5 For each one shall bear his own load.

⁶ Let him who is taught the word share in all good things with him who teaches. —*Galatians 6:1–6*

In Truman Capote's *Other Voices, Other Rooms,* the hero is about to walk along a heavy but rotting beam over a brooding, murky creek. Starting over, ". . . stepping gingerly . . . he felt he would never reach the other side: always he would be balanced here, suspended between land and in the dark and alone. Then feeling the board shake as Idabel started across, he remembered that he had someone to be together with. And he could go on." Isn't this our experience? It certainly has been mine. I shiver at the thought of having to go it alone. I get chills when I consider where I might be if at the right time I had not felt the board shake because someone was walking with me!

The Christian walk is a shared journey. We do not walk alone; others walk with us. In this section Paul is giving us some guidance for our journey together. We will come back to verse 1, but let's begin with verse 2: *"Bear one another's burdens, and so fulfill the law of Christ."*

1. Paul is talking about interrelatedness and interdependence, a principle that is laced throughout Paul's epistles. "If one member suffers, all suffer together; if one member is honored, all rejoice together" (1 Cor. 12:26, RSV). "We who are strong ought to bear with the failings of the weak" (Rom. 15:1, RSV). The new life into which we have been born through Christ is a shared life.

The Greek word used to describe the shared life of the people of God was *koinonia.* Our best word for it in English is "fellowship," but this is far too limited to encompass the meaning of the Greek. *Koinonia* means sharing, all kinds of sharing: sharing in friendship (Acts 2:42), being partners in the gospel (Phil. 1:5), sharing material possessions (2 Cor. 8:4), having fellowship in Christ (1 Cor. 1:9), and sharing life together in the Spirit (2 Cor. 13:14). Above all, *koinonia* is fellowship with God. "That which we have seen and heard we proclaim also to you, so that you may have fellowship" *(koinonia,* 1 John 1:3)—that life we share with the Father and his Son Jesus Christ.

In *koinonia* we are bound to each other, to Christ, and to God. Our life is a shared life, we *bear one another's burdens.*

2. Crucial to living this shared life is *learning to listen.* Is there anything that enhances our feelings of worth more than being listened

to? When you listen to me you say to me, "I value you. You are important. I will hear and receive what you say."

When I really listen to a person—listen with ears and a heart that hears—it becomes revelation, and the Spirit comes alive in the relationship. Certainly that is the primary (though perhaps not the only) mode and place of revelation of Spirit—in relationship. When I listen, the gap between me and the person to whom I listen is bridged. A sensitivity comes that is not my own. I feel the pain, the frustrations, the anguish—sometimes feeling these and identifying a problem even when the other is not actually sharing the problem or these feelings explicitly. I listen in love and the sharing moves to the deep and intimate levels where the person and I really live. The Spirit opens doors and hearts and effects change.

The miraculous thing is that I do not have to have an answer for the person with whom I am sharing. In my listening I become the answer, and if something specific is needed, the Spirit reveals the "answer" in the listening relationship.

3. Another essential for the shared life of the people of God is that persons must be available to each other—available in love. This is what Paul is talking about: *"Bear one another's burdens."*

One of the most available persons I have known is Leo Fessenden, a Christian layman. Now retired, Leo once owned and operated a music store in San Clemente, California. Scores of young people were in and out of his store every day. I saw Leo as a sort of priest to these young people. He wouldn't have seen himself in that fashion, I'm sure, and the young people probably didn't think of him in that light. But they went to him to share their problems and needs, their hopes and dreams, their failures and disappointments. During a five-year ministry in San Clemente, scores of young people who had no contact with our church at all came to see me because of Leo. In most cases, I discovered that Leo had already performed the most important ministry, and I simply added my supportive concern.

I remember a group of these young people coming to see me when they learned I was moving to another city. They were a motley crew, really. Many of the fellows had long hair and beards; the girls were dressed in the rebellious garb of the day. On the street they would have been stereotyped as "hippies," "dropouts," or "delinquents." They would have felt out of place in our congregation on Sunday morning, and many of my parishioners would have felt out of place with them. They were not the kind of youth that are usually in church on Sunday morning. Through misty eyes I looked at those young people and remembered a significant involvement with almost all of them. There was a young lady who had had a baby out of wedlock. There was a fellow who had spent three months in juvenile hall. There was a second fellow who had been caught in the tentacles of drugs. All of them had experimented with marijuana, and many of them had gone on to try LSD and different barbiturates. One had spent a week in our home as a runaway. One of them was, even then, paying me $25.00 per month on a loan I had arranged for him to pay the hospital bill of the young girl he had made pregnant (he repaid the entire amount). One of them had gone through a long period of depression because his mother had committed suicide.

My relationship with these young people had come primarily through Leo Fessenden. Because he was available to them, listened to them, cared about them, did for them what he could, they trusted me when I was recommended by him as a person with whom they could relate.

They gave me a going-away present that day, and I treasure it. But most of all I treasure a note which accompanied the gift. It read:

> We don't really know how to say it—but because "you cared" we are going to miss you. We never attended—much less belonged to your church—but we always felt you were one of us. You never had easy answers for us, but you were there to help when we needed help, and as you will remember the help we needed wasn't simple to give, but you gave it and we are grateful. As we say farewell, we hope that your God is standing outside your window smiling, because we know He is as proud as we are of you. We wished that we could have made this presentation to you before your people, but we are sure you understand. With all our love.

I have had a lot of honors in my life, more than I deserve, but no honor exceeded the honor those young people paid me. I miss the mark of the high calling of Christ much of the time in my life and know that I often fall far short of the glory of God. So memories like this of these young people are important, reminding me that this is the point at which God will ultimately judge me—*whether I have been available in love.*

The marvelous aspect of this principle of availability is that we have to bring to a relationship only ourselves. It doesn't require particular skills and training. We simply have to be open and honest, willing to listen and share ourselves. Above all, we have to love the person, and that completes the principle: we are to be available in love![1]

4. Self-understanding, self-appreciation and self-affirmation mark the integrity of the people of God. *"For if anyone thinks himself to be something, when he is nothing, he deceives himself. But let each one examine his own work, and then he will have rejoicing in himself alone, and not in another"* (Gal. 6:3–4).

Unfortunately, the message that many of us have heard as the "Christian" message gives us little encouragement for self-appreciation. The message has come through as self-depreciation. To be sure, self-denial is at the heart of the gospel, but self-denial is not to be seen as self-depreciation or any form of devaluating of the self.

Akin to misunderstanding this dimension of the gospel is a limited grasp of true humility. Christian humility is not a groveling "doormat" stance. Unfortunately, we have thought of humility only as a recognition and affirmation of weakness and limitation. Not so. The truly humble know who they are; they know their strength as well as their weakness.

So Paul does not stop by admonishing us not to deceive ourselves by thinking we are something which we are not. He goes on to urge us to examine ourselves so that we will rejoice in ourselves. We need to learn to affirm strength. Christian character is not to be thought of in terms of weakness, of self-loathing, and/or anemic living. To be forgiven and accepted by God, to realize that God knows us thoroughly and loves us thoroughly, to be called and commissioned, to be made a *son* and an *heir* is to be made a new person in Christ, to be given a vocation. All of that is accompanied by strength. Thus "to be Christian is to be strong in God, under God, and with God."

5. There are some burdens only I can bear.

Having called for the bearing of one another's burdens, Paul seems to contradict himself. *For each one shall bear his own load* (v. 5). The KJV translates the nouns in verses 2 and 5 the same, "burden." The RSV and the NKJV translate verse 5 "load" rather than burden. In Greek one word is *baros* (burden), the other *phortion* (load). The difference is only slight. The latter, "load," is the word used for a soldier's pack. The meaning is that there are some duties and tasks which we alone can perform, for which we alone must accept responsibility. Others may support us through their prayers and encouragement, through "being with us," but the load is ours to bear.

In this setting the load each of us must bear on our own is the task of self-examination and self-correction. The standard of measurement for our lives is known only by us, for that standard is the calling of Christ to us, the apostolic action He requests of us. Therefore we can never measure ourselves against other Christians, much less non-Christians who may excuse themselves by accusing us of hypocrisy. Paul talked about this in another setting. "But they measuring themselves by themselves, and comparing themselves among themselves are not wise" (2 Cor. 10:12). We look at ourselves in relation to our gifts and calling, and bear the load of judgment in terms of our being and doing as a person *in Christ*.

6. The laborer is worthy of his hire. *"Let him who is taught the word share in all good things with him who teaches"* (Gal. 6:6). Paul is not talking only of material things. Prayer, encouragement, emotional support, the sharing of spiritual gifts—all are essential. Yet Paul *is* talking about material things.

To avoid the charge of preaching for money, for there were many peddling the gospel for a price, Paul continued to work at his trade. He knew, however, that this should not be the general practice. The Christian church needed teachers, persons in residence locally who were trusted, who could stay at the task, and who could give the time necessary for teaching. These persons were to be supported materially as well as otherwise.

7. The ministry of spiritual support, correction, guidance, and restoration.

At the heart of the shared life of the people of God is the ministry of spiritual support, guidance and restoration. This is what Paul is talking about in Galatians 6:1: *"Brethren, if a man is overtaken in any trespass, you who are spiritual restore such a one in a spirit of gentleness, considering yourself lest you also be tempted."*

As Christians we are not incapable of sinning. While we do not live in the "domain of sin," we do sin. We are often "overtaken in trespasses." The word for "trespass" is *paraptoma* and means literally "false step." It could mean a slip that comes in walking on an icy or otherwise dangerous path. Paul is giving us some clear signals:

(1) We are all vulnerable. Any of us may slip. The church should never take the stance of being a "pure" people, a people without sin. We should be careful about spiritual overconfidence. Just when we think we are solidly in the saddle, with firm clutch on the reigns, the wild horse of the flesh may take a sudden turn or make a dramatic buck sending us sprawling to the ground. Or, like Peter, we may be betrayed by overconfidence and end up denying Christ.

Confusion plagues us. It is not always easy to decide what is right. So Paul says, be careful how *you* think of *others'* sins; consider yourself, *"lest you also be tempted."*

(2) Within the shared life of the people of God we are to judge each other, but this judgment is assessment in love, not condemnation. When we are involved with each other, knowing the love we share and our mutual commitment to each other's growth, we can speak the truth in love, we can assist each other in recognizing and acknowledging faults and weaknesses. Without this kind of involvement with and mutual concern for each other we remain locked in our own worlds and there is little chance for change and growth.

(3) Paul defines the kind of mutual support and correction we should provide for each other: *"restore him in the spirit of gentleness."* Remember, *gentleness* is a fruit of the Spirit. Our supporting, correcting, guiding, and restoring activity is in the Spirit of Christ, who is gentle and calls us to gentleness. We handle each person with the kind of gentle care with which we would handle a piece of precious, fragile crystal. We seek to be sensitive to the brittleness of persons, to their high emotional pain threshold. We are firm, seeking never to fall in the ditch ourselves in order to help the sinner; but we are gentle recognizing that the stakes are high—in fact, eternal. We don't burst down doors to make our case. We respect privacy and dignity and self-esteem. We know that what is worthwhile is not accomplished by mere denunciation and rebuke. Our duty is not to condemn but to restore.

THE LAW OF THE HARVEST

[7] Do not be deceived, God is not mocked; for whatever a man sows, that he will also reap. [8] For he who sows to his flesh will of the flesh reap corruption, but he who sows to the Spirit will of the Spirit reap everlasting life. [9] And let us not

grow weary while doing good, for in due season we shall reap if we do not lose heart.

[10] Therefore, as we have opportunity, let us do good to all, especially to those who are of the household of faith.

—*Galatians 6:7–10*

The Interpreter's Bible refers to this section as Paul's call for Christians to engage in "the agriculture of the Spirit." That is a colorful and suggestive thought which aptly describes what Paul is talking about. The law of the harvest is relevant to our spiritual development and describes our destiny.

Judgment Is Certain

A well-known Baptist preacher, R. G. Lee, had a famous sermon he preached hundreds of times, all over America, "Payday Someday." The title alone is gripping and captures the truth.

God has established a law of identical harvest: *"Whatever a man sows, that he will also reap"* (v. 7). And *"God is not mocked"*; the laws by which He governs the universe cannot be evaded. We cannot hoodwink God. His judgment is as inevitable as His love is redemptive.

Paul does not describe the process, but he is clear about the fact: *"He who sows to his flesh will . . . reap corruption, . . . he who sows to the Spirit will. . . reap everlasting life"* (v. 8).

It is probable that Paul knew Jesus' picture of the separation of sheep and goats in Matthew 25. So he is talking about a final judgment when we will be rewarded with "life" or "death" according to how we have sown.

But there is more here.

To Live Is to Choose

Life on earth is life in the making. It involves constant choice and constant conflict—conflict between the different facets of our nature that struggle for dominance; conflict between the causes that vie for our allegiance; conflict between a false suggestion from our exterior world and a true intuition of the inner self; conflict between self-dominance and self-surrender. Through the continuous making of resolute decisions we pattern our lives and we mold our character. William James was right in saying that the hell to be endured hereafter, of which theology tells, is no worse than the hell we make for ourselves by habitually fashioning our character in the wrong way.

126

Life Is Determined by the Choices We Make

The spiritual life is one of growth rather than of anxious human endeavor. It is a process, not an episodic jumping from one phase to another. This is also true of the development of personhood. We mature by process. To really be alive means more than simply passing through the different stages of physical development, more than being pushed along the natural corridor of living and dying. It means embracing life and taking responsibility for it.

In Herb Gardner's *A Thousand Clowns,* an uncle tells of what he wants for his nephew:

> I just want him to stay with me till I can be sure he won't turn into a Norman Nothing. I want to be sure he'll know when he's chickening out on himself. . . . I want him to stay awake and know who the phonies are, I want him to know how to holler and put up an argument. I want a little guts to show before I let him go. I want to be sure he sees all the wild possibilities.. . . And I want him to know the subtle, sneaky, important reason he was born a human being and not a chair.

This is the crux of it. In "the agriculture of the Spirit" we cannot afford to "chicken out" on ourselves. There are two big alternatives, sowing to the flesh or sowing to the Spirit, and in each of those alternatives life is determined by the choices we make.

While there is an ultimate judgment when we will be given "life" or "death," we reap all along the way. The *"due season"* does not have to wait for the Day of Judgment. Our reaping in due season is the harvest of the multiplication of identical seed. The works of the flesh carry with them the germ of their own decay; the work of the Spirit carries with it the fruit of the Spirit multiplied.

The Household of Faith

In reminding us of the law of the harvest, Paul calls us to do good *"as we have opportunity."* By this phrase he does not mean "on such occasions as are opportune," but rather "as long as we have the opportunity to do so."

Then he adds *"especially to those who are of the household of faith"* (v. 10). Do not misread this: Paul is not talking about exclusive concern; the gospel is universal.

Even so, those who are children of God by faith in Christ (Gal. 3:26) must remember that they form a family. He knew that we are not likely to do good elsewhere, if we do not do good in our own household. And the law of the harvest works here as well: doing good in one place flows out in goodness to other places.

GLORY ONLY IN THE CROSS

11 See with what large letters I have written to you with my own hand! 12 As many as desire to make a good showing in the flesh, these would compel you to be circumcised, only that they may not suffer persecution for the cross of Christ. 13 For not even those who are circumcised keep the law, but they desire to have you circumcised that they may boast in your flesh. 14 But God forbid that I should boast except in the cross of our Lord Jesus Christ, by whom the world has been crucified to me, and I to the world. 15 For in Christ Jesus neither circumcision nor uncircumcision avails anything, but a new creation.

—*Galatians 6:11–15*

Ordinarily Paul dictated his letters to a scribe, then added his signature. But in the Galatian letter he does more. At least from verse 11 on they were written in his own hand. How are we to picture this? Did he take the pen in hand to add a personal greeting, a benediction, and his signature? If so, he cannot contain himself with that. His love for the Galatians overwhelms him again. He is carried away with surging thoughts and swelling emotions, so he adds another summarizing appeal—an intimately personal one, restating the claim that *"neither circumcision nor uncircumcision avails anything, but a new creation,"* and putting his life on the line with the crucified Christ.

Another Look at the Issue of Circumcision

Paul comes back again to the issue of controversy—circumcision. Even more pointedly than in Galatians 4:17 and 5:10–12, he states the motives of the Judaizers: (1) *To make a good showing in the flesh.* They wanted to put on a good outward demonstration. (2) *To avoid persecution.* The Romans reorganized the Jewish religion and officially allowed its practice. Since circumcision was the mark of a Jew, it could provide escape should persecution arise. (3) *They wanted to get credit for their influence.* If they could convince the Galatians to be circumcised, they would be able to boast about what they had done.

All these reasons are perverted motives and betray the gospel. There is only one reason for glorying: *the Cross of our Lord Jesus Christ.*

Francis Asbury, the father of American Methodism, knew this was so. Near the end of his notable and fruitful life, he said:

> Were I disposed to boast, my boasting would be found true. I was converted at the age of sixteen. At the age of eighteen I began to preach, and travelled some in Europe. At twenty-six I left my native land, bade adieu to my weeping parents, and crossed a boisterous ocean to spend the rest of my days in a strange land, partly settled by savages. In thirty years I have crossed the Allegheny Mountains fifty-eight times. I have slept in the woods and been without food and covering. Through the Southern states I have waded swamps and led my horse for miles, and in these journeys took cold that brought on the diseases that now prey on my body and must soon terminate in death. But my mind is still the same, that through the merits of Christ and by the grace of God I am saved."[3]

I am sure Asbury remembered Paul and his "reasons" for boasting (2 Cor. 11:21–30): a religious man, persecuted for his faith— "five times forty lashes, three times beaten, shipwrecked, sleepless nights, imprisoned—but *if I must boast, I will boast in the things which concern my infirmity*" (2 Cor. 11:30). Like Paul, Asbury knew that there was nothing to boast in, only the Cross. Do we?

The Cross-Style of Life

Not only individuals but the whole church needs to learn this. There are few churches that do not have a cross at some focal point within their building. But what does the cross really mean in the life of those congregations?

It is a cross-style of life to which Christians are called. The God who so loved the world that He gave His Son for it expects the church likewise to love the world and give itself for it. The words of the Lord's Supper commission us: *my body, my blood.* The Spirit of Christ is given to us to enable us to love with His love, to die in His death, to give our body and blood for others.

The great expression of the Spirit each day is to get the cross out of the church and into the world; to have the power and presence to say not only in liturgy but in life, "This is *my body*, this is *my* blood."

A New Creation

Paul comes back to it, and almost sings it. *"For in Christ Jesus neither circumcision nor uncircumcision avails anything, but a new creation"* (Gal. 6:15).

Paul himself is the witness. In Galatians 2:20 he said he had been crucified with Christ. Now he declares that by the Cross *"the world has been crucified to me, and I to the world"* (v. 14). All the things in life which are imposing and appealing to the "natural" man have lost their attraction and significance for him. He is a new creation in Christ and could say, For his [Christ's] sake I have suffered the loss of all things, and count them as refuse, in order that I may gain Christ (Phil. 3:8, RSV).

Paul did not mean that he was severed from the physical world. He continued to live in the present world and used its good things for the service of the Lord. But the best and the worst of this world which led to trust in self instead of God had no puffing power; he was crucified to that, and that to him.

Paul's testimony is repeated over and over again as persons respond in faith to God's gift of Christ, as they are given His Spirit and become new creations. I heard of such a miracle recently. The American Red Cross was gathering supplies, medicine, clothing, food, and the like, for the suffering people of Biafra. Inside one of the boxes that showed up at the collecting depot one day was a letter. It said, "we have recently been converted and because of our conversion we want to try to help. We won't ever need these again. Can you use them for something?" Inside the box were several Ku Klux Klan sheets. The sheets were cut down to strips and eventually used to bandage the wounds of black persons in Africa.

It could hardly be more dramatic—from symbols of hatred to bandages of love because of the new creation. Nothing else matters, says Paul.

A BLESSING AND A PLEA

¹⁶ And as many as walk according to this rule, peace and mercy be upon them, and upon the Israel of God.

¹⁷ From now on let no one trouble me, for I bear in my body the marks of the Lord Jesus.

[18] Brethren, the grace of our Lord Jesus Christ be with your spirit. Amen.

—*Galatians 6:16–18*

Paul began his letter with a prayer for peace (1:3) and he closes it with the same. In the beginning, peace was combined with grace; here it is combined with mercy, grace being added as the final note:

His opponents and detractors were many, and he was weary. He could not understand why there could be doubt about his commitment to Jesus Christ. All that he was, centered in Christ and his very person, carried the signs: *"For I bear in my body the marks of the Lord Jesus"* (v. 17b).

There is some challenging mental food for reflection here. What do these *"marks"* mean? What is Paul driving at?

The metaphor may have been suggested to Paul, sharp mind that he was, as a contrast with circumcision. "If you are going to have marks on your body, why not have some that have resulted from your battle for the gospel?" Or, "You may wish to be stamped as a son of Israel; I want to be *marked* as belonging to Jesus—and here are the markings."

A second stream of reflection flows from the fact that in that day a master often branded his slaves with a mark that identified them as his. Paul had committed himself to be a slave for Christ. The scars, the result of wounds he had suffered in that role, formed his badge of identity. Not on his apostolic authority, but through his wounds he makes his appeal.

Another thought is stimulated—the *stigmata*. This is one of the great mysteries of religious history—that the markings of the wounds of Christ actually appear on the person of others.

Tradition says it happened to Francis of Assisi. As he fasted on a lonely mountaintop, he received a vision of the Cross on which the love of God was being crucified stretching across the entire horizon. As the vision faded, Francis relaxed. Looking down, the marks of the nails were in his hands, and he bore them to his death.

Reading about St. Francis, I can believe that. He so identified with Christ, so intensely sought to reflect the love, poverty, joy, simplicity, and openness of Jesus' life that he actually communicated Christ through his person. In the tradition of Paul, he bore the marks of Christ.

But what about you and me, as pedestrian saints who are so far below the mark of Paul and Francis?

In my prayerful reflections once I raised that question and made a response.

> The stigmata, Lord—St. Francis received it
> > the sign of your gruesome crucifixion
> > on his own body.
> And Paul—he claimed it
> > "I bear the marks of Jesus branded
> > on my body."
> But what about me?
> > What is my stigmata?
> At least this, Lord—
> > that I will be a sign of your presence to others,
> > your love through my love
> > your forgiveness through my forgiveness,
> > your acceptance through my acceptance;
> that I will give unstintingly
> > in hospitality to others;
> that my heart will be a place of *welcome,*
> > open to every pilgrim or stranger
> > who seeks a listening ear or an embrace of
> > acceptance;
> that I will enter into the pain and joy
> > the tears and laughter of others so completely
> > I will be one with them
> > and because I am one with you
> > that they will receive you, O Christ, from me.

We may not be called on to produce the marks Paul could produce, yet there must be marks which identify us. If we belong to Christ we are branded. Within the shared life of the people of God the *stigmata* is the fruit of the Spirit. And in that body the grace and peace of our Lord Jesus Christ is received and shared.

NOTES

1. This concept of being available in love is developed in Maxie Dunnam, *Be Your Whole Self* (Atlanta: Forum House Publishers), pp. 138ff.

2. Quoted in *Be Your Whole Self,* pp. 62–63.

3. Quoted in John Clyde Turner, *The Gospel of the Grace of God* (Nashville: Broadman Press, 1943), p. 38.

INTRODUCTION OF EPHESIANS

Has there ever been a day when more people were seeking for meaning? What is the place of the individual person in the cosmic order? we want to know. Where do we belong? How do we fit? What does it all mean? And where will it all come out?

Ephesians, in its message of a divine purpose being accomplished by the mighty acts of God in Christ, is a relevant source for our struggle for meaning at a level beyond our "little lives" of getting on as best we can. The central theme of the epistle is that all things are created for ultimate unity in Christ Jesus.

In every age, humans have been conscious of a higher life. They have also been aware of a struggle between powers puffing them in different directions. Biblical writers had a world view completely foreign to our scientific outlook. We speak of evolution, physics, heredity, chemistry, scientific, and materialistic determinism. Paul spoke of personal agencies, "principalities and powers." Whatever the label or explanation, we often feel caught and helpless. Hostile forces war within and without, and we need deliverance. One of the primary messages of Ephesians, supporting the central theme, is that we can obtain liberty through Christ.

Adding further significance to the relevance of this epistle for our day is the teaching that the church is the place—the dynamic center—for the consummation of the unity which is God's divine purpose for His created order. This may in fact be the most distinctive feature of the teaching of this epistle. In our divided world, blacks and other minorities have poured out their blood for civil rights. Women are desperately seeking equality. The elderly, especially in America, are fast becoming a kind of "race" separated from the mainstream of life. The gap between rich and poor is an almost daily widening chasm. The third world is ravaged by revolution because people have "seen" and "tasted" and known that liberation is theirs and they must claim it.

What a vision for the church—the gathering of a divided humanity into one! With what purpose and power might the church be infused if she recovered that self-understanding. The church is the *token* at least, the guarantee, the sign of hope that the work of redemption which will ultimately embrace all things, the entire cosmos, has begun.

Title and Destination

In the Greek manuscripts from the third and fourth centuries the Pauline epistles were supplied with titles: "to the Romans," "to the Galatians," "to the Ephesians," etc. The uniformity of the letters clearly indicates that these titles must have been added by second-century scribes after a collection of Paul's letters had been gathered into a corpus.

While there is justification for these titles in the other letters, not so with *Ephesians.* The words *in Ephesus* (1:1), found in all later manuscripts, are missing from the earliest ones. Most scholars agree that nothing is more certain about the epistle than that it was not written to the Ephesians. Paul had spent three years in Ephesus, and no doubt there were deep and abiding friendships. Also, he had not been away from Ephesus long (some even think the letter was written from there) when he wrote the epistle. Yet, it is clear in the body of the letter, that the writer did not know his readers personally. It is unthinkable that if Paul had been writing the Ephesians that he would not have mentioned persons by name and been *personal* in what he said.

One of the most widely accepted possibilities is that Ephesians was a circular letter addressed to many churches, entrusted to Tychicus for delivery to different congregations, and that there may even have been a number of copies with a blank for the salutation to be filled in as it was delivered to a particular church. Though there is no precedent for this in ancient times, and much evidence to the contrary, if Tychicus was indeed the bearer of the letter, it could have been meant for any one or all of the churches he would be visiting.

Author

Until the beginning of the nineteenth century the claim of Paul's authorship for Ephesians went almost unchallenged. True, Erasmus, the great sixteenth-century scholar, had raised questions on the basis of style, but strong debate has occurred only within the past 150 years.

Before looking at the problems, let it be clearly noted that this book shines brightly as one of the noblest of New Testament writings. This is the best argument for its genuineness, and many feel that not only is Paul the author, this is his masterpiece—"the crown and climax of Pauline theology." While that may be an overstatement, it must be noted that the burden of proof rests on those who disclaim Pauline authorship. The weight of scholarship has produced no unanimous verdict, and scholars of first rank have not been convinced by arguments against Pauline authorship.[1]

The most popular and acceptable specific alternative has been proposed by Edgar J. Goodspeed, who put forth the hypothesis that Ephesians is an anthology of Paulinism, designed to address the second generation of Christians and churches. Goodspeed further suggested that the author was Onesimus, the slave who was the subject of Paul's letter to Philemon. Ignatius had written a letter to the church in Ephesus (ca. A.D. 110), naming Onesimus as the bishop in that city. If these two Onesimuses were the same, it is very possible that Onesimus, the former slave, was the collector of Paul's letters and the writer of Ephesians as an introduction to them. For Goodspeed, this also explains how the tiny personal letter of Philemon got into the collection.

Some have credited authorship of Ephesians to the writer of Luke-Acts. Others, while not proposing a specific writer, think they have adequate data to discount Pauline authorship. I am not convinced that Paul did not write Ephesians. A response to the major problems raised by critics may serve best in this commentary in exploring the question of authorship.[2]

Vocabulary

Arguments concerning vocabulary center on the frequency of use of words not found in other Pauline epistles. Logical explanations exist for most of these, e.g., some of the words cited appear in quotations from the Old Testament, and others are cognates or compounds of words Paul uses elsewhere. It is also argued that some of Paul's "stock" words are used in Ephesians in a non-Pauline sense. But that is a matter of interpretation, taking no account of timing, or the growth and development in thought and expression on Paul's part.

Style

The style *is* different. But this is not a personal letter in the sense of the other Pauline epistles. It does not address pressing immediate concerns with concise, forceful words, staccato fashion. The sentences are long, often involved and loosely constructed, sometimes monotonous. But one need not discount Paul's authorship therefore. He was not consistent in style, even within a single letter. One scholar, Percy, has argued that every stylistic feature in Ephesians can be paralleled in the other Pauline letters. And since a big part of Ephesians is in the form of prayer, it is not surprising that style and language differ from his "logical" presentation in *Romans* and his hot response to the Judaizers in *Galatians.*

Historical Setting

Those denying Pauline authorship contend that the historical setting of Ephesians comes after the death of Paul, the Gentile-Jewish controversy having been settled by the time Ephesians was written. This is a weak argument. For Paul the Gentile-Jewish issue had been settled theologically by the Cross, and ecclesiastically at the Jerusalem Conference (Acts 15).

Disallowers say the reference to the breaking down of the wall of partition between Jew and Gentile in the temple (Eph. 2:14) had to have come after the destruction of the temple by Titus in A.D. 70. But Paul may have been speaking metaphorically here, as he often did, so that the barrier is that of hostility shattered not by Titus, but by Christ on the Cross.

The veneration of Paul and the other apostles in Ephesians causes some to place the writer in the second generation with respect to Paul. Yet Paul made very specific claims about his unique commission in his other letters. Could not the reference to Paul as "the very least of all the saints" (3:8), have come easier from his own pen than from one who wanted to venerate him?

Another contention is that Ephesians reflects an ecclesiastical structure that did not exist in Paul's day. To be sure, what he wrote about the church is far in advance of what he wrote elsewhere. But as Caird has reminded us, 1 Cor. 15 is also far in advance of anything Paul wrote elsewhere about life after death, and Col. 1:15–20 far exceeds in thought anything he wrote elsewhere about Christology. "Should we not expect that, when Paul devoted himself systematically to a fresh theme he would go beyond what he had said in passing reference elsewhere?"[3]

Theology

The theological issues impacting authorship will be responded to in the commentary on the particular texts, but in my opinion there is not enough convincing argument at any of these points to discredit Paul's authorship. Was Paul compelled to include all he believed in every letter, and/or could there not be a development of his thought and a refining of his statement of it in every new setting?

Literary Relationships

Ephesians and Colossians share a remarkably similar structure, and one-third of the content of Ephesians and one-fourth of the actual words have their counterpart in Colossians. Those who reject Pauline authorship regard this literary kinship with Colossians, and, as Goodspeed and Mitton have added, the association of Ephesians with all the other Pauline letters, as the most significant weight of evidence against Paul's authorship. Words and phrases from other letters appear in different combinations and with different meanings in Ephesians, they say, and other letters do not display the immense level of self-quotation. Interestingly, some who affirm Pauline authorship argue that Ephesians contains precisely what one would expect from an author half-remembering, perhaps subconsciously calling forth earlier statements. This is not what an imitator would do.

It is not unlikely that Paul's expressions in Ephesians would be built on what he has written and spoken previously. And it isn't difficult to believe that he wrote Colossians and Ephesians at the same time—Colossians a letter to a particular church, and Ephesians an encyclical letter to many churches. The same ideas would be burning in Paul's mind and find expression, some in the same form, some different, in both letters. The target audience would account for the differences. Eph. 6:21–22 and Col. 4:7–9 suggest that the same courier would deliver both letters.

The evidence for an imitator of Paul is brittle. If the imitator had the whole Pauline collection, why be so dependent on Colossians? If he had the sources before him and intended to reproduce the substance, why did he do the job badly—the hypothesis being that he used Pauline words and phrases in un-Pauline ways? If he was working only from memory, why would he quote verbatim only one sentence about Tychicus (Col. 4:7–9, Eph. 6:21–22)? What purpose would a pseudonym serve? If an incompetent imitator, how could he succeed in producing such a brilliant work of creative genius as generations have seen it to be?

Problems in Ephesians remain puzzling. It is uniquely unlike any of Paul's other letters. To attribute it to Paul without reservation is not supportable. But I feel the difficulties of assigning it to Onesimus or Luke or anyone who might seek to imitate Paul are even greater. Some of the most radical critics in our day accept it as genuine, and those who disallow Paul's authorship do so with degrees of misgiving. So I believe we may accept as valid the ascription, "Paul, an apostle of Jesus Christ by the will of God," and move through the letter with integrity, seeking to appropriate his message for today.

NOTES

1. For those who desire further study, it may be helpful simply to list some scholars who affirm, and some who disallow Pauline authorship. Affirm: Hart, Westcott, Armitage Robinson, E. F. Scott, Caird. Deny: Moffatt, Streeter, W. Knox, Keck, Ralph Martin. Neither is a complete list. Books of special note are: E. J. Goodspeed, *The Meaning of Ephesians*; E. F. Scott, *The Epistles of Paul to the Colossians, to Philemon, and to the Ephesians*, The Moffatt New Testament Commentary; C. B. Caird, *Paul's Letters from Prison*; J. L. Houlden, *Paul's Letters from Prison*; *The Interpreter's Bible*, vol. 10.

2. I am primarily dependent upon Caird's *Paul's Letters from Prison* and E. F. Scott's volume in the Moffatt New Testament Commentary for the bulk of this research.

3. Caird, *Paul's Letters from Prison*, p. 20.

An Outline of Ephesians

I. God's Plan and Our Place in It: 1:1–14
   A. Greeting: 1:1–2
   B. Chosen by God: 1:3–6
   C. Redeemed by Christ: 1:7–12
   D. Sealed with the Spirit: 1:13–14

II. God's Redemptive Power for a New Humanity: 1:15—2:22
   A. Prayer for Masterful Living: 1:15–19a
   B. The Supremacy of Christ and His Incarnation in the Church: 1:19b–23
   C. God's Power for Redemption: 2:1–10
   D. The New Humanity: 2:11–18
   E. A Habitation of God: 2:19–22

III. The Mystery and Meaning of Faith: 3:1–21
   A. The Mystery Revealed: 3:1–7
   B. The Purpose of the Mystery: 3:8–13
   C. The Mystery Revealed in Prayer: 3:14–19
   D. Doxology: 3:20–21

IV. The Church: United in Christ, Propelled by Hope, Equipped for Ministry: 4:1–16
   A. Walk Worthy of Your Calling: 4:1–6
   B. Be Equipped for Ministry: 4:7–12
   C. Grow Up in Christ: 4:13–16

V. The Walk of New Persons: 4:17—5:21
   A. Walk in Newness of Life: 4:17–24
   B. Some Signs of Newness of Life: 4:25–32
   C. The Christian Walk: 5:1–21

VI. Relationships in Christ: 5:22—6:9
   A. A Model of Christian Marriage: 5:22–33
   B. Children and Parents—Reciprocal Respect: 6:1–4
   C. Servants and Masters: 6:5–9

VII. Strong in the Lord: 6:10–24
   A. Put on the Armor of God: 6:10–17
   B. Be Watchful in the Spirit: 6:18–20
   C. Sustain and Comfort One Another: 6:21–24

CHAPTER ONE—GOD'S PLAN AND OUR PLACE IN IT

EPHESIANS 1:1–14

Scripture Outline

> Greeting (1:1–2)
>
> Chosen by God (1:3–6)
>
> Redeemed by Christ (1:7–12)
>
> Sealed with the Spirit (1:13–14)

GREETING

1:1 Paul, an apostle of Jesus Christ by the will of God,
To the saints who are in Ephesus, and faithful in Christ Jesus:

² Grace to you and peace from God our Father and the Lord Jesus Christ.

—Ephesians 1:1–2

Paul begins with the conventional greeting of his other epistles. He identifies himself out of the depth of his most vivid self-consciousness and sense of call—*"an apostle of Jesus Christ by the will of God"* (v. 1).

Paul knew who he was. The NEB leaves out the article *"an,"* and this is good. *Apostle* in Paul's mind did not signify a class, or an office; it was a calling, a vocation. Those of us who are ordained clergy would do well to think more often about fulfillment of our calling than success in our profession. To be sure, there are functions uniquely belonging to the ordained clergy as the church has developed, yet our primary task is to be *representative* ministers in the congregation where all members are a part of the general ministry. To think of ministry should be to think vocationally, not professionally.

Paul's claim to apostleship was that he had seen the risen Christ (1 Cor. 9:1). His calling had come directly from Christ, not from men nor through man (Gal. 1:1). He was commissioned as an ambassador of Christ (2 Cor. 5:20).

Paul also saw himself uniquely called to be an apostle to the Gentiles. H. Chadwick has made the interesting suggestion that the purpose of this encyclical letter was to bring the whole Gentile mission under the aegis of Paul's sole apostleship. Whether so or not, there is truth behind the assumption. Paul saw himself as *the* apostle to the Gentiles. It is in this capacity that he writes *"by the will of God."*

Paul was convinced that God had a plan for his life. Are you? Like Jeremiah, who heard God say, "Before I formed you in the womb I knew you, and before you were born I consecrated you; I appointed you a prophet to the nations" (Jer. 1:5, RSV), Paul knew himself set apart before he was born (Gal. 1:15). His Damascus Road experience brought a dramatic and drastic upheaval in his experience and thinking, but it was a part of the working of God's purpose in his life. As we will see shortly, the purpose which shaped Paul's life was a part of a larger purpose that included not only all humanity, but embraced the whole of creation.

"To the saints" (v. 1). Again the NEB is on target in using "God's people" instead of saints. The word as Paul used it does not distinguish persons from others by moral or spiritual qualities, but as being set apart because they belonged to Christ. They are saints because they have been called by God, and have responded.

Have you ever noted that Paul never uses the word in its singular form? It is always plural, saints. Christians are saints because they are members of the holy community—the community of God. The little girl was right when, remembering the stained glass windows of her church, she answered the question what is a saint, with the telling word, "a saint is a person the light shines through."

"Faithful in Christ Jesus" (v. 1). *Pistos* is the Greek word here for "faithful," and it means "trustworthy." It is also used in the active sense meaning "those who have faith," a meaning that is more appropriate here. However, it must not be connected with *"in Christ"* and taken to mean those who believe in Christ Jesus. This was one of Paul's most unusual words: *"in Christ."* Those who are justified by grace through faith, receive Christ; they enter into union with Him, are made new persons, and incorporated into a new humanity.

CHOSEN BY GOD

3 Blessed be the God and Father of our Lord Jesus Christ, who has blessed us with every spiritual blessing in the heav-

enly places in Christ, [4] just as He chose us in Him before the foundation of the world, that we should be holy and without blame before Him in love, [5] having predestined us to adoption as sons by Jesus Christ to Himself, according to the good pleasure of His will, [6] to the praise of the glory of His grace, by which He made us accepted in the Beloved.

—Ephesians 1:3–6

The first three chapters of Ephesians form an almost continuous prayer, giving the entire letter the sound of music. Though in prison, Paul's spirit is ecstatic.

As indicated in the introduction, this is a different kind of letter. The first three chapters are doctrine set to music, truth that sings, theology from the knees and heart of prayer. Paul is not debating or answering ugly charges hurled against him; he is not using all of his intellectual powers to make reasoned statements. Rather, he prays—and he shares his prayer. He breaks out into joyful praise, then moves into deep intercession.

Yet, this prayer is rooted in the content of Paul's life. Expressed in prayer is a great new understanding that Paul has talked about but never fully developed in other letters: the abolishment of the barrier between Jew and Gentile in the fellowship of one church is not only an integral part of God's plan for them, it is the key to understanding God's plan for the whole universe—His intention to unify the entire cosmos in Christ Jesus. This is big thinking and big praying!

Chosen

Paul says we are chosen by God. Is there anything quite like the feeling that comes when we are *chosen?* I remember how it was growing up in rural Mississippi. We had to manufacture our toys out of tin cans, broomsticks, barrel hoops, and the like. And we had to invent our games or adapt those which had been passed down to us from who knows where, except that they came to us through our older brothers and sisters. Whether playing "stealing sticks" or slow pitch with a string ball, there was nothing quite like the feeling that came when you were chosen for a team.

Can any married person ever forget the joy that came when it was settled—when your mate had accepted your proposal of marriage, or your mate had finally gotten the courage to ask and you could respond *yes?* In human relationships, this is the ultimate in being chosen. Someone selects you as the one person with whom he or she wishes to spend their lives. Then the consummation of the choices comes in the marriage when the decision is sealed with a life commitment of love. Chosen!

Chosen by God

At a much deeper level, but of the same kind, were my feelings when I was baptized, when I finally made a commitment to preach, and then, after years of study and being "on trial," I had hands of ordination laid upon me. Chosen by God!

Paul never thought of himself as having chosen God—it was the other way: God had chosen him. This was Jesus' moving word to the disciples: "You have not chosen me, but I have chosen you" (John 15:16). What bracing power! What motivating inspiration to know oneself chosen by God!

The words and form of Paul's prayer is an effort to mark the bounty of God's gift to us, the boundless extent of the debt of gratitude due Him for what he has done for us. Instead of a simple "I thank God," he is using the melodious liturgical, *Blessed be the God and Father of our Lord Jesus Christ* (v. 3). The word for "blessed" is the same as that for "praise," and the one for "blessing" is the same as that for "gift."

Here Paul's theme of grace is dominant. Grace is God's stance of giving, loving, blessing. The Greek word for grace *(claris)* means favor and gift and blessing. In 2 Corinthians 9:8, Paul says, "God is able to provide you with every *[charis]* abundance" (RSV). The KJV translates that, "God is able to make all grace abound toward you."

Our praise is to the God *"who has blessed* [graced] *us with every spiritual blessing* [gift], *just as He has chosen us in Him before the foundation of the world"* (vv. 3–4).

Thomas Merton asked, "What am I?" and answered, "I am myself a word spoken by God." How we perceive ourselves, who we think ourselves to be, determines the direction of our lives and shapes our relationships. To accept at the depth of our being that we are *chosen by God* is the antidote for our insecurity, our neurotic fears, our striving to be accepted, our self-depreciation.

Chosen for a Purpose

"That we should be holy and without blame before Him in love" (v. 4). In Herman Melville's classic, *Moby Dick*, there is a gripping scene where Captain Ahab tightens a carpenter's vise on his hand. With what appears to be masochistic self-punishment, he screws the jaws tighter and tighter. With grimacing sternness

he says to the sky and sea, but also to himself, "A man has to feel something that holds in this slippery world."

We do need something to hold in a slippery world. And ours is that kind of world. Our wide-open, permissive society has led to the comparing of our times with the period of debauchery in first-century Rome. We do not use words like "debauchery"; we don't take sin that seriously. Our society, though, seems bent on gratifying, titillating, and catering to our wants, whims, and wantonness—all for pleasure.

The permissive society does not provide purpose. "If it feels good, do it" is not adequate direction to find meaning. But God offers a way. He chooses us for a purpose—"to be holy and blameless in love."

"Holy" in Greek always had in it the idea of difference and separation. The Christian is to be distinctly different—set apart by God for His purposes. The church has often mistaken the meaning of this. The *separation* is not *from* the *world*, but a *difference* expressed *in* the world.

The Greek word for blameless, *amomos,* is a sacrificial word; it means "unblemished." Our whole lives are to be an offering to God. This was Paul's admonition in Romans 12:1: "I appeal to you therefore, brethren, by the mercies of God, to present your bodies as a living sacrifice, holy and acceptable to God, which is your spiritual worship" (RSV).

There can be no satisfaction here with second-best; no "Well, I'm only human you know," as if to be human damns us to being something weak, or incomplete, or incapable of Christian morality; no copout: "You can't change human nature." "Chosen for a purpose" means precisely that to be human and Christian is to be holy, and to make our entire lives an offering to God.

In talking about God's plan and our place in it, Paul uses two phrases that deserve serious attention.

1. *"In the heavenly places"* (v. 3). Paul shared the world view of his time—an imaginative picture of a two or three-storied universe. But we should not allow that limited understanding of the structure of the universe to blind us to a perception of the structure of reality that is valid and can speak to us.

"In the heavenly places" was not simply a designation for the habitat of God, or the "place" to which Christians go when they die. Heaven was a part of the created universe. For Paul it is a term of human topography. It was the realm of all unseen reality, good

147

and evil. Not only God, but the evil powers have their operation *"in the heavenly places"* (6:12). Heaven also stands for man's invisible, spiritual environment, as contrasted to the tangible, visible environment of earth.

Paul uses this phrase five times in Ephesians, and it is found only in this letter. He is "stuck" on it, as other words and phrases became "stock" for him at certain times. He is stuck on it because his message is that Christ is supreme and the source of blessing in heaven and on earth. In every realm, good and evil powers struggle to dominate individual and corporate life. The power of Christ is ours as we do battle with all attackers, especially those in the spirit-realm.

2. *"Predestined us to adoption as sons by Jesus Christ"* (v. 5). (See commentary on Gal. 4:5, concerning adoption).

"Predestine" means literally to determine beforehand. This verse virtually duplicates verse 4. The realizing of God's purpose is seen in terms of sonship rather than as being *holy and blameless.*

Unfortunately, in much consideration of the doctrine of predestination, the negative rather than the positive is dominant. We torture ourselves over the issue of hell and heaven as the reward determined beforehand by God for us humans. We get into trouble when we try to devise a doctrine, iron-clad in its logic, about the sovereignty of God as it relates to our chosenness. Is it not enough to know that the destiny of the Christian believer is in the hands of a God who loved us so much that He gave Himself for us in Christ? The Pauline doctrine of predestination does include the fearful doom of the unrepentant, but that does not mean we are destined to be unrepentant. The salvation of Christ is *universal* in the sense that it is available to all. Therefore, this verse is the triumphant expression of the glory of the redeemed—those who have responded to their chosenness, to God's grace.

"According to the good pleasure of His will" (v. 5) has a lilt to it that delivers us from any morbid thoughts of a rigid system. Here is grace abounding—*"the good pleasure of His will."* And to what end? *"To the praise of the glory of His grace."* The old catechism was right in defining the chief end of man as praising God and enjoying Him forever. This is the highest function of the life that God has blessed—that it should praise Him to whom it owes its blessedness.

REDEEMED BY CHRIST

[7] In Him we have redemption through His blood, the forgiveness of sins, according to the riches of His grace [8] which He made to abound toward us in all wisdom and prudence, [9] having made known to us the mystery of His will, according to His good pleasure which He purposed in Himself, [10] that in the dispensation of the fullness of the times He might gather together in one all things in Christ, both which are in heaven and which are on earth—in Him. [11] In Him also we have obtained an inheritance, being predestined according to the purpose of Him who works all things according to the counsel of His will, [12] that we who first trusted in Christ should be to the praise of His glory.

—Ephesians 1:7–12

That we are *chosen* by God is the first affirmation in God's purpose and our place in it. That we are *redeemed* by Christ is the second affirmation. This passage is packed with vivid symbols, behind which is one reality: the power of Jesus Christ to redeem us, to bind us to Himself and to each other, and to bring unity to the whole universe.

Redeemed/Forgiven

"Redemption through His blood" seems a stark phrase in this setting, a matter-of-fact word as Paul moves on. But remember, he is praying. And remember, too, that he is praying out of the depth and content of his whole life. Nothing was more important for Paul than Calvary. The Damascus Road was always viewed by Paul with Calvary on the horizon. It was at Calvary that sin stood condemned once and for all, and after Calvary no one could possibly imagine that sin does not matter to God.

Against the backdrop of God's concern of sin ravaging His children's relationship with Him, Paul saw the Cross as the supreme revelation of love. The marvel of this was overwhelming—that the sinless One would become "sin for us," ready and glad to endure the shame and agony of the Cross on our behalf.

Love and sacrifice go together. We are redeemed "through His blood." This is not a strange word for Paul. For sinners Jesus "made peace through the blood of His cross" (Col. 1:20). We are "justified by His blood" (Rom. 5:9). Those who were once far off *"have been made near by the blood of Christ"* (Eph. 2:13). We need to be careful and clear as we look at this image. There was some connection, but not a literal one, between Paul's use of *"the blood of Christ"* and the Jewish idea of blood sacrifice for sin. If the Jewish image was in Paul's mind, as it probably was, it was a transposed image and the blood of Christ was synonymous with the Cross.

Paul was thinking about sacrifice, but the sacrifice was not an offering being made to secure favor; it is not a price paid to an enslaving power. The obedience of His life, the utter self-abandonment and self-consecration of love—an obedience unto death, "even death on a cross" (Phil. 2:8)—this was Christ's sacrifice. The redemption wrought by this sacrifice is not the regaining of something through purchase, but deliverance by an act of divine power. Power, not price, is the key.

That power is the very power of God because the love that initiated it is God's love. "Just as the flame which flashes out from a volcano momentarily reveals the elemental, unceasing fires burning at the earth's heart, so the love that leapt on one crowning day of history in the sheer flame of the cross disclosed what God's inmost nature is for ever. Jesus . . . made Himself a sacrifice when He poured out His soul unto death: but in the deepest sense, the sacrifice was God's. It was God who made the offering, God who paid the price, God who *having loved His own which were in the world, loved them unto the end* (John 13:1)."[1]

The primary meaning of this redemption is forgiveness. This helps us give meaning to the metaphor of redemption through His blood. The metaphor did have its origin in the Old Testament; it was the release of a slave or of an alienated land by payment of a ransom (Lev. 25:25–55). There was also the regular Old Testament use of the metaphor to denote Israel's release from Egyptian bondage and Babylonian exile. In these instances, no payment of a price was involved, but rather the sheer power of God to deliver. So the idea of ransom was not big in Paul's understanding of redemption. He was not troubled by questions which arose later as to why a ransom was exacted, to whom was it paid, of what did it consist. Paul was talking about deliverance, at a great price. To make that clear, he is specific about the deliverance. This is the crucial part of verse 7: *"the forgiveness of sins, according to the riches of His grace."*

The result of this forgiveness is that we can respond to God *"in all wisdom and prudence."* It is hardly possible to distinguish between wisdom and prudence. They are roughly synonymous. If there is any difference it may be that the word for wisdom refers to intellectual knowledge, and prudence to an understanding of the practical application of wisdom.

Gathered into One

The mystery is now made known. The purpose that had been formed in divine counsel was expressed in the ordering of history: to *"gather together in one all things in Christ, both which are in heaven and which are on earth—in Him"* (v. 10).

The whole thought of the epistle turns on this verse: *the ultimate goal of the cosmic process is to unite all things in Christ.* To get the full impact of this extravagant thought, let us look at it in parts.

1. "A plan for the fullness of time" (RSV) is clearer than "in the dispensation of the fullness of time" (KJV). The Greek word for plan is *oikonomia*, literally, "household management." It can mean the "office of steward." The *oikonomos* was the steward who saw to it that the family affairs were kept in order and functioned smoothly and efficiently.

The word is used three times in Ephesians—here and in 3:2 and 3:9. J. A. Robinson has cited many passages that suggest the meaning is "the actual working out of a policy or project." That is a more elaborate meaning and certainly fits the three passages in Ephesians.

Yet the literal meaning is packed with significance, too. It boggles our minds as it did Paul's—that all history has been a preparation for, a planning and thinking for, an arranging and an administering for the goal of God—that the world would be brought together as one family in Christ. We serve a great God who has given us a great Christ; ours is a great redemption because it meets us where we are and delivers us to what at the deepest core of our being we want and need—a family.

To have a dwelling place, and for that dwelling place to be a family, and for that family to include all creation, and for that "extended" family to be *"in Christ"*—there is nothing greater!

2. *"Gather together in one all things in Christ"* is a rather clumsy statement. The RSV translates it simply "unite all things in him." This is Paul's great thought: the entire universe is to find its cohesion in Christ. All the conflicts, all the diverse strands, all the discrepancies, all the loose ends, all the competing and warring forces, all the estrangements are to be united in Christ.

If that extravagant thought causes your mind too turbulent an upheaval, concentrate on your own small sphere of movement. What disunities you know could be brought together in Christ? That is where it begins. If the open secret is that God's plan is for all humankind, the entire universe, to be united in Christ, certainly it is time for my part of the universe to experience that unity.

SEALED WITH THE SPIRIT

13 In Him you also trusted, after you heard the word of truth, the gospel of your salvation; in whom also, having believed, you were sealed with the Holy Spirit of promise,
14 who is the guarantee of our inheritance until the redemption of the purchased possession, to the praise of His glory.
—*Ephesians 1:13–14*

The first affirmation in God's purpose and our place in it is: "we are chosen by God." The second: "we are redeemed by Christ." And now the third: "we are sealed with the Spirit."

Paul turns specifically now to the Gentiles, to whom he is writing. He stated their development in stages that may describe any person's coming into the faith. They heard the word, received it— the gospel of salvation, in believing and trusting Christ—and were sealed with the Holy Spirit. The last stage is our present consideration: In God's plan and our place in it, we are sealed with the Holy Spirit.

According to Paul, circumcision, was a seal that confirmed Abraham's justification by faith (Rom. 4:11). It is commonly assumed that Paul also saw baptism as the seal of the Christian. The seal was more than an outward sign; it was an inward experience. Christians were sealed with the Holy Spirit.

It is not absolutely certain in this instance that the event of being sealed with the Holy Spirit is to be associated with baptism. Paul could easily have designated baptism if that was his intended reference. Here he is centering on the validation of their faith. The Holy Spirit was not an option in Christian experience. Nor do we possess the Holy Spirit; rather, the Holy Spirit possesses us.

How does the Holy Spirit function? He "is the guarantee of our inheritance until the redemption of the purchased possession." To get the full impact of this statement we need to remember that in the New Testament, salvation is three-sided. It is a past fact (Rom. 8:24; 11:11; 2 Tim. 1:9; Heb. 2:3–4; 5:9; Rev. 12:10). It is a present experience (Luke 19:10; 1 Cor. 1:18; 15:2; 2 Cor. 2:15; 6:2; Phil. 2:12; 1 Pet. 3:21). It is also a future hope (Rom. 13:11; Heb. 9:28; 1 Pet. 1:5). The past dimension is often emphasized more because the accomplished fact can be proclaimed as good news.

The Holy Spirit functions in the present, giving us power and guidance to "work out our salvation." The Holy Spirit also *guarantees* our future salvation. But it is more than a guarantee, it is a present foretaste of the fuller inheritance of our redemption. Charles Wesley, who sang the theology of the Methodist revival, and sang so often in the language of Paul, prayed in song often for the coming of the Holy Spirit. In one verse of one of his most expressive hymns, he portrayed the work of the Holy Spirit, pleading,

> Send the Spirit of Thy Son,
> To make the depths of Godhead known,
> To make us share the life divine,
> Send him the sprinkled blood to apply
> Send him our souls to sanctify,
> And show and seal us ever thine.

The Spirit reveals God, makes effective in our lives the power of Christ's sacrifice, perfects in love (making us holy and blameless), and seals us forever as belonging to God. Like Paul, Wesley knew the Holy Spirit was not an option, but an essential reality in the Christian experience.

NOTE

1. James S. Stewart, *A Man in Christ* (New York: Harper, 1935), p. 239.

CHAPTER TWO—GOD'S REDEMPTIVE POWER FOR A NEW HUMANITY

EPHESIANS 1:15—2:22

Scripture Outline

Prayer for Masterful Living (1:15–19a)

The Supremacy of Christ and His Incarnation in the Church (1:19b–23)

God's Power for Redemption (2:1–10)

The New Humanity (2:11–18)

A Habitation of God (2:19–22)

Some of my most meaningful times have come in small prayer/share groups. To be in a fellowship where people know you thoroughly and love you unconditionally is a great gift. To have such people surround you with concern, lay their hands upon you, and pray for you is a life-strengthening, life-changing experience. Almost as meaningful as that, and certainly the channel of the same power, is to have persons who call your name daily in prayer even though they are not personally present with you. With what energizing power this word from Paul must have come to these new Christians to whom he was writing: *"I . . . do not cease to give thanks for you, making mention of you in my prayers"* (v. 16).

Paul had a pastoral heart. He was not only a man of thought, of action, of vision, of eloquence—he was a *man of prayer*. His shepherd-heart goes out to the churches to whom he is writing, and he prays as he writes. In his prayer we have a dramatic picture of God's Redemptive Power.

PRAYER FOR MASTERFUL LIVING

15 Therefore I also, after I heard of your faith in the Lord Jesus and your love for all the saints, 16 do not cease to give

thanks for you, making mention of you in my prayers: [17] that the God of our Lord Jesus Christ, the Father of glory, may give to you the spirit of wisdom and revelation in the knowledge of Him, [18] the eyes of your understanding being enlightened; that you may know what is the hope of His calling, what are the riches of the glory of His inheritance in the saints,

—Ephesians 1:15–18

The Mood of Paul's Praying

Paul is thankful, thankful for the peoples' *"faith in the Lord Jesus and your love for all the saints"* (v. 15). Can those persons who pray for us express such gratitude?

Prayer that flows out of a deep sense of gratitude is forceful. Our praying should be rooted in thankfulness. When so rooted, our prayer will be punctuated with thankfulness as is Paul's. Not only was he thankful, he was thrilled—thrilled because he knew who God was and what God was doing. Paul S. Rees put it succinctly: "The apostle's mood is one in which, thinking for those *for* whom he prays, he is thankful; and thinking of the God *to* whom he prays, he is *thrilled."*

The way Paul uses words here indicates how thrilled he is. We would have expected him to refer to the "God of glory" and the "Father of our Lord Jesus Christ." But he turns the designations around, saying, *"the God of our Lord Jesus Christ"* and the *"Father of glory."* As he prays is he so excited as to get his tongue twisted? Maybe, and that is O.K.—to be so moved in prayer that our words may tumble out in other than ordinary ways. There is something deeper here, however. *"Father of glory"* is a Hebraism like 2 Cor. 1:3 where God is the "Father of mercies," and James 1:17, the "Father of lights." God, in Himself, is all-glorious, but He is also the source of glory, which glory He has already conferred on Jesus and wishes to confer on us. That is worth getting excited about.

The Marvels for Which Paul Prayed

Paul prays for *"wisdom"* and *"revelation"* (v. 17).

The wording of this petition lends itself to two interpretations. The RSV has the petition, "a spirit of wisdom and revelation while the NKJV has "the spirit." The words may refer to a human disposition, a receptive spirit, a capacity to understand, eagerness to receive truth. Or the words may refer to the activity of the Holy Spirit imparting a particular gift—the gift of wisdom and revelation.

These two interpretations are not incompatible. Paul used the word in both senses. In fact, he used the word both ways in one sentence. "For ye have not received the spirit of bondage again to fear; but ye have received the Spirit of adoption, whereby we cry, Abba, Father" (Rom. 8:15, NKJV). The human spirit is precisely the aspect of our being which is open to the Holy Spirit. And, it is the human spirit dedicated to and informed by God that is the vehicle of the Holy Spirit's activity in the world.

While the two interpretations are not incompatible, and while we may certainly pray for a receptive spirit and inward disposition of eagerness to receive whatever truth God has for us, we need to remember that in the New Testament "revelation" is an activity of God, not a faculty of man. In a recent three-hour conversation I marveled at the way a "new" Christian's "eyes of understanding" were being enlightened. The twenty-year-old man has only a high school education, has come from a culturally deprived background, and has had no contact with the church since he was six. He had been deeply immersed in drugs and the drug culture, and his conversion to the Christian faith a year ago sounds like a story out of the Book of Acts. I was especially moved as he shared a period of struggle through which he had recently gone and the revelation that had come to him. Down on himself, heartsick over his failures, he cried out to God to give him some relief, to ease his emotional pain. It came to him, as clearly as if spoken aloud. God said, "My son, know that my pain is as great as yours. I grieve your failure with you." Tears of deep joy and deep sorrow brimmed over on to the cheeks of my young friend as he talked about his vivid awareness of a *personal* God who cared for him, and whom he had so often grieved.

That hit me like a sledgehammer. How long had it been since I had focused any attention on what my thoughts and action might be doing to God? That revelation was a gift of the Spirit to a "new" Christian and through that "babe in Christ" to one who has been on the way for thirty years.

Revelation is the activity of God, not a faculty of man. We do well to ponder, though, how "new Christians" often seem to be in more *direct* contact than Christians who have been in the faith for years. Could it be that we allow our spirits to be jaded by too much sophistication, too much materialism? We are duped by the pressure of society to be "rational." Thus our spirits are not receptive to the Holy Spirit who would enlighten the eyes of our understanding.

Paul knew that knowledge of God is something more than knowledge of facts about God. Even the objective revelation of God in Jesus Christ is not enough to produce the *knowing of God* we long for and desperately need. So Paul prayed that the Spirit would provide that revelation, that knowing which is ours as the Spirit of Christ becomes a living presence in us. He puts this *knowing* that comes by the Spirit even more graphically in Eph. 3:19. "May you be strong to grasp. . . the love of Christ and to know it, though it is beyond knowledge" (NEB).

For this "higher knowledge," it is necessary that *"the eyes of your understanding be enlightened."* The RSV says "the eyes of your hearts"; NEB designates it "your inward eyes." When we talk of our "heart," other than designating the physical organ, we are usually talking about the seat of our emotions. In biblical days, however, the heart was the whole inner self. In the Old Testament, the heart was the seat of the intelligence, and we find such phrases as "a wise and understanding heart." In the New Testament the mode of speaking is expanded so that "the heart" identified the higher intelligence in which will and emotions cooperated with the mind. This is the reason faith for Paul was an activity of the heart, of the whole inner being— not a mere assent of reason (cf. Rom. 10:10).

The Measure of Our Wisdom and Revelation

As our vision is illumined by the Spirit, our knowledge of God expands and matures. Paul defines that rich dynamic of growth in verses 18–19, piling up a number of synonymous or parallel phrases to emphasize the greatness of the promise of the gospel. Three distinct attributes are carefully noted and described.

1. *The hope to which he has called us.* This hope refers to all the possibilities of spiritual growth open to those whom God has called.

Is there anything more exciting than the unfolding and blossoming of a life yielded to Christ and shaped by His indwelling Holy Spirit? A garden, dazzling with the radiant color of tulips and daffodils, roses and petunias, is beautiful; yet that beauty does not compare to the beauty of a courageous soul who has taken the rough and rugged soil of a stubborn will, a mean temper, and selfish impulses and, by God's grace, through the recreating power of the Spirit, transformed and landscaped it into the likeness of Jesus Christ. Moonlight is beautiful, especially as it reflects on the smooth silk calmness of a glistening lake—but not nearly so beautiful as the unselfish lovelight sparkling in the eyes of one who has been made loving by the Spirit of Christ. A mountain peak, robed in fresh fallen snow, is a magnificently glorious sight, but not half as glorious as a mountain peak personality—one who has been made a giant by the Spirit.

You have seen it as I have—the complete transformation of persons as they allow themselves to be formed and transformed by Christ. This is the hope to which we are called.

But there is in this hope, also, the specific dimension of life after death. Paul could not ignore this dimension of hope. When he was ready to clinch his argument about the ultimate meaning and finality of Christ, he said to the Corinthians, "Lo! I tell you a mystery. We shall not all sleep, but we shall all be changed, in a moment, in the twinkling of an eye, at the last trumpet. For the trumpet will sound, and the dead will be raised imperishable, and we shall be changed" (1 Cor. 15:51–52, RSV).

I once thought lightly—even put down thoughts and talk—about eternal life in the tomorrows beyond physical death. Not any more! I have been in the innerclosets of men and women on their death-beds. I have been invited into the most sacred chambers of persons who, though yet healthy, are seventy-five to eighty years old and are "tired," whose psychic energy is waning. The resonance of their spirits, the hope of their commitment, their longing for life beyond death have brought me to the depth of Jesus' promise, "Because I live, you will live also" (John 14:19, RSV), and the confidence of Paul's assertion, "Death is swallowed up in victory" (1 Cor. 15:54, RSV).

Resurrection is at the heart of the Christian faith—not only the Resurrection of Christ, but our resurrection to eternal life with Christ.

2. Paul has already spoken of the new life as a heritage, here he extols the marvels of eternal life: *"the riches of the glory of His inheritance in the saints."* This is a present experience as well as a future hope.

Paul uses the word "saint" over thirty times to denote Christians. Certainly he is talking about the Christian community here. As "saints" we are one in Christ. He is our peace and *through Him we have access by one Spirit to the Father* (cf. 2:11–22).

There must be here also, though it is not Paul's common use of the word "saint," the hope of our being *among* (in) the saints—the whole company of angels and redeemed persons. Certainly in the context of our hope being rooted in God who raised Christ from the dead *"and set Him at His right hand in heavenly places"*

(v. 20), the thought of our sharing in a "communion of saints" both in this life and the life to come is essential.

A friend of mine, a brilliant young theologian, shared with me a prayer experience. He was using my *Workbook of Living Prayer* as a daily discipline and came to a section where I was emphasizing the power of Jesus' name in our praying. As a meditative prayer exercise I suggested in the workbook that one repeat the name of Jesus over and over—Jesus, Jesus—reflectively, lovingly, deeply, seeking to center in the reality of Jesus until Jesus prayed in and through us.

An amazing thing happened. In the midst of that prayer a vagrant thought invaded his heart, engrossing his attention. Would there be *known* relationships in heaven? Would he be able to *see* God? He tried to dismiss the unsettling intrusion, but, like the "friend at midnight," it kept pounding on the door of his heart. He would return to his "Jesus prayer," but the clamoring thought would intrude again.

Then it happened. He opened his eyes and saw Jesus walking toward him. My friend didn't kneel down in reverence, or back away in awe; but stood and joyfully embraced the Christ. He knew his prayer experience was far more than he expected. One of the deepest longings of his life and one of his most gnawing questions had been answered. He would *see* God, and know Him. He would be *with* Him. He would see and know others, and be known. He had experienced what Paul talked about: *"the riches of the glory of His inheritance in the saints"* (v. 18).

3. The third divine fact of the measure of wisdom and revelation is *"the exceeding greatness of His power toward us who believe"* (v. 19). Until the eyes of our understanding are enlightened to see this, we are missing a huge hunk of the Christian experience. It is one of the fundamental thoughts of Paul, thus the capstone of this prayer, that by faith we lay hold of the power of God.

Why is it that we continue in our anemic life, feebly getting on as best we can? Why is it that we plod along—our Christian walk more a stumble than a stride? Why is it that we give way to trampling defeats and become uninspiring spectacles of spiritual ineffectiveness? Why do we allow the mean carnalities to shape our lives when a glorious heritage of life after "the measure of the fullness of Christ" has been promised?

Why? We do not lay hold of the *"exceeding greatness of His power toward us who believe."* The RSV designates this the "immeasurable greatness," and the NEB translates it the "vast resources" of His power. Paul opens the floodgates of his language-river to try to communicate the dimensions of this power.

1. It is Resurrection power—the power God *"worked in Christ when He raised Him from the dead"* (v. 20).

2. It is *ascension* power—*"and set Him at His right hand in heavenly places"* (v. 20).

3. It is *dominion* power—*"far above all principality and power and might and dominion . . . and . . . has put all things under His feet, and gave Him to be the head over all things to the church"* (vv. 21–22).

That same power of God, which did all of that for Christ, is available to us who believe. Glory!

The call here is to bring the working power of God out of the past into the present. To be sure, we are to celebrate "the mighty acts of God in history," but that should make us even more aware of Christ as present power. This is the paramount miracle—that His immeasurable power is available now to heal the sick, to drive out demons, to redeem our sins, to energize our wills, to renew our spirits, to reconcile our relationships, to bring peace.

THE SUPREMACY OF CHRIST AND HIS INCARNATION IN THE CHURCH

[19] and what is the exceeding greatness of His power toward us who believe, according to the working of His mighty power [20] which He worked in Christ when He raised Him from the dead and seated Him at His right hand in the heavenly places, [21] far above all principality and power and might and dominion, and every name that is named, not only in this age but also in that which is to come.

[22] And He put all things under His feet, and gave Him to be head over all things to the church, [23] which is His body, the fullness of Him who fills all in all.

—*Ephesians 1:19–23*

The Exalted Christ

Nowhere in the New Testament is there a more glorious portrayal of the exalted Christ. As indicated above, three phrases pour out of Paul's surging soul as he seeks to do the impossible—to capture the immeasurable power and glory of God's work in Christ: Resurrection, Ascension, and Dominion. Ephesians has been called the "Epistle of the Ascension," and that it is, because here we meet the exalted Christ.

In the modern church do we make too little of the Ascension of Christ? How much thought do you yourself give it? Does the Ascension explicitly impact your life? Is your religious attention usually focused on the resurrected, preascended Christ? The early Christians were post-Resurrection, post-ascension Christians. They knew the gospel story: a Jesus who had once been a baby in a mother's arms—but He was not that now; a Jesus who had been a carpenter, a teacher, a companion, a friend—but He was not that now; a healing lover who mercifully blessed all He could touch, all He could see and hear and speak to—but He was not limited by time and space now; a self-giving suffering servant who hung on a cross, pouring out His life-blood and blood-love on our behalf—but He was not hanging there now. God had raised Him from the dead, but not only so; this Jesus had ascended and the curtain had gone up on a new act of the drama. Pentecost had happened. The Spirit of this Ascended One had been poured out on His followers and the church was born. The Ascended One had been given lordship over all *"principality and power and might and dominion."* His name was to be exalted over *"every name that is named, not only in this age, but also in that which is to come"* (v. 21). Everything has been put *"under His feet."*

The Incarnation of Christ in the Church

Ephesians is the great church epistle as well as the "Epistle of the Ascension." It is no accident that Paul's understanding of the church is galvanized to the exaltation of Christ. Few passages in the New Testament are bolder than the last two verses of this chapter. The exaltation of Christ is breathtaking within itself, but the connection between Christ and the church is doubly so.

Paul's metaphor for the church is a *"body."* He uses that metaphor over and over, though with varying emphasis. In 1 Corinthians 12:12–27, the multiplicity of functions (gifts) within the church calls for the body, an organic unity, as an apt metaphor. The mutual interdependence of Christians calls for the same body metaphor in Romans 12:4–5. In Colossians 1:18 and Ephesians 4:15, it is the dependence of Christians on their head that makes the body such a useful symbol. In Colossians 1:24, Paul sees the church as an extension of Christ's life and character, thus His body. And in Ephesians 4:4, body is the image Paul uses to emphasize the need for visible manifestation of the unity God provides by His Spirit. In this passage, Ephesians 1:22–23, the church is Christ's body—in unity with Christ and sharing in Christ's exaltation.

The last two verses, especially the last, are difficult. Who is the *"fullness,* "and who or what *"fills all in all"?* G. B. Caird gives a succinct and clear explanation: "It is God who is to *fill all in all 'Now when all things are made subject to Him, then the Son Himself will also be subject to Him who put all things under Him, that God may be all in all'* (1 Cor. 15:28), and this is to be achieved by his filling Christ with his own fullness (Col. 1:19; 2:9), in order that he, as the representative of God's being, may fill the church (Col. 2:10; Eph. 3:19) and subsequently the universe (Eph. 4:10). It is Christ who is here described as the *fullness* of God the all-filler. God's purpose is being achieved in three stages: the fullness of his own divine nature has found complete expression in the man Jesus Christ; he has given Christ, the bearer of his fullness, as his gift to the church, which is to be the first sharer of that fullness; and through the church he intends his fullness to pervade the rest of creation." Some very practical, challenging, and inspiring truths flow from this high and holy understanding of the church:

1. The church is a continuing incarnation of Christ. That means that whatever Christ *would* do, the church *must* do. Isn't that a dazzling thought? As the body of Christ, the church complements and fulfills Christ Himself.

2. Sinful though she may be, the church must furnish bodily hands and feet for her exalted Lord. For Paul, with his Hebrew mind, spirit without body was inconceivable. Christ is Spirit, and resides as Spirit with the church. For the Spirit to act incarnationally in history, the church must be the instrument.

3. As the image, the earthly manifestation of her risen and exalted Lord, the church is the "colony of heaven" (Phil. 3:20, Moffatt). We seek to approximate in this earthly order the eternal design of God— the hope which awaits us in glory.

4. Such bold affirmations call for careful avoidance of presumption. The church, in her institutional extension of Christ, dare not claim

any equality with Him. We need to guard diligently against exalting the church to some imperial status. To label some leaders "princes of the church" is a sign of having fallen into that snare.

5. The Incarnation of God in Christ was sinless. The church as the extension of the Incarnation of Christ is wrought with sin, thus always under judgment.

6. God's plan for the world is in the hands of the church. Though we must always guard against presumption, know ourselves to be constantly under God's judgment, and diligently avoid locking the church into any institutional form we may favor, still we cannot avoid the role God has given His church in His bold scheme. God's intention is that all alien forces, all estranged persons, all warring elements are to be brought to unity. Christ is the center around which that unity is to cohere. The church is the instrument through which the unity will occur, the channel of power to bring it about, the demonstration plot to model the unity as realized fact in nucleus and anticipated universal reality. As hackneyed as it may sound, Christ is counting on His church, and He has no other plan.

GOD'S POWER FOR REDEMPTION

2:1 And you He made alive, who were dead in trespasses and sins, 2 in which you once walked according to the course of this world, according to the prince of the power of the air, the spirit who now works in the sons of disobedience, 3 among whom also we all once conducted ourselves in the lusts of our flesh, fulfilling the desires of the flesh and of the mind, and were by nature children of wrath, just as the others.

4 But God, who is rich in mercy, because of His great love with which He loved us, 5 even when we were dead in trespasses, made us alive together with Christ (by grace you have been saved), 6 and raised us up together, and made us sit together in the heavenly places in Christ Jesus, 7 that in the ages to come He might show the exceeding riches of His grace in His kindness toward us in Christ Jesus. 8 For by grace you have been saved through faith, and that not of yourselves; it is the gift of God, 9 not of works, lest anyone should boast.
10 For we are His workmanship, created in Christ Jesus for good works, which God prepared beforehand that we should walk in them.

—Ephesians 2:1–10

"Tell it like it is" is a phrase that became common in the decade of the sixties, and carried on into the seventies. It had its origin in the personal growth movement, i.e., sensitivity training, when the emphasis was on personal confrontation, honesty, and no-holds-barred sharing of feelings and responses. It spilled over into other areas of life. Politicians, news commentators, and other public communicators have been fond of claiming to "tell it like it is." One popular newscaster on national TV closed his show by saying, "And that's the way it is."

Paul needed no encouragement to "tell it like it is." But not only that, he "told it as it could be." This section of chapter 2 is a graphic presentation of God's power for redemption. The chapter division is arbitrary. There is no break at this point with what he has been saying in chapter 1; the working of God's mighty power is still the theme. That power was wrought in Christ Jesus, raising Him from the dead and seating Him at God's right hand. That power also works in individual members of the body (church), raising us who are *"dead in trespasses and sins"* (v. 1), and making us *"alive together with Christ"* (v. 5) and seating us *"together in the heavenly places in Christ Jesus"* (v. 6).

The predicament and possibility of each one of us is drawn in graphic relief.

Our Predicament

Paul minces no words. We cannot miss what he is saying. *"You were dead in trespasses and sins"* (v. 1). No mild response can be made to such a graphic metaphor. In fact, it is more than a metaphor; death and sin are taken seriously by the Bible, and they go together. "The wages of sin is death" (Rom. 6:23), contended Paul. Biblically, there was a finality to death that has been dropped out of a crack in our modern minds. The immortality of the soul as a natural birthright for humans is an idea foreign to the Bible. It was a Greek concept that crept into our thinking. Death was death in biblical understanding, and only God could do anything about it. Thus our fate beyond death is completely dependent upon how we stand before God and what God chooses to do. Sin cuts us off from God, the source of life; thus we are *dead.*

This is the inevitable nemesis of sin: death. And it is universal. Paul begins with *"you,"* talking of the Gentiles, but he gets only to the third verse before he includes himself and the Jews: *"also we all once conducted ourselves in the lusts of our flesh . . . and were by nature children of wrath."*

A holy God and sinful men—settling things between them is the issue.

Sin is death because it is separation from God. Issues in that death-state beat on the door of our minds with wild fists, clamoring for attention.

1. In sin we are controlled by Satan. *The prince of the power of the air* is a title for Satan (cf. 2 Cor. 4:4; John 12:31). The unredeemed world is described in Colossians 1:13 as the *power of darkness,* and our salvation depends upon being rescued from that realm and brought into the kingdom of His dear Son (Col. 1:13).

2. In sin we walk *according to the course of this world* (v. 2). "Walk" was a verb used frequently in the New Testament, especially by Paul (31 times) to denote moral behavior. Apart from Christ we are pulled to conform to the standards of the present world order. Without Christ we are doomed to the death that is inevitable for those who follow a godless and worldly humanity.

3. Walking *"according to the course of this world,"* we become *"children of wrath"* (v. 3). In Ephesians 4:18, Paul uses another picture: the hardening of the heart. He says we will come to the place where we are *"past feeling"* (4:19). The word translated *"hardening"* is a grim one, and Barclay renders it "petrifying." It is the Greek word *porosis,* coming from *poros,* which meant a stone that was harder than marble.

At 12:21 A.M. on a morning in November 1979, the doctor pronounced Jesse Water Bishop dead in the gas chamber of the Nevada State Prison. Bishop was a career criminal who committed his first armed robbery at the age of fifteen, and spent twenty-two of his last twenty-seven years behind bars. Bishop renounced all efforts to stay his execution for a murder he had committed in 1977. At that time he even waived his right to a jury trial, immediately pleading guilty. He could have been given an appeal of his case even minutes before entering the gas chamber, but he said no, with these words: "This is just one more step down the road I've been heading all my life. Let's go" *(Time,* Nov. 5, 1979, p. 35).

One agonizes about such a life and shudders at such a steel-encased set of the will. But we can also learn.

Sin is not to be played with, not to be taken casually, not to be looked at tentatively as though we can do as we please, order our lives as we will, change when and if we wish, thinking we will always be in control. There is a cumulative effect that builds until our hearts may be petrified and we are past feeling. We really see the horror of that possibility—that sin may kill our wills, and we may thus be doomed to a walk that can only end in death.

The predicament is horrible and clear: *"dead in trespasses and sins."*

The Possibility

As the predicament is excruciatingly painful, the possibility is excitingly clear and beckoning: *"to be made alive in Christ."*

Paul was so convinced and excited about the possibility that he ran ahead of himself. He wanted to "tell it like it is," presenting the predicament in stark boldness, but he did not want that scathing reality to be isolated from the glorious hope of deliverance. So, his first word is, *"you He has made alive."* Only then does he talk about sin and death. In fact, verses 1–5 form a kind of parenthesis to what Paul started out to say—that as Christ has been exalted and enthroned, so we who have been made alive have become a part of a new humanity. All who take part in this new life can equally claim to "sit with Him in heavenly places."

Sin equals death, and God's answer to death is resurrection. That resurrection is a present reality. Christians are those who have already been *"made alive."* The resurrection after death to eternal life promised in the New Testament is the heritage only of those who have been already made alive through Christ in their earthly existence.

We may not like to think of it, but the Bible is clear: the end toward which everything moves is God's judgment. "It is appointed for men to die once, but after this the judgment" (Heb. 9:27). John makes the case especially clear. "Do not marvel at this; for the hour is coming when all who are in the tombs will hear his voice and come forth, those who have done good, to the resurrection of life, and those who have done evil, to the resurrection of judgment" (John 5:28–29, RSV).

The astounding and liberating truth is that we share in Christ's Resurrection now. Christ so identified Himself with us in His life and death that His death was a representative and inclusive event. He died *for us.* His Resurrection is therefore inclusive as well. To be *with* Christ and *in* Christ is to share His new life now.

By Grace through Faith

One of the exciting things about Paul, though often difficult, is his spontaneous expression of truth and conviction. Sometimes this is out of context, sometimes simply not stated in orderly development. In verse 5 he interjects the ringing conviction of his life in a parenthesis, *"by grace you have been saved."* That central thought is taken up and amplified in verses 8–10. These verses are a summary—though generalized—of Romans 1–5, Paul's bold and radical doctrine that utterly denies us anything of which we can boast (cf. Rom. 3:27—4:1; Gal. 6:14). We can do nothing to receive the favor of God; only receive through faith what He has given us (see commentary on Gal. 2:15–16).

There is a slight variance in expression here compared with that in Galatians and Romans. The first variance is at the point of the tense of our salvation: You *have been* saved. This perfect tense expression is new. Uniformly in other letters Paul speaks of salvation as a continuing process: to us who *are being* saved (1 Cor. 1:18); we *shall be* saved (Rom. 5:9). He never hesitated in his insistence "You have been justified," or "You have been reconciled to God," but salvation was to be *completed* by God in His final kingdom.

This perfect tense of our salvation in Ephesians is in keeping with the eschatological attitude and emphasis of the letter. It harmonizes with the declaration of our share in the *"glory of His inheritance in the saints"* (1:18).

Paul has made a distinction before, claiming to be "in Christ" now, and anticipating being "with Christ" in heaven. Now the experience and claim is bolder: the Christian is both "in Christ" and "with Christ" in heavenly places here and now.

Another variance in this passage is the place given to *works*. There is no question we are *"saved through faith . . . not of works, lest anyone should boast"* (vv. 8, 9). But—and here is the slight variance: *"we are His workmanship, created in Christ Jesus for good works, which God prepared beforehand that we should walk in them"* (v. 10).

God has made us what we are; we have absolutely nothing of which to boast. This word "boast" is characteristically Pauline, occurring as a verb or noun over fifty times in his letters. By His own creative imagination, mind, and power, God brought the final person into being; so by the redemptive work of Christ, God makes new persons now.

Redemption means much more than the repair of the ravages and ruptures resulting from humanity's fall. It does not mean the restoration of Eden's innocence, but much more. It is the creation of a new humanity and a new world, which has previously existed only in the mind and purpose of God. This is *"His workmanship, created in Christ Jesus."* This new life does not result from a person's good works; good works are possible and indeed will flow out of the new life that has come to us through God's grace.

THE NEW HUMANITY

[11] Therefore remember that you, once Gentiles in the flesh—who are called Uncircumcision by what is called the Circumcision made in the flesh by hands— [12] that at that time you were without Christ, being aliens from the commonwealth of Israel and strangers from the covenants of promise, having no hope and without God in the world. [13] But now in Christ Jesus you who once were far off have been brought near by the blood of Christ.

[14] For He Himself is our peace, who has made both one, and has broken down the middle wall of separation, [15] having abolished in His flesh the enmity, that is, the law of commandments contained in ordinances, so as to create in Himself one new man from the two, thus making peace, [16] and that He might reconcile them both to God in one body through the cross, thereby putting to death the enmity. [17] And He came and preached peace to you who were afar off and to those who were near. [18] For through Him we both have access by one Spirit to the Father.

—Ephesians 2:11–18

I was visiting with a friend, a minister in a huge midwestern church. Entering his home, we walked through the garage. His son's go-cart was there and I commented on it. This triggered him to share the story of his reconciliation with his father.

His mother and father, after thirty years of marriage, had divorced. The father had been unfaithful to his mother, trampled on her feelings, and spurned her forgiveness and love, returning over and over to his "kept women" even after renewing his commitment and pledging fidelity.

This caused my friend great pain and anguish. Though he loved his father, he became bitter, even hateful toward him. Unable to accept him and the suffering inflicted upon his mother, my friend and his father became estranged. The father, embarrassed by his own actions, eaten up with shame and guilt, was unable to face his son.

About four years after this, the father came to a convention in the city where his son was a minister, and a series of circumstances made it "right" for him to visit his son. They walked through the garage as we were doing that day, my friend leading the way, his father walking behind. The tension was extreme, and my friend was in the house before he realized that his father was not with him. Looking back, he saw his father staring at the go-cart, tears flowing down his face. The memory of his son's childhood, of days when the bond of love was so solid, and the thought of his now-grown son making go-carts for his own son, as he had done for him, overwhelmed him. Barriers were dropped, masks were taken off, emotions including repentance were expressed, love and forgiveness began to flow as honest sharing brought father and son together again.

The Cross is like that for would-be Christians. It is the sign that brings us back to our senses, back to the place of love where reconciliation takes place. We look at the Cross and are reminded of what we have lost—the relationship with Christ we have spurned. Feelings of repentance well up. We open ourselves to God, and, gracious Father that He is, He restores us to fellowship with Him.

Reconciliation

What joyful tones and what solid conviction accompanied these words of Paul for the Gentile reader. The meaning of estrangement had been seared like a burning brand upon their souls. They were contemptuously called the uncircumcision by those who arrogantly claimed that God's love was only for the circumcised and that others (Gentiles) were created "to be fuel for the fires of hell." They felt the burden of *"being aliens from the commonwealth of Israel and strangers from the convenants of promise, having no hope and without God in the world"* (v. 12). These words are like a death-shroud over the spirit, hanging heavily over our souls even now: *"having no hope and without God in the world."* Paul uses the word "aliens" to designate foreigners. Since the Gentiles had never belonged to Israel, Paul must have been using the metaphor of an ancient city-state which was made up of free citizens and also of resident aliens who had no civic rights. The disenfranchisement and deprivation was made more graphic by adding the word "strangers." Gentiles were aliens who were not even resident but outsiders altogether.

The layout of the temple in Jerusalem dramatically marked the estrangement of Gentiles. Inside the temple walls were a series of courts. The innermost court was the hallowed "Most Holy Place" into which the high priest could go—and that only once a year.

Then came the court of priests, just outside the Holy Place; then the court of Israelites; then the court of women; then finally, far back and away from the Most Holy Place, far away from even the priests, separated from men of Israel by a barrier of "lowly" women, was the court of the Gentiles. On the low barrier separating this lowest court from the rest were posted signs in Latin and Greek, giving warning that death would come to any Gentile who sought to advance further toward the Most Holy Place.

Paul uses this familiar layout of the temple to speak metaphorically of what the blood of Christ had done. The warning signs had been smashed, the enmity between Jew and Gentile had been abolished. On Crucifixion day, not only the barriers between outer and inner courts, but even the curtain isolating the Most Holy Place was rent in two from top to bottom.

The way is open for all. Those who *"were afar off"* and *"those who were near"* have been reconciled, brought into one body by the Cross. All—no one is excluded—all *"have access by one Spirit to the Father."*

Revelation and Revolution

Particular aspects of the gospel and descriptions of the new humanity are to be noted in this passage. Here is revelation that brings revolution.

1. *He is our peace.* Is Paul calling to mind Isaiah 57:19, "Peace, peace, to the far and to the near, says the Lord" (RSV)? In its original context this word of Isaiah expresses God's offer of peace to all Jews, whether in dispersion or in Palestine near Jerusalem. The words "near" and "far," however, came to refer to Jews who were near to God and Gentiles who were far from Him.

Paul is saying something radically new and revolutionary. A Gentile is brought near to God—through Jesus Christ: *"He is our peace."* The peace offered in Isaiah's prophecy is now a reality—no longer an abstract idea, but a person; not a state of mind, but a state of being, an actual fact. God has created something new. In Christ God died for both Jew and Gentile, bringing them both into union with himself, in his flesh abolishing the enmity which the law had created. (See commentary on Gal. 3:10–14 in this volume.)

2. *One body through the cross.* Paul speaks of a new humanity in two ways. In verse 15 he says Christ created one new man *"in Himself."*

In verse 16 he speaks of *"one body through the cross."* Both are revelations that bring revolution.

A physical barrier may be removed and the people it once separated remain unchanged. In my hometown of Richton, Mississippi, every day at noon elderly people with limited income come together for a hot nourishing lunch provided by federal funding. They sing together, play games together, share in craft-making together, and though the government may frown upon it, they worship together. There are black and white people in that daily gathering, which would have been unheard of even ten years ago. But the barriers have finally come down. Blacks and whites are no longer forcefully separated in Mississippi.

It doesn't take too much spiritual perception to see that within some the harshest, most demeaning and destructive barrier is still there—inner estrangement and hostility that has the crushing power of ages of forced segregation behind it. It is a revelation to talk to my mom and dad, now in their mid-seventies, who were victimized by a system that would not allow the faintest expression of broken barriers for two hundred years. To see in them the freedom that has come, and to hear them express in genuine human caring terms their concern and relationship with blacks, even though to a marked degree it is still superficial and limited, provides me great joy. I know, as they know, that the removal of the real barriers of estrangement and hostility involves a profound personal change.

That is the change Christ brings. He is the "last Adam," creating a new humanity of which He is the head (1 Cor. 15:45–47; 2 Cor. 5:17). Before Christ all were of the "first Adam." Divisions of all sorts—race and religion, class and sex (Gal. 3:28; Col 3:11)—belong to that old order which must pass away with the advent of Christ in our lives. Smoldering embers of the old Adam may come alive and flame up even in the lives of Christians. But they are dying embers and will be completely smothered by the Spirit of the new Adam maturing within us.

Each who shares in the *"new humanity"* must share with others who belong to the new breed. If we identify with Christ we must identify with others who identify with Him. So we have the second way Paul speaks of the new humanity: *"one body through the cross."* This is the church—not as an ecclesiastical organization but as the new humanity of verse 15. The church is nothing else than the Incarnation of Christ. On a vaster scale, the church fulfills in her life what Christ affected in His own life. All of this, the creation of the church as the "body of Christ" was *"through* the cross." Through the Cross, our only means of reconciliation and redemption, we are brought near to each other as to God.

3. *Access by one Spirit to the Father.* The Greek word *prosagoge,* translated "access," is a technical term for the right of free approach into the presence of a king. In the Persian royal court, there was an official called the *prosagogeus* whose function was to introduce people who desired an audience with the king. The image is beautiful and the truth is clear: through Christ we have open access to the Father. On the Cross Jesus flung the door open—in fact, nailed it open so that it could never be closed again—the door into the presence of God.

A HABITATION OF GOD

19 Now, therefore, you are no longer strangers and foreigners, but fellow citizens with the saints and members of the household of God, 20 having been built on the foundation of the apostles and prophets, Jesus Christ Himself being the chief cornerstone, 21 in whom the whole building, being fitted together, grows into a holy temple in the Lord, 22 in whom you also are being built together for a dwelling place of God in the Spirit.
—*Ephesians 2:19–22*

The content and imagery of this closing section of chapter 2 is beautiful and challenging. All of it evolves around the unity of the church under the Lordship of Christ.

No Longer Strangers and Foreigners

A stranger was a foreigner; a sojourner was a resident alien. It was possible, in theory, for a Gentile to become a naturalized member of the Jewish state by adopting the Jewish religion. Yet, in practice, he was never received as a full son of Abraham; his birth was always remembered and held against him. (The Books of Jonah and Ruth are protests against this rigid racist practice.) The Gentiles could only greet this word of Paul with doxology: they were now *"fellow citizens with the saints."*

The Household of God

The metaphor is changed from commonwealth to family. The church is the household of God—a family. Hitherto the Gentiles have had no privileges, now they are brought into the intimacy of a family circle.

Christ, the Chief Cornerstone

Paul is true to his style—changing metaphor and moving from one meaning of a word to another. From commonwealth and family, he moves to *"building"* and *"temple."* This building is built on the foundation of prophets and apostles, and Christ is the chief cornerstone. Paul is not concerned about literal meaning. He probably had in mind a large stone placed at the corner of the roof to bind two walls together, but that did not limit his image. Christ was the binding stone, giving strength and unity to the entire structure, but the building was incomplete. Every time a new convert trusts Christ for salvation a new stone is added. The building grows as the body is built up (Eph. 4:16).

A Habitation of God

What a picture! How radical the thought was to those who believed that the temple in Jerusalem was God's earthly dwelling place. Paul returned to the thought which led him to a description of the church as a building: *"in whom you also are being built together for a dwelling place of God in the Spirit"* (v. 22). Formerly outcasts, relegated to an outer court in the temple, the Gentiles are now themselves a part of the temple. God has His presence in them. God's people, not a particular place or building, is the dwelling place of God.

The word of the Revelation comes to mind here. "And I heard a loud voice from the throne saying, 'Behold, the dwelling of God is with men. He will dwell with them, and they shall be his people, and God himself will be with them'" (Rev. 21:3, RSV).

The word from 1 Peter also comes to mind: "You also, as living stones, are being built up a spiritual house" (2:5).

The old order is gone—gone completely. God cannot be associated with or restricted to any visible ritual, temple, law, or doctrinal system. *"You will neither on this mountain, nor in Jerusalem, worship the Father,"* Jesus said to the Samaritan woman (John 4:21). "Destroy this temple and I will build it again in three days," He was accused of saying. The truth is glorious and demanding: we who by faith claim Christ as Savior and Lord are the habitation of God. He has redeemed us to be a new humanity in whom His life is expressed in the world.

CHAPTER THREE—THE MYSTERY AND MEANING OF FAITH

EPHESIANS 3:1–21

Scripture Outline

The Mystery Revealed (3:1–7)

The Purpose of the Mystery (3:8–13)

The Mystery Revealed in Prayer (3:14–19)

Doxology (3:20–21)

The bulk of Ephesians 3 is prayer. It is also out of prayer that our life of action flows.

As already indicated, this epistle is unique in the Pauline corpus because the first three chapters are given over almost completely to prayer. Prayer is rooted in the mystery and meaning of the faith; also, in and through prayer we probe the mystery and clarify the meaning of faith. Thus the theme of this chapter:

THE MYSTERY REVEALED

3:1 For this reason I, Paul, the prisoner of Christ Jesus for you Gentiles— **2** if indeed you have heard of the dispensation of the grace of God which was given to me for you, **3** how that by revelation He made known to me the mystery (as I have briefly written already, **4** by which, when you read, you may understand my knowledge in the mystery of Christ),
5 which in other ages was not made known to the sons of men, as it has now been revealed by the Spirit to His holy apostles and prophets: **6** that the Gentiles should be fellow heirs, of the same body, and partakers of His promise in Christ through the gospel, **7** of which I became a minister according

to the gift of the grace of God given to me by the effective
working of His power.   —*Ephesians 3:1-7*

Paul starts to pray, intending to resume his intercession
already begun in chapter 1, but immediately interrupts himself to
remind his readers of who he is and the special role he has been
given in the drama of God's universal purpose. In his interruption, he does not stray from the consciousness that he is offering
a prayer, and thus his language is not that of ordinary speech.
These first three chapters have a musical quality about them—
liturgical music played in a solemn mode. The interruptions are
like parentheses in which he develops further or introduces the
idea of his prayer. Verses 1–13 comprises one of the interruptions.
Here Paul identifies himself and interweaves into his prayer an
exposition of the gospel.

The Prisoner of Jesus Christ

One feature that distinguishes Ephesians, Philippians, Colossians,
and Philemon from the other letters of Paul is his designation of
himself as a prisoner (Eph. 3:1; 4:1; Philem. 1, 9) and the reference
to his bonds (Phil. 1:7, 13, 14, 16; Col. 4:18; Philem. 10, 13) or to his
chains (Eph. 6:20). Paul was fond of vigorous metaphor. Were these
references metaphorical or literal? The RSV uses *"for"* instead of *"of"*
in Ephesians 3:1 to make sure we see Paul's reference to himself as a
prisoner in a literal sense, and I believe that was the case. In 6:20 he
refers to himself as *"an ambassador in chains."* That is an almost
unintelligible, mixed metaphor unless *"chains"* has the literal meaning of imprisonment.

Thus when Paul asks the church at Colossae to remember his
bonds (4:8), it is not likely that he is simply reminding them that
he is in the service of the Lord; his bonds are literal.

Two lessons are immediately obvious. One, *Paul's suffering
clothed him with authority.* He spoke out of the "blood-and-guts"
context of laying his life on the line for what he believed. You can
believe a person's story about his participation in war if he bears the
marks of that involvement. You can believe that a person is hurting
with the starving poor of the world if you know that person is giving his own resources to alleviate that suffering. My affirmation of
love and concern is validated by my willingness to spend myself—
time, energy, presence—with and on behalf of the one I say I love.
Paul's commitment and zeal on behalf of the Gentiles brought his
arrest and imprisonment. His suffering clothed him with authority.

Two, *Paul's imprisonment was being used by God in the fulfillment of His purpose.* Thus he could see himself not as a victim of his enemies, but a *"prisoner of Jesus Christ."* This imprisonment was for the sake of the Gentiles. Paul reminds us that God can use all the circumstances of our lives for the *furtherance of the gospel.*

A slogan that has made its way into the vocabulary of many Christians in recent years is "Praise the Lord anyway." It is a great motto and should never become glib or casual. There is power in praise. To praise God in all circumstances works to keep our eyes focused on Him, to lift us out of the debilitating pain and mire of our circumstance, enabling us to see clearly and to get a vision of how God works in and through us to transform that which may be evil and destructive into something good, creative, and redemptive. This does not mean that God designs and orders the events that bring pain, chaos, confusion, and suffering to us. Not so! It means that God is with us in all circumstances, and can bring good to those who love Him and who seek to respond to His call according to His purposes.

In this Ephesian letter Paul sounds the note of victory in the midst of apparent defeat, and freedom though in prison: *"Therefore I ask that you do not lose heart at my tribulations for you, which is your glory"* (Eph. 3:13).

Dispensation of Grace

After identifying himself by name, and the situation in which his preaching had placed him—prisoner—Paul acknowledges that he might be known by his reputation: *"indeed you have heard."* This is rather decisive proof that he was not writing to the church of Ephesus since they would have known him personally, not only by reputation. He speaks of himself as the one upon whom a special grace has been dispensed (v. 2). Grace cannot mean in this instance the free pardoning love of God shown to all Christians, but rather a singular favor granted to Paul. The best explanation of this passage is found in 1 Corinthians 12, Paul's own account of "spiritual gifts." To all members of the church, the Spirit imparts gifts *(charisma)* for ministry. No matter the apparent worth of the gift, humble or striking by importance, all come through the same Spirit and are essential for building and sustaining the body of Christ. Paul's gift was that of evangelizing the Gentiles. God had chosen him, given him a special commission to be the one apostle of the Gentiles. (See commentary on Gal. 1:11–17, and Eph. 4:11–12.)

How the Mystery Is Made Known

Paul claimed a unique privilege: God had made known to him the mystery (v. 3); it had come through revelation. Paul would contend that revelation comes primarily in two ways, and he alludes to both in this passage. First, revelation comes by prophetic inspiration—God breaks into our lives and speaks to us in a direct way. This had happened to Paul on numerous occasions, the most dramatic being his conversion. It may well be that Paul is referring to this experience as the occasion for God sharing with him the mystery. He told the Galatians that his conversion was a revelation of Jesus Christ, in which he received directly from God the gospel he preached (Gal. 1:11–16).

Second, revelation comes through Scripture. In Ephesians 5:32, Paul makes this clear. *"For this reason a man shall leave his father and mother, and be joined to his wife: and the two shall become one flesh"* (Eph. 5:31) is a quotation of Scripture. Then in verse 32 Paul uses the word "mystery" for the fifth time in this letter. The previous four uses (1:9; 3:3, 4, 9) suggest that God's secret plan is revealed by prophetic inspiration, but here the *"mystery"* is revealed in Scripture. *"This is a great mystery, but I speak concerning Christ and the church"* (Eph. 5:32).

Revelation, either by prophetic inspiration or through Scripture, is a gift the Spirit shares with all Christians (1 Cor. 14:6; 2 Cor. 12:1, 7).

Revelation comes not alone to individuals, but to the corporate community. The record of the body-life of the early church in Acts 2 is a marvelous account of this. The believers "continued steadfastly in the apostles' doctrine and fellowship, and in the breaking of bread, and in prayers. And fear came upon every soul; and many wonders and signs were done by the apostles" (Acts 2:42–43).

But what is the mystery Paul is talking about? *The mystery is not Christ's secret, but the secret which is Christ.* Paul is talking here about one significant phase of God's secret, which is Christ in whom all things are to be united. That particular phase is the calling of the Gentiles to share equally with the Jews *the promise* which hitherto had been seen as only a gift to Israel: *"that the Gentiles should be fellow heirs, of the same body, and partakers of His promise in Christ through the gospel"* (Eph. 3:6).

What fullness of grace!—*"fellow heirs and partakers of the promise."* The promise made to Abraham and to his descendants was that they should *be given the world as their inheritance* (Rom. 4:13). It could not be more encompassing, could it?— *"members of the same body.* This is the body of Christ, the new humanity after the design of the new Adam, replacing the old humanity of the first Adam. And the Gentiles are integrated into that body, sharing the glorious liberty of the sons of God (Rom. 8:21).

THE PURPOSE OF THE MYSTERY

[8] To me, who am less than the least of all the saints, this grace was given, that I should preach among the Gentiles the unsearchable riches of Christ, [9] and to make all see what is the fellowship of the mystery, which from the beginning of the ages has been hidden in God who created all things through Jesus Christ; [10] to the intent that now the manifold wisdom of God might be made known by the church to the principalities and powers in the heavenly places, [11] according to the eternal purpose which He accomplished in Christ Jesus our Lord, [12] in whom we have boldness and access with confidence through faith in Him. [13] Therefore I ask that you do not lose heart at my tribulations for you, which is your glory.

—Ephesians 3:8–13

The Unsearchable Riches of Jesus Christ

The unsearchable riches of Jesus Christ belong to all who belong to Christ. So Paul could write, "Everything belongs to you! Paul, Apollos or Cephas; the world, life, death, the present or the future, everything is yours! For you belong to Christ, and Christ belongs to God" (1 Cor. 3:21–23, Phillips)!

As a recipient of the unsearchable riches of Jesus Christ, Paul refers to himself in two ways. In verses 4 and 5 he makes a bold claim: he possesses a knowledge of the mystery of Christ *which in other ages was not made known to the sons of men.* On the surface that looks like presumption, if not sheer arrogance. In verse 8 Paul sees himself in another light: *"less than the least of all the saints."* Moving up and down these apparently opposite roles of self-assessment, the Christian finds the rhythm of life.

Confidence and humility is the rhythm—a confidence born not out of grandiose thoughts about our own gifts and talents which makes for arrogant self-confidence, but confidence that God has gifted us and will gift us with all the grace needed for masterful living. Humility is not the opposite of that kind of confidence, but the other side of the same coin. We know our gifts but we also know our limitations. And we know that as God has gifted us, He will also make up for our limitations. In either case, we will not claim the power is intrinsically ours, nor will we take the glory. All is *by the effective working of His power.*

The Fellowship of the Mystery

The mystery which is Christ Himself has not only been revealed *to* Paul, it is God's purpose that all people share in *the fellowship of the mystery.*

The radical boldness of that dream is best seen against the backdrop of the era in which Paul verbalized it. The apparent strength of that small band of Christ-believers and followers compared to the strength of the enemy was like the proverbial molehill/mountain comparison. And so today as the evidence of an almost totally secular world order pushes the question: Will the kingdom dream ever be realized? Paul's answer is clear and definite. The world may seem to be moving toward chaos, the end may appear to be a riddle wrapped in mystery, but not so. The solving clue has been made known in Christ. *"Redemption through His blood, the forgiveness of sins, according to the riches of His grace"* (1:7) moves with divine determination. Nothing in earth or hell can prevail against that impelling, impregnable power of God.

This deathless hope that shines throughout Ephesians and Paul's other writings calls us to a recommitment in two areas. One, our witness of this now open secret must be taken to the ends of the earth. Somewhere about 1950 the church of the Western world, especially what we call "mainline churches," began to lose, even to deliberately deemphasize the world missionary enterprise. Ecclesiastical clichés like "Christian imperialism" became the smokescreen we put up to veil our anemic commitment, our burnt-out passion and compassion, our wilted zeal to take the gospel "to the ends of the earth." Two obvious factors undergird a recommitment to world evangelization: (1) the discovery that there are three billion people who are not even nominal Christians in any way that would suggest Christ as the saving alternative to chaos, and (2) the realization that the naive notion of theological liberalism, which claims all religious roads lead to God and are equally valid, has led us not to God but taken us far afield from the centrality of the Christian faith.

Our second area of commitment is that our self-awareness of this now open secret of Christ must be celebrated and cultivated in the communities of faith of which we are a part. That leads to the next big point Paul makes about the purpose of the mystery.

To Be Made Known by the Church

The mystery is to be made known by the church (v. 10). According to Caird, it is hardly an exaggeration to say that any interpretation of Ephesians stands or falls on this verse.

Here again Paul reaffirms that the mission of the church is that of her exalted Lord. Yet here is something new. He has told us that it is part of God's purpose to bring all the principalities and powers under the sovereignty of Christ. Now he tells us that God is going to achieve this end *"through the church."*

Do you get the expansiveness of that? The mission field of the church is the whole cosmos!

Christ has triumphed over all powers, heavenly and earthly. No hostile forces are great enough to hinder the soul's ascent to God when that soul is companioned and championed by Christ. But there is more yet. The church, even in her earthly expression, rises triumphantly with Christ to overcome all the powers of earth or heaven. What Christ said is true, "The gates of hell shall not prevail against her."

The church, then, is two things: (1) a demonstration plot for the breaking down and the final dissolution of the barriers of hatred and suspicion which divide humanity; and (2) the staging ground for the expression of and release of the mighty power of Christ to draw all persons unto Him.

Have you ever stopped to wonder at the marvel of God's creation—the church? The creation of heaven and earth is a wonder. Yes, all stand amazed at it. The creation of humans, rational beings with freedom to respond or rebel against their Creator—that is a marvel that we cannot comprehend. But, marvel of marvels, God, in Christ, woos the rebel back; pours out unlimited love that the rebel can't resist; rebels respond in love and obedience and God creates a new people who live together in a relationship of love and forgiveness—and that's the church. When she is true to her being, Christ Himself is present. His love flows from her corporate life. His forgiveness is expressed in the relationship of her members to each other and to those outside her fellowship. His justice and mercy are made visible in her ministry and mission to "the least of these."

One other great dimension of the church making known the mystery must be noted before we leave this passage. We hinted at it earlier, but it must now be stated explicitly. In his earlier letters (1 Cor. 2:6–8; 15:24–38; Rom. 8:37–39), Paul boldly claimed that the powers had been defeated—"destroying every authority and power. For he must reign until he has put all his enemies under his feet" (1 Cor. 15:24–25, RSV). In this Ephesian passage, as well as in Colossians and Philippians, Paul not only sees the *defeat* of these powers, he sees their *redemption*.

What would happen if the Christian church could get her mind around this claim of Paul—that all powers, all structures, all institutions, all systems can be redeemed—indeed, that it is God's plan to bring everything into harmony of His love in Jesus Christ?

THE MYSTERY REVEALED IN PRAYER

14 For this reason I bow my knees to the Father of our Lord Jesus Christ, 15 from whom the whole family in heaven and earth is named, 16 that He would grant you, according to the riches of His glory, to be strengthened with might through His Spirit in the inner man, 17 that Christ may dwell in your hearts through faith; that you, being rooted and grounded in love, 18 may be able to comprehend with all the saints what is the width and length and depth and height— 19 to know the love of Christ which passes knowledge; that you may be filled with all the fullness of God.

—Ephesians 3:14–19

Paul now returns specifically to his prayer. He has set the prayer in the context of the mystery of God which is Jesus Christ. Here is theology on its knees.

Paul is very specific in the petitions of His intercession. Some see them as three petitions, some as four, some as six, according to the way they understand or interpret the participial clauses in verses 16–19. The number is not important if we appropriate the fact that we may *realize* the mystery of God in prayer. It is convenient to use the introductory word "that" to designate four petitions, and in examining them to get the full impact of Paul's intercession.

Strength in the Inner Man

This is the first petition: *"that He would grant you . . . to be strengthened with might through His Spirit in the inner man"* (v. 16).

The mystery of life baffles us; the mastery of life eludes us. Prayer is the answer for both dilemmas. In prayer we commune with God who gives us light to illumine the mystery, and power to become masterful in our living.

As I lead retreats, preach, and teach at conferences and seminars across the nation, I come in touch with thousands of people.

Because my time with these persons is limited, I have sought to discipline myself to be especially attentive in every encounter—to listen with my eyes and my heart, as well as my ears.

Often an especially sensitive soul can be identified in a group. I can almost feel the vibrations emanating from the person and something in me resonates and I know that what Buber called an "I-Thou" dynamic is taking place. At one conference I identified such a person but did not have the opportunity to share to any degree, so an exchange of letters followed. In one letter he said,

> My past, however, does not reflect the pain from boyhood so much as from a broken marriage. It has not been easy to have had a close friend marry the woman who had been my wife for seventeen years. To have her live in the same community, work in the same school district and see the children exposed to two distinctly different philosophies of living is not easy.
>
> I don't always like the opportunities that are mine to witness to the healing and forgiving Love Christ makes available to me. *The Love that is for my brokenness, however, when I let it, does heal.*
>
> *Yes, and even my ego is in constant need of healing.*

The writer of those words knows the meaning of being strengthened with might in the inner man.

"The inner man" is an expression used by Paul in two other passages, Romans 7:21 and 2 Corinthians 4:11. "For I delight in the law of God, *in my inmost self,*" is the Romans text and is in the setting of Paul's analyzing the experience of the person who is living under the law, torn between his mind and his impulses. Thus "my inward self" may be synonymous with the "I" who wants to do good but does evil. The Corinthians passage is a better parallel to the present use in Ephesians: "Though our outward man perish, yet the *inward man* is renewed day by day." Paul conceives human nature as composed of two elements: (1) the flesh, which is an encompassing term, not merely for the body, but for all the impulses and activities of our earthly lives; and (2) the inner man, or "mind," where the true personality resides. It is the inner self that may be continually renewed and strengthened.

The Indwelling Christ

"That Christ may dwell in your hearts through faith" (v. 17) is Paul's second petition. And this is the lodestar of Paul's theology—

that a person may be "in Christ" and thus live in the Spirit and in the power of the living Lord who indwells.

I remember vividly a morning spent with Dr. James Stewart, the remarkable Scottish preacher and scholar whose book *A Man in Christ* remains a landmark in the interpretation of Paul. This book had fired my faith and I wanted to talk with Dr. Stewart about prayer and the indwelling Christ. I had developed a working understanding of prayer as "recognizing and exercising the indwelling Christ." Dr. Stewart confirmed the direction of my understanding and talked in a moving way about prayer keeping us *in touch with God who at every instant is present.* With a twinkle in his eyes that reflected his brilliant mind and lively faith, he said, "The eternal lives in every instance—you must receive it. And I am sure that at any instant in the day God may be present in us as the living Christ."

In *A Man in Christ,* Stewart describes the new orientation and direction of the person in Christ. The person in Christ is "looking to Jesus" (Heb. 12:2). That means three things, says Dr. Stewart. "First, the sinner is now looking, not inwards, but outwards—trusting not to any merit in himself, but to something outside of himself altogether, the grace and love of an entirely trustworthy God. It means, second, that he is looking not downwards, but upwards, not to sin's alluring shame, but up to the beauty and purity of Christ. It means, third, that he is looking, not backwards, but forwards 'forgetting those things which are behind, and reaching forth unto those things which are before' (Phil. 3:13)."

It is often impossible to distinguish between the Spirit and the indwelling Christ in Paul's thought. I doubt seriously if there was any conscious or clear distinction in Paul's mind—especially when he reflected on experience. Christ the Lord was enthroned in heaven, but He was also an inward, abiding presence. So in the first petition Paul can say *"by His Spirit in the inner man,"* and move without any hesitancy in the second petition to a focus on *"the indwelling Christ."* Union with Christ and possession of the Spirit means the same and is effected by faith.

What matters supremely is that Christ may dwell in our hearts by faith, and when He does we get a new orientation for life. We may not become immediately unentangled from our sins, the weary road back home from the far country may yet be a long and painful one, the marks of our sojourn as prodigals in the far country may still be upon us—and some of the marks we may carry to our graves—but our faces are steel—set in a new direction. Christ is drawing us home. But not only drawing us home—He is remaking us after His image that we might be happy "as sons" at home.

The Boundless Dimensions of Christ's Love

This is Paul's third petition: "*That you, being rooted and grounded in love, may be able to comprehend with all the saints what is the width and length and depth and height—to know the love of Christ which passes knowledge*" (vv. 17–19). The wording of this petition is longer than the others because Paul feels the need to add some explanatory words and descriptive terms to "*the love of Christ.*"

Seeking to talk about something infinitely great, he resorts to dimensions of measurement. But he leaves the terms hanging in air. He would have completed them, if he could. But, instead, as if desperate for words, he adds the phrase which means far more than it apparently says: to know the love of Christ "*which passes knowledge.*"

Paul is not saying that the love of Christ cannot be known. He was contending against the undue exaltation of knowledge for its own sake on the part of the Greeks. He is saying that this love of Christ is far beyond the rational limits of intellect or theory. This is experiential knowing, intuitive and practical.

Paul had confronted this problem with the Corinthians in his first epistle to them. He praised them for their "zeal for knowledge." If Christianity were only a matter of knowing, the Corinthians would have had no need of a teacher. But it was far more than that, so as he dealt with one question after another, he pointed them to a "more excellent way." Love is more than knowledge, and true knowledge is unattainable without love. Knowledge of God is grounded in love. "Every one who loves is born of God, and knows God. He who does not love does not know God; for God is love" (1 John 4:7, 8).

Paul saw the Cross as the supreme revelation of love, and this is the love he wanted his readers to know—boundless love, going even to the limits of crucifixion. The marvel of it is overwhelming—that the sinless One would gladly endure the shame and agony of the Cross for miserable sinners. That is the reason Paul could not finish the description he started. Love so glorious and subduing defies description, for it passes knowledge.

The outstretched arms of Christ on the Cross embrace all humankind, to the ends of the earth and to the ends of time. Bishop Earl Hunt tells a poignant story of how this love impacted and sustained one man. He had a friend who, in his work, often visited a great foundry. A keen observer of persons, he always studied the workmen who labored there. One man, a furnace-tender, always fascinated him. The bones and muscles of this laborer were those of a veritable giant. His face was as strong as granite, his hands as big as hams. It was a striking sight to see him work with his shovel and the coal—huge muscles rippling in unbroken rhythm, face florid with heated blood, and pools of perspiration glistening on his bare skin as the glow from the furnace played across his body. He was rough, uncouth, a man of brawn more than brain. "Once my friend saw him stagger, almost overcome with the intense heat of the fires," said Bishop Hunt. "He looked weary, ill, nearly beaten. But he regained his footing, stepped aside into the cooler shadows, lifted his goggles, and passed a great blackened hand in gentle reverence over something hanging around his neck. It seemed to strengthen him; his strained features relaxed; and in a moment he was back on the job. Curious to know what had happened in that brief respite, my friend peered more closely and discovered that the something around the big workman's neck was a tiny golden crucifix suspended on a short chain. It looked strange against its background of hot, damp flesh. But it did something for this giant of a man with his furnace and fires to have that tiny likeness of the Christ on the job with him. He could touch it and brush weariness aside. It was a fountain of refreshment and strength for him."[2]

Love and sacrifice go together, so Paul would see the Cross as the deed of boundless, infinite love.

This is the penultimate climax of this epistle, the ultimate being the next petition we will consider. The divine mystery is Christ, and here Paul makes it clear that he is not dwelling on an incomprehensible metaphysical plane, nor is he exalting "knowledge" as did the gnostics. The mystery now becomes one with the love of Christ. To know this is to know what is deepest and most characteristic of the nature and purpose of God.

The lofty heights to which this prayer of Paul rises may so fill our minds and hearts with ecstasy that we pass over a phrase that at first glance is insignificant: *"with all the saints"* (v. 18). In the quoting of this passage the phrase is often omitted as unimportant. Not so! Great meaning is here, and all that Paul is driving at in terms of "knowledge" of the mystery is supported by it: *"That you, being rooted and grounded in love, may be able to comprehend with all the saints . . . to know the love of Christ"* (vv. 17–19).

The value placed on knowledge in the Greek church sometimes resulted in arrogance and aloofness. In Paul's later days, small groups of intellectual converts became exclusive, preferring to worship by themselves. Paul countered that. Knowledge that is of Christ—true knowledge—can never lead to fancied superiority. In fact, any knowledge that leads thus is fatal to true knowledge.

A second factor here is that the more persons of faith are united in fellowship with other persons of faith, the more they enter into the fellowship with God. And there is a third factor: love is known best not by isolated contemplation, but by being experienced in community. A fourth factor: the boundless dimensions of the love of Christ—its width, length, and depth—are such that the combined experience of all Christians is essential to comprehend it.

The Fullness of God

The ravishing climax of Paul's intercession, and the ultimate climax of this letter, is in his final petition: *"that you may be filled with all the fullness of God"* (v. 19).

Halford Luccock, one of the most imaginative preachers of the twentieth century, remembered a marvelous phrase from Lytton Strachey's book *Eminent Victorians:*

> In writing about General Gordon, Strachey says, "The Sunday before General Gordon started for the Sudan, he drove around London to a number of churches to take Communion as many times as possible, 'In order,' he said, 'to start thus brim full of God.' Would six Communions in one day supply more of God than one Communion? Hardly. But to begin every day and every enterprise "brim full of God."[3]

Wouldn't that be something—to begin every day and every enterprise "brim full of God"! It is possible, and Paul prays thus—that we be filled with all the fullness of God. Why is it that we barely, if at all, get beyond the passion and death of Jesus? Why do we hang back, refusing to move on to Resurrection and Pentecost? Read the New Testament. Christians are promised *fire,* not a feeble flicker; *light,* blazing, not dim—like that of a city set upon a hill; *joy,* not momentary happiness, abiding joy which flows from the satisfaction of our hungering and thirsting for God; radiant excitement like that of a man finding a treasure hidden in the field.

"Filled with all the fullness of God"—unbelievable, to our natural minds, but believe it we must! Again, we must not get earthbound and language-bound. Paul broke the barriers, but the heights were still beyond him. Of course we cannot contain God's fullness. The creature, even the creature redeemed by Christ and given a glorious liberty, remains a creature. The Creator remains Lord, and the line between creature and Creator are never completely blotted out. Though we cannot contain God's fullness, we can receive it to the full measure of our capacity and to the degree of our yieldedness. This is what it means to be Spirit-filled or baptized with or in the Spirit: to have a relationship with God that is so yielded to Him that He comes to us and dwells with us in intimacy and power, so that we can experience in life all the things Jesus promised the Holy Spirit would do for believers.

DOXOLOGY

20 Now to Him who is able to do exceedingly abundantly above all that we ask or think, according to the power that works in us, 21 to Him be glory in the church by Christ Jesus to all generations, forever and ever. Amen.
—*Ephesians 3:20–21*

It is Paul's practice to offer ascriptions of praise to God to mark the great division of his epistles. More appropriate, perhaps, than any other is this great doxology with which he closes his prayer. He has declared the mystery—the glory of God, fully revealed in Jesus, to be appropriated by the whole church, and to be lived out in the life of every believer so that the whole cosmos may be brought into the harmonious orbit of Christ's love.

He has prayed that God will bestow blessings that transcend our knowledge, and he is confident that these blessings will be granted, for God is love, and *"He is able."*

I doubt if I will ever forget a sermon Dr. John Birkbeck, great Scot preacher, editor of the British Edition *The Upper Room* and Director of the Drummond Press, preached in The Upper Room Chapel, in Nashville, Tennessee. He took this doxology and sang it out with the crescendoing cadences of great Scot preaching.

He is able!
He is able to do!
He is able to do exceeding abundantly!

He is able to do exceeding abundantly above all that we ask or think!

And then he developed his sermon on the power that is available to us by using an acrostic of the word *able*.

Almighty—
Boundless—
Limitless—
Everlasting . . . Power.
Paul would have liked that elaboration of his doxology, and I certainly cannot do better.

NOTES

1. Stewart, *A Man in Christ*, p. 257.

2. Earl G. Hunt, Jr., *I Have Believed: A Bishop Talks about His Faith* (Nashville: The Upper Room, 1980).

3. Halford E. Luccock, *The Power of His Name*, p. 105.

CHAPTER FOUR—THE CHURCH: UNITED IN CHRIST, PROPELLED BY HOPE, EQUIPPED FOR MINISTRY

EPHESIANS 4:1–16

Scripture Outline

Walk Worthy of Your Calling (4:1–6)

Be Equipped for Ministry (4:7–12)

Grow Up in Christ (4:13–16)

For Paul there was always a harmony between doctrine and ethics. Faith was not isolated from practice. Daily conduct always had its footing in doctrine. How one acted grew out of what one believed. Thus justification and sanctification is the double phenomenon of the Good News.

As is often the case, Paul has in Ephesians what may be called a doctrinal section and a practical section. Such was the case with Romans (chs. 1—11, doctrine; 12—46, practical) and Galatians (chs. 1—4, doctrine; 5—6, practical). With chapter 4 of Ephesians he moves to its practical section. Although the first three chapters are in liturgical form, breathed out of the spirit of devotion and prayer, they are an exposition of an expansive doctrine of God's ultimate purpose in creation, the exaltation of Christ, and the church as the initial and primary stage in the accomplishment of God's grand design to *"gather together in one all things in Christ."* Thus these chapters are the teaching, or doctrinal section, and with chapters 4—6 we move from exultation and revelation of doctrine in the setting of prayer to the development of the outgrowth of these meanings in practice.

All of the last three chapters, however, are not given over to the practical. In fact, perhaps more than the other letters, this practical section is rich in new aspects of doctrine, and the ethical instructions are subordinated to the theme so powerfully stated in the first three chapters.

Handley C. G. Moule, in his *Ephesian Studies* (published at the turn of the century, but still a rich mine of sparkling truth and inspiration for the modern reader) captioned the last three chapters, "Holy Results of Heavenly Blessing."

WALK WORTHY OF YOUR CALLING

4:1 I, therefore, the prisoner of the Lord, beseech you to walk worthy of the calling with which you were called, ² with all lowliness and gentleness, with longsuffering, bearing with one another in love, ³ endeavoring to keep the unity of the Spirit in the bond of peace. ⁴ There is one body and one Spirit, just as you were called in one hope of your calling; ⁵ one Lord, one faith, one baptism; ⁶ one God and Father of all, who is above all, and through all, and in you all.

—Ephesians 4:1–6

Paul identifies himself again as *"the prisoner of the Lord"* (v. 1). The RSV says "for" the Lord. As we indicated previously, this identification is not alone metaphorical; it is actual. Yet, the metaphorical meaning is present, too. The phrase, when translated "prisoner *in* the Lord," is an expression of the mystical union captured in Paul's characteristic phrase "in Christ." The truth here is that even in prison the bond of fellowship with Christ holds strong.

The Source

Paul uses one of his favorite metaphors here, repeating it three times. *"Walk worthy of [your] calling"* (4:1); *"walk in love"* (5:2); *"walk as children of light"* (5:8); *"walk . . . not as fools but as wise"* (5:15). There is a sermon there for any preacher, a lesson for any teacher, a truth for any seeker. Christianity is a way to walk.

The humble word *"therefore,"* a mere adverb and conjunction, has real meaning. Here is symbolized in a single word one big difference between Christianity and other religions. Our ethic is not a demand laid upon us, to which we seek to respond only out of the resources of our lives, and the performance of which makes us acceptable to God. In Christianity we do not begin with moral demands, nor do we envision a God whose attention we may get by religious rite or ritual. We know no God whom we must somehow find, or to whom we must somehow by strain and struggle arrive. Ours is a seeking God who has found us. He acts in our behalf. We are justified by grace through faith, not by our effort or merit.

Paul has told that story of grace—the drama of salvation—and now can say *"therefore."* It is after we know that *"by grace [we] have been saved"* (2:5) that we can be *"worthy of our calling."* It is out of His love that we can walk in love. Because He has delivered us from darkness, we *"can walk as children of light."* He has saved us from the devices of our own futile and finite minds, *therefore* we can walk *"not as fools but wise."*

John Wesley enunciated a great doctrine of the Christian faith: "prevenient grace." More than a doctrine, it is an experience. It means God's lovingkindness, His self-giving, His going before us—drawing us on and preparing the way. Our walk is not in the strength of our own might or in the illumination of our own wisdom. It is a "therefore" walk. Our being and doing as Christians are expressions of what God in Christ has been and done for us.

The Signs

Ours is a *calling* and that translation is perhaps the most accurate. I still like the KJV "Walk worthy of the *vocation* wherewith ye are called." For me "vocation" has a more permanent ring to it. Our "calling" is not for a season; it is not something we hear today which may fade or grow faint tomorrow. We are engaged for life. This is our vocation. Two words, "laity" *(laos)* and "apostolate," which we use in the Christian church, add meaning to our calling. All Christians are the laity, "the whole people of God," and are a part of the apostolate, those to whom the ministry of Christ is committed. Our lives are to be a vocation for Christ, and we should be constantly asking, "What apostolic action today will reflect my vocation?"

Paul now records the "signs" that reflect the worthiness of our calling.

1. *Humility, "with all lowliness"* (v. 2). The word translated here as lowliness, *tapeinophrosyne,* was actually coined by the Christian faith, and means humility. In the Greek world there was no word that could communicate what Christians knew was a sure "sign" of their vocation. The Greek adjective from which this uniquely Christian word was compounded always connoted cringing servility, cowering slavishness.

193

Before Jesus, humility was seen as an ignoble quality. Since Jesus, because He personified the meaning, it is set at the forefront of Christian witness. How we need to recover it. A number of years ago the *Wall Street Journal* carried a story of how the movie industry is plagued by pride and rampaging egos. The question is how to resolve which star gets top billing, whose name appears first and in what size letters.

"Months of delicate negotiation are sometimes required to deal with what one writer calls a 'conceit of the industry.' To satisfy two superstars, a studio created two sets of screen titles and two sets of ads with one star named first in each. Then they had to run each ad 50% of the time. In another situation this kind of bizarre compromise was made. A studio placed one star's name on the left (the normal spot for top billing), while the other star's name on the right appeared *a half line higher.* When pictures of both stars were used in ads, again one was placed to the left, while the other on the right was placed slightly higher."

As outrageous as that "conceit of the industry" may appear, the madness for status is epidemic. We need to hear Jesus' word, "Except ye be converted, and become as little children, ye shall not enter into the kingdom of heaven. Whosoever therefore shall humble himself as this little child, the same is greatest in the kingdom of heaven" (Matt. 18:3–4, KJV). Conversion and humility belong together, and to those who are converted and become humble belong the kingdom. (See commentary on Col. 2:8–12.)

2. *Gentleness.* This word is often translated "meekness" and is a twin word to humility. It has nothing to do with weakness. It is strength that knows who it is. It is submission in relation to others for the sake of Christ.

The cross and the basin and towel are the signs of meekness—the cross, submission; the basin and towel, service. Bernard of Clairvaux said, "Learn the lesson that, if you are to do the work of a prophet, what you need is not a scepter but a hoe." Prophets are meek. They know who they are—submissive servants for Christ's sake.

The argument that arose among the disciples in the Upper Room at the Last Supper was over which of them was the greatest (Luke 9:46). Isn't it true that most of the time when there is trouble over who is the greatest, there is trouble over who is the least? Most of us know we will not be the greatest, but we do not want to be least.

Meekness is a willingness to be least if obedience to God requires it. (See commentary on Gal. 5:23.)

3. *Longsuffering.* This word is often translated "patience" as in this case in the RSV and NEB. It describes a spirit, of never giving in or never giving up; a spirit of persistence which sees defeat as a temporary, not final, setback, thus not to be deterred by discouragement and disappointment.

Another more characteristic meaning literally is "a long temper" and thus has to do with relationships. Chrysostom saw it as the spirit of one who has the power to take revenge, but never does. (See commentary on Gal. 5:22.)

4. *Love.* The fourth "sign" of our vocation is love—*"bearing with one another in love."* Humility, meekness, and patience are all dimensions of love. Love is the inclusive Christian virtue. But more than a virtue, it is the dynamic that helps us keep going on our Christian walk.

In 1975 a nine-year-old girl, Marcia Trimble, was murdered in our city, Nashville, Tennessee. The ghastly deed shocked and angered our community, yet all were amazed at the way her parents lived through the ordeal, the strength they exhibited which they attributed to their Christian faith.

Over four years later a person was arrested as the murderer and the police believed the mystery of the killing solved. In the drama of this arrest, one wondered about the response of the parents. What were they feeling? How would they respond? The painful wounds of the loss of a child would be opened again by the ensuing trial. In a newspaper interview it was reported that despite her love for her daughter and the loss and pain she and her family suffered, Mrs. Trimble was not bitter toward the young man police believed had strangled Marcia. "That boy is not guilty until a jury decides that he is," she said. "And I think this community owes it to him to consider him innocent until a jury changes that."

What about her belief in the death penalty? "I really don't know how I feel. . . . I don't think it has anything to do with this case and I am not so sure it is a deterrent to crime. Killing someone certainly wouldn't bring Marcia back, what good would it do anyone?"

What sort of person can make assertions like this in the teeth of such deep personal loss and pain? She answered that. "People have called me a religious nut and a fanatic but I am just a housewife who has suffered and God helped me bear something that I couldn't myself. I have no hatred for Marcia's killer, instead I think I have learned through this how much you can love."[1]

A nut you are not, Mrs. Trimble; a fanatic you may be—but only in the sense of those in whose train you follow, about whom it was said, "My, how these Christians love." It is the crowning sign of our Christian walk—love.

5. *Peace.* The "signs" of our Christian vocation that Paul insisted on result in peace. In fact, he made his case for them here because he is talking about Christian community, the church. Without humility, meekness, longsuffering, and love there can be no real community.

Note what may not be obvious. Each of the previous four virtues depends upon getting self out of the center, and that is what community is dependent upon. That is also what makes for peace. Within community, every member must be willing to give up his own self-interest for the common good. As long as *my* feelings, *my* prestige, *my* interests are the things that matter, there can be no peace. But humble, meek, patient, loving people have mastered the "my," and are committed to "our."

Peace within the community of faith is no mere formal one, imposed and maintained by authority. It is a peace that flows from its members being at peace with each other because they are bound together by love.

The Shape

The *source* of our calling is Christ Himself: we act out of response to His loving action toward us. The *signs* of our vocation are humility, meekness, longsuffering, love, and peace. The *shape* of our vocation is unity—the *unity of the Spirit. "There is one body and one Spirit, just as you were called in one hope of your calling; one Lord, one faith, one baptism; one God and Father of all, who is above all, and through all, and in you all"* (Eph. 4:4–6).

Just as the "fellowship of the Spirit" is the fellowship created *by* the Spirit, the "unity of the Spirit" is the unity which the Spirit creates. It requires human diligence to *maintain* it, but the Spirit creates it.

One, one, one—the word is used seven times in verses 4–6. This sevenfold formula relates the unity of the church to the unity of Christ and God.

The church is one body, and the conditions for that oneness are here fully stated: *"one hope of your calling; one Lord, one faith, one baptism."*

1. *"One hope of your calling."* We cannot claim to be members of one body unless we are prepared to acknowledge, affirm, and express our unity with all other members. This unity within the body is a symbol of unity of all mankind and all creation.

The Taizé Community in France seeks to be this visible sign in a special way. Brother Roger, the founder and leader of the community, has traveled regularly to some of the forgotten corners of the earth, to live with some of the forgotten people—often the poorest of the poor—as a witness of solidarity. In 1977, he spent some weeks in Asia living in different areas. On the China Sea, he and some of the brothers from the community lived for awhile with people housed in junks and shacks built on pilings. They shared their life, on the water, under the same conditions. From that setting he wrote an open letter on December 7, a portion of which vibrates with the singing notes of Ephesians: the unity of the church, and of the whole universe *in Christ.*

> Surrounded by a Chinese population we have been seized by a conviction; every creature, wherever he or she may be, is inhabited by the Spirit of God. Christ is so intimately bound up with mankind that wherever there is a human being, he is present. Whether recognized or not, Christ accompanies every human being. That communion which is the Church has, it is true, visible contours, the contours of the Body of Christ. But, at the same time, it is so much more extensive than the human mind can imagine: in the heart of God, the Church is as vast as humanity itself.
>
> Once again in Asia, we have been made aware how necessary it is that the Church, devoid of powerful means and without the support of human efficiency, be a source and become a ferment of friendship for all humanity. Spread across the world, often hidden among the masses of those with no knowledge of Christ, these small places of sharing are a leaven in the dough which raises the whole and cracks the hardened crust. Their mere presence, with no apparent efficacy, will beget a world of communion for the entire human family.

The one hope of our calling, or better, the one hope inspired and energized by our calling, is the bringing of all persons and the whole universe to unity in Christ Jesus. When a local congregation gets bogged down in the minutiae of heating bills, whether to paint or not to paint the fellowship hall and what color, whether it is proper for youth to sing in the choir dressed in their jeans (boys and girls alike), what kinds of musical instruments are proper for worship in the sanctuary, what is the right mode of baptism and who is qualified to serve Holy Communion, it would be well to have its mind blown by reading this vision of the church in Ephesians. The hope of that high calling would give us a new basis for all our priorities, and a guide for the investment of our energies.

2. *"One Lord, one faith, one baptism."* This is a well-known verse of Scripture, quoted often in support of ecumenical efforts, and also taken as the three essentials on which all Christians are to agree. We worship the same Lord, hold the same faith, and practice baptism as a "sign" of our belonging. All this may be true, but it is doubtful if this was Paul's intention. It is difficult to think that he would mention baptism and not the Lord's Supper if he was seeking to give us the basics on which we were to agree.

The fact is that the whole sentence expresses one fundamental: we all belong to the Lord; faith is the inward disposition of the heart, and baptism is the outward sign by which we are united in one Lord. The Shema of Deuteronomy 6:4, "Hear, O Israel: the Lord our God, the Lord is one," is called to mind by verse 6: *"One God and Father of all.* "This is something more than verse 5; it is the ultimate ground of all unity. The one God and Father of all is *"above all, and through all, and in you all."*

Again it is important to note what may not be obvious. God the Father is sovereign in the universe, but that is not the heart of this affirmation; this has to do with God's relation to His people. That relation is as E. F. Scott has summarized. All Christians are united because "God is *over* them all; His presence *pervades* the church to which they belong; He dwells *within* their very hearts."[2] This, then, is a threefold phrase, each clause emphasizing the same truth: our life is inseparably bound up with God our Father.

BE EQUIPPED FOR MINISTRY

7 But to each one of us grace was given according to the measure of Christ's gift. 8 Therefore He says:
"When He ascended on high,
He led captivity captive,
And gave gifts to men."

[9] (Now this, "*He ascended*"—what does it mean but that He also first descended into the lower parts of the earth? [10] He who descended is also the One who ascended far above all the heavens, that He might fill all things.)

[11] And He Himself gave some to be apostles, some prophets, some evangelists, and some pastors and teachers,

[12] for the equipping of the saints for the work of ministry, for the edifying of the body of Christ,

—*Ephesians 4:7–12*

Three things stand out clearly.

Each Is Gifted

"*To each one of us grace was given according to the measure of Christ's gift*" (v. 7). Every Christian shares in Christ's bounty. No one is unimportant; thus no one can feel useless and negligible in the life of the church. In the charter of the Church of the Savior, Washington, D.C., this truth is affirmed in a beautiful way. "On the ship of the church there are no passengers; all are members of the crew."

There Is a Variety of Gifts

"*And He Himself gave some to be apostles, some prophets, some evangelists, and some pastors and teachers*" (v. 11).

Paul does not forsake his theme of unity. Unity is not uniformity. Personal uniqueness is not suppressed. Unity comes from ministry—the sharing of the common hope of our calling. A variety of gifts is given, needed gifts befitting every believer, enabling every believer to make his or her own unique contribution to the whole.

From the beginning, at Pentecost, the church has had within it a group set aside for specialized functions. Both Protestant and Catholic churches have had "orders" of ministry ever since. In most cases it is the role of the church to "set apart" those who acknowledge a particular call and who have the "gifts and graces" for specific orders of ministry. It is always to be prayed that the church is God's instrument for the effective expression of those who have been called as "apostles, prophets, evangelists, pastors, and teachers."

This listing of Paul recalls the classification of ministries in 1 Corinthians 12:28. The fact that Paul did not repeat the complete list in 1 Corinthians should not be given too much weight.

Certainly that list was not intended as a complete catalogue of gifts any more than this one defines a complete order of ministry. The listing has an important purpose and leads to a third fact.

The Purpose of Gifts

Each one is gifted; there is a variety of gifts and the purpose of gifts is twofold: to equip the saints for the work of ministry and to edify the church.

Eric Sevareid was one of America's most able and popular news commentators. On his retirement, he was reminiscing about his many years as a news correspondent and commentator in the nation's capitol. He talked of another commentator who, he said, knew everyone worth knowing: the president, the diplomats, the senators, the president's cabinet, key bureaucrats, and the socially elite. He had the contacts; he was stuffed with information. There was only one problem, Sevareid said; he never used it; "He forgot what he was here for."

That is a parable for the church. Paul, even in the midst of his glorious vision of the church would not let us forget what it is all about: *"for the equipping of the saints for the work of ministry, for the edifying of the body of Christ"* (v. 12). The NKJV puts a comma after saints; the RSV does the same, using "equipment" rather than "perfecting" of the saints. The meaning is clearer to eliminate the comma as the KJV does. The NEB reads most clearly: "to equip God's people for work in his service."

The Roman Catholic Church, with the most clearly defined and particularized orders of ministry—and historically the most rigid in terms of who can function and how—is breaking out of outmoded forms, and a revival of the *laos,* the whole people of God, is taking place. In the constitution of the Roman Catholic Church which came from the Second Vatican Council is this word reminiscent of Ephesians 1:11–12: "And if by the will of Christ some are made teachers, pastors and dispensers of mysteries on behalf of others, yet all share a true equality with regard to dignity and to the activity common to all the faithful for the building of the body of Christ."[3]

"For building up the body of Christ"—that is the second purpose of gifts. In a day when the Holy Spirit seems especially active, and persons are seeking, receiving, and acknowledging greater portions of His power, there is a danger of individualization of gifts and a temptation to "spiritual pride." There is also the possibility that persons experiencing some dimensions of the Spirit's work "outside the church," in informal gatherings, interdenominational fellowships,

prayer meetings, parachurch movements, will disparage the local church to which they belong because they do not see the Spirit vividly at work there. The error is that they do not get beyond surface demonstrations, and are looking for the most dramatic signs of the Spirit's gifts. Also, some congregations are not open to and seeking the gifts of the Spirit for ministry, and are threatened by outward manifestations of the Spirit's power. Thus persons seeking a deeper experience of the Spirit do not feel "at home."

Whatever the situation, the truth is still the same. The Spirit gives gifts to build up the body of Christ. Paul dealt with the whole matter of the Spirit's gifts in chapters 12—14 of 1 Corinthians. There was great dissension and division in the church over the way people were using their gifts. In 1 Corinthians 14, Paul is dealing with one primary cause of controversy, speaking in tongues, and he gives perspective with this challenging word' "Since you are eager for manifestations of the Spirit, strive to excel in building up the church" (1 Cor. 14:12, RSV).

Paul makes no exception: all the Spirit's gifts are to equip us for ministry and to build up the church. The ministry is a replication of Christ as we become like Him as servants. The word "minister" comes to us directly from the Latin. It translates the Greek word *diakonos* meaning "servant." The church is built up not by cultivating the interior life and fellowship of the church alone, but by calling and training members to be servants, and thus to do their part in Christ's mission to the world.

GROW UP IN CHRIST

[13] till we all come to the unity of the faith and of the knowledge of the Son of God, to a perfect man, to the measure of the stature of the fullness of Christ; [14] that we should no longer be children, tossed to and fro and carried about with every wind of doctrine, by the trickery of men, in the cunning craftiness of deceitful plotting, [15] but, speaking the truth in love, may grow up in all things into Him who is the head— Christ— [16] from whom the whole body, joined and knit together by what every joint supplies, according to the effective working by which every part does its share, causes growth of the body for the edifying of itself in love.

—*Ephesians 4:13–16*

We broke the previous section in the middle of a sentence. How else could we? Verses 12–16 are all one long sentence, packed with powerful truth, and radiating with vivid images. Do not miss the connection, though we are considering the passage in two sections. Verse 13 begins with the conjunction "till" which adds with force something that cannot be separated from what has gone before.

In verse 3 of this chapter, Paul has talked about unity as a possession to be *kept;* here in verse 13 it is a goal toward which we strive. This is not contradictory, but complementary. Unity is a gift of the Spirit, but that which the Spirit gives must be appropriated in fullness and perfected by our own commitment, will, and effort.

So Paul calls us to *"grow up in all things into Him who is the head—Christ"* (v. 15).

1. *We are to mature* **in Christ.** Growth is the dynamic movement of our lives.

The RSV and NEB have "mature manhood" instead of *"perfect man"* in verse 18. This is easier to grasp. Perfection carries a picture of completion when what is called for is a process of growing *"to the measure of the stature of the fullness of Christ"* (v. 13). This *"new man"* (2:15) has been created in Christ, but a long path of growth stretches out before him.

The opposite of maturity is infantile gullibility. An adult, well-founded fidelity to the gospel, to Christ Himself is required. There is a sense in which our faith and life-stance is to be childlike, but this does not rob Paul's metaphor of its meaning. The metaphor of children is clear in relation to its opposite, mature manhood. The Christian is to grow out of a flighty, unsettled, gullible temperament into maturity.

The mixing of metaphors here makes the image more graphic, despite the incongruity. The added metaphor is that of a boat bobbing up and down, veering here and there, controlled and tossed about by changing and erratic winds. Young children tend to believe everything they are told, and rudderless boats, or boats without someone at the helm, tend to go wherever the wind takes them. Christians are to be more mature, wiser, and more perceptive in order to recognize and withstand the *cunning craftiness* of those who would deceive. Of course this is possible only as our minds and hearts are formed *in* Christ.

2. *We are to speak the truth in love.* When Paul talks of speaking the truth in love, he means more than frankness of speech tempered by love. He is talking about the whole inward and outward dispositions of persons being integrated in Christ. So we have the capacity to

apprehend the truth, the desire and power to live the truth, so that all that we are and do will be truth in love. We are growing *"up in all things into Him who is the Head—Christ*—as we are integrated in our whole being around His Lordship in our lives.

Paul brings Ephesians 4:1–16 to a climactic summary in verse 16. He repeats cryptically a lot of what has already been said, but in doing so, gives a picture of the church as a dynamic growing organism, a body whose head is Christ. Every member of the body, however insignificant it may appear, has something to contribute to the well-being of the whole. Every part does its share, and as it does, causes growth to the body for the edifying of itself in love.

We do not need to try to analyze the image too closely. However we view it, Christ is the center around which the organism (church) functions, and from which life and power are derived, and He is the *head* in the sense of authority, guidance, and direction. It is in that sense that we considered this section under the chapter title "The Church: United in Christ, Propelled by Hope, Equipped for Ministry."

Notes

1. *The Tennessean,* August 29, 1979.

2. Scott Ernest Findlay, *The Epistles of Paul to the Colossians, to Philemon, and to the Ephesians, The Moffatt New Testament Commentary* (New York: R. R. Smith, 1930), p. 205.

3. *The Teaching of the Second Vatican Council* (Newman Press, 1966), p. 121.

CHAPTER FIVE—THE WALK OF NEW PERSONS

EPHESIANS 4:17—5:21

Scripture Outline

Walk in Newness of Life (4:17–24)

Some Signs of Newness of Life (4:25–32)

The Christian Walk (5:1–21)

The first sixteen verses of chapter four have acted as a transition into the "practical" section of Ephesians. With verse 17 Paul becomes as direct as one can get, laying down demands of the Christian life, listing specific codes of conduct. In approaching this section (4:17—5:21) we must not forget the first three chapters. If we do, we may see the Christian faith as a nag and a fuss and a whine— a lot of rules and regulations, shoulds and oughts, but little joy. Likewise, though, to take only chapters 1—3 without the practical demands of chapters 4—6 may tempt us to "cheap grace," soft religion without any muscle of responsibility and demand for moral conduct and commitment to righteousness.

The living and doing of the gospel are present in Ephesians— the invitation and the imperative. You are a child of God; now become a child of God. You are a new person in Christ; grow up into that new person. We affirm God's action; that affirmation is an assignment of our task. Faith and response go together. The outgoing of God to persons is grace; the outgoing of persons to God is faith. And the result of that dynamic encounter and relationship is a life of love with deliberate intention to be and do all God requires us to be and do. God takes the initiative, but that movement is short-circuited in our own lives unless we respond.

Paul uses the word "walk" six times in this epistle. It is an action word, encompassing the whole of our lives, the way we think and relate, behave and respond—the way we act publicly as well as the way we "appear" to others.

The "walk of a Christian" is Paul's way of talking about the daily conduct, the morality, the distinctive marks of those who are seeking to grow up in Christ.

WALK IN NEWNESS OF LIFE

17 This I say, therefore, and testify in the Lord, that you should no longer walk as the rest of the Gentiles walk, in the futility of their mind, 18 having their understanding darkened, being alienated from the life of God, because of the ignorance that is in them, because of the blindness of their heart; 19 who, being past feeling, have given themselves over to lewdness, to work all uncleanness with greediness.

20 But you have not so learned Christ, 21 if indeed you have heard Him and have been taught by Him, as the truth is in Jesus: 22 that you put off, concerning your former conduct, the old man which grows corrupt according to the deceitful lusts, 23 and be renewed in the spirit of your mind, 24 and that you put on the new man which was created according to God, in true righteousness and holiness.

—*Ephesians 4:17–24*

Sanctification

The word "sanctification" has been placed on an almost forgotten shelf of the vocabulary of the church. There has been a good and necessary deemphasis of the "do's" and "don't's" of Christianity. Destructive, devastating "social sins" have screamed so loudly in their ravaging evil impact on humanity that the church had to confess her sin of uninvolvement, insensitivity, and apathy, and to invest her energy in the arena of social concern and change. But prophetic ministry and commitment to social justice with Christian integrity can never leave out personal morality. The same blazing light of judgment that condemns social immorality illumines and condemns personal immorality. There is a difference between *personal* and *private*. The Christian religion is personal, but not private. Our sins may be personal, but I find it impossible to imagine any personal sin that does not boil over and poison other relationships.

Sanctification, the misused and forgotten word in the Christian vocabulary, has to do with holiness of life—personal but not private holiness. In Protestantism, especially, we have failed to emphasize clearly enough that *regeneration,* the remaking of life into the likeness of Christ, is the natural result of justification. We have been so neurotically careful that we stay with Paul's conviction that we are justified by faith and not by works that we may have missed a monumental aspect of Paul's teaching. Justification carries the transformation of life with it. "Had there been any law," Paul wrote to the Galatians, "which had the power of producing life, righteousness would really have been due to law:" (3:21, Moffatt). That is an illuminating sentence, revealing the apostle's understanding that justification by grace through faith and the recreation of life (or the creation of *new* life) are virtually synonymous.

Justification creates a new creature, with a new heart, in a new world. The new world is a new realm into which the Christian enters, moving out of the strictures and controls of the powers in the domain of flesh. Thus Paul's word, *"you should no longer walk as the rest of the Gentiles walk"* (v. 17).

The old world is still present, and the temptations and powers of the old world still have a magnetic pull upon us. In most cases most of us may only be "signs" of new life in the midst of deceit and decadence. Brother Roger, and the Taizé community in France of which he is spiritual director, have a challenging understanding of this.

> The time has come to multiply, across the world, places of sharing where struggle and contemplations are closely related in day-to-day living. . . . Those involved in creating such places of sharing will not flee the contradictions of a society which gives rise to inequalities, the pursuit of profit, unbridled consumption, racial segregation, terrorism.
>
> . . . In their struggle for a world of greater justice, they will necessarily come to grips with all these contradictions, sustained by a hidden prayer life, even if at times they are able to share with others nothing but their weakness and their powerlessness.[1]

The personal and the social, the contemplative and the active life flow in and out of each other. Sanctification, life that becomes more and more holy, more and more in the image of Christ, is the walk in newness of life Paul is talking about.

Christ Delivers Us from . . .

Presently in chapters 4 and 5, Paul will extensively catalog debauched and evil attitudes and actions that must be put away from the Christian's life. In this section he makes the big point that Christ delivers us from something to something.

In the *"futility of their mind,"* the pagan Gentiles' understanding had been darkened; their hearts were hardened, *"being past feeling"*; they were alienated from the life of God, so they gave themselves *"to lewdness, to work all uncleanness with greediness."* It would be difficult to make a stronger case, or express it more descriptively. That, says Paul, is what you have been delivered from. Does that sound foreign to your experience, your perception of reality? Does the language sound too archaic to have present-day meaning? Consider this word from a young mother who, through her husband, became hooked on heroin.

> One day, God in His mercy, allowed me to find a "Hook Card" that had the address and phone number of the Los Angeles Teen Center. On the other side, the card said: "Society says, 'Once an addict, always an addict.' But Jesus says, 'I am the way and the truth . . . and the truth shall set you free." Curious to know what all this meant. . . I went to the Teen Challenge Center . . . I was a bitter woman. Mentally, spiritually, and physically sick. No purpose in life. But as I listened to the Gospel of Christ, a glimmer of hope was beamed to my heart. Perhaps there was hope for me. . . . At last, I decided to commit my wasted life to Christ. I asked Him into my heart. And he made me a new creation in Christ Jesus. Old things passed away. All things became new.[2]

Other examples, less dramatic but just as poignant, could be piled high. The language Paul uses is packed with suggestive contemporary meaning.

1. *"Alienated from the life of God."* The long sentence which includes vv. 17, 18, and 19 is rather complicated with descriptive phrases describing descriptive phrases. By the continued and cumulative denial of the truth, understanding is darkened. That is a lesson we have yet to learn. The more we deny truth, the less capable we become in understanding and apprehending truth. Every surrender to temptation *encrusts* the heart (i.e., the will), hardens its sensitivity and narrows the range of

future choice. To reject God *alienates us from the life of God,* thus destroying the source of mental, moral, and spiritual health.

2. *"Being past feeling."* The NEB translates this "dead to all feeling"; Phillips, "stifled their consciences"; and the RSV, "they have become callous." The Greek word is a medical term *(apalgeo)* which suggests another, *apelgekoles,* which implies a paralysis of conscience. Sometimes we have dramatic examples of such insensitivity. A man named Gary systematically kills and buries twenty-eight young men under his house or in his yard in a suburb of Chicago. An Idi Amin systematically decrees the death of thousands of his political enemies in Uganda. Antagonistic forces in Cambodia continue their warfare as millions of people starve, and nations of the world look on with a kind of pitiful and feigned impotence. We seem to have lost the capacity for moral outrage.

There is a less dramatic condition, difficult to diagnose, but epidemic in its devastation—what Karl Helm points to when he speaks of the "serene secularist." Dull in sensitivity and conviction, such persons ask no ultimate questions, and are not even concerned that they are not concerned. We need to be saved from *"being past feeling."*

3. *"To work all uncleanness with greediness."* The result of what has happened to the pagan Gentiles—the hardening of their hearts, the darkening of their hearts, being alienated from the life of God—was that they gave themselves over to lewdness, *"to work all uncleanness with greediness."* That is strong language. Lewdness is the worst excess of evil conduct, passions gone wild, issuing in horrible prevalence of sexual, especially homosexual vice (Rom. 1:24, 26–27)—and all of this in an atmosphere of greediness. The basest passions were flaunted; every kind of impurity in self-indulgence was rampant.

From this, Paul says, you have been delivered. Most readers may think the degree of debauchery too blatant to be an apt description of our time. But that assumption needs questioning. Venereal disease has reached an epidemic level in the United States, ten million cases reported in a recent year. Many, perhaps most, of the one million runaway children in our nation each year are not gathered into the arms of a compassionate society, but are exploited by evil adults for prositution and pornography. Child pornography is a multi-million dollar business. In 1978, in Los Angeles alone, more than 30,000 boys and girls were exploited for child pornography and prostitution.

Reacting to that statistic, Dr. Harold Voth, Senior Psychiatrist of the Menninger Foundation, asks a searing question: "Do you see how these facts reflect what is happening to the American character, to the Spirit of America?"

If what such data suggest about the fabric of our national life seems removed from us, consider that the word "greediness" in this passage is sometimes rendered "covetousness" (Eph. 5:5; Col. 3:5). In the New Testament the word generally has the specific connotation of adultery—covetousness of a neighbor's wife. There is, however, a more general basic meaning. *Pleonexis* (greedy, covetous) is the vice of self-assertion, an unbridled concern for the satisfaction of one's own impulses, ruthless disregard for the rights of others. Maurice Sendak once wrote a story of a pampered dog which is a parable of the vice of *pleonexia,* dressed up in modern terms. The dog had her own pillows, comb and brush, a red wool sweater, two windows to look out of, two bowls to eat from, and a master who loved her. Despite this, she left home, explaining, "I am discontented. I want something I do not have. There must be more to life than having everything."

There are two lessons here. One, when we are greedy, no matter what we have we want more. Christ saves from greed—the greed that runs the gamut of wanting more and more things, more and more recognition, more and more status, to the greed of passion that turns into licentiousness. There is a second lesson in Sendak's story of the dog. "There must be more to life than having everything." There is. So Christ not only delivers us *from,* He delivers us *to.*

Christ Delivers Us to . . .

Paul Tillich, with penetrating insight, diagnosed ours as a negative age characterized by meaninglessness, by guilt, and by death. The point to be made here is that we may have experienced the forgiveness and acceptance of Christ; we may be *justifed,* thus to a marked degree, we may be free from guilt and meaninglessness—even from the threat of death; yet we may still be bound up, tied in knots, functioning at a much lower level as a person than the possibility Christ offers. Christ frees us to something. So Paul called us to *"be renewed in the spirit of your mind, and that you put on the new man which was created according to God, in true righteousness and holiness"* (vv. 23–24).

Christ delivers us to the freedom to be *"a new man which was created according to God."* Too often in thinking about *being*

Christian we become victims of what I call a *slavish consistency*, the sort of thing Paul argued against in Galatians (see commentary on Gal. 5:1).

Jesus does not call us into a slavish consistency. He calls us *from* it. To seek to be a carbon copy of another, however Christian that other might be, is to smother the uniqueness of our own personhood. This is not to say that there are not particular Christian manners, or codes of Christian conduct, or a Christian ethic. Nor is it to say that there are no attitudes and approaches to life that are uniquely Christian. It is to say that we have our own *élan*, our own individual freedom of expression. Christ frees us to live according to the mode that is appropriate to us as persons.

Have you ever noted the way Christ dealt with people? His way with the rich young ruler is completely different from his way with the Samaritan woman at the well. Rather sternly Jesus said to the rich young ruler, "Go, sell your possessions and give to the poor, and come, follow me" (Matt. 19:21, NEB). With the Samaritan woman he was not nearly so stern and direct. He tenderly accepted and carefully led her to a new understanding of her need to fill the gnawing emptiness of her life. Jesus recognized that she was going from one man to another, seeking love and belongingness—but He wasn't condemning. With the warmth and love she so desperately needed, He pointed to a satisfying water of relationship that would quench her deep thirst.

To them both Jesus was seeking to give the personal identity which had been distorted, destroyed, or never discovered. The rich young ruler needed a life task; his success and riches had not brought satisfaction. The Samaritan woman needed to have the vacuum of her life filled; all the men she had known contributed little or nothing to eliminate her feelings of emptiness. Jesus offered them the freedom to be, to cut themselves loose from their enslavement to false selves. This is the way He always related to people—on the basis of the wonder and glory that belongs to each of us as persons.

SOME SIGNS OF NEWNESS OF LIFE

25 Therefore, putting away lying, *"Let each one of you speak truth with his neighbor,"* for we are members of one another. 26 *"Be angry, and do not sin"*: do not let the sun go down on your wrath, 27 nor give place to the devil. 28 Let him who stole steal no longer, but rather let him labor, working with *his* hands what is good, that he may have something to

give him who has need. [29] Let no corrupt word proceed out of your mouth, but what is good for necessary edification, that it may impart grace to the hearers. [30] And do not grieve the Holy Spirit of God, by whom you were sealed for the day of redemption. [31] Let all bitterness, wrath, anger, clamor, and evil speaking be put away from you, with all malice. [32] And be kind to one another, tenderhearted, forgiving one another, even as God in Christ forgave you.

—Ephesians 4:25–32

Paul now gives us some specific directions for living the new life Christ has given us. This involves *putting away* certain things, and beginning to act and relate in certain ways. The new ways of acting and relating are signs of newness of life.

Our Speech

Paul refers to our speech in verses 25, 29, and 31. In the first two instances he sets the positive way of our speaking against the negative. *"Putting away lying, let each one of you speak truth with his neighbor"* (v. 25). *"Let no corrupt word proceed out of your mouth, but what is good for necessary edification, that it may impart grace to the hearers"* (v. 29).

One scholar has written, "Of all deeds, words are the most revealing, the most instantly available, the most freighted with personal significance." The thought that words are deeds is fresh, but not new. In Hebrew, thought, word, and deed are not distinct from one another; indeed word and deed have the same root. To say something was to do something.

Dietrich Bonhoeffer had discovered this, and he witnessed to it in the Flossenberg Prison during World War II where he had been condemned to die. He walked the narrow corridors visiting the cells, speaking to prisoners and encouraging them, laughing and joking with them, reminiscing with them and praying with them. His words were his primary means of ministry. Still his words were deeds. He wrote: "God has put His Word into our mouths in order that it may be communicated to others. The Christian needs another Christian who speaks God's Word to him. He needs that friend again and again and again."

Words are powerful, and Paul calls us to use them as deeds of love, for edification, that they *"may impart grace to the hearers."*

There may be such a thing as "small talk," but even small talk is powerful in the result it may have in some lives. Persons who are hurting, crying out for hope, famishing for some word of affirmation and encouragement, may go from us still crying in their pain and starving in their hunger because we have given them "small talk" when we could have imparted grace by our words. Talk is not cheap; words are powerful.

Our Temper

Verse 26 is a rendering of Psalm 4:4: "Be angry, but sin not; commune with your own hearts on your beds, and be silent."

In this and verse 31 where Paul mentions *"bitterness, wrath, anger, clamor"* and *"malice,"* Paul is talking about our temper. Newness of life is seen in the way we control and express our temper.

There has been a false notion abroad in the church that to have strong feelings and to express those feelings is sinful. Not so. We are created with the capacity to feel. Earlier in this chapter Paul has spoken condemningly of those who are *"past feeling."* We have become less than human when we are dulled and numbed to feelinglessness. Having and expressing feelings is not a sin-issue. What we do with feelings, how we express them, and how our feelings affect others determine Christian action and attitude. So Paul would say, *"Be angry and do not sin"* (v. 26).

Our anger can turn into hatred and malice. If we harbor it, it can become seething bitterness or issue in wrathful action. The impulse toward anger is a natural one. The Christian witness is hampered by thinking that being a Christian precludes angry indignation. But anger is dangerous and must be kept under the restraint of the Spirit of Christ. So Paul cautions, *"do not let the sun go down on your wrath."*

Our Work

Paul calls us to honest labor as a sign of newness of life. *"Let him who stole steal no longer, but rather let him labor, working with his hands what is good, that he may have something to give him who has need"* (4:28).

It is interesting that Paul gives added meaning to our labor. Stealing is selfish and sinful. *Working with our hands,* honest labor, is good, but it can also be sinful. How much of our work is a means to a selfish end. Jesus warned about laboring for plenty and hoarding what we harvest or earn—tearing down our barns and building bigger barns (Luke 12:13–31).

Paul seeks to provide an antidote for that kind of neurotic need for material security. We are to labor in order to *have something to give him who has need* (v. 28). John Chrysostom put this clearly years ago. "The words 'mine' and 'yours' are empty of meaning; they do not express any reality. You are stewards of the goods of the poor, even when you have acquired them through honest labour or by inheritance."

What a challenging sign of newness of life. No more preoccupation with "building bigger barns," accumulating huge estates to leave to our children when we die. No more frantic activity at the expense of what really counts—human tenderness, family love, and togetherness. No more compulsive earning and spending as victims of a consumer society. Guards up against media manipulation that would turn our whole society into a waste heap and each of us into human garbage disposals.

Our labor should have meaning. If meaning is not intrinsic in what we actually do, the way we labor and what we do with the result of our labor can have tremendous meaning, and can be a sign of newness of life.

There is another dimension of this sign that we may easily miss. Verse 28 is a forceful reminder that many of the converts in the Gentile church came from the dregs of society (cf. 1 Cor. 1:28–29; 1 Pet. 4:16). Many of them were slaves, and among slaves, stealing was regarded as normal. Paul's charge *"let him who stole steal no longer"* was a literal one. But Paul enlarges the eighth Commandment by suggesting an alternative: honest labor. Living at the expense of others is a kind of thieving. Not to pay a worker a fair wage is theft. For workers not to give the one who has hired them a full day's labor is a form of stealing. So the key to what Paul is saying is that we are interdependent and Christians are to feel that they are responsible for each other's well-being.

Our Way of Relating

"We are members of one another" (v. 25), Paul says. *"Be kind to one another, tenderhearted, forgiving one another, even as God in Christ forgave you"* (v. 32). This is a beautiful description of how we are to relate to others. The pattern has been given us by Christ. Paul can never get away from the Cross, nor can any Christian. The old gospel hymn's question, "Are you living in the shadow of the cross?" has special relevance to how we relate to others.

In no area of our lives is the cross's way of relating—forgiving one another, being kind to one another, and treating one another kindly—more needed than in the family. The popular columnist Erma Bombeck has talked often about the problem of relationships within families.

In one of her columns she made the point that the trouble with families nowadays is that no one answers anyone. Every time someone asks a question, that person responds with another question. One of her readers noticed it too, and wrote to her that a few days earlier his sixteen-year-old daughter had yelled down from upstairs, "Has anyone seen my new sweater?"

Her father yelled back, "You mean the one that cost $20?"

Her sister replied, "You mean the one you won't let me wear?"

Her brother responded, "You mean the stupid one that makes you look fat?"

Grandma answered, "You mean the one with the low neckline?" Her mother grumbled, "You mean the one that has to be washed by hand in cold water?"

Everyone was talking about the same sweater but no one answered her question.

We need to listen and hear, to sense and understand, especially in the place where we are best known and our lives are most intricately intertwined. Practicing there, we may be able to carry that style of relationship into all of life.

Who Determines Our Way?

Paul has two warnings to which the Christian must give constant heed: do not *"give place to the devil"* (v. 27) and *"do not grieve the Holy Spirit"* (v. 30). When we express our anger in bitterness, wrath, and undisciplined passion, we are obviously giving the devil a place and grieving the Holy Spirit. The question for the Christian is always *who will rule in my life,* who will call the signals? The devil or the Holy Spirit?

THE CHRISTIAN WALK

5:1 Therefore be imitators of God as dear children.
2 And walk in love, as Christ also has loved us and given Himself for us, an offering and a sacrifice to God for a sweet-smelling aroma.
3 But fornication and all uncleanness or covetousness, let it not even be named among you, as is fitting for saints;
4 neither filthiness, nor foolish talking, nor coarse jesting, which are not fitting, but rather giving of thanks. 5 For this

you know, that no fornicator, unclean person, nor covetous man, who is an idolater, has any inheritance in the kingdom of Christ and God. 6 Let no one deceive you with empty words, for because of these things the wrath of God comes upon the sons of disobedience. 7 Therefore do not be partakers with them.

8 For you were once darkness, but now you are light in the Lord. Walk as children of light 9 (for the fruit of the Spirit is in all goodness, righteousness, and truth), 10 finding out what is acceptable to the Lord. 11 And have no fellowship with the unfruitful works of darkness, but rather expose them. 12 For it is shameful even to speak of those things which are done by them in secret. 13 But all things that are exposed are made manifest by the light, for whatever makes manifest is light. 14 Therefore He says:

"Awake, you who sleep,
Arise from the dead,
And Christ will give you light."

15 See then that you walk circumspectly, not as fools but as wise, 16 redeeming the time, because the days are evil.

17 Therefore do not be unwise, but understand what the will of the Lord is. 18 And do not be drunk with wine, in which is dissipation; but be filled with the Spirit, 19 speaking to one another in psalms and hymns and spiritual songs, singing and making melody in your heart to the Lord, 20 giving thanks always for all things to God the Father in the name of our Lord Jesus Christ, 21 submitting to one another in the fear of God.

—Ephesians 5:1–21

In J. F. Powers's short story "The Trouble," there is an especially moving scene in which a young black fellow expresses a profound truth. In the midst of a race riot in a major American city, a black family watches the fighting in the streets from the safety of their apartment. The mother of the family has been hurt and taken back to the apartment. The family has gathered around to care for her; the doctor and the priest have come.

A terrified small boy of the family joins his grandmother at the window to observe the chaos in the street. It is bedlam and horror: whites chasing blacks and blacks chasing whites. All of a sudden the boy notices a white man running down the street. He turns the corner and heads down the alley behind the building, just ahead of a gang of black youths. The man has made a fatal mistake, for the alley is a dead end, and now there's no escape for him.

The gang comes around the corner and the boy recoils in horror, terrified at what he is about to see. But just then, down in the alley, the back door of the apartment house opens. The boy's grandmother, seeing the plight of the man, has left the security of her observation window and gone down to help him.

The boy's mind swirls with these thoughts: "I was very glad for the white man until I suddenly remembered Mama all broken to pieces on the bed. And then I was sorry that Grandma did it. And then again, I was happy that she did. Then I got ahold of this funny idea. I told myself that the trouble is, somebody gets cheated, or insulted, or killed. And everybody thinks that they can make it come out even by cheating, and insulting, and killing the cheaters, and the insulters, and the killers. Only they never do."

The boy is right: the endless cycle of cheating, insulting and killing never stops. That is, until persons begin to walk a new way—to *"be imitators of God as dear children"* (v. 1).

Paul continues to catalog the "old way": fornication, all uncleanness or covetousness, filthiness, foolish talking, and coarse jesting—none of these can be a part of any one who wishes an *"inheritance in the kingdom of Christ"* (v. 5).

Apart from the catalog of evil deeds and attitudes, Paul sets up three beacons which illumine and mark the Christian walk.

Walk in Love

The RSV translates 5:1, *"be imitators of God, as beloved children."* This has a stronger, clearer ring than "be followers of God." The principle of the imitation of God is one that Jesus took from the Old Testament. "The Lord said to Moses, "Say to . . . Israel, You shall be holy; for I the Lord your God am holy" (Lev. 19:2, RSV). Jesus said, "You, therefore must be perfect, as your heavenly Father is perfect (Matt. 5:48, RSV). "Be merciful, even as your Father is merciful" (Luke 6:36, RSV).

In this passage the idea of imitation is tied to a particular aspect of God's nature and action: *"forgiving one another, even as God in Christ forgave you"* (Eph. 4:32) and *"walk in love"* (5:2). Paul also uses the favorite image of Jesus, "children of God." Is there a connection here with Jesus' word in Matthew 5:43, that we are to love even our enemies that we may be children of God? Certainly it is not too much to affirm that these words of Paul, in the style, content, and spirit of Jesus' teaching, embody a core principle of the gospel. As children of God, we are to imitate God. We are to act in our own little spheres as God acts in His universe, and thus prove that God is our Father.

Walk As Children of Light

Dorothy Sayers, the theologian and mystery novelist, likened our thoughtless, purposeless, rote participation in public worship to those "bit actors" who appear at the studio, play through the brief scene and shots to which they are assigned, and leave, unaware of the meaning of the drama in which they are cast, ignorant of whether it is comedy, tragedy, drama, or melodrama.

Is not this the Christian problem? We want to be "bit actors," moving in and out of the drama of redemption—the new life of justification and sanctification—as we please. It can't be so. *"For you were once darkness, but now you are light in the Lord. Walk as children of light"* (Eph. 5:8).

The passage calls to mind two other passages: (1) the familiar words of John 12:35, 36: "Walk while you have the light . . . that you may become sons of the light"; (2) the passage in Rom. 13:8–14 which has the same challenging ring and makes the same contrast as this passage—"Let us cast off the works of darkness and let us put on the armor of light; let us walk properly as in the day" (vv. 12, 13). The Romans passage closes with that favorite image of Paul: "Put on the Lord Jesus Christ." We are not "bit actors." Paul does not say, "You belong to the light"; he says, *"You are light"* (Eph. 5:8). Living as *children of light,* our new nature partakes of the highest element in which we now dwell and manifests itself in our conduct.

My preacher friend Don Shelby shared a dramatic and descriptive story of one who moved from darkness to light, and began to live a new vision:

> One morning while serving the church in San Diego, I was called into the sanctuary upon my arrival at the study. The custodian wanted me to see a strange offering which had been placed at the very center of the altar. Upon examination we discovered it to be a pair of brown corduroy trousers, a belt, a white T-shirt, a pair of tan suede boots, and a note. There were blood stains on the shirt and on the note. The note had been written on one of the pledge cards

which we had placed in the pews for that year's Loyalty Sunday. A name was written large and underlined three times. Then the plea, also underlined, *"Please listen to God."* On the reverse side an address had been written and also a phone number. Where a signature was called for, a name was signed. I made a call to the number listed and reached a young man, the one who had written that note. I need not share all the details, but this young man of 19 years, after a long wandering in a wasteland of drugs, dropping out of sight, severing contact with his family, and getting involved in one mess after another, had come home. The night before he had finally reached bottom. There had been a struggle on the streets, a fight and an almost fatal beating. After making sure the victim of his uncontrolled assault was going to be all right in the emergency room of a nearby hospital, this young man came by the church, found an unlocked door and went into the sanctuary. He said he stayed there the rest of the night, praying and pondering. He asked God to forgive him and to show him the way to go. He said all at once the presence of God became very real. He knew he had been forgiven. A wonderful peace came. He committed himself to follow Christ. He determined to make things right which he had messed up. To symbolize his commitment, he had put on some clean clothes he had in his bedroll and left the others as a kind of offering, giving God his old life. He said he walked out the door a new person with a new vision and a new hope.

From the passage encompassed by verses 8 through 14 of chapter 5 of Ephesians, three specific frameworks of truth may be gleaned: (1) Light is productive; evil is barren. By its own nature, evil can only destroy. (2) Christians are to have no fellowship with, but expose the works of darkness. (3) Light not only illumines but transforms.

The light of Christ shining anywhere burns with cleansing, purifying transforming power. That light need not be diffused as it shines through *"children of the light."* The effect of a Christian life in any community is first to reveal, and in that revealing to "rebuke by exposing." Then there is this hopeful fact: whatever the light shines on—if it shines clearly enough, consistently enough, and long enough—it must, in the end, transform.

Walk in Wisdom

The Christian walks in love and in light and *"also in wisdom. See then that you walk circumspectly, not as fools but as wise"* (v. 15).

Wisdom—this is the ultimate for which, according to philosopher and moralist, all persons and civilized societies are to strive. "How much better to get wisdom than gold!" (Prov. 16:16). Wisdom—the most precious of people's individual and corporate possessions. Paul shattered most notions about the nature of wisdom by denouncing "wisdom of the world." "The foolishness of God is wiser than men . . . God chose what is foolish in the world to shame the wise, God chose what is weak in the world to shame the strong" (1 Cor. 1:25, 27, RSV).

Here Paul was contradicting the Greek idea that religion was man's climb upward to a divine realm, to God. The gospel is the drama of divine descent, not of human ascent. This was the "foolishness of the cross"—that God came to us, that He forgives us and accepts us apart from our effortful striving.

Though we recognize and acknowledge that much which has been touted as "wisdom" by the "wisest" persons of history may sometimes be contradictory to the gospel of the Cross and a God who "stoops to conquer," this does not excuse us from intellectual, philosophical, and ethical struggle and pursuit. The Christian faith gives no license to intellectual laziness and shallow thinking. Christians are under as great an obligation as any person ever felt himself to be—to live *"not as fools, but as wise"* (v. 15).

Paul is making a case for a special wisdom; not a philosophical wisdom that boasts of itself and has as its focus "to be wise"; not a worldly sophistication that is calloused to the "foolishness of the cross" or is numb to God's choosing the weak to shame the strong; not a mind-trip that finds security in isolation from the nitty-gritty environment of common folk—*but a practical wisdom that makes conduct consistent with faith.*

Four distinct markings suggest a contour of such a wisdom.

1. *'Redeeming the time"* (v. 16). This charming and challenging metaphor suggests even more than its powerful particular meaning in this setting. It is used in Colossians 4:5 in the same fashion as here. *"The time"* for the realization of God's plan is short, desperately so, Paul thought; thus Christians are to make the most of the time available.

"Because the days are evil" indicates that Paul is making a connection with the commonly accepted belief that a period of crisis would precede the coming of the Messiah. Because the Lord is

going to come soon to judge the world, the time is precious. This is not an occasion for surrender, or withdrawal, but one for renewed commitment and earnestness in sustaining the Christian walk.

There are some other lessons here. While Paul is addressing a situation in which the present return of Christ was expected and the time evil and thus to be redeemed, his words suggest a truth for Christians who still await the return of Christ. One, Christianity is not a religion of escapism from history. Our faith is a sanctuary for strength and renewal, comfort and hope, but it is also a staging ground for battle. It is a fortress against the principalities and powers of the present world, but also an embassy of God's kingdom set right down in the center of whatever evil orders may be struggling for dominance. Withdrawal from the world has no credence in New Testament Christianity.

A second truth is that the debasement of contemporary society can never be an excuse for relaxing our witness, or acquiescing to lower moral standards. There have been few, if any, periods of history in which it was not necessary to struggle for decency and right. Battle is a rather descriptive metaphor for the Christian faith's struggle for justice, righteousness, and truth.

A third truth is that we must read "the signs of the time" through bifocal lenses. We look at the world as it is, recognizing and identifying the evil which is rampant. We do not hide our eyes from the wrong which appears forever on the throne, as right hangs painfully on the scaffold. Yet the other focus of our lenses enables us to see in such a way that we do not identify Christian hope with secular optimism. Our willingness to work for the kingdom, to "wager our lives" on the triumph of justice, is not dependent upon social progress. That brings us to the second distinct marking of the contour of Christian wisdom.

2. *"Understand what the will of the Lord is"* (v. 17). The Christian's duty, and thus the mark of wisdom, is to look for the will of the Lord. In the setting of this epistle, the crisis of the times, with evil rampant and the expectation that the Lord would soon return, it was of crucial importance that Christians keep their senses awake in order to perceive in every situation and on every occasion what God would have them do. Is the need less for any who would be Christian in any age?

We dare not neglect the regular disciplines of prayer, Scripture reading, corporate worship, and sharing in koinonia, for through these we listen to the Word, we talk with the Lord and with others who are talking and walking with the Lord, and so we clarify His will. Yet, to see these sources of piety as piety itself, to think the keeping of these disciplines is the doing of God's will, is a perversion of New Testament Christianity. Authentic piety depends upon prayer, Scripture study, worship, and sharing as channels of power, revelation, and guidance, but never as ends within themselves. The end is to repeat God's life in the world—to imitate Him in His outpouring of love, forgiveness, and sacrificial service.

This is a distinct mark of the contour of wisdom.

3. *"Be filled with the Spirit"* (v. 18). The warning against drunkenness in verse 18 strikes abruptly and seems out of place until we see that Paul is making a contrast which would be readily understood: the contrast between a short-lived ecstasy that is destructive, and the genuine ecstasy of the Spirit that is creative and upbuilding.

Verse 18 is a partial citation from Proverbs:

> Do not look at wine when it is red, when it sparkles in the cup and goes down smoothly. At the last it bites like a serpent, and stings like an adder. Your eyes will see strange things, and your mind utter perverse things. You will be like one who lies down in the midst of the sea, like one who lies on the top of a mast. "They struck me," you will say, "but I was not hurt; they beat me, but I did not feel it. When shall I awake? I will seek another drink" (Prov. 23:31–35, RSV).

Paul's warning is direct and literal. It needs serious consideration, for our modern church gives too little attention to the problems of the use of alcoholic beverages. Christians should be able to at least agree on this precept: "Do not get drunk with wine, for that is debauchery." This RSV translation is strong, as it should be. "Debauchery" is often rendered elsewhere as "profligacy" or "dissipation." It denotes the ruin of life in dissolute living. The Greek is *asotia,* a negative formation from a root closely related to *soteria,* meaning "salvation." That comparison of root meaning suggests the contrast Paul is making. Is it too much to say that many seek salvation in wine? At least in terms of immediate deliverance or escape, the bar draws more people than the church. So Paul is not sketching an antithesis between wine and Spirit, but between the two states resulting from being filled with either: intoxication from wine (or any alcoholic drink or drug) which leads only to the dissipation of life, and vitality with the Spirit which brings progressive fulfillment and meaning.

The impact of this contrast is fuller when we remember the setting. In ancient religions (and this carries over to today) high value was placed on ecstatic mood. It was thought that people could approach God only as they were drawn out of themselves in rapturous ecstasy. Exciting music, dancing, and—chief of all—intoxication were employed to produce their ecstasy. Greek religion found its highest expression of this style in the worship of Dionysus.

Paul affirmed joy and enthusiasm, even ecstasy, as the mood in which we find fellowship with God, but condemned drunkenness as the reversal of this mood. Instead of intoxicating themselves with wine, the mark of wisdom is to seek the fullness of the Spirit. We lose the force of the words in the usual translation, "Be full of the Spirit." E. F. Scott says that the thought is rather "Find your overflow of soul in the rapture which the Spirit will give you." Persons are truly lifted out of themselves as they are possessed or *filled with the Spirit.* They rise into that higher mood in which they can commune with God and understand His will.

Three characteristics of Spirit-filled people sharing and worshiping together are given in the final verses of this passage (19, 20, 21).

The early church, Spirit-filled, was a *singing* church. The dominant theme was joy. It was a *thankful* church. Knowing who God was, and what He had done; keeping at the surface of their awareness the fact that they were the recipients of unmerited mercy and grace, gratitude was the keynote of their life. They saw themselves all "in the same boat," so they respected one another. Struggle for status was not yet pronounced, so they willingly *submitted to one another in the fear of the Lord.* That is the third distinct mark of the contour of wisdom which Paul outlines, and that is the theme of our next chapter: Christian submission.

NOTES

1. Letter from Taizé, January 1978.

2. Helen Gonzales, *Report,* Southern California Teen Challenge, vol. 3, no. 3, Fall 1967.

CHAPTER SIX—RELATIONSHIPS IN CHRIST
EPHESIANS 5:22—6:9

Scripture Outline

A Model of Christian Marriage (5:22–33)

Children and Parents—Reciprocal Respect (6:1–4)

Servants and Masters (6:5–9)

It is a fact of history that no persons owe more to Christ than women and children. What Christ and the impact of His gospel did for women and children triggered perhaps the most dramatic social revolution of all ages.

Within the modern movement of women's liberation Paul is often seen as an oppressor—certainly a "conservative" who championed the status-quo, subservient position of women, and allowed that position to be the norm within the church. Those who make such glib assertions need to take a longer and harder look at Paul. Even concentration on this one section (Eph. 5:22—6:9) will prove him to be a radical rather than a conservative.

The scope of this volume does not allow a comprehensive study of Paul's understanding of social relationships. However, one fact, to be applied to all of Paul's statements, must be noted: He expected the imminent return of Christ. All his pronouncements on social relationships and other ethical issues are flavored by this conviction that Christ would soon return and earthly history would be culminated. We must always view Paul against this, his eschatological horizon.

Leander E. Keck provided an accurate and pertinent perspective in this regard:

> Once the sense of the imminent end is gone, Paul comes through as a social conservative who urges that everyone stay in his or her place regardless of how long history

and society continue. Appealing to I Corinthians 7 to say that Paul argues against all social change actually stands the apostle on his head. Paul does not sanctify the status quo as a divinely ordained order but insists on precisely the opposite—it is doomed to pass away. Neither society's inherent goodness or rightness, nor God's sanction of the way things are, causes Paul to urge Christians not to change their relation to social structures or the social structures themselves, but the conviction that God will soon change everything anyway. Actually, then, by depriving the status quo of its divine sanction, of its inherent rightness and permanence, Paul opened the way for Christians to change the world, once they ceased to rely on God's impending act to do so. Paul's ethic is really not conservative at all, but lays the foundation for an ethic of social involvement. He himself built very little on this foundation. Yet here too, one might recall Paul's own word in 1 Cor. 3:10: "According to the commission of God given to me. . . I laid a foundation and another. . . is building upon it. Let each . . . take care *how* he builds upon it."[1]

One other general fact must be noted before we move to consider this specific passage. Paul's ethics is primarily pastoral, oriented to and motivated by his concern to "build up" the Christian community. He is chiefly concerned about the impression non-Christians get from the actions of Christians. This section of Ephesians, then, has a direct bearing on the main theme of the epistle. God's purpose is to reconcile all things in Christ, and the church is the instrument through which the work of reconciliation is to be fulfilled. Paul now brings that reconciliation to a particular focus—the family.

What insight! *The unifying work of the church must begin in the family.* It is no accident that Paul compares the relationship of husband and wife to Christ and the church. The effecting of reconciliation in every area of life is an extension of what is begun in the home. No institution more desperately needs the attention of the church than marriage and family. Not only the church, but the whole world depends on what happens in this arena of the most intimate relationships—the home. We need to heed what Paul has to say.

A MODEL OF CHRISTIAN MARRIAGE

^{22} Wives, submit to your own husbands, as to the Lord.
^{23} For the husband is head of the wife, as also Christ is head of the church; and He is the Savior of the body. ^{24} Therefore, just as the church is subject to Christ, so let the wives be to their own husbands in everything.

^{25} Husbands, love your wives, just as Christ also loved the church and gave Himself for her, ^{26} that He might sanctify and cleanse her with the washing of water by the word, ^{27} that He might present her to Himself a glorious church, not having spot or wrinkle or any such thing, but that she should be holy and without blemish. ^{28} So husbands ought to love their own wives as their own bodies; he who loves his wife loves himself. ^{29} For no one ever hated his own flesh, but nourishes and cherishes it, just as the Lord does the church. ^{30} For we are members of His body, of His flesh and of His bones. ^{31} "For this reason a man shall leave his father and mother and be joined to his wife, and the two shall become one flesh." ^{32} This is a great mystery, but I speak concerning Christ and the church. ^{33} Nevertheless let each one of you in particular so love his own wife as himself, and let the wife see that she respects her husband.

—Ephesians 5:22–33

If we can get beyond the "turn-off" words in this passage, we will discover a beautiful and challenging model for Christian marriage. The "turn-off" words are those which call for wives to submit, to be subject to their husbands, and the designation of the husband as the *"head of the wife."* To understand and overcome what some see as a putdown of women, we need to look at two facets of Paul's vision: the meaning of submission and the shape of love.

Submission

In the previous chapter we noted that verse 21, *"submitting to one another in the fear of God,"* was one of the distinct markings of the contour of Christian wisdom. This is a call to all Christians, not to a particular group. While verse 21 is a conclusion to the previous section, it is also an introduction to what follows: thus the admonition for wives to submit to their husbands must be seen in the context of the call to all Christians that *their attitude to one another must be one of mutual service.* Paul enunciates this style of relationship in the metaphor of marriage. It is bereft of full meaning apart from an understanding of and commitment to the more inclusive discipline of submission to which all Christians are called.

In the seventies, there took place a resurgence of emphasis upon submission. New congregations grew up around a structure of submission in which people submitted themselves to the oversight, care, and direction of an "elder." There may be wisdom in this, but there is also danger of some glaring, manipulative perversions.

Also, there has been a resurgence within many congregations of an emphasis on a wife-to-husband submission, with and without the emphasis on the husband as "head" of the house. Again, perverted and damaging expressions have occurred. Unfortunately, the fact is that most of us have been exposed to such a limited or mutilated form of biblical submission that we have either embraced a deformity of the real thing or we have rejected the discipline altogether.

The clearest and most challenging expression of the biblical meaning of submission is Mark 8:34–35 (RSV): "And he called to him the multitude with his disciples, and said to them, 'If any man would come after me, let him deny himself and take up his cross and follow me. For whoever would save his life will lose it; and whoever loses his life for my sake and the gospel's will save it.'"

We cower back from such a hard word. Self-fulfillment and self-actualization touch our ears gently. Self-denial cuts to the quick of our feeling and challenges us at the core of our being. No one need remind us that we are self-seeking, self-serving, self-indulging people. Yet this is something we have not wanted to talk about. The blatant emphasis on self-seeking and self-serving that flowered in the sixties and the seventies may be one of the most telling signs of our decadence. A spate of books on such themes as self-assertion and "winning through intimidation," have touted a philosophy of getting ahead and exercising personal power for selfish gain—a perversion of self-actualization or self-fulfillment.

Jesus knew, and Paul was echoing the truth, that self-fulfillment involves self-denial. But self-denial does not mean self-hatred or self-mortification nor the rejection of our individuality. Self-denial is a way by which we realize that our happiness and fulfillment are not dependent upon having our own way or getting what we want. Self-denial is the willingness to consider the needs of others above our own self-interest. It is a commitment to live in relationships where the worth of all persons is valued and where "getting my own way" gives way to considering the concerns, needs, and interests of others.

Self-actualization or self-fulfillment is not the opposite of self-denial. Self-denial, according to Jesus, is the only road to self-fulfilment. We save our lives by losing them for Christ's sake. Willingness to be "last" makes us "first." Again, it must be made clear—if we are to have a creative, redemptive understanding of submission—that self-denial is not the same thing as self-contempt. Unfortunately, some expressions of Christian piety have equated the two. To a marked degree, the monastic movement was a world-denying, self-mortification movement that stimulated an ascetic spirituality in which the flesh was evil and had to be "whipped" into subjection to the Spirit. This was rooted in a misunderstanding of Paul's teaching about "flesh and spirit" (see commentary on Gal. 2:17–21), and denied God's affirmation of His creation as *good*. Thus, self-denial issued in self-contempt. To practice self-denial out of a stance of self-contempt never produces the abundant life of joy which is the birthright of persons *in Christ*.

Jesus made the ability to love ourselves the foundation for loving and reaching out to others (Matt. 22:39). Self-contempt says we have no worth; self-denial declares that we are of infinite worth—as are others—and life is found in the rhythm of affirming ourselves and others in the act of "loving others as ourselves." It is in this context that submission is to be understood and practiced.

Submission is an ethical theme that runs throughout the New Testament. It is to be the posture of all Christians because we are to follow the crucified Lord who emptied himself to become the servant of all. Submission is the cross-style to which we are called. Jesus not only died a cross-death, He lived a cross-life of submission and service.

Here we come to the radical nature of Paul's teaching, which is really a specific commentary, in the context of the family, on the revolutionary teaching of the New Testament. "Be subject to one another *out of reverence to Christ*" (Eph. 5:21, RSV) is the general principal by which all Christians are to be guided. We are commanded (not just women, but all persons—men and women, parents and children, masters and slaves) to live a life of submission not because of our station in life, but because Jesus lived a life of submission and showed that such is the only way to "find life."

It is almost impossible for us to understand the radical nature of this teaching because we are so far removed from the world of Paul's day. In that day—and this persists in some cultures even now—persons were bound into a certain "station." The Greeks held that was the way the gods had created things; persons had no choice. This was especially true of women. Women were seen as chattel, things to be used at whim and fancy, without rights, little more than slaves. Those to whom first-century culture afforded no choice were addressed by Paul as *free;* they could decide. This was revolutionary. Why would he call wives, children, and slaves to submission? That was their lot already. But something had happened to them. The gospel had freed them from a subordinate station in society. Second-, third-, and fourth-class citizenship was challenged by the gospel, and those *condemned* to those classes knew it. Paul, then, is not calling for submission on the basis of the way things were, the station in which the gods had ordered matters. No New Testament writer did that. All contemporary customs of superordinate and subordinate were completely ignored. Everyone was "to esteem others better than themselves" (Phil. 2:3) and be subject to one another out of reverence for Christ.

Wives were to be subject to their husbands not because that was a part of the natural order, but because submission is the style of all Christians. When wives and others began to live this way, the status quo was deprived of its divine sanction, of its inherent rightness and permanence, and a revolution of mutual respect, affirmation, and service began. As will presently be seen in Paul's admonition to husbands, there are no "high" or "low" positions in Christian marriage and home, nor in the entire Christian family. A new order has been born in which all participants regard themselves as servants of one Master, Jesus Christ, and give themselves in mutual service to one another because of Him.

The biggest heresy in marriage is an alphabetical one—" big *I,* little *u.*" A cartoon pictured it at a superficial but probing level. Husband and wife—from their appearance, still in their teens—are in a marriage counselor's office. The girl clutches a teddy bear close to her breast, and the boy says with a superior air, "I think you know our problem, doctor. She keeps taking the teddy bear away from me." It is funny, but tragic, because it describes a cancer which will devastate any marriage: selfishness.

More common than selfishness, because it is more subtle and slower in its destructible work in marriage, is unconcern. We don't care enough. The question is not whether marriage will work, but whether we will *work our marriage.* Marriage is demanding, and not enough of us are willing to invest enough of ourselves in the relationship to grow an exciting, enriching, effective marriage.

Caring is the key, for caring is love translated into the practical everyday requirement essential for the mutual affirmation necessary for marriage-aliveness. As in his admonition to wives, so in his admonition to husbands: Paul could not get away from the Cross of Christ. *"Love your wives,"* He said, *"just as Christ also loved the church and gave Himself for her"* (5:25).

Caring is the closest identification we have with the Cross of Christ in our marriages. Having pain, or suffering because we have done something wrong, is not what bearing a cross means. To bear a cross means that we care enough to deliberately enter another's life, even if it involves suffering and pain, which it always does in marriage. To care means that I am *with* and *for* my mate, no matter what the circumstance. To care means that I cherish and appreciate my partner, and so I commit my energies, my self, my time, to his or her fulfillment.

So, married love looks like the Cross. The love which flows from the Cross, and which must be the dynamic of marriage, is not a love you can achieve but the love you have received. Christ empowers us to implement in marriage the love with which He has loved us.

The Church and Marriage

In this passage Paul uses a reciprocal metaphor. Through the relation of Christ and the church he pictures the love that should characterize the relationship of husband and wife, and he uses marriage to throw light on the relation between Christ and the church.

The husband as *head* is a metaphorical return to Genesis 2:18–24 where the process of creation is beautifully described, climaxing with the creation of woman from a rib taken from the side of man. Man says, "This is now bone of my bones and flesh of my flesh" (Gen. 2:23, RSV). Then comes the model of faithful love which should be forever etched on the consciousness of the human race: *"Therefore a man leaves his father and his mother and cleaves to his wife, and they become one flesh"* (v. 24, RSV).

To interpret the passage literally is to miss the breadth and depth of meaning that can be grasped only as the passage is seen as a whole. Paul always insisted that the church's submission to Christ was not obedience to His dictation, but faith. Faith is the acceptance of Christ's free and unconditional grace. With that acceptance come the constraints of love which grace entails. "For the love of Christ controls us, because we are convinced that one has died for all; therefore all have died" (2 Cor. 5:14, RSV). That speaks luminously of Christ's love for the church, and the love of husband and wife. Note this, too: *Christ loved the church not because she was lovable but to make her so.* Love is decision, commitment, and caring.

Verse 26 introduces an allusion to baptism: *"with the washing of water by the word."* The reference, however, is not to an individual being baptized but to the cleansing and consecration of the whole church. *"By the word"* means the gospel by which Christ has declared the church His own and has set her on the road to perfection. In like manner, Christian marriage is God's declarative act of oneness: *"What God has joined together let no man put asunder"* (Matt. 19:6, RSV); and the commitment of marriage, sustained by the decision to love and nourished by caring, moves a couple along the road to perfection in love. As the church reflects the kingdom of Christ, so marriage may be a cameo of that kingdom.

CHILDREN AND PARENTS: RECIPROCAL RESPECT

6:1 Children, obey your parents in the Lord, for this is right. **2** "Honor your father and mother," which is the first commandment with promise: **3** "that it may be well with you and you may live long on the earth."

4 And you, fathers, do not provoke your children to wrath, but bring them up in the training and admonition of the Lord.

—*Ephesians 6:1–4*

Paul's teaching about parent-child relationships in this section does not turn on his quotation of the first Commandment which bids children to honor their father and mother, but rather on the call to parents to respect their children: *"Do not provoke your children to wrath, but bring them up in the training and admonition of the Lord"* (v. 4).

Of course, honor of parents is an essential virtue and certainly in need of cultivation. The unthoughtful and irresponsible emphasis on permissiveness has created a desperate need in modern America to return to a strong emphasis on discipline and obedience in the home. Yet, the word of Paul, so radical in his day, and still the key to making the family what Christ would have it be, is reciprocal respect between parents and children.

Statistics indicate that more twins are being born than previously. When a teacher mentioned this to her third grade class, one of the pupils said, "I guess more twins are being born because little children are afraid to come into this world alone." Humorous, but true in fact. Children need love and respect, affirmation and support. Other statistics make crucial the need for us to hear Paul's word about reciprocal respect in the family. In 1978 there were 1,600,000 documented cases of child abuse in the United States. Probably more than that many were undocumented. Who knows the terror of unloved and unrespected children?

All sorts of fall-out has resulted from the deterioration of the family and the lack of love and respect in bringing children to maturity. In a recent year one billion dollars' worth of property damage was done by children to our schools; 70,000 assaults were made on teachers; and 100 murders were committed. Suicide is the second highest cause of death among the young. Is there a connection between these statistics and what is not happening within the home?

To a world in which the father had absolute power over a child, in which that power was regularly expressed in casting female babies away and drowning sickly or deformed children; to a world in which children were property, chattel to be held, used, or disposed of according to the wishes of the father—to this world Paul spoke a revolutionary word about the infinite value of all persons, and the respect parents should have for their children: *"Do not provoke your children to wrath."* In Colossians 3:21, he adds a phrase to this injunction: *"lest they become discouraged."* Continuous criticism and rebuke, discipline that diminishes rather than affirms self-worth, breaks the spirit of a person. Though discipline is essential, it needs the context of reciprocal respect. (See Commentary on Col. 3:18—4:6.)

SERVANTS AND MASTERS

5 Bondservants, be obedient to those who are your masters according to the flesh, with fear and trembling, in sincerity of heart, as to Christ; 6 not with eyeservice, as men-pleasers, but as bondservants of Christ, doing the will of God from the heart, 7 with goodwill doing service, as to the Lord, and not to men, 8 knowing that whatever good anyone does, he will receive the same from the Lord, whether he is a slave or free.

⁹ And you, masters, do the same things to them, giving up threatening, knowing that your own Master also is in heaven, and there is no partiality with Him.

—*Ephesians 6:5–9*

Paul's word to servants must be heard in the same context as his word to wives, husbands, and children. Here one significant understanding must be noted. Paul's ethics, and especially his ethics of relationship and societal status, was thoroughly influenced by his expectation of the imminent return of Christ. This produces what appears to be a "conservative" stance, for he actually urges his readers to remain in their present roles in society. In 1 Corinthians 7:17–24, for example, he applies this ethic to three situations: circumcision, slavery, and marriage.

While Paul may have been cited as a champion of the status quo and in support of oppressive systems, this is a misuse of his message. Because he expected Christ to return soon, he expected the institution of slavery to be abolished without human effort. Even so, he called for a transformation of attitude and thus of relationship within external strictures of slavery. The obedience of a slave to a master was to become a heart response *"as to Christ,"* not a response in cowering, manipulative *"eyeservice, as men-pleasers."* Masters were to relate to their servants in the same way, as to Christ—how radical!—*"giving up threatening, knowing that your own Master also is in heaven, and there is no partiality with Him"* (v. 9).

The lessons are clear and relate to all. (1) The slave who becomes a Christian is the Lord's freedman though he may still belong to an earthly master; likewise the free person who becomes a Christian is Christ's slave. (2) Inner freedom is not tied to external status. In Paul's thinking, with the expectation of the parousia, to attempt to change one's status would have been a tacit denial of the fact that one's relation to God is a matter of trust/faith; Paul's conviction that inner freedom is what matters caused him to see that attempts to change one's situation makes the externals more important than they really are.

NOTE

1. Leander E. Keck, *Paul and His Letters* (Philadelphia: Fortress Press, 1979), p. 98.

CHAPTER SEVEN—STRONG IN THE LORD

EPHESIANS 6:10–24

Scripture Outline

Put on the Armor of God (6:10–17)

Be Watchful in the Spirit (6:18–20)

Sustain and Comfort One Another (6:21–24)

Paul closes his letter to the Ephesians by giving us the building plans for a life in Christ. He shows us the way to *be strong in the Lord.*

PUT ON THE ARMOR OF GOD

10 Finally, my brethren, be strong in the Lord and in the power of His might. 11 Put on the whole armor of God, that you may be able to stand against the wiles of the devil. 12 For we do not wrestle against flesh and blood, but against principalities, against powers, against the rulers of the darkness of this age, against spiritual hosts of wickedness in the heavenly places. 13 Therefore take up the whole armor of God, that you may be able to withstand in the evil day, and having done all, to stand.

14 Stand therefore, having girded your waist with truth, having put on the breastplate of righteousness, 15 and having shod your feet with the preparation of the gospel of peace; 16 above all, taking the shield of faith with which you will be able to quench all the fiery darts of the wicked one. 17 And take the helmet of salvation, and the sword of the Spirit, which is the word of God;

—Ephesians 6:10–17

To be strong in the Lord and in the power of His might, we must put on the whole armor of God (vv. 10–11). Strength and power are necessary because we are in a battle for our own souls and the souls of others.

Some may think that life for ancient people was more terrifying than for us today. Demons, devils, and evil spirits haunted every corner of the ancient world. The whole universe was a battleground. But ask my teenage son, Kevin, about terror. In school he has learned about the ominous power of the split atom. On television he has been confronted with raging masses in the streets of Iran; 100,000 Russian troops "armed to the teeth" moving into Afghanistan. He knows that enough power is stockpiled in atomic weapons by either the United States or Russia to destroy the whole human race, and he knows that what is happening in Poland or in the Israeli-Arab world may determine whether the button is pushed and the shades drawn on civilization. It is no wonder that when the evening TV news glaringly reminds us of the dark abyss on the edge of which we are perilously balanced, he asks me to stay with him as he goes to bed. In the dark of the night before sleep comes we talk of the future, of war, of death, of evil in the heart of men, of hope, of God, and of heaven.

Paul's words about wrestling *"against principalities, against powers, against the rulers of the darkness of this age, against spiritual hosts of wickedness in the heavenly places"* (v. 12) do not strike Kevin's ears with strangeness. Nor mine. Kevin trembles in the presence of the evil of a chaotic world that is going mad and is seemingly bent on its own destruction. One day, if we escape the portended atomic nightmare, Kevin will tremble as surely as he recognizes evil expressing itself within himself—in those dark nights of his soul when opposing powers will pull him with person-rending might in opposite directions. Already he has hints of the working of those powers as his sexual passions become more intense, as he wrestles with the "easy" way of cheating rather than studying for good grades, as he sorts out his instincts and drives, his needs for affirmation and acceptance.

At least by hint, Kevin knows what most of us have discovered, that Paul was writing of forces which invade the world, our inner- and interpersonal worlds, to make us sin, even to destroy us. So we must be strong in the Lord. To be so requires putting on the whole armor of God.

In the first half of his letter Paul prayed that his readers would come to know the power of God which was demonstrated and is operative in the Resurrection of Christ. That power had been demonstrated, too, in the readers' conversion to Christ. Each person's conversion is a Resurrection from the deadness of sin to life in Christ and deliverance from the prevailing forces of sin. Now, in this last chapter, Paul reminds his readers that in all their future they will have to rely on the same Resurrection power. We may be tempted to think that our enemies are human and then to seek to fight with worldly weapons. But our real enemies are the spiritual forces that stand behind all institutions and seek to control the lives of persons and nations.

If Paul wrote this epistle from prison, as well he may have, the spectacle of Roman soldiers marching or standing guard was always before him. His military metaphor may have been inspired by this. Deeper, however, is the imagery of Scripture on which he falls back. This passage becomes a patchwork quilt of Old Testament allusions, especially from Isaiah (see Is. 11:4–5; 52:7; 59:15–17). With that dual perspective—the ever-present soldier and the scriptural knowledge of what protects and sustains the warrior of God—Paul describes the armor in detail.

Belt of Truth

A girdle was a belt. Its most immediate and practical use for a soldier was to gird (hold tight) his tunic so he might be free in his movement; it also provided a place to hang his sword. The imagery here is that truth holds together all other virtues and makes them effectual.

Breastplate of Righteousness

Paul talks about the belt of truth and the breastplate of righteousness in the same breath and the same verse. If he is following Isaiah 59:17, as he seems to be doing, the warrior "puts on righteousness as a breastplate." Yet Paul gives it a more specific meaning. As the purpose of a breastplate is to guard the most vital parts of the body, so the Christian protects himself by righteousness. When persons are clothed with righteousness, they are impregnable. In what sense?

1. *Passions are redeemed and redirected.* Do not forget that righteousness, as Paul sees it, is first of all a gift. God, through the Cross, imputes righteousness; that is, He looks at us as though we were without sin. The imputed righteousness of God is appropriated by our faithful and obedient response to Him. Thus we are regenerated—made over into new creations by Christ dwelling within us by the power of the Holy Spirit. Our passions, then, are redirected.

237

The drives and instincts of our lives move under the sway of the indwelling Christ.

2. *Death loses its sting.* The most devastating aspect of death is our fear of it, especially our fear of what lies beyond death in the mysterious abyss of eternity. When we accept the grace of God, extravagantly given us in the Cross of Jesus Christ, death is defeated. We know that He who gave himself in Christ holds our future and beyond death we have nothing to fear.

Sandals of the Gospel of Peace

The *caligal,* military boots, was one of the most important parts of the Roman soldier's equipment. They were designed for marches over every kind of tough terrain. It has been said that the attention given to soldiers' boots was the secret of Roman conquest. So, Paul uses this image in verse 15: *"having shod your feet with the preparation of the gospel of peace."*

Even though we may not grasp the precise meaning of this metaphor, two possibilities can add to our strength in the Lord.

1. In the gospel the believer is prepared for all difficulties. The gospel gives us the stability of sure footing. We can march over the rough terrain of life, over the mountain passes of excruciating pain, through deserts of fear and terror, without falling out.

2. We must be ready to carry the gospel any- and everywhere. The prophetic message of Isaiah 52:7 must have been in Paul's mind. *"How beautiful upon the mountains are the feet of him who brings good tidings, who publishes peace, who brings good tidings of good, who publishes salvation, who says to Zion, 'Your God reigns'"* (Is. 52:7, RSV). Missionary spirit, evangelical zeal, preparedness, and readiness to carry the gospel everywhere—that is at least one meaning of wearing the sandals of the gospel.

Some of the keenest observers of the current scene are intimating that the times are coining when what is happening now in Latin America and many other countries, may happen in the United States—persons being imprisoned, persecuted, even killed for the faith. To be ready for that our feet must be *shod with preparation of the gospel of peace.* Is there any meaning in the striking paradox that the soldier should be equipped for battle with a declaration of peace? At least this: "Not by might, nor by power, but by my spirit, saith the Lord of hosts" (Zech. 4:6, KJV).

The only "power" the Christian can trust is the power of the Spirit, and the manifestation of the Spirit is love.

Shield of Faith

One of the most dangerous weapons of ancient warfare was the fiery dart. The heads of the darts or arrows would be wrapped with flax or hemp fiber, soaked in pitch, then set afire before they were thrown. A wooden shield could be set afire by them. For that reason, the shields were covered with a layer of hide and were large enough to protect the whole body. Even though the dart may pierce the shield, the fire would be quenched.

What a picture! Faith is a shield, guarding the believer against all attacks of invisible and visible enemies. Be careful, though. Paul never uses the word *"faith"* glibly as we moderns do. We use it to refer to what we believe, and of the act of believing. "I have faith," or "I believe" rolls off our tongue easily because we express ourselves in such vague ways. We may be noting our belief in a person: "I have faith in her," or indicating our rational assent to certain dogma or beliefs. For Paul, trustful obedience was always involved in faith (see commentary on Gal. 2:16). Justified by faith, we live by faith, in trustful obedience to Jesus Christ. This faith, Paul says, will *"quench all the fiery darts of the wicked one."*

The highway of life is strewn with the wreckage of Christians who never discovered how to combat *"the wicked one."* They depend on their own moral strength. Sanctioned and supported by ethical wisdom, high ideals and precepts, committed to social and personal justice and righteousness, they face evil in naked encounter. And some victories are won: temptations are escaped, sin is labeled ugly and overcome, social crime is exposed and condemned. Even the strength that comes from the fear of the consequences of our sin often becomes a source of power in resisting evil.

But none of them are ultimately adequate. Moral strength or the driving inspiration of a high ideal, at times wears down, and we wear out. We need more. We need the resources of Christ who stands with us and fights *with* and *for* us against every onslaught of sin.

We need to recover viscerally the meaning of justification by faith, for this is good news not merely at the point of our acceptance, but in the resource for daily living it affords. Jesus addressed a parable to those who "trusted in themselves" (Luke 18:9–14). This is a message for us who have fallen into the snare of "moralistic

Christianity"—a works-righteous stance that believes, consciously or unconsciously, that with our own resources of moral goodness, ethical responsibility, and high Christian ideals we can withstand *"the fiery darts of the wicked one."* Faith, our trustful obedience, our utter commitment and dependence upon Christ for *daily,* as well as ultimate salvation, is our only shield.

Helmet of Salvation

Paul returns to his reminiscence of Isaiah who pictures God with "a helmet of salvation upon His head" (59:17). The helmet does not protect, but symbolizes God's power and readiness to save others. Paul sees this helmet of salvation, worn by the Christian soldier, as the guarantee of divine protection and ultimate deliverance. The future consummation of the Christian's life is secure because salvation has been given by God. If we *"fake"* (receive) that helmet we are safe—not only in the sense of being delivered from conflict and suffering, or removed from the arena where fiery darts are flung in all directions, but safe from the destructive powers of evil forces.

Salvation, then, is not only forgiveness of past sins, it is strength to overcome, even conquer, present and future sins.

Wearing this helmet, we have confidence—confidence that nothing, absolutely nothing, can separate us from the love of God. So if God be for us, it does not matter who is against us (see Rom. 8:31–39).

Sword of the Spirit—the Word of God

Goodspeed sees this phrase as a parallelism for all that has preceded it. There is a sense in which that is true. Truth, righteousness, the gospel, faith, salvation, are all of the Spirit who speaks the Word of God. But the more complete meaning is to see this phrase in the way we have seen the other words of Paul—not as technical theology but as descriptive analogy. And, as with the other items of Christian armor, this one should not be allegorized too rigidly.

The sword of the Spirit is the Word of God, and that word *"is living and powerful, and sharper than any two-edged sword"* (Heb. 4:12). In the New Testament *"the word of God"* is never a general reference to "the Holy Scriptures." It means *the word which God gives us to speak.* We must be rooted in Scripture, for the Scripture is the primary source of God's Word. But the challenge of Paul's suggestion is that the Christian may be open to and can always depend on receiving the needed word from God. It may be a word of comfort for one's emotional turmoil, a word of hope for one's quivering soul, a word of courage for trembling knees, a word of challenge to one's apathy, a word of condemnation for one's sin, a word of prophetic judgment for one's uninvolvement and insensitivity. It may also be the word which the Christian is to speak—witness to be made, judgment to be shouted, prophecy to be uttered, teaching to be shared.

Our sword, then, is the Bible, but it is more. It is the word of the Bible made alive by the Spirit for our edification and for witness, admonition, and exhortation with others. It is also the inbreaking of God by His Spirit, speaking to our spirits, and through our spirits to others.

That brings us to the next area essential for those who would *be strong in the Lord.*

BE WATCHFUL IN THE SPIRIT

[18] praying always with all prayer and supplication in the Spirit, being watchful to this end with all perseverance and supplication for all the saints— [19] and for me, that utterance may be given to me, that I may open my mouth boldly to make known the mystery of the gospel, [20] for which I am an ambassador in chains; that in it I may speak boldly, as I ought to speak.

—*Ephesians 6:18–20*

Verses 18–20 can be summed up in the phrase "be watchful in the Spirit." All the armor will be of no avail in Christian warfare without the dynamic power that comes in this way.

To be watchful in the Spirit is to stay alive, to be alert. This instruction was a part of the early catechetical teaching of Christianity. We find it in 1 Corinthians 16:13; Colossians 4:2; 1 Thessalonians 5:6; 1 Peter 5:8; Revelation 3:2; 16:15. The teaching is repetitive of Jesus' words "Take heed, watch" (Mark 13:33), and "Watch therefore and pray always that you may be counted worthy to escape all these things that will come to pass, and to stand before the Son of Man" (Luke 21:36). What does it mean—to be watchful in the Spirit?

To Be Watchful in the Spirit Is to Remember

Experience is the word we use to designate a remembered past. We do not have to do everything we do as if for the first time. We are the beneficiaries of those who have gone before us. It is not necessary for each generation to discover the law of gravity or relativity. The electric light bulb and the principle of steam power are ours without having to discover them anew. No research scientist would think of ignoring the findings of his predecessors. He may not be bound by their methods and conclusions, but would surely be instructed in both. Why is it that we do not recognize and build on this principle in our religious, moral, and ethical life? The experiences of the crusades, the witch trials in Salem, the ovens of Dachau are ours to call upon. The Old Testament prophets and Jesus are relevant to every age.

We have the history of the race and our own personal histories to equip us so that we do not have to relearn everything daily. This has special meaning for Christians. The Bible is the great source book of our remembered past—our experience. The church is the gathering of God's people who recall and celebrate the experience. The whole range of the drama of the mighty acts of God and our personal appropriation of those saving acts in experience are ours to remember and to make us strong in the Lord.

The power of remembering as an element of being watchful in the Spirit is illustrated poignantly in the Psalms. Psalm 77 is graphic. "I cried out . . . my spirit was overwhelmed . . . so troubled I cannot speak. . . . Will the Lord cast off forever?. . . Has God forgotten to be gracious? Has He in anger shut up His tender mercies?" What is the answer to such debilitating despair?

> *1 will call to mind the deeds of the Lord;*
> *yea, I will remember thy wonders of old.*
> *I will meditate on all thy work,*
> *and muse on thy mighty deeds.*
> *Thy way, O God, is holy.*
> *What god is great like our God?*
> *Thou art the God who workest wonders,*
> *who hast manifested thy might among the*
> *peoples.*
> *Thou didst with thy arm redeem thy people,*
> *the sons of Jacob and Joseph.*
> —Psalm 77:11–15, RSV

The psalmist reclaims, in the present, God's salvation and is lifted out of despair. This is one of our primary sources of power: to return again and again to the foundation of our faith, the drama of salvation and its record in the Bible. To be watchful in the Spirit is to remember.

To Be Watchful in the Spirit Is to Pray

One ingredient of prayer is memory. God speaks to us through our memory, but remembering also stimulates us to speak with God. This speaking is prayer—whether verbal dialogue or the sharing of thoughts and feelings in the depths of our spirits.

If we have genuinely experienced God's forgiveness through the Cross of Christ, either in a cataclysmic conversion or in a final explicit yes that we spoke to the gentle but persistent wooing of God's love, we have a weapon of incomparable power. We can begin each day in freedom, released from the burdens of past sin, our consciences cleansed by repentance. In prayer we repent and receive the life-giving power of forgiveness.

And there is more. We may again sin and our consciences be soiled, but we need not allow guilt to build up into a mountain because of our failure to repent. Nor need we be enslaved by sins to which we may be especially vulnerable. We are no longer victims of our weaknesses. In prayer we claim the fact of our living "in Christ." We cultivate His indwelling presence. We live, then, not in our own power but in the power of Christ who lives within us.

To Be Watchful in the Spirit Is to Be in Communion with the Saints

"I believe in the communion of saints" is an item of the Apostles' Creed—the response of most Christians to that affirmation, if they consider it at all, is vague puzzlement about meaning—the thought that it is another archaic language statement that has no meaning today.

Only in the past few years have I begun to appropriate the power that can be ours through communion with the saints. My brother was killed in an inexcusable industrial accident in 1975. He died seeking to save the lives of three men who had been overcome by poisonous gas in the hold of a ship at a shipbuilding plant. His death was one of my most painful emotional experiences because it was only in the last three or four years of his life that we had grown especially close, and had begun to share deeply a brother-love that had been prevented by a lot of circumstances and separations.

Not long after his death I was sharing in a communion service in which the liturgy gave very pointed reference to "our departed loved ones," and gave deliberate opportunity for prayer for these. I began to pray for Lloyd in a way I had not done before. I had thought a lot about him, my memory often alive with the joy and pain of our lives together. But something else began to happen. I began to "share" with Lloyd rather than "think about him."

A part of the meaning of the communion of saints came alive that day. Since that experience I spend most of my personal prayer time in communion services, remembering, praying for, and communing with the saints. I do it at other times as well, but in the Eucharist as I await my turn to receive the bread and the wine, or after I have received the elements and am reflecting upon the meaning and power of Christ's presence in the community of faith, the time for "communion with the saints" becomes very special. The writer to the Hebrews knew the immediate and vital power of this. After rehearsing the great movement and personalities of faith in Hebrews 11, he begins chapter 12 with that vivid reminder: "Therefore, since we are surrounded by so great a cloud of witnesses. . .

SUSTAIN AND COMFORT ONE ANOTHER

21 But that you also may know my affairs and how I am doing, Tychicus, a beloved brother and faithful minister in the Lord, will make all things known to you; 22 whom I have sent to you for this very purpose, that you may know our affairs, and that he may comfort your hearts.

23 Peace to the brethren, and love with faith, from God the Father and the Lord Jesus Christ. 24 Grace be with all those who love our Lord Jesus Christ in sincerity. Amen.

—*Ephesians 6:21–24*

To be strong in the Lord requires that we sustain and comfort one another. From beginning to end Ephesians is the great church epistle. The community of faith, with the exalted Christ as the head, is the focus. So Paul closes the previous section by asking his readers to pray for him as he continues, despite his imprisonment, boldly to *make known the mystery of the gospel* (v. 19).

Dr. Karl Menninger, the famous Kansas psychiatrist, was once asked at a forum what he would do if he felt a nervous breakdown coming on. If the questioner anticipated the doctor saying, "I would go see a psychiatrist," he must have been shocked at Dr. Menninger's response. "If you feel a nervous breakdown coming on, lock up your house, go across the railroad tracks and find someone in need, and do something for him."

Whether that advice could always be taken literally may be questioned, but the truth behind it is unquestionable. Preoccupation with self is emotionally distressful and destructive. Moving out of ourselves in love and care for others is healthful. At the center of the Christian community is the love of Christ which connects us with one another. So Paul sent his letter by Tychicus, but also instructed Tychicus to share with the recipients so *"that you may know our affairs, and that he may comfort your hearts"* (v. 22).

There is no way to make it alone. The Christian life is a shared life. Within the Christian community every person has a gift which is essential for the whole. So Tychicus, whose name we hardly know, shares with Paul, whose name is written large in the history of the church, in making us strong in the Lord. He does so in the ministry of sustaining and comforting one another—a ministry for which we are all equipped.

The great source of our strength is captured in Paul's benediction. The form of this benediction makes it clear that this is a circular letter, to be shared with many churches. So the benedictory greeting is for the whole Christian fellowship. The blessing of peace recalls Paul's fundamental theme: the peace between Jew and Gentile which has come in the church and which is the first fruits of the cosmic peace which Christ is bringing to all creation. *Love with faith,* added to peace and the hope of ultimate unity in Christ Jesus, suggests the recurring Pauline triad of 1 Corinthians 13; faith, hope, love. Also here is recalled that great phrase in Galatians 5:6: "In Christ neither circumcision availeth anything, nor uncircumcision; but faith which worketh by love."

The last phrase, though loaded with meaning, offers some difficulty. This phrase has no parallel in any other New Testament benediction. The key word is *aphtharsia,* which literally means "immortality" or "incorruption." So the translation here, *Grace be with all those who love our Lord Jesus Christ in sincerity* misses some of the meaning. The RSV has it "with love undying." But that, too, does not seem to get at what Paul is communicating in the context of his letter. The difficulty perhaps is in the fact that Paul compressed his thought too much. Some believe he was saying, "those who love our Lord Jesus Christ and share in his undying life." That fits Paul's tone and the message of his letter, and Robinson's comment is justified: "So the epistle which opened with a bold glance into the eternal past closes with the outlook of an immortal hope."

In that hope we can be strong in the Lord!

INTRODUCTION TO PHILIPPIANS

The church at Philippi was Paul's "joy and crown" (4:1). Of all his churches it gave him the least trouble, perhaps no trouble at all, and the most satisfaction. So Philippians is a letter of joy, brimming over with expressions of gratitude, affection, and love.

Philippians is also a letter desperately needed by the modern church. It provides a picture of a church that takes seriously who she is as partners with Christ in the gospel, who accepts Jesus as Lord and patterns her ministry after Him—"taking the form of a servant," always exalting the Lord and being strengthened by Him, living in hope "that He who has begun a good work in you will complete it" (v. 6), expressing the fruits of the Spirit, living as witnesses to our servant-Lord on earth, but knowing our citizenship is in heaven.

Paul and Philippi

The vivid story of Paul's visit to Philippi is told in Acts 16. In a few lines, the work of the Holy Spirit guiding the missionary endeavor of Paul and his companions is boldly stated. The Holy Spirit had prevented them from going to Bithinia, so they went to Troas, where Paul had a vision of a man of Macedonia, calling, "come and help us." As the pattern of his life had been established by his obedience to the heavenly vision on the Damascus Road, Paul, along with Silas, Timothy, and probably Luke, set out for Macedonia, "concluding that the Lord had called us to preach the gospel to them" (v. 10).

They made their way to Philippi, a Roman colony, "the leading city of the district of Macedonia." There a Christian church was born, beginning with the conversion of Lydia, a dealer in purple, whose entire household responded to the gospel and were baptized with her. A church began in her house. Dramatic events followed in which Paul, in Jesus' name, freed a slave girl from a spirit which made her a source of gain for her owners. Paul and

Silas were arrested, flogged, and imprisoned, but this only became the setting for another display of the Holy Spirit's power as the jailer and his household were converted and baptized.

On the entreaty of the city fathers, who were alarmed by the discovery that they had flogged a Roman citizen, Paul left Philippi. We may assume that Paul returned about five years later, when at the close of his ministry in Ephesus, he "departed to go to Macedonia," giving "much encouragement" as he passed through the districts of that country (Acts 20:1, 2). Paul next went to Greece, returning to Macedonia three months later on his last visit to Jerusalem. We are told that he sailed from Philippi after the days of unleavened bread. So, three times Paul was in Philippi.

Writing the Epistle

That Paul wrote this epistle goes without serious question. It is the most personal of Paul's letters and bears the mark of authenticity in almost every sentence.

From the epistle itself we learn that Paul was a prisoner when he wrote it. Though an influential group of scholars claim the letter came out of an imprisonment in Ephesus, most still contend that it came out of Paul's imprisonment in Rome. Reference is made to the palace guard (1:13), whose headquarters were in Rome, and a greeting from the saints among the imperial slaves is included (4:22). Reflected in the epistle is the fact that the church in the place where Paul is imprisoned is strong and energetic—this would fit Rome; and Paul is facing the possibility of execution—also the situation of his Roman imprisonment. As with Colossians and Philemon, which came from Rome, Timothy is included in the situation.

Several points of harmony of Philippians with Ephesians and Colossians indicate a connection in time and setting for the writing of these letters. Philippians 3:20 and Ephesians 2:12, 19 provide a picture of the church as a city, a commonwealth, and of our true citizenship being in that realm. This is distinctive from other metaphors of Paul. Also, the personal glory of Christ, His grace and majesty, are present in Ephesians, Colossians, and Philippians in a way hardly hinted at in earlier letters, reflecting a profound and expanded revelation given through Paul (cf. Phil. 2:5–11 with Eph. 1:17–23, 2:8, and Col. 1:15–19; also cf. Phil. 2:10 with Eph. 1:20 and Col. 1:20). The blessedness of *knowing* Christ in Philippians 3:10 is expressed in the same glowing language of Ephesians 3:19—"to *know* the love of Christ." Though present in other epistles, this idea reaches its fullest prominence in these three prison letters.

Whether late or early in his two-year imprisonment we cannot be certain; thus we date the letter within the years 61 to 63.

The occasion for the writing, as indicated in the epistle, was Paul's gratitude that the Philippians had sent him *another* gift. Not only that, they had sent Epaphroditus to deliver the gift and to be a personal servant to Paul. What generosity! When Epaphroditus later became ill and homesick, Paul sent him home. To prevent any misunderstanding, Paul gave him a marvelous testimony: *"Receive him . . . with all gladness . . . because for the work of Christ he came close to death"* (2:29–30).

The occasion of Epaphroditus' return gave Paul the opportunity to encourage the Philippians in the trials through which they were going (1:28–30), and to make a plea for unity. Through Epaphroditus Paul had heard that a tendency to party-spirit and some personal antagonism between two women converts were threatening the peace of the congregation. Thus we have the most descriptive passage in Scripture of the Lord as servant, and the call for us to have the same mind of Christ (2:1–11). Too, Paul had learned there were false teachers seeking to dissuade the Philippians from the true path, and he urged them to "beware" and to "have no confidence in the flesh"—to rejoice only in Christ Jesus.

Out of concern for one person, Epaphroditus, and for an entire congregation, the Philippians; out of joy and thanksgiving for a people of faith who were partners with him in the gospel, and a passion to glorify Christ, Paul wrote to the church at Philippi and the Holy Spirit made that letter a word for the church forever and ever.

Two things, on the surface unimportant to the letter and its ministry, claimed my attention as I was doing the research for this writing, which I believe deserve to be noted.

One, Paul has been accused of being "down on women." But note the role women played in the church at Philippi. Lydia was the first convert there, and the church began in her house. Euodia and Syntyche were obviously leaders in the church or their disagreement with each other would not have been so important to Paul (4:2). The gospel message of the worth and dignity of women was not missed or downplayed by Paul.

Two, the feeling of solidarity between the church of Philippi with the whole Christian mission is an inspiring pattern for the church in every age. The Macedonian converts to Christianity were as a class, very poor (2 Cor. 8:1), but their liberality was conspicuous, far exceeding their ability. One wonders about the connection between being "poor in spirit" and being poor in fact. Is there a connection between missionary liberality and economic status? In some of the poorest nations of the world the Christian gospel is spreading more rapidly, and there is a sense of Christian solidarity among these people, that is missing, for the most part, in the developed nations of the world.

I visited Philippi some years ago and was troubled by the fact that not much is left of that once flourishing Colony of Rome. But out by the river, where Lydia was converted and perhaps baptized, I gained a helpful perspective. The most winsome church of the apostolic age probably never had a separate building; it was "the church in Lydia's house" or in the house of another. If there was a particular building for the church itself, not one of its stones stands upon another! No monument was there to mark the church which stood foremost as a witness of faith and love. But the river continues to flow there in Philippi, rushing to its final destination in the sea. And the message that went out from that church in Philippi and the letter written to that church continues to glow with light and power.

I returned to Philippi not long ago and discovered that a handsome chapel had been built near the river where Lydia was converted. I'm pleased with that, but it was not necessary for the witness. Acts 16 and the Philippian Letter is the river of the gospel that will forever flow into the hearts of those who are looking for a word from the Lord.

Outline of Philippians

I. Partnership in the Gospel: 1:1–30
   A. Participants in the Gospel: 1:1–11
   B. Proclaimers of the Gospel: 1:12–18
   C. The Gospel through the Person: 1:19–30
II. Servants of the Servant Who Is Lord: 2:1—3:1
   A. Our Common Life in Christ: 2:1–4
   B. The Servant Who Is Lord: 2:5–11
   C. Working Out Our Salvation: 2:12–18
   D. The Fellowship of Servants: 2:19—3:1
III. What Really Matters: 3:2–19
   A. Knowing Christ: 3:2–11
   B. The Prize of the High Calling: 3:12–14
   C. Conduct Consistent with Commitment: 3:15–16
   D. Judgment: 3:17–19
IV. Citizens of Heaven: 3:20—4:23
   A. In the Kingdom Now: 3:20—4:3
   B. Living While You Wait: 4:4–7
   C. You Are What You Think: 4:8–9
   D. The Sufficiency of Christ and the Support of His People: 4:10–23

CHAPTER ONE—PARTNERSHIP IN THE GOSPEL

PHILIPPIANS 1:1–30

Scripture Outline

Participants in the Gospel (1:1–11)

Proclaimers of the Gospel (1:12–18)

The Gospel Through the Person (1:19–30)

Every time Paul thinks of his friends in Philippi, he is filled with joy. The entire letter throbs with personal intensity. Most of Paul's letters include in the greeting a prayer of thanksgiving, but none of these prayers compares in depth of feeling with this one. Affliction, gratitude, confidence, and joy fill the mind of Paul, even though he is in prison, as he thinks of the one church which never caused him trouble or anxiety.

While a number of themes are woven into the first chapter, they may all fall under the theme *partnership in the gospel.*

PARTICIPANTS IN THE GOSPEL

1:1 Paul and Timothy, bondservants of Jesus Christ,

To all the saints in Christ Jesus who are in Philippi, with the bishops and deacons:

2 Grace to you and peace from God our Father and the Lord Jesus Christ.

3 I thank my God upon every remembrance of you,

4 always in every prayer of mine making request for you all with joy, 5 for your fellowship in the gospel from the first day until now, 6 being confident of this very thing, that He who has begun a good work in you will complete it until the day of

Jesus Christ; [7] just as it is right for me to think this of you all, because I have you in my heart, inasmuch as both in my chains and in the defense and confirmation of the gospel, you all are partakers with me of grace. [8] For God is my witness, how greatly I long for you all with the affection of Jesus Christ.

[9] And this I pray, that your love may abound still more and more in knowledge and all discernment, [10] that you may approve the things that are excellent, that you may be sincere and without offense till the day of Christ, [11] being filled with the fruits of righteousness which are by Jesus Christ, to the glory and praise of God.

—*Philippians 1:1–11*

Paul begins his epistle with a customary greeting, which includes a prayer. This greeting, with characteristic intensity, reveals the commanding passion of Paul's life—his devotion to Christ. This has added meaning because of the relationship of Paul to the Christians at Philippi. They are his friends, so the tone of the letter is set in the fact that this is a letter from a friend to his friends.

Three times in the first two verses he speaks the name of his Lord. These references to Christ are the cord binding Paul, and Timothy, Epaphroditus and other companions in the Roman prison with the band of faithful and joyful Christians at Philippi. They are all *participants in the gospel.* Though we may never grasp the full meaning of this, three words begin to plumb the depths of what it means to be participants in the gospel.

Privilege

The privilege that is ours is spelled out in the first two verses and the three pivotal references to Christ. We are *in* Christ; this is the state of our being: *"saints in Christ Jesus."* We are in a relation *to* Christ. That relationship is one of servants: *"servants of Jesus Christ."* Blessings *from* Christ and God our Father are ours to receive: *"Grace to you and peace from God our Father and the Lord Jesus Christ."*

The *New English Bible* expands a phrase in verse 1 to give even greater meaning to the thrilling designation of who we are: "to all those of God's people, *incorporate in Christ Jesus."* Isn't that exciting? We have not simply taken on a new religion with a new belief system, we have a new status in relation to God, have been given a new life, and are now a part of a new community.

254

Get that firmly in mind and rejoice in the sublime privilege that is ours: a new status in relation to God—forgiven and accepted, a new life, and a new community. The gospel is universal, the gift of God of Himself in Jesus Christ is offered to all. Yet, the privilege is an *exclusive* one, belonging to those who by faith belong to Jesus Christ.

In a similar greeting to the Ephesians (1:3–6), Paul spells this out completely. It is absolutely breathtaking. God chose us *in Christ* to be holy, adopted us as sons and daughters *through Christ,* freely bestowed His grace upon us *in the Beloved,* and *in Him* has given us redemption and the forgiveness of our sins.

Promise

We may have passed too quickly over three aspects of the privilege that is ours as participants in the gospel: (1) a new status in relation to God, (2) a new life, and (3) a new community. The promise that Paul sounds in verse 6 stops us and calls us to look again, especially at the second aspect: *a new life in Christ Jesus—"being confident of this very thing, that He who has begun a good work in you will complete it"* (v. 6).

The new status that is ours is that of being justified or accepted by God. Do not miss this: it is *in Christ* that we are justified (Gal. 2:17), and *in Christ* that we are new people, living a new life. We are always in need of keeping together the new status and the new life God gives us.

This illustration is a simple one, but it will make the point. A down-and-outer—some would call him a bum—comes to you in dire need. His dirty ragged dress is only the outer sign of his destitution and need. He is hungry and sick. You give him a bath and a change of clothing, but that is not enough. He is undernourished and sick, needing food and a doctor. Perhaps more, he needs love and friendship, healing of hurts, restoration of dignity, new purpose and meaning. So we come to Jesus, not in dirty rags but clothed in the garments of sin, spiritually starving and sick unto death. We are welcomed by Christ, accepted—bathed in His love and forgiveness. We are clothed in his grace, received as children—as though we were sinless. God sees us as righteous *in Christ;* this is our new status.

But that isn't enough, nor is it all. Christ, the Physician, knows we are sick, so He gives us His Spirit to reside within us, to heal and strengthen, to provide direction and give new life.

There are two snares into which we often fall as Christians. One is the snare of thinking that receiving a new status before God, being justified, is everything needful. The second snare is despondency into which we sink when the tide of our Christian experience ebbs low. We become life-less. No fruit of the Spirit seems to be growing in us. We are battered by one failure after another and feel forsaken by God. Temptation is especially appealing and we feel the joy of our salvation will never return. Remember: God did not start His work within us to abandon it. He does not do things half-measure. We have the promise: He will complete what He started. Let us claim that promise and come to Him again in faith, in the same yieldedness as when we first gave our life to Him.

There is something else to be said here. The Christian life is not an achiever's game. The Christian has no right to expect to fare any better in his own self-efforts than the non-Christian. What the Christian can count on is a God who keeps faith. The truth of Philippians 1:6 runs throughout Paul's theological stance. He persistently insists, "God is faithful" (1 Cor. 1:9; 10:30; 2 Cor. 1:18; 1 Thess. 5:24). Because God is faithful and is going to complete what He started within us, we can appropriate the cross-resurrection way of life. We can "go on to perfection" because God has already invested his total self in us. We can face the coming judgment without fear for our relationship with God has been made right through Christ; we can expect the Christian mission to be vindicated and finally accomplished.

Partakers

"You all are partakers with me of grace," Paul says in verse 7. He celebrated his fellowship with the Philippians *"in the gospel from the first day until now"* (v. 5).

The *"first day,"* not to be confined to twenty-four hours, was packed with tender memories as Paul remembered going to Philippi the first time. Finding no synagogue to which he could go on the Sabbath and speak with the Jews, he went down to the river where a group of women were said to meet on the Sabbath. After he told them the story of Jesus, one of the women, Lydia, opened her heart to the Lord. On *"the first day"* he cast an evil spirit out of a slave girl, and her owners were incensed to the point of having Paul flogged and imprisoned. But on *"the first day"* God worked miraculously again and the jailer was converted, then his family, and the Christian community grew in Philippi.

This was a big idea for Paul because it was a big experience. One of his most graphic ways of saying it was, "For as in Adam all die, so also in Christ shall all be made alive" (1 Cor. 15:22). Two communities are designated: the fallen community which with Adam we all have shared, by birth and by choice; the redeemed community which in Christ we share by *new* birth and choice. Once united to Christ by faith we are members of a new community which God is creating. In this new community "there is neither Jew nor Greek, . . . neither slave nor free, . . . neither male nor female; for you are all one in Christ Jesus" (Gal. 3:28). In this new community we are all *servants of Jesus Christ* (see commentary on Phil. 2:5–11) and we share a common life in Christ (see commentary on Phil. 2:1–4).

Prayer for Participants in the Gospel

In verses 3 and 4 Paul expressed how he thanked God *"upon every remembrance of you,"* and how in joy he prays for the Philippians. In verse 8, the depth of his longing and yearning for his friends is expressed—*"with the affection of Jesus Christ."* He even calls God as witness to the depth of his feeling before sharing his prayer in verses 9–11.

1. *It is prayer for love. "That your love may abound still more"* (v. 9). It is on target that this would be Paul's great intercession for those who are participants in the gospel, because love is the core word of the gospel. In English, "love" is an appallingly overworked word, diminished in power. The Greek words for immoral passion, sexual feeling, fraternal and family affection are all translated "love." A fourth Greek word for "love," *agapē* was lifted out of obscurity into immortality by the New Testament. Writers like John and Paul selected that word for the love expressed in what God chose to do in Jesus Christ "for us men and our salvation." The spontaneous, unmerited love and favor God has shown us rebellious and pride-filled creatures is *agapē:* "The Son of God loved me, and gave himself for me."

In the gallery of word pictures signifying love, none come close to "the width, and length, and depth, and height" of *agapē* the love of Christ which passes knowledge (cf. Eph. 3:16–19). In language we are poverty-stricken to convey the richness of the meaning of *agapē*, and so pictures are necessary: a father welcoming home a wayward son, a forgiven woman pouring precious perfume on Jesus, a shepherd risking the wilds to find one lost sheep. Dare we hang the portrait *par excellence* in the same gallery?—the Son of God hanging on a cross, spilling every ounce of blood in love for us sinners, acting out everything He said: "Greater love has no one than this, than to lay down one's life for his friends" (John 15:13).

Paul felt poverty-stricken in language, too, so he pictured *agapē* in Jesus, urging us to read into the meaning of the word the mighty acts of God, culminating in God's choosing to do in Christ something never done before and never to be done again: to be born, to live, to teach, to suffer, to die, to rise again—all "for us men and for our salvation." And the way that *agapē* looks in our lives is etched immortally in Paul's hymn of love: "Love is patient and kind, not jealous or boastful or arrogant or rude, does not insist on its own way, is not irritable or resentful, bears all things, believes all things, hopes all things, endures all things" (1 Cor. 13)—*and all for the sake of others.* That we who are participants in the gospel may abound more and more in that kind of *agapē-love* is the prayer of Paul.

2. *It is prayer for light.* "That your love may abound still more and more in knowledge and all discernment" (v. 9).

Who coined the phrase "love is blind!" That is 180 degrees off course. In this verse we separate light from love only for the sake of clear reflection. Paul's prayer shows us that we can hardly pray for growing love apart from a greatening light. Both the Phillips rendering and the NEB make this sublimely clear. "My prayer for you is that you may have still more love—a love that is full of knowledge and every wise insight" (Phillips). "And this is my prayer, that your love may grow ever richer and richer in knowledge and insight of every kind" (NEB).

Love calls for and seeks after knowledge. It is not blind. It does not overlook faults and weaknesses in others, but sees them clearly, looking beyond them to "the heart of things" and continuing to love. Love does not downplay truth, or speak in circles or opaquely to avoid confrontation, but speaks the truth that change and healing may be possible.

The light for which Paul prays is seen in its connectedness and in its connectedness but with a difference from love in Bishop Moule's paraphrase of this verse: "that your love may abound yet more and more *in the attendant and protective blessing* of spiritual knowledge and all needed discernment." Spiritual knowledge and discernment are gifts of the Spirit (1 Cor. 12:4–11) and are desperately needed, especially in our time of moral and spiritual confusion. Interestingly, the Greek word *aisthēsis,* translated "discernment," is used only in this one verse in the New Testament. Cognates of it are used in Luke 9:45 and Hebrews 5:14.

The Luke verse follows the story of the disciples' inability to cast an evil spirit out of a young boy and Jesus performing that miracle. They were mystified by the wonder this evoked and Jesus' challenge to the people to let His words sink into their minds and be stored up there. "They did not understand this saying, and it was hidden from them, so that they did not perceive it." (Luke 9:45).

The Hebrews verse that uses a cognate of *aisthēsis* ("discernment") has to do with Paul's referring to teaching God's Word with the metaphors of milk and solid food. "But solid food is for the mature, for those who have their faculties trained by practice to distinguish *(diakrisis)* good from evil" (Heb. 5:14, RSV).

These two passages give meaning and power to Paul's petition that we may grow in the gift of discernment and spiritual knowledge. At least two dimensions must be noted. One is a quality of *judgment,* a sharpness of perception, very much like that of the art critic, enabling us to distinguish between the real and the phony, the authentic and the superficial. A second dimension of spiritual knowledge and discernment is a kind of "sixth sense," a penetrating intuition that has been practiced, cultivated, and disciplined. Both these dimensions are at the same time gift and growth. They are gifts of the Spirit, but they grow and mature in effectiveness as we intentionally and consistently wait on the Lord, open to Him in prayer, and as we immerse ourselves in His Word through which His revelation comes. Let us remember, too, the exercising of the gifts is essential for their effectiveness. We must wrestle with hard issues in the light of the teaching of Jesus and the living Christ within. The result of that wrestling and the discernment that comes must be applied to the practical issues of daily life. Only then are we living in the light.

3. *It is a prayer for life.* Everything that Christ does *in* us must reflect itself *through* us. So the prayer is for life, life lived in a special way because the love of Christ is abounding within us, spiritual knowledge is increasing, and the capacity of discernment is being sharpened. How does this life express itself practically? What does it look like?

"That you may approve the things that are excellent" (v. 10). Is the word *discriminating?* To be able to differentiate not only between good and evil, but between good and better, between better and the best. *Excellence* is the quality we must seek.

The categories of experience within which our choices are to be made are multiple and seem to be growing in geometric proportion each decade. Categories of good and evil, decent and indecent are too broad. The opportunity of the Christian to impact with transforming power the environment in which he lives comes at this very point—being confronted with a choice between the decent and the excellent, the good and the best. What we read, the entertainment we seek, how we relate the content of our conversation, the degree to which we discipline ourselves, how we respond to and participate in our "sensate culture"—this tells the tale of our lives, how discriminating we are.

Our culture is so far gone down the path of sexual promiscuity, selfish indulgence, moral indifference, flabby thinking that only those who consistently choose the superlatively good can make a difference. Tennyson put the words that describe how discriminating we must be on the lips of Queen Guinevere.

> It was my duty to have loved the highest;
> It surely was my profit had I known;
> It would have been my pleasure had I seen.
> We needs must love the highest when we see it.

"That you may be sincere and without offense." Weymouth renders this "that ye may be men of transparent character." Moffatt also uses the word "transparent" for what the NKJV translates "sincere" and the RSV translates "pure."

As an adjective, the Greek word is *eilikrinēs* and appears in the New Testament only in this verse and in 2 Peter 3:1. The noun form, *eilikrineia,* occurs in 1 Cor. 5:8; 2 Cor. 1:12 and 2:17. Neither the noun nor the adjective form is common in classical Greek, and the derivation of the words is not clear. One suggestion of etymology has a challenging meaning when applied to our lives: The word may come from a combination of two Greek words—*heilē* which means "the sunlight," and *krinein* which means "to judge." The word would thus literally mean "sun-tested" and "sun-judged."

Two ancient practices provide insight for relating the meaning to our lives. One came about because there were slipshod sculptors who would produce statues from blemished, defective stones, filling the cracks with wax and painting over the blemishes. In time the sun would melt the wax, peel the paint, and reveal the glaring imperfections. Thus "sun-tested"—to be free from pretense and sham.

If you have been in the shops of the old city of Jerusalem, you know the necessity of a second ancient practice that gives meaning to this word. The bazaars and shops are small and dark. In that setting you cannot properly judge an article of pottery, glassware, or cloth. You have to move out of the shadowed recesses of the shop to the nearest available sunlight *to* appraise the value, to detect whatever faults or flaws may be in the article.

"Sun-judged"—to be able to stand in the clear sun of God's judgment and the judgment of our sisters and brothers, with no need to hide, or to conceal our thoughts and desires. "Live like men who are at home in daylight," Paul urged the Ephesians (5:8, NEB). That is what it means to be transparent, sincere and without blame.

A second suggestion of the derivation of the word has equally challenging meaning. *Eilikrinēs* (sincere or transparent) may have been derived from *eilein,* a Greek word which means "to shake to and fro in a sieve" until all foreign matter is extracted and the remaining substance is absolutely pure. Isn't that a marvelous picture of a character cleansed and purified by the grace of God because of willingness to be completely exposed and receptive to that grace.

Eilein also means to test "by rolling and rocking." That has the nuance of suffering, of conflict, of temptation, of challenge. We are purified, made whole by such testing. Viktor Frankl told how in the Nazi concentration camp everything was reduced to the basic, the elemental, the *human reason* for being. Those who survived somehow discovered the essence of existence, their reason for being—meaning through loving, acting, and suffering.

"Being filled with the fruits of righteousness." This is a beautiful expression for our life as participants in the gospel: *fruitfulness.* We would expect Paul to pray in this fashion. He knew the work of the Spirit in his own life—the Spirit producing the fruits of love, joy, peace, patience, kindness, goodness, faithfulness, gentleness, and self-control, which were now being tested in prison as he faced his own execution. *"Being filled with"* puts us in mind of trees whose every branch produces in this earthly life "the fruit" Paul described in Galatians 5:22–23.

PROCLAIMERS OF THE GOSPEL

12 But I want you to know, brethren, that the things which happened to me have actually turned out for the furtherance of the gospel, 13 so that it has become evident to the

whole palace guard, and to all the rest, that my chains are in Christ; 14 and most of the brethren in the Lord, having become confident by my chains, are much more bold to speak the word without fear.

15 Some indeed preach Christ even from envy and strife, and some also from goodwill: 16 The former preach Christ from selfish ambition, not sincerely, supposing to add affliction to my chains; 17 but the latter out of love, knowing that I am appointed for the defense of the gospel. 18 What then? Only that in every way, whether in pretense or in truth, Christ is preached; and in this I rejoice, yes, and will rejoice.

—*Philippians 1:12–18*

Paul's vocational passion is stated with bell-ringing joy and trumpetlike clarity in verse 18. *"What then? Only that in every way, ... Christ is preached; and in this I rejoice."*

Paul's friends are worried about him. He is in prison and soon must face trial. They are naturally concerned about the outcome, knowing all too well that death may be Rome's judgment on him. In his effort to reassure them, Paul laid down, perhaps inadvertently, three great principles. We can proclaim the gospel *anywhere*. We are to proclaim the gospel *everywhere*. When the gospel is proclaimed, the Spirit guarantees a harvest.

We Can Proclaim the Gospel Anywhere

Paul was in prison, but he did not allow this to hinder his missionary work. In fact, his imprisonment had *"turned out for the furtherance of the gospel"* (v. 12).

Paul portrayed the results of his imprisonment, thus proving that the gospel can be proclaimed anywhere. Verse 13 shows the impact upon those *outside* the Christian community. He witnessed to the soldiers who guarded him. Through them the word had spread to the whole praetorian guard that he was in prison not because he was a criminal but because he was a Christian.

Verse 14 shows the impact upon those *within* the Christian community. Because Paul remained faithful to Christ, and continued to witness joyfully despite the awfulness of his circumstance, the other Christians in Rome were *much more bold to speak the word without fear* (v. 14).

We need to remember this: the fruits of our proclaiming the gospel are not only in the winning of persons to Christ, but the encouragement we give others to be bold in their Christian living and witnessing.

We Are to Proclaim the Gospel Everywhere

Whether through Paul, a prisoner, or the guards, or the servants in Caesar's household, or the ordinary Roman citizens, the gospel was to be proclaimed everywhere.

I preached one Sunday not long ago at the Ocean Grove Camp Meeting. This has been one of the notable camp meeting centers in America, a great preaching place on the beautiful New Jersey Atlantic Coast, known as "God's Square Mile."

My wife and I went a couple of days early to get a little rest. On Saturday afternoon, we were strolling around when we came upon a park—not very big, but quiet and cool, with beautiful trees. Squirrels were scampering all around, a few children were playing kickball over in a corner, and, on a bench in the center of the park, a man sat smoking a cigar.

We greeted him as we passed—just a casual, "How are you?" We didn't expect his answer. In fact, we almost missed it.

I didn't really hear what he said. I guess I had not expected any honest answer. Thank God for the Spirit making us sensitive. The fellow mumbled something about not being well. Not many words, and half-joking, but miraculously we picked up on it and stopped to visit.

Ah, how the Spirit works when we are responsive. Within minutes, strangers were sharing deeply and intimately. He told the story of his wife, ravaged with cancer, in their retirement home only a block away, dying but not knowing it. A big strong man with no inner resources to face his crisis, he trembled with fear and tears flowed freely. He apologized as though he should not be crying in the presence of strangers. He was as terrified of the future as a child is of the dark night when alone.

He said he had no one to talk to, no one with whom to share. That struck me as being strange, very strange. He was in "God's Square Mile," yet had no one with whom to share. How ironic!

My wife and I shared God's good news of love and care, prayed with him—and my wife, the hugger in the family, embraced him. Dogs barked and chased around the trees; children squealed joyously in their games as a divine transaction took place on that bench in the center of that park. I preached the next morning to four or five thousand people, but I remember little about that service. But my memory is still alive with that experience in the park.

I spoke to a man for God, shared the gospel in that unlikely setting, and he heard, and was helped by the grace of Christ.

We are to proclaim the gospel everywhere.

The Spirit Guarantees the Harvest

Paul's presence in Rome, his imprisonment, and his proclamation of the gospel affected people—interestingly, the Christians—in various ways. The members of the church might have taken his imprisonment as a signal for them to stay quiet, to do nothing that would attract the attention of the authorities. This may have been the case with a few; but most of them gained courage and confidence and began proclaiming the word with fresh vigor.

Paul's honesty is so refreshing. He recognized and recorded the fact that some Christians were prompted by good will towards him and were challenged to be as faithful as he. Others were interested in success for its own sake. Jealous of Paul, they were determined to show that they could be successful and that the church could prosper without him. How "human" the church, then as now! So there was strife and envy. As disappointed in that as Paul was, he was undaunted in his belief that even confused and impure motives do not annul the power of the gospel. When Christ is proclaimed, the Spirit guarantees the increase.

THE GOSPEL THROUGH THE PERSON

[19] For I know that this will turn out for my deliverance through your prayer and the supply of the Spirit of Jesus Christ, [20] according to my earnest expectation and hope that in nothing I shall be ashamed, but with all boldness, as always, so now also Christ will be magnified in my body, whether by life or by death. [21] For to me, to live is Christ, and to die is gain. [22] But if I live on in the flesh, this will mean fruit from my labor; yet what I shall choose I cannot tell. [23] For I am hard-pressed between the two, having a desire to depart and be with Christ, which is far better. [24] Nevertheless to remain in the flesh is more needful for you. [25] And being confident of this, I know that I shall remain and continue with you all for your progress and joy of faith, [26] that your rejoicing for me may be more abundant in Jesus Christ by my coming to you again.

[27] Only let your conduct be worthy of the gospel of Christ, so that whether I come and see you or am absent, I may hear of

your affairs, that you stand fast in one spirit, with one mind striving together for the faith of the gospel, [28] and not in any way terrified by your adversaries, which is to them a proof of perdition, but to you of salvation, and that from God. [29] For to you it has been granted on behalf of Christ, not only to believe in Him, but also to suffer for His sake, [30] having the same conflict which you saw in me and now hear is in me.

—*Philippians 1:19–30*

The confidence of Paul in the gospel, expressed in this passage, shines like the noonday sun. Despite the fact that he is shackled because of the gospel, his hope is unshaken. Even this *"will turn out for my deliverance through your prayer and the supply of the Spirit of Jesus Christ"* (v. 19).

The NEB translates a portion of verse 20 in this fashion: "the greatness of Christ will shine out clearly in my person, whether through my life or through my death." This is an ultimate truth to be marked in red—the gospel is communicated through the person. Note the way Paul underscores this truth throughout the passage, not only by reference to himself, but by his call to us.

To Live Is Christ

Verses 21–26 form one of these marvelous passages in which Paul opens the door of his innermost being and invites us in to visit. Though addressing his readers, Paul is talking to himself, working out his feelings as he shares his unedited thoughts. He is ambiguous in his desires. Oh, for the transparency of commitment and hope that will enable us to struggle honestly and openly with our deep longings and desires. I want to go and be with Christ, he says; what joy that would be. Yet, what about the fruit of my labor? I'm hard-pressed to decide whether I want to go and be with Christ, or stay with you. How precious and revealing. Interwoven in the struggle is one of the boldest of Paul's claims: *"For to me, to live is Christ, and to die is gain"* (v. 21). Isn't that the highest, clearest point to which our faith can take us? When we arrive at that juncture of our spiritual pilgrimage, we will then be able to live with joyful, self-giving abandon, welcoming every bit of life, and without fear of death.

Do you see the possibility?—that with Paul we may come to the place where the earthly distinctions of life or death will mean little to us. The only death that matters is the one we die when we are "baptized into the death of Christ" (Rom. 6:3). But do not make the error of interpreting *"to die is gain"* to mean that our continuing bodily life is something we should be glad to escape. *"To live is Christ,"* and physical death neither adds to nor takes from that glorious fact. Christ has transformed both life and death.

When we pause to think, we realize that Paul had no actual choice in whether he lived or died—the Roman judge would decide that. He was wrestling with which verdict to hope for. That adds more depth to his conviction that to live is Christ and to die is gain.

The phrase *"depart and be with Christ"* (v. 23) gets the attention of most commentators. In my outline of this passage, I had ignored it because I believe what I have already said focuses the crucial content of these verses. Yet, I found myself drawn back to this notion—the desire to depart and be with Christ. This desire was much, much stronger than the translation indicates. The powerful pressure of Paul's feeling can be sensed when we note that the verb used here is also used in Luke 12:50 ("How I am *constrained* until it is accomplished," RSV); in Acts 18:5 ("Paul was *completely absorbed* in preaching," Phillips); and in 2 Corinthians 5:14 ("The love of Christ *controls* us," RSV).

The way Paul expresses himself implies that he expected to find himself in the presence of Christ immediately after death. On the surface this notion seems contradictory to Paul's teaching in his earlier letters (1 Thess. 4:13—5:10; 1 Cor. 15:35–55; 2 Cor. 5:1–10; Rom. 8:18—25) that Christians who die remain in a state of sleep until the Advent of Christ, who will then raise them to eternal life, give them a "new body," transforming their mortal nature into immortality. Expositors have strained to provide a solution to this apparent contradiction. But the big question is, *is it a contradiction?*

Paul did believe that there is a real analogy between sleep and death. There is a sense in which the experience of sleep obliterates the passage of time. In terms of consciousness, when I fall asleep my next awareness is that of waking. It does not unduly stretch Paul's notion to think that when a Christian falls asleep in death, the next awareness is that of the great awakening on the Day of Christ. This does not negate Paul's thought about the trumpet of God awakening the dead for judgment. All who die in Christ, in terms of conscious awareness, come simultaneously into His presence, and our communion with Christ is uninterrupted by the "sleep" of death. This belief is undergirded by Paul's expression of longing in 2 Corinthians 5:8, "we would rather be away from the body and at home with the Lord," and Jesus' promise to the criminal who died with him, "Today you will be with Me in Paradise" (Luke 23:43).

Mystery will always surround death and our "passage" from this life to the next, but that mystery does not diminish our hope. We live in the certainty of Paul: *"to live is Christ, and to die is gain."*

Conduct Worthy of the Gospel

Paul never allowed anyone to get away from the ethical/moral demands of a life in Christ. The slurring comment about the man who was "so heavenly minded that he was no earthly good" could never be made of Paul, nor of any Christian whose perspective is clear. Our arena of life is the practical everyday sphere where we live—our home, job, school, church, neighborhood—and in that arena, our conduct must be worthy of the gospel.

"Only let your conduct be," or as the RSV has it, "let your manner of life be," is a translation of a single word, *politeuomai.* By derivation it means "to exercise the rights and duties of a citizen." Paul was saying, "Live your citizen-life." You are a Christian; your citizenship is in heaven (see Phil. 3:20). The Philippians could easily identify with Paul's image. Philippi was a colony of the Roman empire. Every Roman colony was a little of Rome planted in distant settings throughout the world. A Roman citizen, no matter where he was, never forgot that he was a Roman. So the Philippian Christian understood Paul's word. There are *common* principles and actions that are to characterize our life as citizens of the kingdom.

We do well, even in our day when persecution is not expected to come upon those who live the Christian citizen-life in the United States, to reflect on Paul's admonition about our being together in *one spirit* as Christians.

"Stand fast." How wishy-washy are we in our convictions? How are our convictions shaped? What influence does our environment, our current circle of friends, the social standards of our day have upon our convictions?

"With one mind striving together for the faith of the gospel." Am I a part of a local church that is driven by a passion for the faith of the gospel which is a compassion for souls—"that none should perish but all come to new life in Christ"? If not, what am I doing to infuse that fire of passion into our citizen-life? When

did I last expend significant energy, make any sacrifice, invest time and talent to strive with one mind with my brothers and sisters for the faith of the gospel?

"Not in any way terrified by your adversaries." Do we even have any adversaries? That speaks loads about our integrity in proclaiming the gospel. How often are we in tension and conflict, as a church and as individuals, with the values of the community in which we live? What are the social and political issues to which the church must speak if she is faithful to her Lord which may bring forth adversaries: rights of women and children; violence in the home; the cheapening of human life by easy abortion; inattention to the elderly, the poor, the homeless; outrage against the rising crime rate that makes us calloused to persons caught in a cycle of "living outside the law"? It may be that a church can measure the effectiveness of her prophetic ministry by the adversaries who emerge to question and challenge her gospel.

Believing and Suffering

The Cross is at the center of the Christian life—not just Golgotha's cross, though that is our salvation, but the Cross as a way of life. Prior to Golgotha, Jesus suffered persecution, rejection, hostility, and misunderstanding. He promised His followers nothing less in their ministry in His name: "In the world you have tribulation; but be of good cheer, I have overcome the world" (John 16:33, RSV).

Paul, in prison and suffering, has a vision of the victorious Christ, so he can talk about being granted the privilege of suffering. No doubt he remembered Jesus' beatitude: "Blessed are those who are persecuted because of righteousness, for theirs is the kingdom of heaven. Blessed are you when people insult you, persecute you and falsely say all kinds of evil against you because of me" (Matt. 5:10, 11, NIV). He was also remembering his call. Had Ananias told him what the Lord had said to him about Paul? "This man is my chosen instrument to carry my name before the Gentiles and their kings and before the people of Israel. I will show him how much he must suffer for my name" (Acts 9:15, 16, NIV). This was after Calvary, remember. Jesus had already suffered for the sins of the world; Paul would suffer, not as a repetition of Calvary but as an extension and expression of it, in the name of Christ for the sake of others.

Even though we may not be imprisoned for the cause of Christ, and we don't hear much of martyrs in our day, don't miss the meaning of this. Because of the love Paul received from the cross, he was also to love, in spite of the cost. It costs to love, in any time, in any place. The costs may not be chains or death, but they are no less real. It costs to take into your home a young pregnant woman who has been disowned by her parents and needs love and care to pass through the most traumatic time of her life. It costs to turn your home into a "place of hospitality" for wanderers, for misplaced, unsettled persons, to give up your privacy and the comfort of routine for a season, that another might have the *space* and *time* in a warped and confused life journey to convalesce and think in the setting of love and acceptance. It costs to be "on call" for prayer and listening and counseling as your church seeks to minister to those outside the church as well as those within.

The word of Paul for us here is that the love of Christ on the Cross is both the means of our salvation and the mandate for our ministry. We are called to be faithful to Christ, to love with His unlimited giving and forgiving love—and that often requires suffering. We are to count such suffering a privilege.

It is interesting, and worth a long look, that Paul put *believing* and *suffering* together in verse 29. The Greek word here for "believe" is *pisteuō*, and the most useful word to assist in getting its meaning is "trust." When Paul talked about believing, the primary response he sought was not consent to the truth of his statements, but a personal entrustment of oneself to what the gospel announced. To trust is to commit oneself. To be granted the privilege of believing in Christ is to be given the opportunity of entrusting our lives to Him.

Here is the most challenging truth of this particular passage. Who we are is determined by whom and what we trust. Our identity is formed and transformed by our network of trusts. Believing in Christ calls for a reconfiguration, a reformation of the self. Christian "believers" are not persons who major in believing, who delight in correct doctrine and systematic propositions. Rather, they are persons who entrust themselves to Him whom the gospel proclaims as Lord and seek to live as worthy citizens of His kingdom by acting and relating as the gospel calls us.

It is natural, then—inevitable—that those who believe are also given the privilege of suffering. They are conformed to the One in whom they believe, and that is the theme of the next chapter.

CHAPTER TWO—SERVANTS OF THE SERVANT WHO IS LORD

PHILIPPIANS 2:1—3:1

Scripture Outline

Our Common Life in Christ (2:1–4)

The Servant Who Is Lord (2:5–11)

Working Out Our Salvation (2:12–18)

The Fellowship of Servants (2:19—3:1)

In October 1979, Pope John II visited the United States. The details and intricacies of the preparation were mind-boggling. The planning required precision and thoroughness. Out of the detailed preparation accompanying the excitement there were elements of humor. The newspapers reported one such turn of event.

In Chicago, the nation's largest Roman Catholic archdiocese, officials preparing for the Pope's arrival discovered to their dismay that the local papal throne was missing. It is customary in the Roman Catholic Church for each archdiocese to maintain a "throne room" in case of a visit by a Pope. But since a Pope had never visited Chicago and hope of one ever coming had been abandoned, the throne room in Cardinal John Cody's residence had been turned into a committee room. The week before the Pope's visit, workmen were busy reinstalling a platform for the throne. Officials panicked momentarily when no one could remember what happened to the throne. It was found, however, with other discards in a storage room at a nearby Catholic college.

A parable: *No one could remember what had happened to the throne.* The personal tragedy of many of us is that we have no throne room in our lives. Or, we sit upon the throne of our own lives. Or, as Christians, we proclaim Jesus Lord but refuse to reckon with who He really is, and what He requires of us. This chapter is about the Lord who is Servant and about those who would be followers of such a Lord.

OUR COMMON LIFE IN CHRIST

2:1 Therefore if there is any consolation in Christ, if any comfort of love, if any fellowship of the Spirit, if any affection and mercy, 2 fulfill my joy by being like-minded, having the same love, being of one accord, of one mind. 3 Let nothing be done through selfish ambition or conceit, but in lowliness of mind let each esteem others better than himself. 4 Let each of you look out not only for his own interests, but also for the interests of others.

—Philippians 2:1–4

Paul is always concerned about the church. He has concentrated on his own situation in chapter 1 because he knows what is uppermost in the minds of his friends at Philippi; he needs to assure them that he is confident in the faith and high in spirit.

He is first and foremost a pastor, so in 1:27 he begins to express his concern for them and the witness they must make. Whether he ever returns to them or not, they are to live as citizens worthy of the kingdom of Christ. They are to stand fast in the gospel and not be intimidated by adversaries. They are to count it a privilege to suffer because they *believe;* they have entrusted their lives to Christ.

In the first four verses of chapter 2, Paul gives a succinct, radiantly clear description of our common life in Christ. Thus he underscores the challenging fact that the Christian life is always a shared life: *"With one mind striving together for the faith of the gospel"* (1:27).

The Harvest Yield of Our Common Life in Christ

Paul begins with an *"if,"* but the if is not used the way we normally use it—as the condition upon which what follows depends: if there is good weather, adequate rain, and sunshine, and if the frost doesn't come too early, the trees will bear an abundance of fruit. He turns that around, first naming the harvest and then the conditions that will produce the harvest. And what is the harvest of our common life in Christ?

The NEB has translated these verses 1, 2, and 3 in a way that makes this metaphor of harvest yield, and seed and conditions which produce or prohibit an abundant harvest clear. The verses begin "If then our common life in Christ yields anything to stir the heart . . ," then go on to name the harvest yield.

1. *Loving consolation.* The RSV uses the word "encouragement" for "consolation." The Greek word is *paraklesis,* variously translated in other New Testament passages as "comfort," "exhortation," and "incentive." What is to be sensed here is the strong, upholding support that is ours within the Christian community.

As a pastor I could tell story after story of the ministry of *"loving consolation"* carried on by members of the church. One vivid experience comes to mind. A man was unfaithful to his wife, walked all over her, used her, and went his perverted, selfish way. But he kept coming back, asking his wife to accept him and promising to be faithful. That story was repeated over and over again until the woman couldn't take it any more. She committed suicide.

The woman had a friend in our church who had experienced much the same thing with her husband. This church member told me the story of her friend's suicide. As she wept she confessed, "That has been my temptation. You don't know how many times I've been on the verge of suicide. I couldn't follow through on my temptation because of the love and support of Christ through this church. I want you to know that Mary and Jim, Bob and Karen, Ben and Ann have kept me alive."[1]

2. *Fellowship of the Spirit. Koinōnia,* the Greek word here for "fellowship," may be translated "participation," "communion," or "sharing." Paul used the same word to suggest what happens in Holy Communion. "The cup of blessing which we bless, is it not a participation in the blood of Christ? The bread which we break, is it not a participation in the body of Christ?" (1 Cor. 10:16, RSV). It is the essence of our common life in Christ and implies all that Paul's threefold benediction explicitly states: the grace which Christ supplies, the love which God bestows, and the fellowship which the Holy Spirit creates (2 Cor. 13:14). The Holy Spirit gives us the gift of *koinōnia,* of fellowship. We do not create it. As Christ supplies grace, God bestows love, so the Spirit creates a deep sharing among us which makes us one.

3. *Affection and mercy.* This is a restatement of *"loving consolation,"* but with added meaning. In this verse and in Philippians 1:8, the KJV

says "bowels" instead of *"affection."* While it is somewhat inexact and certainly inelegant, the word gets our attention enough to cause us to want to explore the deep meaning of it. The Greek word is *splagchnon,* literally, "inward parts." As Paul used it, it did mean the viscera, but not the lower viscera, the intestines; rather, it meant the heart and lungs. That becomes a powerful metaphor. The Hebrews used a comparable metaphor for the feelings, which literally meant bowels. *"Affection"* thus takes on far more power than we usually credit to it. This is no light, soft word that is far less than love. It is active love, expressive love, and, for the Christian, nothing less than loving with the love of Christ.

Lightfoot paraphrases 1:8 in a fashion that helps us understand what "bowels" and "affection" really mean. "Did I speak of having you in my heart? I should rather have said that in the heart of Christ Jesus I long for you." Lightfoot then adds the comment, "A powerful metaphor describing perfect union. The believer has no yearnings apart from his Lord; his pulse beats with the pulse of Christ; his heart throbs with the heart of Christ."[2]

What a compelling characteristic of relationship for those who share a common life in Christ. Affection and mercy *(splagchnon and oiktirmos)*—the deepest and tenderest of feelings for one another, and the manifestation of these feelings in compassionate yearnings and actions. (See commentary on Col. 3:12, where Paul talks about putting on the "bowels of mercies".)

The Seeds That Produce the Harvest

"If then our common life in Christ yields anything to stir the heart, . . ." Paul begins. Then he names those things we have been discussing: loving consolation, fellowship in the Spirit, affection and mercy. *"Fulfill my joy by being like-minded, having the same love, being of one accord, of one mind"* (v. 2), he continues. Though clumsily stated, I believe Paul is saying that these are the seeds that produce the harvest yield of our common life in Christ. If they are not the seeds, then certainly they are the conditions in which the harvest grows.

The NEB translates the verse clearly: ". . . fill up my cup of happiness by thinking and feeling alike, with the same love for one another, the same turn of mind, and a common care for unity." Paul is not asking for uniformity of belief, nor is he talking about doctrinal orthodoxy. He is calling for harmony of relationship, mutual concern and love for one another, a caring for the quality of fellowship in order that Christ may perform His ministry through the body.

Overarching all of this is what Paul says in verses 3 and 4, which capture the burning uniqueness of our common life in Christ. Abraham Maslow, one of the giant thinkers of the twentieth century, brought a radical shift of perspective to psychology and began an entirely new approach to therapy as he realized the importance for persons to find purpose outside themselves. Since Freud, practitioners in the field of psychology and psychiatry were oriented toward the pathological. They studied sick people, dysfunctional persons. Maslow took the opposite approach, studying people who were vitally alive and fully functioning, radiantly happy *whole* persons. In the process, he developed a theory called self-actualization, and described a composite person whom he designated *self-actualized.* In his search for the secret of self-actualization he wrote, "Without exception, I found that every person who was sincerely happy, radiantly alive, was living for a purpose or a cause beyond himself."

Maslow's discovery has been a great blessing for the cause of mental and emotional wholeness. It is no wonder he named Jesus as a fully-actualized person. And it is no wonder Paul, in the style of Jesus, as we will see in the next section, called us to do nothing *"through selfish ambition or conceit,"* and not to *"look out only for [our] own interests, but also for the interests of others"* (2:3–4).

THE SERVANT WHO IS LORD

5 Let this mind be in you which was also in Christ Jesus, 6 who, being in the form of God, did not consider it robbery to be equal with God, 7 but made Himself of no reputation, taking the form of a bondservant, and coming in the likeness of men. 8 And being found in appearance as a man, He humbled Himself and became obedient to the point of death, even the death of the Cross. 9 Therefore God also has highly exalted Him and given Him the name which is above every name, 10 that at the name of Jesus every knee should bow, of those in heaven, and of those on earth, and of those under the earth, 11 and that every tongue should confess that Jesus Christ is Lord, to the glory of God the Father.

—*Philippians 2:5–11*

If I had to designate one big idea that has characterized the mood and movement of people during the past ten to fifteen years, I would say it has been a time of aggressive self-expression. Perhaps the most graphic reflection of that is the advent of "assertiveness training." This has been formalized in books, seminars, and workshops. For many people, winning is everything—even if you win by intimidation—and success is measured by achievement and position. The question seems to be "Can I get what I want out of life, and how soon?"

This is no new phenomenon, though the expression of it is getting a kind of Good Housekeeping Stamp of Approval in our day. James and John, the brother disciples of Jesus, were bitten by the bug of winning—of being number one—so they asked Jesus for the privilege of sitting at His right and left hand in His coming kingdom. They had not only missed the central facet of Jesus' teaching, they were totally unaware of the nature of the kingdom Jesus established. But Jesus, unwilling to stoop to intimidating or humiliating others for any reason, did not rebuke them in the presence of their friends. He simply asked a question to force further thought, "Are you able to drink the cup that I drink, or to be baptized with the baptism with which I am baptized?"

James and John still missed it. Without hesitation they responded, "We can." But Jesus knew they did not know, so He pressed His teaching about the nature of His kingdom, concluding, "whoever would be great among you must be your servant, and whoever would be first among you must be slave of all" (Mark 10:43, 44, RSV). And to disallow any mistake of what He was talking about, He added, "For the Son of man also came not to be served but to serve, and to give his life as a ransom for many" (v. 45).

Had Paul heard that story? In verses 3 and 4 he laid the claim upon the Christians of Philippi not to be served but to serve. Now in verses 5–11, he shows clearly what that means. He gives us one of the most beautiful pictures in all Scripture of the nature and character of Christ, and one of the most demanding challenges to those who would be His followers.

The Lord as Servant

This section of Scripture is packed with meaning and is a hinge passage of Paul, affirming the pre-existence of Christ and describing the nature of the Incarnation. Verses 6 and 7 graphically state the case: *"who, being in the form of God, did not consider equality with God something to be grasped, but emptied Himself by taking the form of a servant, and coming in the likeness of men."*

I am almost breathless before such a passage and tremble at the thought of commenting on it—that I may say too little or too much and detract from the majestic truth that is here. There are intriguing theological nuances, aspects of interpretation that could occupy pages—especially questions about what it means to be in the form of God, or having God's nature, and possessing equality with God.

H. R. Mackintosh has summarized the conclusion to which most scholars would come in commenting on the passage, and these questions about Christ "being divine by nature": "It is asserted—and on the assertion hinges the thrilling moral appeal of this passage—that before He came as man, Christ's life was Divine in quality, not merely *like* God but participant in His essential attributes."[3]

Not only here, but in numerous other passages, Paul embraced with certainty the preincarnate as well as the incarnate life of Christ being of divine nature. In this passage though, he grabs our attention with a puzzling suggestion: Christ *"did not consider equality with God something to be grasped."* We need to put this verse in different words to understand the meaning.

Caird suggests the clearest restatement of it: "Christ, being in the form of God, was equal with God, but did not count this a prize to be clutched." The idea is so mountainous that we may never scale it, but that is all right. To be in awe, even puzzled awe, in contemplating God's coming to us in Jesus Christ is a proper Christian response. We can ascend to great heights of the mountainous truth, however, by comparing Christ and Adam. Paul did this often (1 Cor. 15:21–22, 45–49; Rom. 5:12–14; Eph. 4:22–23; Col. 3:9–11). Adam the man grasped at equality with God; Christ renounced equality with God to become man.

Thus the phrase in verse 7 is crucial: Christ *"emptied Himself."* The KJV translation, "made himself of no reputation," is inadequate to capture the expansive meaning and power of what Christ did. It is easy to get confused here, and commentators disagree. Some contend for the extreme—that Christ emptied Himself of His divine nature—or to a lesser degree, but still extreme—that it was of His *equality with God* that He emptied Himself. I can't agree.

The Greek word, *huparchein,* translated "being" in our text, is not the common Greek word for "being." It describes what a person is in essence—that which cannot be changed; the innate, unchangeable characteristics of a person. Through chances, changes, and all circumstances this being—essence *(huparchein)* remains the same. Paul, I think, would not regard as possible the surrender by Christ of His divine nature. Paul's own experience of the risen Lord was such a vital factor in the formation of his thought that, as He who had come to mean so much to him surely did not begin to exist when Jesus was born in Bethlehem, so the nature of this one did not change in essence, when He became man. He did empty Himself, though, of the glories of heaven, of the prerogatives of being divine; He emptied Himself of rank, privilege, and rights. *The Lord became a servant.* Doesn't this harmonize with Jesus' prayer in John 17?— "I glorified thee on earth, having accomplished the work which thou gavest me to do; and now, Father, glorify thou me in thy own presence with the glory which I had with thee before the world was made" (vv. 4, 5, RSV).

More clearly than any place else in Scripture, the shape of the incarnation is described here: humiliation, weakness, and obedience (see also 2 Cor. 8:9). *"He humbled Himself and became obedient to the point of death, even the death of the cross"* (v. 8). Was Paul thinking of the Suffering Servant in Isaiah 53, especially verse 12?—*"Therefore I will divide him a portion with the great, and he shall divide the spoil with the strong; because he poured out his soul to death, and was numbered with the transgressors; yet he bore the sin of many, and made intercession for the transgressors"* (RSV).

The Mind of Christ in Us

In many ways verses 5–11 make up the greatest and most moving passage that Paul ever wrote about Jesus—certainly the most descriptive. But not only is this a vivid description of who Jesus is, it is a call to us. Thomas A. Langford has expressed this as clearly and as succinctly as is possible.

> In Jesus we find embodied the self-giving of God to persons and the self-giving of a person to other persons. Jesus is the Lord who is servant, and Jesus is the servant who is Lord. As the Lord who is servant, Jesus identifies with human life so as to establish a redemptive relationship. As servant who is Lord, Jesus calls us to acknowledge his lordship through our servanthood. The grace of God in Jesus Christ calls us to a graciousness which is a self-abandonment to the love of God and the love of the neighbor.[4]

Paul introduces this great theological statement of who Jesus is to support his call to the Philippians to look out not only for their own interests, but also for the interests of others. His toughest word was in verse 3: *"in lowliness of mind let each esteem others better than himself."* In what stark contradiction that is to the rampant self-interest being expressed by most. It is scathingly clear: the call of Christ is that our ultimate concern must be for others, and that concern leaves no room for indulgent self-concern. The call is to have the mind of Christ who emptied Himself, and became a servant.

Not many of us want to be servants, do we? And those who have the notion that Christianity centers in service need to realize that there is a vast difference between the kind of serving most of us do and the willful decision to become a servant. Most of us serve by choosing when and whom and how we will serve. We stay in charge.

Jesus calls for something else. He calls us to be servants, and when we make this choice, we give up the right to be in charge. Then, amazingly, we experience great freedom. We become available and vulnerable. We lose our fear of being stepped on, manipulated, taken advantage of. Aren't these our fears? What joy comes, what energizing of life, when we act out of the desire to be a servant, rather than the pride of choosing to serve now and then, when and where and whom we wish.

Carl Jung told of a man who asked a rabbi, "How come in the olden days God would show Himself to people, but today nobody ever sees God?" The rabbi said, "Because nowadays nobody can bow low enough." Let this mind be in us which was in Christ Jesus, who bowed low, emptied Himself, and became a servant—then we will see and know and share with God!

The Servant/Lord Exalted

It is the paradox of the Christian gospel that the last become first, the humble are exalted, the servant becomes Lord, the poor become rich. The Beatitudes (Matt. 5:3–11) are Jesus' catalog of the way things are turned upside-down, inside-out in the new economy of God's kingdom. So Jesus' enunciation of the humble being exalted (Matt. 23:12) was gloriously fulfilled in His own case. He ascended after the Resurrection and now sits at God's right hand; *"Therefore God also has highly exalted Him and given Him the name which is above every name, that at the name of Jesus every knee should bow, of those in heaven, and of those on earth, and of those under the earth, and that every tongue should confess that Jesus Christ is Lord, to the glory of God the Father"* (vv. 9–11).

WORKING OUT OUR SALVATION

[12] Therefore, my beloved, as you have always obeyed, not as in my presence only, but now much more in my absence, work out your own salvation with fear and trembling; [13] for it is God who works in you both to will and to do for His good pleasure.

[14] Do all things without complaining and disputing,
[15] that you may become blameless and harmless, children of God without fault in the midst of a crooked and perverse generation, among whom you shine as lights in the world,
[16] holding fast the word of life, so that I may rejoice in the day of Christ that I have not run in vain or labored in vain.

[17] Yes, and if I am being poured out as a drink offering on the sacrifice and service of your faith, I am glad and rejoice with you all. [18] For the same reason you also be glad and rejoice with me.

—Philippians 2:12–18

Would this have been a shocking word to the Philippians? It is to us: *"Work out your own salvation with fear and trembling."* Those Paul was writing were already Christian. What can this mean—work out your salvation?

The word "salvation" comes from the same Latin root word as "salve," an ointment for healing. To be saved is to be made whole. In Greek the word is *sōtēria,* meaning not only salvation, but preservation.

While there is a beginning point in our salvation experience, the point of repentance and justification—the time of our faith commitment to Jesus Christ—this is only the beginning. We are to *"work out"* our salvation, to grow into maturity, into the full stature of Christ.

Paul does not mean for this section to be a complete dissertation of how we work out our salvation. In truth almost everything Paul wrote was to that end. In this passage, however, these are some signal clues for us.

Obedience

Sōtēria, salvation, involves faith (Eph. 2:8; 2 Tim. 3:15; 1 Pet. 1:9). Paul's great message of salvation was that we are justified by grace through faith. We do not properly understand Paul's meaning of faith unless we know that the primary ingredients of it are *trust* and *obedience.* (See commentary on Gal. 2:15–16.) When Paul talked about the Thessalonians' coming to faith (1 Thess. 1:8), he wrote of their *obedience.* In Romans 1:8 he wrote of "your faith" and in Romans 16:19 of "your obedience," clearly meaning the same thing. In Romans 1:5, he used the actual phrase "obedience of faith," probably meaning "obedience which is faith."

"*Do all things without complaining and disputing,*" Paul says in verse 14. He is talking about the Philippians' style of getting along with each other, to be sure. But since this follows the admonition to work out salvation with fear and trembling, it also suggests the content of what they are to do without murmuring and disputing. They are to obey—to take God at His word, to act with the conviction that the promises of God in Christ are true.

Dag Hammarskjøld, a rare example of a modern mystic who was also a man of the world, while living his busy, productive life, bore an eloquent and challenging witness to the meaning of obedience: "I don't know who—or what—put the question, I don't know when it was put. I don't even remember answering. But at some moment I did answer *yes* to Someone—or Something—and from that hour I was certain that existence is meaningful and that, therefore, my life, in self-surrender, had a goal."[5]

This statement not only witnesses to obedience, but to servanthood. And the *who* who puts the question is God. If you want a biblical example, none is clearer than that of Mary, the mother of our Lord. *Behold, I am the handmaid of the Lord; let it be to me according to your word* (Luke 1:38, RSV).

Abandonment

Obedience is the one essential to working out our salvation. For Paul there was a degree of obedience that deserves special note: abandonment. The extravagance of his obedience is almost shocking: "*I am being poured out as a drink offering on the sacrifice and service of your faith*" (Phil. 2:17).

My biggest problem, not only as it relates to how I express my obedience to Christ but in my basic approach to life, is an unwillingness to give up control, to abandon myself in faith to the Christ-life process. When I press myself, I have to confess that I can't believe my life is going to be good unless I can control it, unless I can make the plans and dream the dreams and then work for their fulfillment. I am not alone in this, and I believe it is the source of a great deal of our human misery. Our trust in Christ must bring us to the point of abandonment, a willingness to "pour out our lives," believing that we don't need to, nor can we, control the future. The future belongs to God.

It is easy to miss another important point Paul is making as he talks about abandonment. We pour out our lives *as a drink offering,* as a sacrifice, for the sake of others. Jewish as well as pagan sacrifices were normally accompanied by a libation of wine (2 Kin. 16:2; Jude 7:18; Hos. 9:4). Priests not only poured libations of wine, but of blood, thus the connection between the two in Christian liturgy. Though such literal priesthood and sacrifice were replaced by the once-for-all offering of Christ, Paul found the metaphor meaningful. As an apostle of the Gentiles, Paul saw himself as the priest presenting to God the Gentiles as an acceptable offering. He also saw himself as an offering, a sacrifice on behalf of others. We need to recover that dimension of the priesthood of all believers—the willingness to offer ourselves, to abandon ourselves in sacrificial ministry for others.

Rejoicing in All Circumstances

Even though I am in prison, Paul says, being poured out as a sacrifice, *"I am glad and rejoice with you all . . . you also be glad and rejoice with me"* (vv. 17–18). This recurring theme of Paul's is an essential ingredient in working out our salvation.

"In fear and trembling," then does not mean nervous apprehension with which some would say we are to face the Last Judgment. The word translated fear *(phobos)* does not here denote fright or dismay or alarm in the face of danger or loss. As often in the New Testament, it denotes the awe that persons experience in the presence of God. With trembling wonder, they are to recognize God's presence. In all circumstances, even in pain, suffering, loss, death, prison, uncertainty, perplexity, the salvation process is going on for those who love and trust the Lord. So, rejoicing is the order of every day.

A few years ago I did a film conversation with Archbishop Anthony Bloom, the Russian Orthodox who has written so helpfully about a life of prayer. When I questioned him about ordinary persons living the contemplative life in the everyday world, he used an image he said he had gotten from Evelyn Underhill. This is a marvelous picture of happy obedience, of rejoicing in all circumstances: "A Christian should be like a sheep dog. When the shepherd wants him to do something, he lies down at his feet, looks intently into the shepherd's eyes, and listens without budging until he has under-stood the mind of his master. Then he jumps to his feet and runs to do it. And the third characteristic, which is not less important: at no moment does the dog stop wagging its tail."

THE FELLOWSHIP OF SERVANTS

[19] But I trust in the Lord Jesus to send Timothy to you shortly, that I also may be encouraged when I know your state. [20] For I have no one like-minded, who will sincerely care for your state. [21] For all seek their own, not the things which are of Christ Jesus. [22] But you know his proven character, that as a son with *his* father he served with me in the gospel. [23] Therefore I hope to send him at once, as soon as I see how it goes with me. [24] But I trust in the Lord that I myself shall also come shortly.

[25] Yet I considered it necessary to send to you Epaphroditus, my brother, fellow worker, and fellow soldier, but your messenger and the one who ministered to my need; [26] since he was longing for you all, and was distressed because you had heard that he was sick. [27] For indeed he was sick almost unto death; but God had mercy on him, and not only on him but on me also, lest I should have sorrow upon sorrow. [28] Therefore I sent him the more eagerly, that when you see him again you may rejoice, and I may be less sorrowful. [29] Receive him therefore in the Lord with all gladness, and hold such men in esteem; [30] because for the work of Christ he came close to death, not regarding his life, to supply what was lacking in your service toward me.

[3:1] Finally, my brethren, rejoice in the Lord. For me to write the same things to you *is* not tedious, but for you *it is* safe.

—Philippians 2:19—3:1

This section is a great description of *the fellowship of servants.* Paul talks specifically about sending Timothy to the Philippians. He knows that Timothy *"will sincerely care for your state"* (v. 20). He mentioned, at length, Epaphroditus, *"my brother, fellow worker, and fellow soldier, but your messenger and the one who ministered to my need"* (v. 25). For the work of Christ, Epaphroditus *"came close to death, not regarding his life"* (v. 30).

Some years ago Alexander Irvine wrote a novel entitled *My Lady of the Chimney Corner.* In it there was the incident in which "the lady" went to comfort a neighbor whose boy lay dead. As gently as falls an autumn leaf, she laid her hand on Eliza's head:

"Ah, woman, God isn't a printed book to be carried aroun' by a man in fine clothes, nor a cross danglin' at the watch chain of a priest. God takes a hand wherever he can find it, and just does what he likes with it. Sometimes he takes a Bishop's hand and lays it on a child's head in benediction, and then he takes the hand of a doctor to relieve pain, the hand of a mother to guide a child, and sometimes he takes the hand of a poor old craither like me to give comfort to a neighbor. But they're all hands touched by His Spirit, and His Spirit is everywhere lukin' for hands to use."

That is the fellowship of servants—those who have in them the mind of Christ who emptied Himself, and became a servant. This is what the Christian faith does for us: it leads us out of ourselves, freeing us from ourselves, binding us to Christ and to our brothers and sisters.

NOTES

1. Maxie Dunnam, *Barefoot Days of the Soul* (Waco, TX: Word Books, 1975), pp. 101–2.

2. J. B. Lightfoot, *St. Paul's Epistle to the Ephesians* (Grand Rapids: Zondervan Publishing Co., 1953), p. 85.

3. Hugh Ross Mackintosh, *Doctrine of the Person of Christ* (Naperville, Ill.: Allenson, 1912), p. 67.

4. Thomas A. Langford, *Christian Wholeness* (Nashville: The Upper Room, 1978), p. 15.

5. Dag Hammarskjøld, *Markings* (New York: Alfred A. Knopf, 1964), p. 205.

CHAPTER THREE—WHAT REALLY MATTERS
PHILIPPIANS 3:2–19

Scripture Outline

Knowing Christ (3:2–11)

The Prize of the High Calling (3:12–14)

Conduct Consistent with Commitment (3:15–16)

Judgment (3:17–19)

There are some who believe that a part of three letters Paul wrote to his friends in Philippi are combined in this one epistle. One of the arguments for this theory is that Philippians 3:2–19 is an abrupt change in tone. Two chapters of love, expressions of affectionate intimacy, are followed by a passage of scathing denunciation.

It is true that if you take these verses out and in your reading follow 3:2 with 3:20, you have a harmonious expression. However, who can doubt that Paul was capable of writing in both veins—of warm affection and challenging exhortation? There are abrupt breaks in other Pauline letters (e.g., 1 Cor. 15:58 and Gal. 6:10). It is important to note that the change of tone is not sustained in these nineteen verses, and there is no sustained reason for believing that Paul's attitude toward the Philippians changes in the course of the letter. He sounds a scathing denunciation against *"dogs"* who distort and pervert the gospel, those who pride themselves in being "the circumcision" (*"beware of the mutilation!"*) *"For we are the circumcision who worship God in the Spirit, rejoice in Christ Jesus, and have no confidence in the flesh"* (v. 3).

This entire chapter is Paul's presentation of What Really Matters, and we will treat it under that theme. Written under the shadow of a low-lying and ominous cloud, from a dark, dismal cell, out of dreary and encumbering circumstances, the epistle resounds with a note of joy. If there is an interruption in that note, it serves only to make real Paul's ardent and unfaltering commitment to what really matters.

KNOWING CHRIST

2 Beware of dogs, beware of evil workers, beware of the mutilation! 3 For we are the circumcision, who worship God in the Spirit, rejoice in Christ Jesus, and have no confidence in the flesh, 4 though I also might have confidence in the flesh. If anyone else thinks he may have confidence in the flesh, I more so: 5 circumcised the eighth day, of the stock of Israel, of the tribe of Benjamin, a Hebrew of the Hebrews; concerning the law, a Pharisee; 6 concerning zeal, persecuting the church; concerning the righteousness which is in the law, blameless.

7 But what things were gain to me, these I have counted loss for Christ. 8 Yet indeed I also count all things loss for the excellence of the knowledge of Christ Jesus my Lord, for whom I have suffered the loss of all things, and count them as rubbish, that I may gain Christ 9 and be found in Him, not having my own righteousness, which is from the law, but that which is through faith in Christ, the righteousness which is from God by faith; 10 that I may know Him and the power of His Resurrection, and the fellowship of His sufferings, being conformed to His death, 11 if, by any means, I may attain to the Resurrection from the dead.

—Philippians 3:2–11

What really matters is knowing Christ, Paul says. *"Beware of dogs"*; beware of anything or anyone that would divert you from this center.

Not My Own Righteousness

It is not the external things that count, but what has happened and is happening inside. Salvation is *to be found in Him, "not having my own righteousness, which is from the law, but that which is through faith in Christ, the righteousness which is from God by faith"* (v. 9). Paul chose not to boast except about what Christ had done for him. Had he been prone to boast otherwise, he had enough external privileges to put him out front in any comparison. He listed four special items for his external pedigree.

One, he was born of orthodox parents, circumcised, as the law required, on the eighth day. Two, he was *"of the stock of Israel,"* more precisely "an Israelite by race." He was not just "of the people of Israel" as the RSV has it. Proselytes could be called "people" of Israel. The word Paul uses is *genos,* meaning "race, family, or kind," so he was speaking of blood descent. Three, he was *"of the tribe of Benjamin."* This was a matter of special pride. Priests had to prove their lineage, and the father of any girl who was to marry a priest had to prove his Israelite descent for three generations. Tribal identities had blurred, and many had become no more than ideal entities. But the tribe of Benjamin was one of the two southern tribes existing in actuality and remaining true to the house of David and to Jerusalem as the center of the faith of Israel. Possibly Paul's parents named him Saul after the first king of Israel, who was also of the tribe of Benjamin.

Paul crowned all his enumeration of privileges of which to boast by claiming to be *"a Hebrew of the Hebrews."* This had very special meaning. Jews were dispersed all over the world. Tens of thousands were in Rome. Alexandria had more than a million. Most of these Jews stubbornly refused to be assimilated into the nations of their residence, tenaciously retaining their own religion, culture, customs, and laws. Many of them, however, forgot their language, and spoke the language of the dominant people around them. A Hebrew was not merely a Jew, he was a Jew who with great effort and arduous discipline retained the Hebrew language and taught it to his children. So Paul claimed not only to be a full-blooded Jew, he was a Hebrew who had learned and never forgotten his mother tongue, though he was born and reared in the Gentile city of Tarsus.

What reasons for which to boast. But there was more. He was ardent in his religious practice, a trained Pharisee, blameless in keeping the law, and zealous in persecuting the Christians. What he was by birth and what he had become by conviction and achievement were enough to tally a high level of superiority compared to any who might be preaching circumcision and righteousness by the law.

Privileges of birth and human achievement, however noble, count nothing.

In the Greek text of these verses, the word for "gain" is plural and for "loss" singular, so a good translation of verse 7 would be "For Christ's sake I have learned to count my former gains a loss." In this dramatic abruptness there is a notable contrast. Each of the outward privileges in Paul's catalog had at one time been a distinct and separate gain, individual items of profit. Now—they are all one big bundle of loss; loss because they are useless. Everything is *rubbish* compared to gaining Christ. Righteousness which is from the law is illusory, short-lived; now we have it, now we don't. It is dependent upon our efforts at meeting obligations, keeping laws, doing right. But the righteousness of God is conferred upon us by God in response to our faith in Jesus Christ.

Too many of us Christians have yet to appropriate this freedom-bringing, wing-giving truth. We keep one foot in the law domain where "doing" prevails, hoping that our *doing* will lead to our *being* righteous. We forget that we do not strive to live by the Spirit in order to be in the Spirit. It is the reverse. Because we are in the Spirit we live by the Spirit. And because we have been conferred the righteousness of God, we do deeds of righteousness. We do righteous works not to get in right relationship with God, but because He has already justified us. We are in right relationship with Him by faith. Our righteousness is *that which is through faith in Christ*.

That I May Know Him

Phrase is piled upon phrase to underscore *knowing Christ* as the core of what really matters: ". . . *these I have counted loss for Christ*" (v. 7); ". . . *the excellence of the knowledge of Christ Jesus my Lord, for whom I have suffered the loss of all things, and count them as rubbish, that I may gain Christ*" (v. 8); "*be found in Him*" (v. 9); "*that I may know Him*" (v. 10).

What does this mean, this most crucial of all matters—knowing Christ? Verse 10 answers the question.

1. *The power of His Resurrection.* Paul is talking about *now*. To know Christ is to have His Resurrection power *now*. At conversion, when we repent and make a faith commitment to Christ, we are united with Christ. God does something which we accept by faith. Once accepted, this becomes a fact of experience. We must now come to *know Him* in whom we now live.

Suffering, death, and Resurrection tell the story of Jesus' life. But *knowing Christ*, as we are privileged to do, is not knowing His suffering, death, and Resurrection as episodes in the gospel. Rather, it is knowing these dimensions of Christ's life as present and active forces in our lives. So, it is not by chance Paul began with "*the power of His Resurrection.*" We must be convinced of Christ's Resurrection and rise to the new life of God's new creation (2 Cor. 5:17; Col. 3:1) before we can learn the secret of Christ's suffering, and be conformed to His death.

The power of His Resurrection—wow! We can know it. Here is a hint of it: Artur Rubinstein, even at eighty, reached greater heights than he had known in his long career as a peerless artist. In an interview he was asked how, after all the long years of perfection, he still kept his interpretations fresh and inspiring. Rubinstein answered, "Every day I am a new man and every occasion is a new moment for me. When I play, it is no longer I but a secret power takes over."

If that is true of a great artist, as certainly it is, it should be even more so for a Christian who knows the power of Christ's Resurrection.

2. *The fellowship of His suffering.* It is a harsh, hard, difficult, demanding, but essential truth. We do not know Christ completely until we know Him in the fellowship of His suffering.

Go Out in Joy is the moving story of Nina Hermann, a chaplain at a children's hospital. She wrestled, as any sensitive person exposed to the daily suffering of children would, with intellectual problems, questioning how this suffering could be balanced out with a good God. She could keep that question in a quiet corner of her mind as she did her daily work in the hospital, expressing concern and compassion for those who were suffering. But when the day was over and she was at home at night, the question would stir again and clamor for attention: "Where is God in all this?"

One cold night, alone in her apartment reading a book by a cozy fire, with one part of her mind she was struggling with the problem when the phone rang. A mother of a former patient, who had just readmitted her daughter to the hospital in an emergency, was calling, insisting that Nina Hermann come to the hospital at once. Nina had gone through this with the family before and there had been many false alarms. She didn't want to go. It was cold, the fire and comfort of the apartment were enticing.

But she said yes, headed out through the snow walking to the hospital, feeling very ambivalent about it all, yet dimly sensing some responsibility and still plagued by the problem of suffering and the goodness of God.

It was a false alarm. When she arrived at the hospital the child was all right. Instead of returning home immediately, she sat down for a talk with the mother. In that conversation it happened—the Cross and Christ's suffering finally hit home, meaning clicked, and it all made sense. It made sense to the mother also, and as a result of that conversation the mother received new hope and new courage for her own ordeal.

Nina Hermann wrote of that discovery: "I had read about God and Jesus Christ participating in the human experience, participating in suffering, knowing rejection, knowing aloneness and pain and fear, knowing anger, even anger at God. I had read it, but it had never been a revelation. Until now."

And that's the significant point of her story. She had received this revelation, by following her conscience, in doing what she determined to be her duty. "Reading about these problems is vital, but alone it is not enough," she said. "Meditation on written words is good, but alone it is not enough. Do when you don't want to do. Go when you don't want to go. Plod through the snow. Wrestle with the cold and wind. Go when you don't want to go. And when you least expect, you may glimpse through an open door a revelation."

The fellowship of suffering has special meaning for our life of prayer. Accepting the fact that we are raised to newness of life with Christ, we celebrate this liberating power of the Resurrection through praise and thanksgiving. To our prayers of rejoicing gratitude, we also link intercession for all those who suffer, who have not experienced wholeness through forgiveness and healing. Intercession is a difficult work. Somehow—and who can tell us how?—our task is to cultivate awareness and become so sensitive to the suffering of others that in prayer, and to the degree possible in our action, we take upon ourselves their suffering.

Prayer, especially intercession, is an expression of our greatest love. Instead of keeping pain away from us, loving prayer leads us into the suffering of God and of others. The deeper our love of God, the deeper our love of others. The deeper our love, the more we will suffer. The more we suffer, the more we will pray.

Our suffering and the suffering of others is embraced by the compassionate Christ. In a way that we may never fully understand, our intercession, through identity with suffering, becomes a channel of Christ's liberating power.

3. *Being conformed to His death.* This was another recurring theme for Paul: "I have been crucified with Christ" (Gal. 2:20). "You have died, and your life is hid with Christ in God" (Col. 3:3).

Paul means more than knowing Christ through the fellowship of His suffering. The Christian is to die to the old order

(Rom. 6:5; Gal. 6:14), must pass through death to life, must yield his life to a process of letting the old die that the new man be born. (See commentary on Gal. 5:16–26 and Col. 3:5–17).

There is a sense in which knowing Christ in the power of His Resurrection and being conformed to His death are one dynamic process. In His death and Resurrection the old humanity (the old Adam) came to an end and a new humanity began (2 Cor. 5:14–17). In the representative dying and rising of Christ, I pass through the death and Resurrection of the old Adam (Rom. 6:4–8; Eph. 2:4–6; Col. 3:1–4). However, the implication of this must be lived out. I must consider myself dead to sin and alive to God (Rom. 6:11). I must allow the Spirit to renew my inner nature and transform me from stage to stage into the likeness of Christ (2 Cor. 3:18; 4:16; Eph. 3:14–21).

4. *Resurrection from the dead.* Paul doesn't stop with what really matters *in this life.* Knowing Christ means that life goes on beyond death. An actual experience which becomes a powerful parable is our best commentary on this mountain-peak truth. Harry Pritchett, Jr. tells the story:

> Once upon a time I had a young friend named Philip. Philip lived in a nearby city, and Philip was born a mongoloid. He was a pleasant child—happy, it seemed—but increasingly aware of the difference between himself and other children.
>
> Philip went to Sunday School. And his teacher, also, was a friend of mine. My Sunday School teacher friend taught the third grade at a Methodist Church. Philip was in his class, as well as nine other eight-year-old boys and girls.
>
> My Sunday School teacher friend is a very creative teacher. Most of you know eight-year-olds. And Philip, with his differences, was not readily accepted as a member of this third grade Sunday School class. But my friend was a good teacher, and he had helped facilitate a good group of eight-year-old children. They learned and they laughed and they played together. And they really cared about each other—even though, as you know, eight-year-olds don't say that they care about each other out loud very often. But my teacher friend could see it. He knew it. He also knew that Philip was not really a part

of that group of children. Philip, of course, did not choose nor did he want to be different. He just was. And that was just the way things were.

My Sunday School teacher friend had a marvelous design for his class on the Sunday after Easter last year. You know those things panty hose come in—the containers look like great big eggs. My friend had collected ten of these to use on that Sunday. The children loved it when he brought them into the room. Each child was to get a great big egg. It was a beautiful spring day, and the assigned task was for each child to go outside on the church grounds and to find a symbol for new life, put it in the egg (the old panty hose containers), and bring it back to the classroom. They would then mix them all up, and then all open and share their new life symbols and surprises together one by one.

Well, they did this, and it was glorious. And it was confusing. And it was wild. They ran all around, gathered their symbols, and returned to the classroom. They put all the big eggs on a table, and then my teacher friend began to open them. All the children were standing around the table.

He opened one, and there was a flower, and they oohed and aahed.

He opened another, and there was a little butterfly. "Beautiful," the girls all said, since it is very hard for 8-year-old boys to say "beautiful."

He opened another, and there was a rock. And as third graders will, some laughed, and some said, "That's crazy! How's a rock supposed to be like new life?" But the smart little boy whose egg they were speaking of spoke up. He said, "That's mine. And I knew all of you would get flowers, and buds, and leaves, and butterflies, and stuff like that. So I got a rock because I wanted to be different. And for me, that's new life."

The teacher opened the next one, and there was nothing there. The other children, as 8-year-olds will, said, "That's not fair—that's stupid!—somebody didn't do right."

About that time my teacher friend felt a tug on his shirt, and he looked down and Philip was standing beside him.

"It's mine," Philip said. "It's mine." and the children said, "You don't ever do things right, Philip. There's nothing there!"

"I did so do it," Philip said, "I did do it. It's empty—the tomb is empty!"

The class was silent, a very full silence. And for you people who don't believe in miracles, I want to tell you that one happened that day last spring. From that time on, it was different. Philip suddenly became a part of that group of eight-year-old children. They took him in. He entered. He was set free from the tomb of his differentness.

Philip died last summer. His family had known since the time that he was born that he wouldn't live out a full life span. Many other things had been wrong with his tiny little body. And so, late last July, with an infection that most normal children could have quickly shrugged off, Philip died. The mystery simply enveloped him completely.

He was buried from that church. And on that day at that funeral nine eight-year-old children marched right up to that altar—not with flowers to cover the stark reality of death. Nine eight-year-olds, with their Sunday School teacher, marched right up to that altar, and lay on it an empty egg—an empty, old discarded holder of panty hose.[1]

"If, by any means, I may attain to the Resurrection from the dead" (v. 11). Paul is not harboring or expressing doubt about his eternal destiny. He uses this hypothetical form to put his passionate longing into brilliant light. From start to finish, Paul could never forget that salvation, which includes Resurrection from the dead, is a gift of God and we dare not presume on divine mercy. *"Attain"* does not mean self-achievement, but gift, gift from God. Only those for whose earthly lives Resurrection would be an appropriate crowning climax would *attain*. And such ones are those who know Christ, the power of His Resurrection, the fellowship of His suffering, and conformity to His death.

THE PRIZE OF THE HIGH CALLING

[12] Not that I have already attained, or am already perfected; but I press on, that I may lay hold of that for which Christ Jesus has also laid hold of me. [13] Brethren, I do not

count myself to have apprehended; but one thing I do, forgetting those things which are behind and reaching forward to those things which are ahead, [14] I press toward the goal for the prize of the upward call of God in Christ Jesus.

—*Philippians 3:12–14*

What really matters, says Paul, is the prize of the high calling of God. The price of a vital faith is a continuous struggle. The quest is perennial. We were created by God to grow; we were recreated by Christ to grow. Not only to grow, but to become our whole selves—the new creation we *are* in Christ Jesus. So Paul sets it out in this word about pressing toward the goal for the prize of the high calling. The pattern is clear.

Recognize Who and Where You Are

Verse 12 is one of those hinge verses in Paul's thought to which we need to return and ponder often. It comes in the text with striking abruptness. The apostle has passionately set before us what really matters, the guiding purpose of his life and that of all Christians. The commanding motive of knowing Christ and all that means has led to his scathing renunciation of everything less worthy. His word now is an explosive disclaimer: *"Not that I have already attained, or am already perfected."*

It is obvious that Paul does not want his readers to misunderstand what he has just said, for of all people, Paul was aware of how far below the possible glory God had in store for all Christians he was. There was perhaps another equally important reason for this disclaimer. There were among his readers those who maintained that they themselves had arrived at perfection. Some scholars contend that in this verse, and in 4:12, Paul used technical terms drawn from the vocabulary of the Greek mystery cults. He makes this disclaimer because a group in the church regarded their baptism as initiation into a state of perfection to which nothing needed to be added.

Whatever the situation, whether Paul was being careful to state his own case, or was addressing a specific problem in Philippi, the message for us is clear. The Christian life is a journey, a process of growth in which we seek to *"lay hold"* of the fullness of that which has been given us, *"that for which I was also laid hold of by Christ."* We *are* Christians; we must now *become* what we are. We have been saved; now we must work out our salvation with fear and trembling.

We are caught in tension. The demand is that we live in the now as those who have "died with Christ" to sin, yet are still sinners. We have been reckoned by God as righteous and He has accepted us by our faith in Christ. Yet we are in fact unrighteous and any claim we make to righteousness is "as filthy rags." That is the tension. But it is creative tension. We are not caught in impersonal forces to which we are victims. We are drawn by the powerful impulsion of a personal relationship with Christ. He has already made us His own. The impulsion of this love makes it necessary for us to be—and to become—what we are: new persons in Christ.

Every day, then, we begin where we are—claiming boldly and confidently that Christ has made us new creatures, but confessing humbly that we have not become in fullness what Christ wants us to be.

There are two frames of reference out of which we tend to operate, either of which is debilitating to our Christian growth and service. One is a false humility that refuses to name and claim our gifts. The second is a confidence that claims too much for ourselves and is not dependent enough on the power of Christ. In verse 12 Paul calls for a balance between these two. We make no claim to perfection, but we have an unshakable confidence that Christ Jesus has made us His own.

We walk the tightrope of naming and claiming our gifts and struggling against the deep hold pride has on our hearts, and the tendency to fall into self-justification.

Leave the Past Behind

Acknowledging who and where we are is necessary at every step along the way to the prize of the high calling. Likewise, every day we must *leave the past behind*. In the last chapter I quoted Dag Hammarskjøld. From the time of saying yes to the call, he was certain that existence had meaning, and this life, in self-surrender, had a goal. He concluded that witness by saying, "From that moment I have known what it means 'not to look back,' and 'to have no thought for the morrow.'"

The Christian, drawn by the powerful impulsion of a personal relationship with God through Jesus Christ, is uniquely equipped to leave the past behind. Yet, how many of us do not. The dimension of our past that continues to drag us back, weigh us down, and make our movement stumbly at best, is our sense of failure, our guilt over past sin, our pain from past hurts. Does not this inability to leave the past behind contradict everything we confess about the healing, forgiving, redeeming power of God?

Film producer Ingmar Bergman is one person in the movie world who uses that media to express his understanding of the world, of God, and of persons. Whether we agree with him or not, he provokes us to think. In his 1978 film, *The Serpent's Egg*, set in Berlin in 1923, he speaks of our need for and relationship to God because of our need for forgiveness. In the film, Manuela, a displaced circus performer, goes to a church to seek some relief from a priest for the guilt she feels over her husband's suicide.

At first, the overworked priest puts her off but then, sensing the depth of her despair, he suggests they kneel and pray together. He says: "We live far away from God, so far away that no doubt he doesn't hear us when we pray to him for help. So we must help each other. We must give each other the forgiveness that a remote God denies us. I say to you that you are forgiven for your husband's death. You are no longer to blame. I beg your forgiveness for my apathy and indifference. Do you forgive me?" Manuela says softly, "Yes."

A poignant commentary, not alone on the state of the church in Germany in the 1920s, or the vitality of the priest's faith, or a descriptive word about human need for forgiveness. More is there. We cringe at the word of the priest limiting forgiveness to being operative only between humans because "a remote God denies us" that forgiveness. But how true to the reality of our practice is the priest's piercing candor? If God is not remote, and if He does not deny us the forgiveness we desperately need, why do we refuse it? "Refuse it" may be too harsh, but we certainly do not appropriate it. Thus the past is always with us, robbing us of freedom, making us heavy-hearted, preventing us from being able to use all our spiritual energy and gifts for coping with the new and moving with joy into the future.

Have a Goal

To take no thought of tomorrow does not mean that we have no aims in life, no goals toward which we are moving. It means that the focus of life is in the here and now, and our energy is expended in living to the fullest the life Christ gives us today. A part of that energy for present investment comes from the divine purpose of our life. So Paul says *"I reach forward. . . I press toward the goal."*

A minister friend, Don Shelby, recalled an incident out of the illustrious life of Winston Churchill which underscores the need for a goal. It was in the critical days of World War II, and England faced the need for increased coal production.

The Prime Minister called a meeting of labor leaders to give them the facts and enlist their support in his inimitable way of using imagination and power oratory. He closed his presentation by picturing in their minds a parade which would surely be held in Picadilly Circus after the war was over. There would come the men of the Royal Navy whom everyone would know had kept the vital sea lanes open. There would pass the Army who had come home from Dunkirk and then gone on to defeat Rommel in Africa and fight under Montgomery in Berlin. There would come the Air Force who had driven the Luftwaffe out of the sky and beat it at its own game. Then, he said, last of all, there would come a great host of sweat-stained, soot-streaked miners. Someone would cry out from the crowd, "Where were you?" And from ten thousand throats would come the answer: "We were deep in the earth with our faces against the coal." Winston Churchill sat down to a wildly cheering throng, many with tears running down their cheeks.

The man at the top had shown the power of a purpose, the need for a goal, how everyone working together would mean victory.

Concentrate on the Path

There is no question about the power of an ideal, the energy that is produced by a driving passion, and the likelihood of our achieving what we set our hearts on. How important it is that we choose our goals wisely. That suggests another piece in the pattern of what really matters as we seek the prize of the high calling of God: *concentrate on the path*, run the race with your eyes on the course and your attention to your present steps.

Earlier we discussed forgetting the past. Another facet to that theme deserves noting here. There is debate about whether Paul is talking about his pre-Christian days, or specifically about his life since the Damascus Road, or his whole life. It is clear, since his metaphor is that of a foot race, that he is not talking about his pre-Christian life. Nor is he referring alone to past failures. In this entire passage one thing he is combatting is self-satisfaction. Therefore included in what must be left behind are our achievements as well as our failures.

In the race of life we concentrate on the path and we forget as we run. We may store our achievements in our memory, but we do not allow them to slow us in our present running. We may take them from our memory storehouse on occasion, but we do so not to rest on our laurels, but to be energized for the race ahead.

I had the exhilarating joy of seeing Eric Heiden win two of his five gold medals in ice skating at the Winter Olympics in Lake Placid in 1980. I have never witnessed anything quite like it. Through his skin-tight gold suit, one could see the rippling movement of the muscles, especially in his legs, as he made his laps before me, straining and stretching toward the final mark. His posture was that of perfect balance, gliding swiftly over the ice, and it was as though he was so eager to reach his final goal that he was trying to touch it from his present position. Past laps did not matter. The laps that remained and the goal ahead was everything.

And don't forget the goal of the Christian's race: *"the prize of the high calling of God in Christ Jesus."* This does not mean the *calls* that come to us all along the way, the summons to duty here, and unselfish service there. It is the ultimate bliss to which God summons us. The author of the Epistle to the Hebrews refers to it as a "heavenly" call (Heb. 3:1), and Paul writes to the Thessalonians of "the God who called you to His own realm and glory." It was the call that came to Paul on the Damascus Road and that call never ceased to summon him onward.

CONDUCT CONSISTENT WITH COMMITMENT

15 Therefore let us, as many as are mature, have this mind; and if in anything you think otherwise, God will reveal even this to you. 16 Nevertheless, to the degree that we have already attained, let us walk by the same rule, let us be of the same mind.

—Philippians 3:15–16

Paul calls now for conduct consistent with commitment, for a congruence between the level of spirituality we have attained and the practical way we daily live: *"To the degree that we have already attained, let us walk by the same rule, let us be of the same mind."*

The essential discipline of Christian growth is learning to say yes to Christ in every area of our lives every day. This is the way we *become* the new creations we *are* in Christ. The Bible makes the point over and over again—that our consent is necessary for Christ to act transformingly in our lives. Christ does not force Himself upon us. He comes to us and abides in us as we say yes to Him. He doesn't take command against our will. He works in us according to our obedient response to Him. And that response must be new and fresh every day. New occasions demand new duties. New situations call for new responses.

John Wesley was turned around by Christ in the experience at Aldersgate, and he could say, "I felt my heart strangely warmed. I felt I did trust Christ, trust Him for my salvation. Eight months later this is what he wrote in his *Journal:*

> My friends affirm I am mad, because I said I was not a Christian a year ago. I affirm that I am not a Christian now. . . . For a Christian is one who has . . . love, peace, joy. But these I do not have. Though I have given, and do give, all my goods to feed the poor, I am not a Christian. Though I have endured hardship, though I have in all things denied myself and taken up the cross, I am not a Christian. My works are nothing; I have not the fruits of Christ. Though I have constantly used all the means of grace for 20 years, I am not a Christian.

We may have difficulty with the extreme way Mr. Wesley makes the case, and the way he uses the word "Christian," but we must not miss the point of his turmoil. He is wrestling with himself, and agonizing as Paul did in Romans. "I know that nothing good dwells within me, that is, in my flesh. I can will what is right, but I cannot do it" (7:18, RSV).

No question about it—Wesley *was* a Christian. He had been laid hold of by Christ. But, like Paul, he would make no claim to have *"attained"* the fullness of what he knew was his by gift and promise. That must be the Christian's stance—to be aware of what is yet lacking in our *being perfected,* and to press on to *"lay hold of that for which Christ Jesus has also laid hold of me."*

We may state this truth in another way, which applies to each of us, no matter where we are on our journey. *Fidelity to truth already attained is a condition of receiving further and fuller truth.* None of us are without some measure of revelation and understanding, none of us are bereft of truth, all are at some level of maturity—let us be true to that.

This leads to Paul's closing word in this section, which is a word of judgment.

JUDGMENT

[17] Brethren, join in following my example, and note those who so walk, as you have us for a pattern. [18] For many

walk, of whom I have told you often, and now tell you even weeping, that they are the enemies of the Cross of Christ: 19 whose end is destruction, whose god is their belly, and whose glory is in their shame— who set their mind on earthly things.

—*Philippians 3:17–19*

In this passage Paul does that which is always dangerous to do—designating oneself as an example. Those who would do this become vulnerable, setting themselves up for failure. One has to be either extremely arrogant, or transparently humble to project oneself as a model. The world is full of the arrogant who send the message, "I have arrived; you would do well to follow me." Modern advertising uses that scheme. Superstars and the supersuccessful are presented as models, the glamorous and luring lie being that if we use the commodity these persons use we will be like them.

Rarely does a call to imitate come from the humble. Thus this is a rare passage. Paul has confessed his limitation: "I have not attained—I am not perfect." And here his deep feelings are captured in his words, "I tell you even weeping" (v. 18, NEB). He is pleading for folks to follow him not in his failures and limitations, not in his achievements, but in that which really matters—*being laid hold of by Christ Jesus.*

Not to be responsive to that, not to press on to attain the prize of the high calling of God has serious consequences. So, Paul makes an unequivocal statement about judgment, and provides a frightful description of those persons whose manner of life makes them *"enemies of the Cross of Christ."*

Who are they? They are those *"whose god is their belly and whose glory is in their shame."* "Belly" is a metaphor that suggests far more than mere gluttony. It covers all that belongs to the bodily, fleshly life of humans; also for the satisfaction of the carnal nature. But it covers even more than that. Paul uses this word as he uses the word *flesh (sarx)* to denote the old, earthbound humanity from which Christians have been rescued into the new humanity of Christ. It is equivalent to "the natural man" (1 Cor. 2:14), "the old manhood" (Rom. 6:6), "the first Adam" (1 Cor. 15:47).

That this is Paul's meaning is understandable when we remember that he is talking about people who are within the church of Christ. That makes the pronouncement of judgment even more searing. Within the church there are those whose fate is *destruction* because they turn their freedom into a perverted liberty; their primary interest is selfish—self-serving, self-seeking, and self-justifying. Their minds are still *"set on earthly things."*

Do not mistake the meaning of this. Paul is not advocating an otherworldly religion. He is stressing the fact that some Christians have simply missed it. They are still circumscribed by an earthbound life, refusing to be open to the gracious and transforming influences of heaven. By failing to accept the *once and for all* death of the old life, they disqualify themselves for the new. *Their fate is destruction.*

But such does not have to be the case. Paul's compelling passion to know Christ and the power of His Resurrection in this life, has added to it the invincible confidence of the coming of our Lord who will complete His saving work by transforming *"our lowly body that it may be conformed to His glorious body"* (3:21). In that confidence we can stand fast as "alien residents," and *"rejoice in the Lord always"* (4:4).

That is the theme of the next chapter.

NOTE

1. From *St. Luke's Journal of Theology.*

CHAPTER FOUR—CITIZENS OF HEAVEN
PHILIPPIANS 3:20—4:23

Scripture Outline

In the Kingdom Now (3:20—4:3)

Living While You Wait (4:4–7)

You Are What You Think (4:8–9)

The Sufficiency of Christ and the Support of His People (4:10–23)

We are citizens of heaven. That is our uniqueness as Christians. Those who set their minds on earthly things are enemies of the Cross of Christ.

We really live in the tension of a dual citizenship. In citizenship language, in the United States we refer to some people living within our bounds as "resident aliens," persons who belong by birth to another country, but are currently choosing to live here. That is a descriptive designation for Christians. We are citizens of heaven, "resident aliens" of earth.

Two hours ago, as I worked on this particular passage, I had a telephone conversation with a young musician. Three years ago she had a dramatic conversion, a Damascus Road type. Rarely have I seen the power of Christ demonstrated in the life of a person in such a radical, transforming way. She was brought out of a debauched life of drug abuse, sexual promiscuity, perverted values. The change was incredible. Her sense of being pardoned and cleansed was exhilarating and overflowing. She was a clear picture of the twice born.

She was a songwriter and was on the way to the top. Her closest circle of friends were already "at the top." So overwhelmed was she by this experience, so deeply grateful for what God had done for her, she committed all her talents and energy to writing gospel music. Life has been tough. She was in deep depression this morning when she called, and her confession had a note of despair in it: "It's hell—this music world—cocaine, alcohol, madness for money and success. I don't know how I can make it. I want another world, Maxie. I don't want to live like the people in this world, but I'm being pulled into it. It's almost impossible to resist. I need your support and prayers."

As her conversion was dramatic, her present situation is a vivid witness to the Christian being a resident alien. We may not feel the tension as unendurably strong as she, but the tension is real and it cannot be allayed. We are forever pulled by the *"high calling of God in Christ Jesus,"* we have been *"laid hold of by Christ,"* and what really matters is to know Him. The only way we can live as citizens of two kingdoms without being torn apart and going to pieces is to claim the power of His Resurrection.

IN THE KINGDOM NOW

20 For our citizenship is in heaven, from which we also eagerly wait for the Savior, the Lord Jesus Christ, 21 who will transform our lowly body that it may be conformed to His glorious body, according to the working by which He is able even to subdue all things to Himself. **4:1** Therefore, my beloved and longed-for brethren, my joy and crown, so stand fast in the Lord, beloved.

2 I implore Euodia and I implore Syntyche to be of the same mind in the Lord. 3 And I urge you also, true companion, help these women who labored with me in the gospel, with Clement also, and the rest of my fellow workers, whose names are in the Book of Life.

—Philippians 3:20—4:3

Philippi, as already stated, was a Roman colony, a miniature Rome in distant Macedonia. Many of the inhabitants of Philippi were Roman citizens, probably the aristocracy of the city. There was an intense pride in being a citizen of Rome (see Acts 16:20–21). We have no way of knowing how many, but certainly some of these proud Roman citizens had become Christians. Were they being accused by their compatriots of belonging to a fellowship disloyal to Rome and the Emperor?

What buckling courage and heartening comfort Paul's words provided for citizens of Rome who had become Christians. There was an emphasis on the word "our"—our citizenship is in heaven—which has meaning if Paul had some other citizenship in mind.

Though a citizen of Rome, you are in Christ's kingdom now. Because we are in that kingdom now,

We Can Live in Great Expectation

We eagerly wait for the Savior (v. 20). The Greek word *apekde-chomai*, translated *"wait for,"* denotes a waiting that is eager and intense; it means "expect anxiously." It was the favorite word to use of the expectation of the Parousia, the return of Christ. (See Rom. 8:19, 23, 25; 1 Cor. 1:7; Gal. 5:5; Heb. 9:28; 1 Pet. 3:20). Their expectation was a cardinal element in the life of the early church and it gave them great moral power.

In Paul, and all early Christian preaching, there was this telescopic view of history—hope centering in the return of Christ. While centered in this, Christian expectation and hope overflows into the whole of life. We hope because we believe that God is in control, and His intention is to make the kingdoms of this world the kingdom of our Lord and Christ. Reinhold Niebuhr, the great theologian, was talking to Harry Emerson Fosdick, the great preacher. Niebuhr was a pessimist; Fosdick, an optimist. They were talking about the future of civilization and agreed that there was not much light; things looked dismal and bleak. They concluded with Niebuhr saying to Fosdick, "If you will be a pessimist with me, decade by decade, I will be an optimist with you, century by century."

A good Christian philosophy of history! Because human beings exercise their freedom and use their power for evil, we are sometimes made pessimists about the present. But because God has done it time and again, and will continue to do it—take human deeds meant for evil and turn them into blessings—and because God controls the by-products of the movements of men, and always has the last word, we can be optimists about the future. The most destructive snare into which we can fall is to believe that the problems of the world are insoluble.

As those who live in the kingdom now we can live in great expectation. Also despite what the current situation is, we can

Stand Fast in the Lord

With the hope of the coming of the Savior, and the fact that *He is able to subdue all things to Himself,* we can live resolutely, with courage, in the moment. All that Paul has written in chapter 3 is a commentary on what it means to stand fast. The most conspicuous characteristic and result of standing fast is joy (v. 4). Here is a contemporary witness shared by Will Campbell in *Brother to a Dragon Fly*.

> I tell you about Mrs. Tilly, a little Methodist woman from Atlanta who never weighed more than a hundred pounds in her life, who looked about eight years younger than God, who joined forces with a group of forty thousand women in the thirties and forties in what they called the Association of Southern Women for the Prevention of Lynching. Later she was active in advocating the desegregation of public schools and got a lot of obscene phone calls, calling her everything but the gentle woman she was. She did not let the calls deter her. No one could intimidate her. She knew racism was evil and she knew that as a white woman she was through with it and wanted her town, her state, her country, the world to be rid of it, too. But she would not stoop to the tactics of the intimidators. She had an engineer hook a recording machine to the telephone and when persons called her late at night to spew out their venom, the answer they heard was a baritone soloist singing the Lord's Prayer. The calls soon stopped.

Of the Same Mind in the Lord

Euodia and Syntyche were obviously important and influential members of the church. Paul has concentrated on the theme of unity throughout his letter, and here he focuses on two persons who must have represented centers around which the fellowship and power of the church revolved. Paul learned about their quarreling, and pleaded for their reconciliation.

Life in the church is the expression of our life in the kingdom now. In that fellowship we must be of the same mind in the Lord.

LIVING WHILE YOU WAIT

4 Rejoice in the Lord always. Again I will say, rejoice!

5 Let your gentleness be known to all men. The Lord is at hand.

6 Be anxious for nothing, but in everything by prayer and supplication, with thanksgiving, let your requests be made known to God; 7 and the peace of God, which surpasses all

understanding, will guard your hearts and minds through Christ Jesus.

—*Philippians 4:4–7*

It is obvious from the way Paul begins this section that his mind is not preoccupied with heaven. We are energized by the promise of the coming of the Savior, but we must live now while we eagerly await His coming.

Dag Hammarskjøld spoke of the way that we are being constantly summoned on by God, "It is not we who seek the way, but the Way which seeks us." Then he continued with a word that speaks to our living while we wait. "That is why you are faithful to it, even while you stand waiting, so long as you are *prepared*, and act the moment you are confronted by its demands."[1]

There are distinct qualities that mark the life of those who live in expectation of the coming of the Lord, and who know themselves to be citizens of heaven, though resident aliens of earth.

Undaunted Joy

Two times in the letter Paul urged the Christians at Philippi to *"rejoice in the Lord"* (3:1 and 4:4). This second time he repeats the call twice, *"Rejoice . . . again I will say rejoice!"* and adds the word *"always."* The joy of the Christian is not a passing quality. Rejoicing is not to be reserved for special times of worship or praise. It is to be uninterrupted and unbroken.

For Paul to repeat twice in 4:4 the injunction to rejoice must mean that conditions in Philippi were such as to make the call to rejoice seem unreasonable. So he is saying, in spite of circumstance—in spite of annoyance, disagreement, persecution—rejoice! This was a theme of the apostle's life. In a letter to another Macedonian church he wrote, "Rejoice at all times" (1 Thess. 5:17), and in 2 Corinthians 6:10 he speaks of himself as "grieved but always glad."

The Lord is risen and reigning, the power of His Resurrection is available; to rejoice is to appropriate and rest upon the redemption won by Him for us, and to live in the freedom His redemption provides.

Gentleness

The Greek word *(epieikēs)* in verse 5 for "gentleness" is one of the most untranslatable Greek words, according to William Barclay. The baffling difficulty is seen in the way both the old and new translations of the Bible have rendered it. The KJV—"moderation";

Wycliffe—"patience"; Tyndale and Cranmer—"softness"; The Geneva Bible—"the patient mind"; the Rheims Bible—"modesty"; Moffatt and the RSV—"forbearance"; NEB—"magnanimity."

It is a fruitful exercise to reflect on these different translations and question ourselves as to whether the words describe us. I come to *"patient of mind"* and am condemned. How often do I appear gentle, try to be gentle and understanding, but my mind is in high gear—questioning, judging, filled with unkind thoughts, even condemning. *Magnanimity!*—that's a big word for a big heart, a heart that is open enough, soft/tender enough, understanding enough to accept another as the other is, to receive another into relationship unconditionally, without prejudging. Robert Frost said, "Home is something you somehow haven't to deserve." If we are magnanimous, our hearts are homes to which persons may come without being worthy or deserving.

Our translation uses the word "gentleness." It is a lost word, I'm afraid, as a description of Christians. Our way of relating is shaped by the brusque world in which we live—a world of assertiveness, bluntness, curtness, presumption. What yeast in the leaven might we become if we cultivated gentleness. This is no "soft" virtue, but rather a bent of character that controls our capacity for rage and activates our capacity to love. The gentle are courteous and kind; exercise restraint; practice reticence in speech, knowing that words can wound and silence may be more affirming than chatter; do not intrude into another's life but are available to and responsive to others' needs. It is no wonder Paul names gentleness as a fruit of the Spirit. (See commentary on Gal. 5:16–26.)

Peace Through Prayer

When I read verses 6 and 7, I think of a phrase that somewhere along the way I tucked in a niche of my memory as important: "Take yourself lightly so that like angels you can fly."

"Be anxious for nothing"—an admonition that touches the quick of every person. Anxiety, in the popular use of the term, is our most common problem. Worry, confusion of mind, pressures of daily life, uncertainty about the future—if we began to catalog specific aspects within these general categories, we would soon run out of space. Depression is the most common emotional problem in America today, and one of the most difficult with which to deal. Often the severity of depression requires hospitalization, but those who are hospitalized, even those who are under the care of

a doctor for this malady, represent only a small portion of our population who are functioning far below the level of effectiveness as persons, who are weighed down so oppressively by anxiety that they cannot even dream of taking themselves "lightly so that like angels they can fly."

In his study of "self-actualizing" persons, the psychologist Abraham Maslow found that they shared, in varying degrees, certain attitudes. One of these was *tolerance for uncertainty*. They seemed to know how to live with the unknown without feeling threatened or frightened. Taking a cue from Maslow, psychologists are talking a great deal about a "tolerance for ambiguity." How much to the point. Uncertainty and ambiguity—not knowing about the future, and a confusion about value and things as they are—are characteristics of life. How we need to appropriate Paul's word, *"Be anxious for nothing."*

Anxiety, in the way Paul is using the term, and the way we most often experience it, is the futile, frustrating, debilitating attempt to bear the burdens of life and especially of the future, ourselves, alone. The Christian answer to anxiety is confident prayer which issues in *"the peace of God which surpasses all understanding"* (v. 7).

This is no glib word, no pious cliche, no easy moralizing about complex issues. Remember, Paul was in prison. Ponder for even a minute the immediate circumstances out of which this word came, and let the movement of his life be flashed, however quickly, upon the screen of your mind. At every step of his Christian journey, the hound of anxiety was snapping at his heels. And even when the hound was not in biting distance, its howl must have sounded loud in his ears. Fears, uncertainty about the future, persecution, physical disease, mental anguish—again the list could become a catalog. Paul's word comes from the sweaty arena of life where his word needs to be heard, and from a person who has experienced the answer he is offering.

His offer of prayer is not an easy solution; no magic formula here, no bedtime or morning rote repetition of words that we have labeled prayer. He is talking about the serious business of bringing our lives before God, examining our dependence upon God, placing our lives in God's hands to be used, remembering and celebrating what God has already done, confessing our needs and dedicating our gifts, commiting ourselves and all that we are to make our common cause God's kingdom, not our own kingdom. When prayer is seen in that fashion, then it is not glib to say that anxiety is an attempt to carry the burden of the present and the future oneself; prayer is yielding it to and leaving it in the safe hands of God.

Prayer, supplication, and requests are not to be separated; they are synonyms. Thanksgiving is prayer also, and gratitude for the past benefits of God cultivates confidence in future ones.

There can be little question that Paul was familiar with the teachings of Jesus. This is one of the many instances verifying that knowledge (see Matt. 6:25ff). Maslow has stated that the creativeness of "self-actualizers" is "like that of unspoiled children." Jesus said we must become "like children" to possess the kingdom. The childlike capacity to trust, to trust God for the present and the future, is characteristic of "Christian-actualizers." We cultivate the capacity to trust through our life of prayer. As our capacity to trust expands, our tolerance for uncertainty and ambiguity grows and our anxiety diminishes.

The peace of God then *"guards [our] hearts and minds through Christ Jesus."* The opposite of anxiety is peace. Not numbness nor unconcern, not the absence of inner and outward struggle, but God's *peace,* the peace that is from Him, giving us hope and confidence, strengthening us to carry on with joy when the burdens are heavy and the pathway rough. This has little to do with outward circumstances, which is why Paul said the peace of God would *guard our hearts and mind.* The word in Greek *(phroureō)* for *"guard"* or "keep" was employed when speaking of a company of soldiers keeping watch over a city—a good metaphor. God's peace is an inward sentinel protecting us, keeping watch that we be not invaded by all the alien forces that would disrupt and ravage our minds and hearts, making us important by crushing us with anxiety. Let Paul witness to the guarding power of this peace within his own life.

> No wonder we do not lose heart! Though our outward humanity is in decay, yet day by day we are inwardly renewed. Our troubles are slight and short-lived; and their outcome an eternal glory which outweighs them far. Meanwhile our eyes are fixed, not on the things that are seen, but on the things that are unseen: for what is seen passes away; what is unseen is eternal (2 Cor. 4:16–18, NEB).

We began this section with the word, "Take yourself lightly so that like angels you can fly." I keep another word in the same niche of my memory. It tells me *how* to take myself lightly. "The way to be anxious about nothing is to be prayerful about everything."

YOU ARE WHAT YOU THINK

[8] Finally, brethren, whatever things are true, whatever things are noble, whatever things are just, whatever things are pure, whatever things are lovely, whatever things are of good report, if there is any virtue and if there is anything praiseworthy—meditate on these things. [9] The things which you learned and received and heard and saw in me, these do, and the God of peace will be with you.

—Philippians 4:8–9

The body of evidence grows almost daily, yet every person has to learn the lesson for himself: *we are what we think.* Sour dispositions create not only sick souls but also sick bodies. Feelings of worthlessness, bitter resentment and self-pity diminish us to fragments. A possessive nature, self-indulgence, self-protectiveness, and self-centeredness shrivel the soul, create dysfunctions within us, distort perception, blur perspective, and prevent any healing we need.

The opposite of this is also true. Those who fill their minds with positive affirmations, who concentrate on the noble virtues that make life meaningful, set the stage for healing and make possible the wholeness that is God's design for all. Two thousand years before psychologists were teaching this truth, Paul discovered its power. *"Meditate on these things,"* he said—things that are noble, just, pure, lovely, of good report. We are what we think.

There is a hospital for children in Tiburon, north of and near San Francisco, called "The Center for Attitudinal Healing." It concentrates on cases of children suffering from traumatic diseases or from severe accidents that have disabled them. It is a remarkable place with a unique philosophy. Rather than the children simply being patients, or victims needing professionals to attend them, the children are encouraged to take responsibility for their own healing and for the healing of other children. As a result of this philosophy, a community of love and concern which brings healing has developed. A newspaper article about the hospital quoted one of the responsible persons there as saying, "We feel that much healing takes place by asking the simple question, do I want to have peace of mind, the peace of God, or do I want to experience conflict? If we want to experience peace of mind we will choose to extend our love to others and experience the love extended to us. If we want to experience conflict we will want something or want to evaluate why we're not getting it."

The purpose of the hospital is to stimulate *attitudinal healing* that enables the children to triumph over their adversity. The center has a marvelous saying, "If you can help somebody else you're not disabled," and is a modern institutional witness to the fact that we are what we think.

So powerful is this truth that it must be kept in perspective. The list in verse 8 is not unlike a catalog of virtues one could find in the writings of Greek moralists. If this verse is taken in isolation, we have no more than the great virtues of pagan morality, but Paul was urging the Philippians not to ignore their value. That is a challenge to Christians of any age—we must never be "less good" than those who make no claim to being Christian. At the same time, we must make no claims to a "superior goodness" as a basis for our salvation.

There is still another huge lesson here. How we use the dynamic power of our thinking determines whether it is "Christian" or not. Almost our total culture reflects a perversion of this power. The "power of positive thinking" is the biggest tool suggested to make us millionaires, to turn us into self-serving people bent on satisfying all our desires. Thus we have a consumer economy of indulgence and waste. It is not arrogant, I think, for Paul, as he calls people to meditate on the great virtues, to add, *"the things which you learned and received and heard and saw in me, these do, and the God of peace will be with you* (v. 9). You cannot separate what Paul said from the style of his life and his passionate commitment to Christ as Lord of his life. The Christian can never use with integrity "the power of positive thinking" without keeping foremost where our thinking is to be centered. *"Let this mind be in you which was also in Christ Jesus. . . made Himself of no reputation . . . taking the form of a bondservant . . . humbled Himself and became obedient to the point of death"* (2:5, 7, 8).

For Christians, what we think must always have the shape of the Cross about it. A young girl, upon walking into the church and seeing for the first time the Cross on the altar, asked her father-preacher, Joseph Cotton, "Daddy, what's that plus sign doing up there?" Bishop Melvin Wheatly set that description of the Cross as a plus sign over against what he called the most distasteful description of the Cross he ever heard: "The cross symbolizes the 'I' crossed out."

Said Wheatley, "That description implies that the Cross is a *minus* sign. I submit to you that the Cross does *not* symbolize the minus sign but the plus sign—not the 'I' crossed out but the 'I' stretched out—reaching down into the ground of being, up into the infinity of becoming, and out toward as many others as it can touch."

THE SUFFICIENCY OF CHRIST AND THE SUPPORT OF HIS PEOPLE

[10] But I rejoiced in the Lord greatly that now at last your care for me has flourished again; though you surely did care, but you lacked opportunity. [11] Not that I speak in regard to need, for I have learned in whatever state I am, to be content: [12] I know how to be abased, and I know how to abound. Everywhere and in all things I have learned both to be full and to be hungry, both to abound and to suffer need. [13] I can do all things through Christ who strengthens me.

[14] Nevertheless you have done well that you shared in my distress. [15] Now you Philippians know also that in the beginning of the gospel, when I departed from Macedonia, no church shared with me concerning giving and receiving but you only. [16] For even in Thessalonica you sent aid once and again for my necessities. [17] Not that I seek the gift, but I seek the fruit that abounds to your account. [18] Indeed I have all and abound. I am full, having received from Epaphroditus the things sent from you, a sweet-smelling aroma, an acceptable sacrifice, well pleasing to God. [19] And my God shall supply all your need according to His riches in glory by Christ Jesus. [20] Now to our God and Father be glory forever and ever. Amen.

[21] Greet every saint in Christ Jesus. The brethren who are with me greet you. [22] All the saints greet you, but especially those who are of Caesar's household.

[23] The grace of our Lord Jesus Christ be with you all. Amen.

—Philippians 4:10–23

The closing section of this letter is a marvelous witness to the sufficiency of Christ and the support of His people for each other. There is nothing systematic about the statement. It is personal, flowing out of the deep well of Paul's love and appreciation for the Philippians, and the trust and confidence he has in the all-sufficiency of Christ which was not to be superseded by anything else.

He has already referred twice to the gift he has received (1:5; 2:25–30) which was the primary stimulation for writing the letter. But he waits until the end to express himself fully. It is obvious that Paul has difficulty doing what he wants to do—express adequate thanks for the support he has received through the years from his friends. All sorts of thoughts and emotions flood his mind and heart. How can you adequately say thanks when the gift comes from people who can't afford it? The church in Philippi was poor and through the years, with other Macedonian churches, had given beyond their resources. How can you be a gracious receiver when your material needs and wants are so few? Paul does the best anyone could do—expressing gratitude in a low key, enough to prevent his friends from thinking he needs more; then in a high key, enough to cause them to realize that he remembers all their past generosity and rejoices in their continuing affection.

Shining through this collage of emotion, love, sensitivity, commitment, and appreciation is a picture of the people of God supporting one another, materially as well as through prayers. There is a beautiful description of this in 2 Corinthians where Paul talks about the Macedonian churches, of which Philippi was one.

> We want you to know, brethren, about the grace of which has been shown in the churches of Macedonia, for in a severe test of affliction, their abundance of joy and their extreme poverty have overflowed in a wealth of liberality on their part. For they gave according to their means, as I can testify, and beyond their means, of their own free will, begging us earnestly for the favor of taking part in the relief of the saints—and this, not as we expected, but first they gave themselves to the Lord and to us by the will of God (2 Cor. 8:1–5).

Sprinkled throughout this section are some verses that capture signal truths.

We Have Amazing Coping Powers

Viktor Frankl spent years in a Nazi prison camp where persons were subjected to subhuman and antihuman treatment that threatened annihilation of decency, of the worth and dignity of persons, as well as physical being. Out of that experience Frankl developed a psychotherapeutic process called logotherapy and wrote an inspiring and insightful book entitled *Man's Search For*

Meaning. From his death camp observations, he documented the amazing coping powers of humans to retain inner freedom. He wrote: "We who lived in concentration camps can remember the men who walked through the huts comforting others, giving away their last pieces of bread. They may have been few in number, but they offer sufficient proof that everything can be taken from a man but one thing: the last of the human freedoms—to choose one's attitude in any given set of circumstances, to choose one's own way."

This last inner freedom, the freedom to choose one's own way, gives us an amazing capacity to cope. Paul witnessed to it: "I know how to be abased and how to abound—I can be content in whatever state I find myself."

Theodore Parker Ferris was one of the great preachers of this century. After his death, the vestry of the church in Boston honored him by collecting and printing what they believed were the best sermons Dr. Ferris had preached during his thirty years as their pastor. One of the sermons was entitled "When Things Don't Go Well." In it he gives us some handles on which to take hold as we seek to cope. (1) "Remember that there is nothing that can happen to you that has not happened to millions of others." (2) "Remind yourself that as a human being you run the risk of this kind of thing happening." The human condition is that life is fragile and love makes us vulnerable; we are going to be hurt, but our hurts will pass; some dreams will be shattered while others will come to fruition. (3) "Remember there are people who became great facing what you must now face." (4) "Say, 'I don't know how I'm going to handle this, but I can. I know that from sources of which I am not conscious help will come, not necessarily the help I ask for, but help that I know nothing about right now will rise up in me, will appear suddenly from all sorts of unexpected places.'"

There Is Support in the Christian Fellowship

Paul recalls and is grateful for the support of the Christian fellowship. You *"shared in my distress"* (v. 14). *"You sent aid once and again for my necessities."* It was financial and material support, and more. It is the mood of all of Paul's letters that the Christian fellowship is bound together in mutual support.

Lefty Gomez is one of baseball's all-time great pitchers. When this was affirmed by his induction into the Baseball Hall of Fame, someone asked him his secret. He responded cheerily, "Clean living and a fast infield." The first may be questioned, but not the second. We are all where we are and what we are because of other people.

Paul used an expressive word to state his appreciation for the support of his friends: *"a sweet-smelling aroma, an acceptable sacrifice, well pleasing to God"* (v. 18). He changed his metaphor from that of commercial accounting to language frequently employed in the Old Testament to describe an offering pleasing to God (Gen. 8:21; Ex. 29:18; Lev. 1:9, 13, 17; Ezek. 10:41). That perspective is needed. What we do for each other is to be done as a *"sacrifice pleasing to God"*—not that we have to sacrifice to serve and support others, though that may sometimes be a part of it; but that we act on behalf of each other, knowing that we are acting for the sake of God.

Our Ultimate Sufficiency Is in Christ

Volumes could be written on verse 13. It is the Mount Everest affirmation of Paul's life: *"I can do all things through Christ who strengthens me."*

We have amazing capacities to cope. The support of the Christian fellowship is essential. But ultimately we are cast back on the bedrock of the Christian faith: the all-sufficiency of Christ.

The eminent preacher, Harold Bosley, recalled a story out of the days of the Great Depression in the early 1930s. A panel of speakers including Clarence Darrow, the distinguished attorney and professed atheist, were addressing a meeting of people from Chicago's Southside—most of them black. The economic conditions were at their worst: money and jobs were scarce and Darrow used that fact to point out the plight of the black people. He summed up their woes, concluding, "And yet you sing? No one can sing like you do! What do you have to sing about?" Quick as a flash, a lady in the congregation shouted, "We got Jesus to sing about!" And her response was followed by many "Amens" and "Yeses" and "That's rights."

Uncharacteristically, Darrow for once was stopped dead in his tracks. He had no response, for he was face to face with that which cannot be rationalized, hardly even talked about, in human terms—people who can sing through tears and above their fears because they walk with the One who strengthens them to do all things.

My preacher friend, Doyle Masters, was stricken with cancer. In early November 1978, his doctor informed him of the seriousness of his illness—inoperable malignancy. Doyle wrote an open letter to his congregation. The letter sings with confidence and joy in the sufficiency of Christ despite the circumstances. Here are parts of the letter.

> The options open to me medically are minimal and at best do not promise renewed energy nor longevity. The other option is to turn this over to God in faith for His healing and ultimate will. This we have been directed to do by God after much prayer and spiritual surrender. What the future holds we do not know, but we know God holds it.

✧ ✧ ✧

> These past few days have rolled over us like an avalanche, leaving in their wake some central certainties which make up my Thanksgiving list. Out of the dark night of the soul has come the sunlight of God's love. I am thankful for God who is real and personal, for a Christ who is present in power, and for the Holy Spirit who is by our side in every struggle.
>
> My gratitude overflows for a faith that is unwavering in the face of seemingly unsurmountable obstacles, and for the personal practice of prayer that brings all God's promises to bear in any situation.

✧ ✧ ✧

> My Thanksgiving list is made this year not from what I have but from who has me—a God who is able to do exceedingly abundantly above all I ask or think.

Doyle knew, with Paul, the all-sufficient Christ.

Though not different in quality from the claim that he can do all things through Christ who gives him strength, Paul makes another statement that deserves separate consideration. *"My God shall supply all your need according to His riches in glory by Christ Jesus"* (v. 19). What extravagance! But through the ages Christians have found it unquestionably so.

My friend, Doyle, died at the too-early age of forty-eight. As I sat in his memorial service seeking comfort for my grief, I reflected upon my friend's life and our relationship.

I had heard him preach only once. The outline of that sermon, obviously present deep in my consciousness because of its simplicity and profoundness, came vividly to my mind. His theme was "One Day at a Time." He made three points:

1. Today is all you have

2. Today is all you need

3. Today is all you can handle

What powerful thoughts! What a legacy to leave his friends.

We can live with greater intention and purpose if we keep in mind that this day is all we have. We can only live *now,* and so we must make the most of it.

To know that today is all we need helps us to focus our lives creatively. There are many things we can do and need to do today. Even in relation to our larger plans and life goals, there are some steps that we can take today—and those are the only steps we need to take.

Today is all we can handle—*but we can handle today.* What freedom comes when we take our anxious eyes off the future, when we cease anticipating all the problems and difficulties of tomorrow and focus our energy on the present! We know that Christ's power is sufficient for every day, but that power is available only moment by moment.

My reflections on my friend's life and death were interrupted by a nudge from another friend who had sat down beside me. He handed me a note. Through blurring tears I read, "Maxie, I'm so glad on this day that we share a Resurrection faith."

Doyle's life and faith, and the only sermon I ever heard him preach was a marvelous commentary on the whole of Philippians, especially these last verses. So Paul's letter ends. He wrote it to say thanks for the gift he had received from the Philippians. He now sends them the only gift he can, the greetings of the saints in Christ Jesus, including those in Caesar's household, and *the grace of our Lord Jesus Christ.* Of course, he would say, there is no greater gift.

NOTE

1. Hammarskjøld, *Markings,* p. 120.

INTRODUCTION TO COLOSSIANS

Colossians has a powerful message for our day: the centrality of the all-sufficient Christ. Like the Colossians, we have lost our focus and have been engaging in the futile effort to find meaning by blending together religions of one kind or another or blending religious expression with ideas of philosophy. This is an age-long phenomenon known as "syncretism," and we have been witnessing its outcropping in expressions ranging from the secular mysticism of Transcendental Meditation to the extreme fundamentalism of "The Children of God," and "the Moonies."

Paul knew that false, syncretistic teaching was getting the attention and adherence of Christians as Colossian teachers sought to combine elements that had been adamantly kept apart: from Judaism, the demands of rigid codes—keeping the Sabbath, observing prescribed festivals, avoiding unclean things; from pagan cults, emphasis on mysterious rites and ascetic discipline, and the worship of angels.

This Colossian expression was one among many as all over the empire men were at work, trying to create new religions out of different combinations of the old. These men were sometimes profound thinkers, sometimes crazed fanatics, sometimes imposters. They were strangely attracted to Christianity because they saw in this the values which they could exploit for their own self-interests and beliefs.

If the Christian missionaries had been willing to compromise, they would have secured for Christ a place in such syncretistic systems. This letter addresses the issue: it is not a place but *the* place which the Christian faith requires for Christ. Christianity cannot be just an element in some form of composite religion. We may press that further: we cannot take Christ as just one element of influence in our lives, rather than the centrality, the core, the dynamic around which and by which our lives move and are motivated and empowered.

The Recipients

"To the saints and faithful brethren in Christ who are in Colosse" (Col. 1:2). At the time of writing, Colosse was in decline midway between fame and decadence. Situated in the Lycus valley, it stood along the easiest and most popular route from Greece and Italy to Syria and Mesopotamia. Even though it was by now inferior in rank to the neighboring towns of Laodicea and Hierapolis, Colosse still retained some influence and a significant population. The fact that Paul addressed his letter to those in Colosse seems to indicate their church was the strongest of the three in number and quality.

Scholars have differed as to whether Paul ever preached at Colosse, though it is now considered fairly certain he never reached the town. The logical assumption is that the gospel was carried to Colosse, Laodicea, and Hierapolis and other interior districts of Asia Minor by friends and colleagues who had been converted during Paul's three-year stay in Ephesus (Acts 19:10). Epaphras, Paul's personal representative and a native of Colosse (Col. 4:12), was the most important of these. He was credited with founding the church in his hometown (Col. 1:7), and had pastoral care of the churches in Laodicea and Heirapolis (Col. 4:13).

Onesimus, the slave, also belonged to the church in Colosse. Thus it may be inferred that Philemon, the master of Onesimus, was also in Colosse and had a church meeting in his home, having been converted by Paul (Philem. 2, 19). Philemon's son Archippus held some sort of office in the church (Col. 4:17). Though not certain, it is probable that Paul was personally acquainted with Nymphas in whose house the church met in Laodicea (Col. 4:15).

Unlike Ephesians, this letter is addressed to a specific church, and its purpose is clear. Paul regards the churches as his. He agonizes over them and assumes that they will listen to what he has to say. His connection with them is intimate, though not first-hand.

The Occasion of the Letter

There are many allusions to the heathen past of those to whom Paul writes. He reminds them that once they were estranged, with hostile minds and involved in evil deeds (1:21). They were dead in sins and in uncircumcision of the flesh (2:13), heathen who had heard the Good News through Epaphras and accepted it (1:7 f. and 4:12 f.). They had experienced in baptism the creative power of God who raised them to new life (2:12), who forgave their sins (1:14; 2:13), and called them to conduct their lives under the dominion of Christ (1:13 f.).

Until now the community has been faithful to what they have received. Their faith in Jesus Christ and love for all the saints (1:4) is enough to cause Paul to say, *"We give thanks to the God and Father of our Lord Jesus Christ, praying always for you"* (1:3). Yet, Paul is worried. He has received news that "false" teachers are deceiving the community, dazzling them with a "philosophy," and leading them away from the centrality and sufficiency of Christ.

This teaching, commonly designated by scholars as "the Colossian heresy," has been described as "an incipient form of Gnosticism." The name comes from the Greek *gnosis*, meaning "knowledge." Claiming a superior and esoteric wisdom *(gnosis)*, the Gnostics asserted that God was separated from the world, distantly so, and had not directly created the world. Rather, creation took place as a result of a series of emanations—each more distant from God, until those furthest from Him created the material world. This theory preserved a rationalization that matter was evil and spirit was good. Since God was spirit and therefore good, the evil material world could have no contact with him.

One can immediately see what a challenge this was to basic Christian understanding of Christ as the incarnation of God. The Christian teaching that God came in the flesh of Jesus Christ, loved, forgave and reconciled the world could not be, argued the Gnostics. If Jesus was the Son of God, He could not dwell in the flesh because all matter is evil. So Jesus must have been an "emanation" from God; at most, one of a gradation of angels. Following that line of reasoning, they contended that Jesus did not really live as a man; His suffering on the Cross was not real; there was no point of a Resurrection because He had never really lived as a material being in evil flesh.

Some Gnostics did concede the uniqueness of Christ, but held tenaciously to the dichotomy of good and evil, spirit and matter. Their teaching, though recognizing a uniqueness in Jesus, still projected the false picture that the Spirit hovered over Jesus from the time of His baptism but left Him at the time of His Crucifixion.

To what degree "the Colossian heresy" was an incipient form of Gnosticism we can only surmise. Paul does not need to describe the teaching he is attacking, but only to make allusions to it, because his readers knew it first hand. In contrast to his vehement denunciation of the advocates of the Law and his indignance with the Galatians for listening to them, Paul is kind and persuasive with the Colossians. He approaches the dispute by slow degrees after affirming his readers and assuring them of his confidence and appreciation for their loyalty. The false teachers had offered a criticism of the gospel and Paul was grateful for the opportunity to respond. He gently but firmly insists that the gospel of the crucified, resurrected and exalted Lord is the exclusively valid answer which applies to all man's questions and searchings.

The Author, Date, and Place of Writing

I have been referring to Paul as the author of this letter. There are those who argue against his authorship, using much the same data as they use to debate his authorship of Ephesians. The fact is that Ephesians, Colossians, and Philemon must be taken together for consideration of authorship and time of writing.

Colossians and Philemon are intimately related because both were evidently written at the same time, and sent to the same town by the same messenger. Colossians is a letter to a church, dealing with large issues of faith and conduct; Philemon is a private note to a person in that church, dealing with a personal matter. Though differing in purpose, Colossians and Ephesians reflect the same mood of thought and repeat the same ideas in much the same words. Their obvious similarity has been ground for suggestions that one of them was written by an "imitator." (See pp. 136–37 for a response to this argument.)

We cannot claim without doubt, as we can with Ephesians, that this letter was known and used by Christian writers of the early second century. The earliest evidence comes from Marcion (ca. A.D. 140), who included Colossians in his canon of Pauline letters; from Irenaeus, who cites it as a letter of Paul; and from the Muratorian Canon. The most weighty argument to compensate for earlier attestation is Colossians' striking resemblance to Ephesians. This, as I insisted in the introduction to Ephesians, despite its difficulties still remains the strongest case for Paul's authorship of both Colossians and Ephesians. If we accept Ephesians as Paul's letter we must accept Colossians as such. If we do not accept Ephesians as Paul's, we then must see it written by an imitator who knew Colossians and believed it to be by Paul.

I make much the same case for the authorship of Colossians as for Ephesians. The weight of the centuries comes down for Paul's authorship, thus the burden is upon those who would disprove.

Even those such as Edward Lohse who disclaim his authorship, make the case that Colossians contains Paul's basic message and preaching.

The intimate relationship between Colossians, Ephesians, and Philemon suggests they were all written during the same period of Paul's life. Since they were written from prison, the long Roman imprisonment, when Paul was awaiting trial in the emperor's court, seems the natural place of origin. The majority of scholars hold this view, although there is significant support for Ephesus as the setting for these epistles, and a few have made the case for Caesarea, as Paul was imprisoned in both cities.

In my opinion, there is not sufficient reason to abandon the generally accepted view that the epistles date from the Roman captivity. The style and theology of Colossians and Ephesians differ from 1 and 2 Corinthians, Galatians, and Romans. Since these latter letters were written shortly after Paul's long stay in Ephesus, it is argued that a gap of time before writing Colossians and Ephesians would be inevitable. Rome was the center of the ancient world and there Paul might well find himself in company with many of his old friends. Runaway slaves would be attracted to Rome as being safer from discovery there than anyplace else. Also, no evidence exists that Paul's imprisonment was as prolonged in Ephesus as in Rome. These prison letters suggest long periods of leisure to receive and consider reports from churches afar, to ponder and think deeply, then to carefully write well- developed and weighty thoughts. Paul's references to the "Praetorium" and to "Caesar's household" point most naturally to Rome.

From there, after long and arduous years of fighting the good fight and keeping the faith, after punishment and suffering of all sorts, after confrontation and conflict with opposition within and outside the church, Paul makes his final argument for the centrality and supremacy of Christ. Christianity can never be one element in any form of composite religion. In Christ we have everything we need. He is our hope and life. Only in Him can we find salvation.

An Outline of Colossians

I. A Question of Identity: 1:1–14
   A. Greeting and Gratitude: 1:1–8
   B. Saints in the Light: 1:9–12
   C. In Whom We Have Redemption: 1:13–14
II. The Centrality of the All-Sufficient Christ: 1:15–23
   A. Christ and Creation: 1:15–17
   B. Christ and Re-Creation: 1:18–20
   C. New Creation by Reconciliation: 1:21–23
III. The Secret: Christ in You: 1:24—2:19
   A. Christ in You: 1:24–29
   B. A Person, Not a Philosophy: 2:1–10
   C. The Cross: God's Answer to Our Deepest Needs: 2:11–19
IV. The New Life in Christ: 2:20—3:17
   A. Life Hidden with Christ: 2:20–3:4
   B. Put to Death the Old: 3:5–11
   C. Put On the New: 3:12–14
   D. The Fellowship of New Persons in Christ: 3:15–17
V. A Christian Style of Relationships: 3:18—4:18
   A. The Family: A Place for Persons: 3:18–21
   B. Relationships Outside the Family: 3:22—4:6
   C. The Game Is for a Team: 4:7–18

CHAPTER ONE—A QUESTION OF IDENTITY
COLOSSIANS 1:1–14

Scripture Outline

Greeting and Gratitude (1:1–8)

Saints in the Light (1:9–12)

In Whom We Have Redemption (1:13–14)

Roots was the most talked-about book in the 1970s. Millions read and millions more saw this epic story covering more than 200 years and six generations of the family of the author, Alex Haley. It centers initially in Kunta Kinte, Haley's great-great-great-great-great grandfather, as the first chapter describes the tribal customs concerning birth, and especially the signal event of naming a child on the eighth day. The description is poignant:

> Omoro (the father) then walked out before all the assembled people of the village. Moving to his wife's side, he lifted up the infant and as all watched, whispered three times into his son's ear the name he had chosen for him. It was the first time the name had ever been spoken as the child's name, for Omoro's people felt that each human being should be the first to know who he was.

And, as if trying to place the truth of the child's identity in proper dimension, chapter one of *Roots* closes with the father taking his infant son out into the night, lifting him face-up to the heavens and proclaiming: "Behold—the only thing greater than yourself."

It was a great celebration of identity, a ritual to recall that a person might always know who he or she is. Nothing is more important—to know who we are. In Colossians, Paul addresses the question of identity. He rehearses the Good News of the gospel as the touchstone for our always remembering who we are and whose we are.

GREETING AND GRATITUDE

1:1 Paul, an apostle of Jesus Christ by the will of God, and Timothy our brother,

2 To the saints and faithful brethren in Christ who are in Colosse:

Grace to you and peace from God our Father and the Lord Jesus Christ.

3 We give thanks to the God and Father of our Lord Jesus Christ, praying always for you, 4 since we heard of your faith in Christ Jesus and of your love for all the saints; 5 because of the hope which is laid up for you in heaven, of which you heard before in the word of the truth of the gospel, 6 which has come to you, as it has also in all the world, and is bringing forth fruit, as it is also among you since the day you heard and knew the grace of God in truth; 7 as you also learned from Epaphras, our dear fellow servant, who is a faithful minister of Christ on your behalf, 8 who also declared to us your love in the Spirit.

—Colossians 1:1–8

Naming Who We Are

As in all his letters, Paul identifies himself in his greeting: *"an apostle of Christ Jesus"* (v. 1). By this designation he does not place himself in a class, as the holder of an ecclesiastical office. His identity is in the commission he has received. The risen Christ has appeared to him and called him. His orders have come "not from men nor through men" (Gal. 1:1), but from the Lord Himself, who has commissioned Paul to speak and act in His name.

Paul knew himself to be Christ's ambassador (2 Cor. 5:20), and he was always ready to offer proof of his claim—those "signs of a true apostle" (2 Cor. 12:12): healings, conversions, the establishment of churches. Such signs made it clear that the power of God was working in and through him.

There is no consistent organizational structure in the New Testament, so there is really no question of whether we have deacons and elders, and whether those terms designate lay or clergy people; or whether we have presbyters or bishops. Rather, the question is: do we have a church that recognizes, affirms, and seeks to equip persons *called by God* to minister in a set-apart, representative kind of way? Maybe an even more important question than that is: do we who are ordained bear the fruit of ministry which are "signs of a true apostle," and do we operate out of the empowering, self-conscious conviction that we are *"apostle[s] of Christ Jesus by the will of God"*?

Paul's burning awareness of his being especially called as an apostle did not make him class-conscious. In fact, his bold affirmation of the gospel shattered the boundaries and barriers of class and position. Especially was this so in the church. There is tenderness, intimacy, warmth, and the pulsing sense of belonging and family in his reference to Timothy, *"our brother,"* and his address: *"To the saints and faithful brethren in Christ who are in Colosse"* (v. 2).

"Brethren" is Paul's favorite designation for his companion Christians; he uses this designation in all his letters. There is no chauvinism here as we may need to guard against in our day; sisters and brothers were in Paul's mind. He made clear the dynamic power of women in the early church and in the spreading of the gospel. Lois, Eunice, Lydia, Nympha, Prisca, and Julia are linked with Tychicus, Achaius, Fortunatus, Apollos, Hermes, Nereus, and Olympas to make up the *family.* That is the way Paul thought of the church—as a family. For that reason he seems little interested in the organization of the church. The natural, organic unity of the family is more important than the way it may organize itself to function.

The church needs to remember who she is—a family. In a family, the well-being of every member is important, and members of the family should be willing to sacrifice themselves on behalf of other members.

The church is a special kind of family. It is a fellowship of *"saints."* As an adjective the word means "dedicated" or, a bit stronger word, "consecrated." Those to whom Paul wrote were saints not because they are distinguished from others by their moral and spiritual qualities, but because they have received and responded to a divine calling, they are set apart by belonging to Christ.

That is our identity as Christians: We are saints because we belong to Christ. We have been called and we are to be faithful to that call. Whether lay or clergy, ordained or unordained, deacons or elders, presbyters or bishops, we are brothers and sisters, members of the family.

Celebrating Who We Are

Along with naming who we are, we need to *celebrate* who we are. At the heart of celebration is gratitude. In the ordinary structure of a Greek letter it was customary to express a few words of thanksgiving for the welfare of the recipients, and to pray for their continual well-being. This was usually done in a single stereotyped sentence or two. Paul does more: he expresses heartfelt thanks focused on what he knows is going on among the people he is addressing, and he uses the thanksgiving to lead to the theme of his letter. Here is a description of who we are as Christians—at least, who we *should* be—which we celebrate.

(1) Paul gives thanks for *"your faith in Christ Jesus"* (v. 4). Paul is the champion of justification by grace through faith. This was the heartbeat of his preaching. We will never plumb the depths of this great truth; we can only celebrate it and rejoice. Matthew Henry said, "Faith opens the door of the soul to receive Christ; faith admits him, and submits to him." Pungent! Faith is the door; faith is the hinge on which the door swings; faith is the key that unlocks the door; faith is the impulse to open the door when the knock comes; faith is the willingness to invite the guest in; faith impels surrender which allows the guest to become master of the house.

(2) Paul is thankful for the Colossians because he has heard of their *"love for all the saints"* (v. 4). This is something to celebrate.

The Indian philosopher, Bara Dala, brother of the great poet Rabindranath Tagore, once said: "Jesus is ideal and wonderful, but you Christians—you are not like Him." He did not say it bitterly but sadly. How different it should be—when the Christian knows who he is and whose he is. Love is the style. Kagawa of Japan is one of the clearest signs of this style in the twentieth century, demonstrating always a passionate devotion to Christ which expresses itself in selfless *love for all the saints*—and for those who are not saints. In Kagawa's home town there once toiled a missionary named Logan. Someone asked Kagawa if he knew Dr. Logan. A radiant smile spread over Kagawa's face as he responded, "He was the first one who showed me the blueprint of love." Would that Tagore's brother Bara Dala had known Logan rather than the Christians he knew! Love. The Colossians had love and Paul was thankful.

(3) Hope was the final characteristic Paul named: *"because of the hope which is laid up for you in heaven "* (v. 5). Here is the great triad of Christian virtues, describing the Christian style:

faith, hope, and *love.* These abide though all else may perish (1 Cor. 13).

This passage is a unique expression of the three elements and defines what Paul means by them. Faith is directed *to* Christ and is *in* Christ; love is *to* and *for* the brethren; hope is *for* the coming of full salvation. There is also a unique expression of the connection of faith and love with hope. Interestingly, the *"hope which is laid up for you in heaven "* is not a *reward* for our faith and love. Rather, the hope that is ours is the *source* of faith and love.

Affirming the Power of the Gospel and Its Witnesses

Verses 5–8 are a compacted affirmation of the power of the gospel and its witnesses.

First, **the witness:** *". . . you also learned from Epaphras, our dear fellow servant, who is a faithful minister of Christ on your behalf."* Too often we fall into the snare of thinking that the gospel has moved across the face of the earth through the zeal, passion, and commitment of superstars like Paul. Not so! To be sure, there are occasional fiery beacons who light up the sky of history—Paul, Augustine, St. Francis, Luther, Wesley. But were they alone in their witness, the sky of history would be bereft of the luminous light of the gospel. The sky is lighted only because of thousands of "lesser" stars: Epaphras, Onesimus, Eunice, Aquila, Grandpa Lewis, Brother Grissom, Murdoc and Cora, Clara Mae Sells, Nettle Beeson. You can extend the list to include those through whom the gospel came to you as lively experience which set you on the path to and in Christ.

In his letters Paul mentions fourteen fellow workers, four fellow prisoners of war, two fellow soldiers, two fellow slaves, and one yokefellow. Enough for us to know that Paul knew his was not a solo ministry, nor could he provide adequate witness to win the world for Christ which was his passionate dream. No less than Paul, Epaphras was an apostle, a messenger or witness. What are the marks of an apostle? (1) an experience of the risen Christ (1 Cor. 9:1); (2) a sense of divine call (Gal. 1:1); (3) a demonstration of the signs of an apostle (2 Cor. 12:12). Then there is a fourth which undergirds the others, especially the second—belief that preparation for apostleship begins at birth (Gal. 1:15). With this understanding of apostleship, why do we continue to argue about *apostolic succession* (hierarchical ministry) in our discussions of church unity? The question is not historic apostolic *succession,* but apostolic *experience* in the present. Are our churches apostolic *now?* Do we perceive in the church's worship and her witnesses the risen Christ? From her and in her do we sense a divine call? Are there gifts of the Spirit operative in her common life, fruit of the Spirit growing from her fellowship and ministry *(koinonia* and *diakonia)?* This is what ministry is about—not a hierarchy of order but a fellowship in which all the people are the apostolate, all members being given by the Spirit gifts to minister. We need to get our identity straight and affirm the *laos,* the whole people of God, the Epaphrases and the Pauls.

Paul not only affirms the *witness,* he affirms the **power of the gospel**. At the time of this writing, Paul's words must have seemed a wild exaggeration. The gospel *"which has come to you, as it has also in all the world, and is bringing forth fruit, as it is also among you since the day you heard and knew the grace of God in truth"* (v. 6). The church was only a tiny handful of rag-tag folk, almost unnoticed in a great empire. But Paul affirmed the power of it. The seeds were being sown and the harvest would be bountiful.

Two words describe the gospel's power as Paul affirmed it: *universal* and *effective.* The gospel must be local. Paul addressed the saints in Christ *"at Colosse."* There is always the local setting, our own environment where the gospel is to be proclaimed and lived out. Often this is an environment alien to our hopes, indifferent to our faith and love. We are always at Colossae, or Mt. Juliet, or Atlanta, or London; put down in some particular place to spend the particular days of our lives. But the gospel we live and proclaim *at Colosse* is universal. Paul wanted the Colossians to remember that. The gospel builds a worldwide community, and the saints at Colossae are a part of this great whole. Paul strikes that note frequently (Rom. 1:8; 10:18; 2 Cor. 2:14; Col. 1:23; 1 Thess. 1:8). How much power would be released in our little corners if we would remember the universality of the gospel.

Universal—and *effective!* Paul constantly celebrates the effects of the gospel—*bearing fruit and growing.* His metaphor is that of a tree which bears fruit at the end of a season and puts forth the buds for the next. The gospel bears fruit in the conduct of believers, and subsequently, by their witness, wins new converts. The bearing fruit and growing cycle repeats itself over and over. The guarantee of growth is a surety because the gospel is God's grace and He will bring the increase.

SAINTS IN THE LIGHT

[9] For this reason we also, since the day we heard it, do not cease to pray for you, and to ask that you may be filled with the knowledge of His will in all wisdom and spiritual understanding; [10] that you may walk worthy of the Lord, fully pleasing Him, being fruitful in every good work and increasing in the knowledge of God; [11] strengthened with all might, according to His glorious power, for all patience and longsuffering with joy; [12] giving thanks to the Father who has qualified us to be partakers of the inheritance of the saints in the light.

—Colossians 1:9–12

The Kingdom in Which We Live

With verse 9 Paul begins to share with his readers the prayer of intercession he has made for them. Even in his praying he raises the question of identity. He does so by offering thanks for who we are: *"giving thanks to the Father who has qualified us to be partakers of the inheritance of the saints in the light"* (v. 12).

The imagery here is powerful and suggestive. The contrast between light and darkness, common with Paul and also with John, was more than figurative. There is here a reference to the gnostic heresy with which Paul was dealing (see introduction), as well as the common belief that certain angelic beings had fallen or had been expelled from a higher world, and had created this material world in which they were in control. This led to the gnostic view of the evil of that which is material, thus to the heresy of the non-humanity of Jesus.

The pervasive idea which Paul also seemingly held, was that people are subject to the "powers of the universe," "the potentates of the dark present" (Eph. 6:12, Moffatt), the rulers of darkness. By His death and Resurrection Christ has overcome these powers and rescued us from their tyranny.

Two very important lessons are here. One, there are two kingdoms: light and darkness, flesh and spirit, good and evil. We have been rescued from the darkness and brought into the kingdom of light. If Paul's terminology is archaic, or if his understanding of the system of angelic powers that rule in the elements seems outdated, the truth of his message is not less relevant, or the power of the promised deliverance any less needed.

How impotent we feel in a technological society—how helpless in the clutches of mechanical law, scientific determinism! How often do we give in to the overwhelming feeling that we have no control—that everything is determined by heredity, environment, natural powers, economic and social forces. How ominous is the power of sin! We move along as best we can, propelled by the forces around us, bobbing erratically along the torrential river of life as though we were Ping-Pong balls in a mountain stream. Paul says *no!* We have been delivered into a kingdom of light, of freedom. We have a destiny about which we can decide, and we have access to the power of Christ to live against the tide of determinism. We are *"saints of the light,"* and the darkness will never prevail against the light (John 1:4–5).

The second lesson in this identification of Paul is that we are now residents of the new kingdom; it is not something that is ours in some distant future. We have already been removed from a world which is subject to evil forces into a realm in which Christ is King. He is Lord, and He alone has ultimate authority over us. With what confidence we may live if we appropriate this truth experientially. No darkness can overcome us, no power can overwhelm us, no experience can completely devastate us. Sin cannot hold sway in our lives. We belong to Christ; His is the kingdom, the power and the glory. We have been qualified to be *"partakers of the inheritance of the saints in the light."*

Power to Live as Saints in the Light

Barclay says that this passage teaches us more about the essence of prayer's request than almost any other passage in the New Testament. From this passage C. F. D. Moule says we learn that prayer at its best makes two great requests: (1) for the discernment of God's will, and (2) for the power to perform God's will.

God's will *is.* He has a plan for the universe and for our lives. Discerning God's will is our task, and that is not easy. It is a surrender of our identity as human beings and a blasphemy against God to give in to the pain, hopelessness, and helplessness we feel, the gnawing doubts that haunt us by passing through our struggles, conflict, pain, disillusionment, and despair with the superficial affirmation, "It's God's will." Such glossing over is a straw bridge which will not hold as we pass over or through the debilitating depths to which we are often plunged. Such shallow, facile words are empty and do not affirm the *almightiness* of God as we presume they do. Nor does such an easy slogan authenticate our faith. The will of God is often enshrouded in darkness, clouded in ambiguity; silence as well as speaking marks His communication with us. In prayer we struggle to discern God's will. We talk. We listen. We ponder scripture. We reflect. We wait. And graciously the response comes. Not according to our timetable, nor in the form and mode of our design, but in God's timing and in His way. That is one of the two great requests that should preoccupy our praying: for the discernment of God's will.

The second request is for power to perform God's will. Discerning God's will is only one part of the hard stuff of prayer. We know far more than we do. Two things are essential: the will to do and the power to do.

The line between the will to do and the power to do may not merit such a clear distinction. I draw the line to underscore the need for power beyond our own human resources, and the willingness to acknowledge that need. The greatest problem in life is not to know what to do, but to do it—to have the will and the power to act according to what we know.

Paul uses a quaint phrase to name our need and to affirm the power that is available to us: "strengthened with all might, according to His glorious power. . ." (v. 11). Weymouth translates that "strengthened with strength of every kind," and Moule has it "according to the might of His glory." What an extravagant possibility. Strength of every kind!

Worthy of the Lord

Overarching these two great requests at the heart of our prayer is the end to which we pray: "that you may walk worthy of the Lord, fully pleasing Him, being fruitful in every good work and increasing in the knowledge of God" (v. 10).

Prayer is practical. It is not an escape from reality. The end of prayer is not "spiritual." We do not seek a mystical communion alone with God. In prayer we struggle with being in the world as those who "walk worthy of the Lord." As Christians in prayer we are looking for the power not to be translated to some "third heaven," but to be made transparent witnesses of Christ's glory in us, bearing fruit of His Spirit. Paul is talking about holiness, a holiness that is personal and social. The person who would walk worthy of the Lord boldly orders his life in obedience to God, seeking what is pleasing to God, thus doing justice, loving kindness, and walking humbly with the Lord (Mic. 6:8).

Now we know that we can never live a life fully pleasing to Christ if the measure of that is moral purity, untainted ethical performance, sinless perfection. Paul is talking about our *affections,* what we deeply desire; our *direction,* what we truly seek; our *disposition,* the set of our wills. He is talking about the shape and substance of our commitment: are we passionately eager to please Him?

The Result of Obedience

Patience, longsuffering, and joy are needs and characteristics of those who walk worthy of the Lord (v. 11). We focus on obedience, and the Spirit gives us patience and enables us to be longsuffering. Joy, is both the result of our obedient living and the witness that we are saints in the light.

These three, *patience, longsuffering,* and *joy,* are the great gifts that are ours when we are empowered with all-power. Obviously, these are gifts—the result of Christ's "glorious might" working within us.

Patience and longsuffering are twin words with a slight but significant difference in their use here. G. B. Caird makes this distinction: Longsuffering (in other translations "endurance") is "the refusal to be daunted by hard times"; patience is "the refusal to be upset by perverse people." How strong the distinction should be made is questionable, but the point is that there are difficulties through which we pass for which we can find no relief or release; we need the power to endure. The promise is that in every situation adequate power to "suffer through" (longsuffering) and to remain whole and triumphant can be ours through the Holy Spirit. Likewise there are people with whom we live and to whom we relate who try us, provoke us, spitefully use us, scorn us—some deliberately, others unconsciously. They are dull to our feelings, callous to our needs, demanding but never giving. We need patience in relationships, power to endure rejection and injury, the capacity to keep on loving, forgiving, and accepting when all human responses are spent and all natural juices of good will are drained from souls.

The outward manifestation of the inner grace of the Lord Jesus is joy. Joy, *chara,* flows from grace, *charis.* It is a distinctively Christian quality (Gal. 5:22; Phil. 1:18; 2:17; 3:1; 4:4). It is significant to note that it is constantly linked in the New Testament with hardship and suffering. There is nothing superficial about it. It is in the category of "blessed," the benediction of Jesus upon those who hunger and thirst for righteousness, who are merciful, who are pure in heart and make peace, those who are persecuted, scorned and falsely accused (cf. Matt. 5:3–11).

So, joy is no flippant exuberance, no gushy bubbling of surface feeling self-conjured up. It is the subdued ecstasy of knowing and being known, of loving and being loved by God. Joy stirs within and expresses itself sometimes only in quiet confidence, in determined obedience that is not morbid or stoical—always giving forth from the one who is gifted with it a sort of glow more like the early morning dawn than the brilliant noonday sun, more like indirect light that illumines a room without announcing its source than a flashing neon or a brilliant spot. No wonder we sing the ancient song, "The joy of the LORD is your strength" (Neh. 8:10). Joy, unlike happiness, is not dependent on circumstances and people. Joy is the expression of Christ indwelling us, the fruit of the Spirit even growing out of the soil of difficulties and suffering.

IN WHOM WE HAVE REDEMPTION

13 He has delivered us from the power of darkness and conveyed us into the kingdom of the Son of His love, 14 in whom we have redemption through His blood, the forgiveness of sins.

—Colossians *1:13–14*

Not only our identity, but the identity of Christ is defined, described, and affirmed especially in this first chapter, but also throughout Colossians. He is the one *"in whom we have redemption."*

In the closing of his prayer in verse 12, Paul announced the kingdom in which we live. We live in this kingdom as *"saints in the light"* (see commentary on preceding section). He builds on this theme in verse 13. We are delivered by Christ and translated to a new kingdom.

Paul describes the entry of the Gentiles into the church—our entry into the Christian life—with an image of the defeated people of a nation being taken to a new land and later being liberated. It was a common practice in the ancient world that when one nation was defeated by another, people living in exile in that now-conquered nation would often be liberated to return to their homeland. This imagery would be familiar to the people in a Roman province such as Colossae.

Paul gives specific meaning to the metaphor. As God had rescued the Hebrew people from oppression in Egypt, so now He has rescued the new Israel from the dark principalities and powers which rule the present world order. Once exiled, and without hope, these sojourners from the promise are settled in the kingdom of Christ. Verse 13 is a continued development of verse 12: The Father has *"qualified"* us to live in the new kingdom.

Note clearly that we do not qualify ourselves. We are qualified by God. Only by His grace can we enter the new kingdom. *Faith* is the path we walk into that new land. Our redemption is in the Cross, Christ's death for us. *"We have redemption through His blood"* (v. 14).

Just as clear is the assertion that we are *"delivered."* To get this clear in our mind and let it saturate our total beings is precisely our struggle in the Christian life. We preoccupy ourselves anxiously with what we ought to be and do. Thus we are constantly stirring up all sorts of passions, inflaming these passions with new power. Our energy is wasted as we focus on our efforts rather than releasing ourselves to be empowered by Christ within us.

Christ, who is now our Lord, has won the victory over sin and death. That is not our battle. He draws our whole being into this victory, giving us a complete Resurrection as persons. We have been *"raised with Christ"* (3:1); our life *"is hidden with Christ in God"* (3:3).

The powerful meaning of this work of God through Christ is best seen as we look at the specific things that have been done for us by Him *"in whom we have redemption."*

We Have Been Transferred From Darkness to Light

In the dark we cannot see things as they really are, nor can we see where we are going. So, there are two facets of truth in this image. In Christ we have *perception;* we can see things as they are. A tourist in the National Museum in Washington, standing before a masterpiece, said in a kind of snide tone, "I don't see anything in that." Another tourist, with a kind of inspired genius, whispered in reply, "Don't you wish you could?" In Christ's kingdom of light we have perception; we can see things as they are—sift the wheat from the chaff, decipher the real from the imagined, the authentic from the superficial.

The other facet of truth in this image of being transferred from darkness to light is that *in Christ we have direction.* Perception: to see things as they are; direction: to see and know where we are going. Have we a more desperate need than direction?

We Are No Longer Slaves, but Free

The Greek word for redemption is *apolutrōsis,* which is also the word for ransoming and deliverance. It is the word that was used for the emancipation of a slave, and for the buying back of something which is in the power of someone else.

It is next to impossible for us who have never been slaves in the literal sense, or actually imprisoned behind bars, to sense the depth of this image. Charles T. Robinson, an inmate in maximum security at the Colorado State Prison, is helping me probe the depth of this experience. I know that only with a quickened capacity for vicarious experience can I even penetrate beyond the surface. But I am trying. Through exchange of letters and Charles' unusually sensitive poetry, I have begun to get just a hint of the experience of being "inside." Here is one of those poems.

> Serenely now,
> We name the same clouds
> in the same blue sky;
> from different sides.
>
> We lie down
> beneath the same dust flecked night,
> under the same awesome moon:
> on different sides.
>
> We speak the same prayers,
> our words going up
> to the same quiet air;
> petitioning the same quiet God,
> from different sides.
>
> You dream dreams
> that come to pass
> as I dream nightmares
> I pray will not.
>
> And we sleep the same sleep,
> in different beds,
> on different sides.

The fourth verse captures the difference of being "inside" and free. "You dream dreams that come to pass as I dream nightmares I pray will not." But we need freedom no less than Charles—freedom from all the passions, forces, influences, habits, and relationships that have us in bondage. The list is almost endless: neurotic fear of the future that makes us impotent; jealousy that breaks out in rage, destroying someone we love, or smolders within to destroy our capacity to truly love; indecisiveness that immobilizes us; prejudice that fences us into a narrow plot of acquaintances and robs us of the richness of friendship; ambition that numbs us to being feelingly human and drives us to trample over the needs of others; sexual lust which, like ambition, is insensitive to the needs of others, allowing us to use persons as playthings and handle the precious gift of sexuality with self-indulgent grasping hands; the passionate drive for immediate gratification and satisfaction that turns the holy into the profane. Or, we could turn the list into the kind Paul makes in Colossians 3:5–8: fornication, uncleanness, passion, evil desire, covetousness, anger, wrath, malice, blasphemy, filthy language. In these *"you yourselves once walked when you lived in them"* (3:7). It does not take much probing to locate the chains from which we have been freed by Christ; and it does not take much perception to be aware that we can become slaves again. So we stay conscious of and celebrate the fact that we are no longer slaves, but free.

We Have Been Transferred from Condemnation to Forgiveness

In every letter Paul sang the joy of this experience. "There is therefore now no condemnation to those who are in Christ Jesus" (Rom. 8:1). The Cross is our proof that God has accepted us and no power in the universe can separate us from His love (Rom. 8:33–39).

We Are No Longer under the Power of Satan, but under the Power of God

We have been delivered by God *"into the kingdom of the Son of His love"* (v. 13).

The forces of evil affect our lives in a variety of ways, but be sure of this: *the power of Satan controls us only as we give him assent.* As residents of the kingdom of the Son of God's love, evil has no control over our lives as long as we say *no* to evil and *yes* to Christ.

So we know who we are, saints in the light; and we know who Christ is, the one *"in whom we have redemption"* (v. 14). Throughout Colossians, the identity question as the key to our life in Christ recurs over and over, with the resounding affirmation of the allsufficient Christ as the undermoving theme. We specifically turn to that theme in the following section.

CHAPTER TWO—THE CENTRALITY OF THE ALL-SUFFICIENT CHRIST

COLOSSIANS 1:15–23

Scripture Outline

Christ and Creation (1:15–17)

Christ and Re–Creation (1:18–20)

New Creation by Reconciliation (1:21–23)

Whenever we claim anything distinctively Christian we have to do it in the context of our experience of Jesus. The Christian gospel is the proclamation of an event, the event of Jesus Christ. In the Christian view of reality, Jesus is final. He is the revelation of God and the revelation of true humanity. This paradoxical tension—the humanity of Jesus and His divinity—is the essence of the gospel proclamation. It was the center of the "Colossian heresy," and thus a preoccupation of Paul's letter. The Gnostics could not accept the full humanity of Jesus Christ because they could not accept the possibility that anything material, earthly, or human could be an expression of, or be filled with the divine. The "false teachers," trying to *"deceive with persuasive words"* (2:4), were demeaning Christ, proposing a substitute philosophy for the gospel Paul preached, which gospel the Colossians had received through Epaphras.

So Paul soars eloquently, in a sweeping crescendo, as he tells the Colossians about the all-sufficient Christ. He uses dramatic, impelling, somewhat philosophical language to present the case for the irreplaceable centrality of the all-sufficient Christ.

CHRIST AND CREATION

[15] He is the image of the invisible God, the firstborn over all creation. [16] For by Him all things were created that are in heaven and that are on earth, visible and invisible, whether thrones or dominions or principalities or powers. All things

were created through Him and for Him. [17] And He is before all things, and in Him all things consist.

—*Colossians 1:15–17*

This is a very difficult passage, but crucially important. Paul was not writing in a vacuum but addressing a very specific situation in Colossae. A tendency of thought in the early church was flowering among the Colossians—an expression of Gnosticism that sought to turn Christianity into a philosophy and to align it with other philosophies. Those fostering this effort were *the intellectual ones* who were dissatisfied with what they considered the rude simplicity of Christianity. They began with one basic assumption—that matter is altogether evil and spirit is altogether good; that matter has always existed, and that out of evil matter the world was created, thus the world and all its material expression is evil. A distant emanation of God, not God Himself, created the world, because God could not touch evil.

This general understanding issued in some specific expressions. (1) The creating god is not the true God, but a distant emanation ignorant of and even hostile to the true God. (2) Jesus was not unique, but merely an emanation, one of the many intermediaries between God and man. Jesus may stand high, even highest, in the series of emanations from God, but Still He was one among many. (3) Jesus was not truly and fully man. This argument proceeded from a general presupposition: if material flesh is evil, He who was the revelation of God cannot have a real body; He cannot have real flesh and blood, as we are flesh and blood. So, the Gnostics insisted that Jesus was a spiritual phantom in bodily form. (4) The Gnostics refused to see Christ as the center or the source of salvation. They insisted that the task of humankind is to find the way to God, climbing up a ladder, as it were, getting past each emanation of God by special knowledge, special passwords. Thus there was great mystery, and the Gnostics claimed to hold the key to the mystery—the key being elaborate knowledge.

I have tried to simplify and give the basic outline of the philosophy that was inifiltrating the church, and forging the "Colossian heresy" which Paul was combatting. This brief synopsis will help us understand Paul's terminology in describing the person and work of Christ.

The Image of the Invisible God

That was Paul's first assertion: Christ is *"the image of the invisible God"* (v. 15). The Greek for "image" is *eikōn*. Scholars have continued to seek the precise meaning of this, entranced by the possible meanings behind the words. Some work within a construct of Greek thought about the *Logos*, "the word, the reason of God." John used this word in the introduction to his Gospel: "The Word (Logos) became flesh." It was the Logos which created the world and put sense into the universe.

Other scholars work from the Hebrew understanding of wisdom. Wisdom was said to be co-eternal with God, and was present with God when He created the world. Wisdom was the image of the goodness of God, thus Christ as image is that goodness of God in creation.

Still other scholars work from a much simpler Hebrew expression of creation: God created everything out of nothing and the culminating act of creation was man. "God said, Let Us make man in Our *image*. . . . So God created man in His own image, in the *image* of God He created him. . ." (Gen. 1:26, 27). It is this image that Jesus is.

Out of all this thinking we can conclude powerful truth, revolving around the word "image," *eikōn*. An *eikōn* was a representation, or reproduction with precise likeness. A portrait of a person's likeness or an image of a sovereign or hero on a coin was an *eikōn*. Paul says Jesus Christ was that—a representation of God the Creator-Father. But more. The word *eikōn* also means manifestation. More than being in the likeness of God, as are all persons created, Jesus was God Himself in human incarnation. The Colossians knew that Paul was countering the Gnostic philosophy that Christ was one expression among many emanations from God, or that He was not truly and fully human. Paul made it clear: in the body of one human, Jesus of Nazareth, God was incarnated. How much this says to those of our day and of every age who fallaciously talk about the many roads that lead to God—Christ being one way, and not the *only* way!

There has been, for thirty or forty years now, a widespread and popular effort to diminish the importance of dogma, the contention being that doctrine is irrelevant to the life of the average person. The problem is not at the intersection of doctrine and the average person, but the irrelevant way doctrine is presented by the religious professional. The doctrine of the Incarnation is the test of relevancy. If Christ were *only* man, then he is irrelevant to our thought of God. If he were *only* God then he is irrelevant to any experience of human life. It is becoming devastatingly clear that you cannot have Christian principles without Christ, and that the validity of Christian principles depend on Christ's authority. His authority depends on who He is—and that must be clear.

When we talk about the Incarnation, about Christ *the image of the invisible God,* we are stuck with the limitation of words. But words are not all we have—we have our lives to offer up as reflections of *the Word become flesh* becoming flesh in us. Still we have to talk about it. How?

I spent five years as a pastor in Gulfport, Mississippi. Though not an ardent fisherman, I fished enough to observe an interesting phenomenon which became a parable for Christ, the image of the invisible God. Near the Bay of Biloxi and the Mississippi Sound, the level of the bayous changes with the high and low tides. These bayous feed the ocean, emptying their waters into the larger body at low tide. But at high tide, the ocean feeds the bayous, raising their level. To the fisherman, there is significance other than the tide. Up the bayous for a certain distance, the water is brackish, flavored by the salt of the Gulf waters. White and speckled trout, whose natural habitat is the Gulf, are bountiful in this brackish water. But further inland the waters lose their salt content, and freshwater fish such as green and rainbow trout hover in the cool depths.

This is a long analogy to say one thing: the bayous went to the ocean, but the ocean also came to the bayous. Though limited, as all our words and parables are, it is a picture of Christ *the image of the invisible God.* He shows us what God is; He also shows us what all persons are meant to be. "Found in the fashion of man," he was human, revealing the model of our humanity—the *image* in which we were created, which image was shattered by sin when things went tragically wrong in the garden. Also, in Him, the "ocean of God" has come to us. So He is the *eikōn* of God: a window through which we see the very nature of God; and a mirror, revealing our human possibility, by picturing our fallenness and the fallen state of all life against the image of our divine destiny.

Christ is the *eikōn,* the image of God: a *representation* perfect enough to be a *manifestation* of God among us. Also, representation and manifestation of what we are meant to be—and which, through Him, we can be.

Christ Is "the Firstborn over All Creation"

This designation of Christ and the elaboration of it in verses 16 and 17 is one of three New Testament passages used as examples of *Wisdom* or *Logos* Christology (John 1:1–14; Heb. 1:1–4), the most familiar of which is from John 1:1–4.

Again, the work of scholars is complex and somewhat contradictory. Debate still swirls around this and the sister passages. Was Christ uncreated, forever sharing in the being of God? Was Christ Himself the Creator? Paul was affirming in the face of the Gnostics and/or the syncretistic Jews infected with the Gnostic spirit—had he been in verbal debate he would have been vehement—that Christ was uncreated and was Himself the Creator. He is pre-existent, one with God in personality and work before the human expression in Jesus.

Our problem, as modern thinkers, centers around the idea of "preexistence." How can we conceive of something *being* before it exists? The ancients did not have the problem we modern "rational" thinkers have. Both Hebrew and Greek thinkers knew that "existence" characterized the world of time-space, but this was not the only reality: "Whereas existence in time-space was real, the other existence was 'really real,' eternal rather than temporal." In Jewish thought the Torah and the name of the Messiah were a part of this super-real existence. In Greek thought, the Logos (Word) was in this category. Leander E. Keck has clearly and succinctly put the New Testament understanding of the pre-existence of Christ in the context of the ancient modes of thinking.

> When NT authors wrote of the pre-existence of Christ, they were applying to him a sophisticated way of thinking which was deeply established in Hellenized Judaism, which in turn was deeply influenced by Greek thought. Paul could assume that he need not explain or justify speaking of an eternal reality which manifested itself in time-space. *Because it "was" before it "became," it could be spoken of as preexisting. What early Christians claimed was that this pre-existing reality became Jesus. They did not hold that Jesus pre-existed; rather what pre-existed was God's son who became Jesus. All incarnational Christology rests on such a conceptual basis.* [1]

However the debates go, and however puzzling the mystery, clear truth emerges: Christ has priority, and sovereignty over creation; He is the sole mediator between God and man. The *New English Bible* translates it, "His is the primacy over all created beings."

In Jesus the complete being of God came to dwell. Nothing is left out. He is the full and final revelation of God; all sufficient, and nothing more is necessary for our salvation.

CHRIST AND RE-CREATION

18 And He is the head of the body, the church, who is the beginning, the firstborn from the dead, that in all things He may have the preeminence.

19 For it pleased the Father that in Him all the fullness should dwell, 20 and by Him to reconcile all things to Himself, by Him, whether things on earth or things in heaven, having made peace through the blood of His cross.

—Colossians *1:18–20*

In these verses Paul underscores what he has been declaring. In Christ we must seek ultimate meaning of and for the world. Everything, *absolutely everything*, exists for the spiritual ends which were supremely represented and manifested in Jesus' life and teaching. Apart from the Christ-event—life, death, and Resurrection—the universe has no meaning.

A friend of mine, Donald English, a brilliant Bible teacher from England has a marvelous way of expressing profound truth in simple fashion. Commenting on "In Him all things were created," he says this is not a scientific but a theological statement. What is being said is that in Jesus Christ we see the clue to God's purposes of creation. "I sometimes put it by saying: the heartbeat of the created universe is that which we have seen in Jesus Christ. His love, His self-giving, the way He liberates people, His sense of the presence of God everywhere, His way of reading life so that there is time and eternity intimately mixed up—all of this is the heartbeat of the created universe."

This means that *in Christ* is the basic clue for answering all the world's big questions—war, racism, starvation, illiteracy, ecology, pollution—for Christ is the "heartbeat" of the entire created universe. It is necessary, then, to talk about *re-creation* as well as creation.

The Church as the Expression of Re-creation

Paul makes a bold leap in thought with verse 18. Having presented Christ as the source of universal life, he now presents Him as the source of that new life which is operative in the church.

The church as the body of Christ was Paul's favorite metaphor. To be such an expression, the church must remember two things: (1) *the church originated with Christ;* the church is Christ's doing, not ours; (2) the church depends on Christ continually as the source of energy and power. He is *the head of the church,* not merely in the sense of being the most important member or having control; but rather in the sense that all the forces of the body are brought together in the head. The *head* is the seat of life and will which permeates all the members, uniting them into an organic whole. Christ, as head, energizes the Body, giving life and power.

The Resurrection is the fact behind this bestowal of life and power. So Paul refers to Christ as *"the firstborn from the dead"* (v. 18) and in Romans 8:29 as "the first-born among many brethren." Christ's Resurrection was the beginning of a new humanity, a re-creation in which we as Christians participate. United with Christ, we share a new and higher life. We will consider this more as we look at chapters two and three of this letter.

The Whole Universe to Be Brought under Christ's Lordship

G. B. Caird summarizes his commentary on verse 18 in this clear, succinct sentence: "Christ is the head over the Church, in order that he may become head over everything else." He is picking up on the last part of the verse: *"that in all things He may have preeminence."*

Verses 19–20 continue the thought by stating the dream of God to reconcile all things *"on earth"* and *"in heaven"* to Himself through Christ. This is the cosmic Christ. I wonder if we have even begun to grasp the greatness of the Lord Jesus Christ? He who is the head over the Church, is to become head over everything else. And the church is to play a role in that.

Donald English, whom I quoted previously, tells a quaint English story that gives this perspective.

> In Birmingham, England, there is a store called Lewis's. It's a great chain store in one of the main streets, and wanted to extend. Right in the way of the extension was a little chapel of the Quakers, a Friends' meeting house. Lewis's sent a letter to the leaders of the Friends' meeting house saying, "Dear Sirs, We wish to extend our premises. We see that your building is right in the way. We wish therefore to buy your building and demolish it so that we might expand our store. We will pay you any price you care to name. If you'll name a price we will settle the matter as quickly as possible. Yours sincerely."
>
> They got a letter back by reply which said, "Dear Sirs: We in the Friends' meeting house note the desire of Lewis's to extend. We observe that our building is right

in your way. We would point out, however, that we have been on our site somewhat longer than you have been on yours, and we are determined to stay where we are. We are so determined to stay where we are that we will happily buy Lewis's. If therefore you would like to name a suitable price we will settle the matter as quickly as possible. Signed, Cadbury." Here is the clincher. The Cadburys are the great chocolate-making, candy-making people in England. They have an enormous spread of business all over the country and the Cadburys are Quakers. They could very well have bought Lewis's many times over.

The point is that it is not the size of the building that counts, but who signs the letter. One thinks of Paul's word to the church at Corinth: "You are a letter from Christ. . . written not with ink but with the Spirit of the living God" (2 Cor. 3:3, RSV).

The church is never in a defensive position as long as she remembers who she is—the body of Christ through whom He intends to become *head over everything else*. Christ Himself signs the letter of the church. It is Christ with whom every power in the universe must reckon, and we who make up the church are not operating out of human wisdom and strength alone. We are a new creation, a fellowship of Resurrection life. We are a letter of Christ; His seal is upon us.

NEW CREATION BY RECONCILIATION

21 And you, who once were alienated and enemies in your mind by wicked works, yet now He has reconciled 22 in the body of His flesh through death, to present you holy, and blameless, and above reproach in His sight— 23 if indeed you continue in the faith, grounded and steadfast, and are not moved away from the hope of the gospel which you heard, which was preached to every creature under heaven, of which I, Paul, became a minister.

—Colossians 1:21–23

The universal is verified as it becomes local. Having dwelt on the universal significance of Christ, Paul now brings it down to the people in Colossae. The thought of the first chapter as a whole began with redemption and now returns to redemption. *"He has delivered us from the power of darkness"* (v. 13). *"And you, who once were alienated and enemies in your mind by wicked works, yet now He has reconciled"* (v. 21).

The big word in verses 20 and 21 is *"reconciled."* We participate in the new creation by reconciliation. Before we consider the meaning and richness of that word, there are some implicit truths in this passage that need to be explicitly stated.

Always Remember Who You Are

Phillips translates verse 21, "and you yourselves, who were strangers to God, and, in fact, through the evil things you had done, his spiritual enemies. . . ." We are not to glory in our past sins, but we must not forget them. If we are Christian, and if we are growing as Christians, we must never assume that we have always been what we are. And we are what we are as Christians by the grace of God.

Martin Luther insisted that persons must confront their own sinfulness in all its ravaging depths before they can enjoy the comforts of salvation. There is truth in this. Though we need not be astringently sin-conscious, we must always remember who we are: forgiven sinners.

The seventies in America was a decade of "personal growth." "Fulfillment," "potential," "self-actualization," "self-expression" were key words in the vocabulary of the movement. I profited from the emphasis and thus do not scorn it; however, I am certain that "sin," "repentance," "confession," "estrangement," "fractured" are necessary words and concepts to fully describe human reality. A modern Roman Catholic who is appreciative of the renewal and reformation of his church flowing from Vatican II, made a telling confession.

> Like most Catholics, I go to confession less often than I used to, although I am not sure why. The idea of it still appeals to me. Probably the greatest problem with it, so far as I am concerned, is the discrepancy between what it promises to be and what it is, subjectively speaking— so often it turns out purely routine and perfunctory. Still, the forgiveness is pronounced and the grace imparted. At the least it is a reminder that we are constantly under God's judgment. A seminarian once said to me, "I'm a Christian to help prevent me from being myself," and that seems to me exactly right. Nothing in the "new church" seems to me more ill-conceived

than the apparent general optimism about human nature which is now so pervasive. My vision of evil is of pure and unbridled egotism, and we live in an age which appears systematically to encourage this[2]

To be preoccupied with sin is unhealthy spiritually and otherwise. Yet, to forget who we are and who we have been is the doorway to spiritual pride and, to change the metaphor, the roadblock to spiritual growth. It may be self-dramatizing and to some degree untrue to say that we must sense in ourselves the capacity for every kind of sin, yet some approximation of this reality is necessary for spiritual development. Remember who you are.

Remember Who Christ Is

Paul has soared to the heights in his effort to describe the person and work of Christ. He is *the image of the invisible God:* He reveals to us something that has never been seen before. *In Him all the fullness of God was pleased to dwell:* God has written Himself into history, has put something in the flow of time that can never be taken out. Christ is *the firstborn of all creation:* He is prior in importance, superior to everything else; He has primacy of all things. *All things were created by Him and for Him:* He is the heartbeat of the created order; creation has meaning only through Him; He is the clue to the answers for all the big questions.

We are almost breathless as we read this hymn-passage on the preeminence of Christ, exalted above all "thrones, dominions, princedoms, virtues, powers." We are more breathless yet when we realize that the preeminent, cosmic Christ is *personal.* In Him *the divine Fullness willed to settle without limit,* but He came to Colossae, said Paul. In His resurrected power, through the preaching of Epaphras, He came to *you who were once alienated.* Remember who Christ is. He is *"the One in Whom we have redemption"* (v. 14). That brings us to the theme of this section.

Reconciliation

P. T. Forsyth described the cause for the deadness and impotence of the modern church with devastating simplicity: "We have churches of the nicest, kindest people who have nothing apostolic or missionary, who never knew the soul's despair or its breathless gratitude." We do not remember who we are or who Christ is. Paul had an apostolic passion because he knew the soul's despair—"O wretched man that I am"—and was driven by a breathless gratitude. He reminded the Colossians that their case was the same: they had been enemies of God, estranged from Him and without hope, but now they *"were reconciled in the body of [Christ's] flesh through death"* (v. 22).

The word "reconcile" is pivotal for Paul. It is the key to his thought about what Christ has done for us. He uses a group of words, all having basically the same meaning, to express the central experience of the Christian faith. William Barclay, perhaps the most popular New Testament commentator of the twentieth century, has reminded us that all these words are compound forms made from the simple verb *allassein* which means "to change."

In the New Testament, with two exceptions (1 Cor. 7:11 and Acts 7:26), the word *katallassein* (from *allassein)* and its related forms are always used to designate *the restoration of the relationship between persons and God.* In 2 Corinthians 5:18–20, there is a series of uses of this word: "God has *reconciled* us to Himself by Jesus"; "God was in Christ *reconciling* the world to Himself"; *"we* pray you to be *reconciled* to God." In Romans 5:11, he uses a noun form, speaking of Christ: "through whom we have now received our reconciliation *(katallagē)."* Some translate that *"atonement,"* which in English has the deep meaning of being brought together, at-one-ment. In Romans 5:10, Paul uses the same image he uses in the Colossian passages: "while we were enemies we were reconciled to God by the death of His Son."

The meaning should be clear. Through what Christ did, the lost relationship between persons and God is restored.

Let it be emphatically noted that Paul does not speak of God being reconciled to persons, but always of persons being reconciled to God. The pivotal reconciliation passage (2 Cor. 5:18–20) to which we referred above speaks three times of God reconciling persons to Himself. God's passionate yearning for His children's return home is never abated; the fire of love burning in His heart is unquenchable, constant, and continuous. Nothing lessens that love or turns it into hate. God is that "hound of heaven" who pursues us down the nights and days, who "moves my soul to seek Him seeking me," who loves us to the Cross. I am the one to be reconciled. I am the one to be moved to penitence and surrender.

It is not likely that I will be thus moved, nor is it likely that I will continue vibrantly alive in my reconciliation unless I have a quickened sense of sin and separation. We need to break through the contemporary disguises of sin. The subtlety of sin is that it always travels incognito. Though clearly identified and labeled in the fourth century as the seven deadly sins—pride, envy, anger, sloth, avarice, gluttony, and lust—these now parade in modern garb and are often given status by being cast in psychological company: self-expression, self-fulfillment, assertiveness, identity, taking care of my own being, the right of my own space, therapeutic enhancement. All these terms express deep emotional, psychological, even spiritual needs, but unfortunately they also become the easy snare of sin's entrapment. With what ease we justify adultery and other non-Christian uses of sex by talking about self-expression and personal freedom. Without any sense of responsibility we become *unavailable* to others because we must seek our own space. We callously trample on the being and feelings of others because we want *to assert who we are . . .* and on it goes. Sex is reduced to lust; we become gluttonous as we move from one effort at satisfaction to another; our neurotic need to belong makes us envy, and our accomplishments fill us with pride.

We are our own center of reference, thus we are estranged. The emptiness we know, the feeling that we are driven, our lack of confidence, our fear of relationships and our terror of the future, our hoarding of ourselves and our talents, and our profane extravagance and waste of material resources—all these witness to the fact of sin and its tenacious pull upon our lives. Even when the strangle-hold of sin is broken, we do well to remember: *"And you, who once were alienated and enemies in your mind by wicked works, yet now He has reconciled"* (v. 21).

I am sure that is the reason Paul put a kind of proviso in verse 23: *"if indeed you continue in the faith grounded and steadfast, and are not moved away from the hope of the gospel . . ."* This is the theme of the balance of Paul's letter—living a life *in Christ*.

NOTES

1. Leander E. Keck, *Paul and His Letters*, Proclamation Commentaries (Philadelphia: Fortress Press, 1979), p. 43.

2. James Hitchcock, "Ever Ancient, Ever New," in *On the Run*, ed. Michael McCauley (Chicago: Thomas More, 1974), pp. 34–35.

CHAPTER THREE—THE SECRET: CHRIST IN YOU

COLOSSIANS 1:24—2:19

Scripture Outline

    Christ in You (1:24–29)

    A Person, Not a Philosophy (2:1–10)

    The Cross: God's Answer to Our Deepest Needs (2:11–19)

Someone said, and I agree, that the idea of redemption in a world of sin and tragedy constitutes the noblest concept ever to enter the mind of God or the awareness of a human being. Paul would also agree. The theme of redemption is woven into the fabric of everything he wrote. He repeats that theme over and over in *Colossians,* affirming that God's implementation of His idea of redemption is the love-gift of His Son Jesus Christ on the Cross. We cannot get away from this central theme.

There is a nuance to the theme that is picked up in Colossians 1:27: *"Christ in you, the hope of glory,"* and is elaborated in the balance of the letter. We are inspired to recall his word to the Romans: "For if while we were enemies we were reconciled to God by the death of His Son, much more, now that we are reconciled, shall we be saved by His life" (5:10, RSV). Our reconciliation is by the death of Jesus Christ, but our complete redemption, our salvation, our being presented *"perfect in Christ Jesus"* (1:28) is by the life of Christ—the risen Christ living in power within us.

Paul says this is the secret, the answer to the mystery which God has now made known to us.

CHRIST IN YOU

²⁴ I now rejoice in my sufferings for you, and fill up in my flesh what is lacking in the afflictions of Christ, for the sake of His body, which is the church, ²⁵ of which I became a minister according to the stewardship from God which was given to me for you, to fulfill the word of God, ²⁶ the mystery which has been hidden from ages and from generations, but now has been revealed to His saints. ²⁷ To them God willed to make known what are the riches of the glory of this mystery among the Gentiles: which is Christ in you, the hope of glory. ²⁸ Him we preach, warning every man and teaching every man in all wisdom, that we may present every man perfect in Christ Jesus. ²⁹ To this end I also labor, striving according to His working which works in me mightily.

—Colossians 1:24–29

The Revelation of Mystery

The hinge verse in this section is verse 27. Paul says the revelation of *"the mystery which has been hidden from ages and from generations"* (v. 26) has now been revealed. The mystery? *"Christ in you, the hope of glory"* (v. 27).

Paul's great definition of a Christian was "a person *in* Christ." He used that picture over and over again. The phrase "in Christ" or its equivalent is used at least 172 times in Paul's epistles. His most vivid description of his own life in Christ was written to the Galatians: "1 have been crucified with Christ; it is no longer I who live; but Christ who lives in me; and the life I now live in the flesh I live by faith in the Son of God, who loved me and gave himself for me" (2:20, RSV). In one of the boldest prayers ever prayed, Paul interceded "that through faith Christ may dwell in your hearts in love . . . so may you attain to fullness of being, the fullness of God Himself (Eph. 3:17, 19, NEB).

What a revelation: Christ in you, the hope of glory!

Paul believed that in all His dealings with humanity God had been working on a deep plan, with a secret purpose that can only be discovered by the illumination of the Spirit. Throughout his epistles he lays emphasis on the deeper element of the gospel. The circumstances which elicited this letter and the setting must also be kept in mind. In the Gnostic systems the terms "ages" and "generations" were applied to the heavenly hierarchies. Ages is literally *aeons*, and this was a term chosen by the Valentinians for those emanations from the Divine which in their system consisted of a hierarchy of angelic powers mediating between God and the material world. Assuming that this Gnostic term was in use in Colossae, the RSV in a marginal note translates "ages" and "generations" as "angels and men." In 1 Corinthians 2:6–8, Paul speaks a similar word. God's plan was concealed from "the rulers of this world," the spiritual powers which conspired to crucify Christ.

The distilled meaning of these references is that God's mysterious secret which has been hidden *"even from the angels,"* which men have sought to probe and decipher, has now been revealed. That mystery is Christ, but more, it is *"Christ in you, the hope of glory."*

Here then is the secret, the revelation of the mystery that has been hidden for ages and generations, but is now revealed to God's saints: *the indwelling Christ.*

Our Share in the Mystery

1. *We are the recipients—Christ dwells in us.* The clue to the whole Christian experience, the core of the gospel, is that Christ, by whom and through whom all things were created, who is before all things and in all things, in whom God was pleased for all His fullness to dwell, the firstborn over all creation, the image of the invisible God; this Christ who has primacy over all things, in whom all things hold together, who is the head of the church— this Christ, who will stand at the end of time and be the final judge and triumphal Lord, *lives in us by the Holy Spirit.*

This is not a sideline thought of Paul, not a peripheral detour of truth. This is the heart of it: Christ the Lord of Creation may live in us. *His dwelling in us is the hope of glory.*

We talk about becoming Christian in ways like this: accepting Christ, inviting Christ into our lives, receiving Christ, surrendering our lives to Christ, giving our lives in faith to Christ, being born again by allowing Christ to be born in us, receiving Christ as Savior. Whatever the language, the faith and experience is that as we confess and repent of our sins, we are forgiven; we are accepted by God and enter into a new relationship with Him. We are saved, reconciled, forgiven by His grace. He then lives in us through the power of His Spirit as the indwelling Christ.

I remember well when the first glow of this glory began to dawn in my soul. I was a pastor in one of the fastest-growing congregations in Mississippi. I was a "success" in every way ecclesiastical success is measured. I had just graduated from seminary and this was my first full-time appointment. It was the Cinderella church of the conference. I was the organizing pastor of the congregation, and to see a congregation develop "from scratch" is a unique joy. The membership expanded rapidly; we built beautiful buildings, raised lots of money, and did many exciting things. I was the "envy" of my colleagues, but in my heart of hearts I grew weary. There was an inexplainable emptiness. Lives were not being vividly transformed. There was a fellowship in the church—but it was not too distinct from the country club. We were highly programmed and the organization hummed efficiently.

Then the racial crisis in Mississippi in the early 1960s shattered our surface fellowship and set friend against friend. I was in the throes of despair, completely exhausted, bereft of power other than my own driving commitment for social justice, which power was also activated by my desire for "professional success." At that point I received an invitation to which I responded, and which changed my life. A dear friend, Tom Carruth, invited me to a Christian Ashram led by E. Stanley Jones. In my desperate search for deeper meaning in my ministry, for energy to struggle through the racial upheaval with integrity of preaching and action, for something more vital than my own lagging, almost non-existent spiritual life, I had gathered a few people into a prayer-study group, and a member of that group introduced us to Stanley Jones's then-new book, *In Christ*.

We were just getting into the book when the invitation came to attend the Ashram. The word itself sounded strange and unattractive, but I had read enough of Jones to know he had something I desperately needed. I went to the Ashram and that was the beginning of *new life* for me, a life consciously *in Christ*. It was not that I was not Christian. I had been following Christ to the best of my ability. By faith I had received the gift of Jesus' death and Resurrection *for me*. I knew myself forgiven and accepted by God. But here was something I had missed—myself the dwelling place of Christ, the Spirit-stream of the living Lord flowing in me.

I remember vividly the experience at an altar at the close of that Ashram. Brother Stanley asked probingly as Jesus had asked two thousand years before, "Do you want to be whole?" The only possibility for wholeness, he affirmed, was the indwelling Christ. I responded longingly and with certainty, *yes—yes!* I yielded myself more cornpletely than ever before to Christ, inviting Him

356

to live His life in me; and I made a new commitment to ministry—a ministry in which I would allow Christ to minister through me.

I have not always lived up to that commitment, but it has been the shaping power of my life. I have discovered that praying is not what it once was—going to Him and struggling to discover His guidance. Rather, prayer is recognizing and cultivating an awareness of His indwelling Presence, and seeking to give expression to His Presence in my life and work. This does not mean I have not struggled or that spiritual formation and growth have been consistent and smooth. It does not mean that there has not been suffering, doubt-wrestling, dark nights of the soul, failure in relationship and ministry. All of these, to excruciating depths and degrees, have been my lot. But I can trace a pattern. When I have been intentional in cultivating the awareness of the indwelling Christ, yielded and responsive to that Presence, I have known wholeness of life, a vibrancy of spirit and joy, and my ministry has been marked by an obvious spiritual quality that genuinely blessed others. When I have been slack in that intentional effort at staying alive to His aliveness in me, then my joy diminishes, my confidence deteriorates, what accomplishments I experience seem ponderous and hard-gained, and I discover that no matter how noble my purposes, I am often without power or my power has soon departed.

This is our glory. Can we grasp it?—that at our invitation, responding to our response of faith, Christ enters our lives, becomes a part of our beings, indwells us. What this means will be probed more in the next chapter as we look at the concept of dying and rising with Christ, living a *new life* in Him.

2. Not only are we the recipients, *we are the communicators* of the mystery. *"Him we preach, warning every man and teaching every man in all wisdom, that we may present every man perfect in Christ Jesus"* (v. 28).

A friend told me recently of a woman in Africa who had discovered the secret, and was the recipient of the mystery. Overwhelmed with gratitude, she wanted to do something for Jesus and the kingdom. But she was blind and seventy years of age; therefore her contributions did not seem to be very significant. She was uneducated, but she came to the missionary with her French Bible and said, "Would you mind underlining John 3:16 in my Bible in red?" The missionary was very intrigued to see what she was going to do. The woman took her Bible and sat in front of a boys' school in the afternoon. When school was dismissed, she would call to a boy or two and say to them, "Boys, come here please. Do you know

French?" Very proudly, they said that they did. Then she would ask, "Please read to me this passage underscored in red in my Bible." They did. Then she would ask, "Do you know what it means?" They would say, "No, we don't know." And she would tell them the story of Jesus. Twenty-four young men became pastors due to the work of this blind woman, touched by the contagion of the light in her which Christ brings.

What does that say about our passion to communicate the mystery, to share the secret which Christ wants to be an open secret?

3. *We suffer that the secret may be fully known.* There is something special to note about our being communicators of the mystery. Paul makes two very shocking statements in verse 24: *"I now rejoice in my sufferings for you, and fill up in my flesh what is lacking in the afflictions of Christ."* The words leap boldly from the page.

If *"I rejoice* in my sufferings" sounds lacking in reason, then "I make up for *what is lacking in the afflictions of Christ"* is wildly foolish, even mad.

The theme of joy in the face of suffering is present throughout the New Testament (e.g., Matt. 5:12; Acts 5:14; Heb. 10:34). Remember too, Paul is in prison. Momentarily, in verse 23, he remembers his call to the ministry, then comes back in mind to his present imprisonment. It takes no philosophical straining on his part to put his being in prison in perspective. He is there as a natural expression or corollary to his apostolic mission. He stated that explicitly in Philippians: "my imprisonment is for Christ" (1:13). To know joy in our suffering is not a trick of the mind. Christians are not stoics or baptized masochists who are able to laugh in the face of pain. Rejoicing in pain has nothing to do with "stiff upper lips" or deriving pleasure from being mistreated in some way. *Suffering has meaning if and as it puts us in deep fellowship with Christ.*

Christ lives in the church, in the fellowship of His followers—His body. He makes our sufferings His own; and as we suffer for the gospel we make His sufferings our own.

What is lacking in Christ's affliction has nothing to do with the limitation of the Cross. He never uses the word "affliction" *(thlipsis)* to designate the Crucifixion. The death of Christ for our redemption was complete, a once-and-for-all, never-to-be-repeated atoning work.

We do not suffer as a repetition of Calvary but as an extension of it—as an expression of Christ-life which, like our Master, is a cross-life. (See commentary on Phil. 1:19, in this volume.)

4. *His power works in and through us.* A part of the secret, our share in the mystery, is that the power of Christ works in and through us: *"To this end I also labor, striving according to His working which works in me mightily"* (v. 29). The NEB gives more clarity: "To this end I am toiling strenuously with all the energy and power of Christ at work in me."

Paul is his own best witness of the secret of the indwelling Christ. He toils strenuously in his apostolic labor; it is his toil, but the *energy* is Christ's. Paul was most himself when he was least dependent on his own resources. So it is for all persons *in Christ.* We are not reliant on our own energy, but that of Christ whose Presence works mightily within us.

A PERSON, NOT A PHILOSOPHY

2:1 For I want you to know what a great conflict I have for you and those in Laodicea, and for as many as have not seen my face in the flesh, ² that their hearts may be encouraged, being knit together in love, and attaining to all riches of the full assurance of understanding, to the knowledge of the mystery of God, both of the Father and of Christ, ³ in whom are hidden all the treasures of wisdom and knowledge.

⁴ Now this I say lest anyone should deceive you with persuasive words. ⁵ For though I am absent in the flesh, yet I am with you in spirit, rejoicing to see your good order and the steadfastness of your faith in Christ.

⁶ As you therefore have received Christ Jesus the Lord, so walk in Him, ⁷ rooted and built up in Him and established in the faith, as you have been taught, abounding in it with thanksgiving.

⁸ Beware lest anyone cheat you through philosophy and empty deceit, according to the tradition of men, according to the basic principles of the world, and not according to Christ. ⁹ For in Him dwells all the fullness of the Godhead bodily; ¹⁰ and you are complete in Him, who is the head of all principality and power.

—Colossians 2:1–10

Karl Valletin of Munich, Germany, was a master among that rare group of performing artists we call clowns. The scene for which he is best remembered took place on a darkened stage illumined only by a solitary circle of light thrown by a street lamp. Valletin, with long-drawn face and deeply worried expression,

359

walks around and around this circle of light, desperately looking for something. A policeman enters the scene and asks, "What have you lost?" "The key to my house," replies the clown. The policeman then joins the search, but they find nothing. After a while the policeman inquires, "Are you sure that you lost it here?" "No," says the clown, pointing to a dark corner of the stage, "over there." "Then why on earth are you looking for it here?" asks the policeman. The reply, *"There is no light over there."*

Clowns are not only performers, they are pedagogues, teaching us by their ridiculous parables, and by becoming themselves absurd expressions of our common frailty. Valletin's parable is a picture of the snare in which we become entangled. We go to whatever promise of light is available. Not unlike the Colossians, we respond to explanations that appeal to rational thought, to offers of salvation that put us and our efforts in the center, to any philosophy that defines clearly and closes all the gaps of mystery. So Paul warned: *"Beware lest anyone cheat you through philosophy and empty deceit, according to the tradition of men, according to the basic principles of the world, and not according to Christ"* (v. 8).

In this section Paul is contending that the secret is in a person, not in philosophy. His argument is against all those who would *"deceive you with persuasive words"* (v. 4). The *secret* is in the person of Jesus Christ.

Christ Is the Fullness to Fill Our Emptiness

Paul is not anti-intellectual, nor down on philosophy. He is one of the great minds of the ages. He simply knew that as important as it is, knowledge is not the answer to meaning in life. We do not think our way through to reality.

An experiential relationship with Jesus Christ, not assent to dogma or doctrinal propositions, is the foundation for the Christian life. This does not mean we can be sloppy in our thinking; the world demands and deserves the best thinking of which we are capable. Right thinking does not make us righteous, only the Cross can do that; but right thinking—right in the sense of being hard, honest, clear, disciplined—is essential if we are going to communicate the gospel effectively to a huge segment of the world. Though we Methodists rightfully make much of our emphasis upon Christian experience, we talk about the "Wesley quadrilateral," which joins *scripture, tradition,* and *reason* to *experience* as our approach to theology. Paul is not demeaning philosophy, great learning or intellectual growth; he was warning against the subtle mixing of Christian thought with false philosophy, and the effort to syncretize the Christian message with the vogue philosophy of the day. He was also warning the Colossians against subjecting themselves to the regulations and practices of religion, falsely thinking this might provide meaning (see vv. 21–22).

No generation escapes being confronted with this temptation. Our present generation is inundated, especially through the persuasive medium of television, with offers to fill our emptiness—from toothpaste and deodorants to where we live and the cars we drive. All of this media manipulation is an expression of overarching philosophies offered as the key to meaning: the "playboy" philosophy which glamorizes indulgent hedonism—anything that feels good must be good, so "if it feels good do it"; the self-realization philosophy which says that self-expression is the only way to fulfillment and meaning, so remember "I am number one"; the materialist philosophy that reduces us to consumers and producers—what we are is what we acquire, our worth is in our productivity. And on it goes: astrology, scientism, scientific determinism, *ad infinitum* and often *ad nauseam*.

You are complete in Christ, Paul says. Possessing Him, or being possessed by Him, you are fulfilled. Having Him you have all you need. This is the supreme reality: the complete being of God is revealed in Jesus Christ; in Him the completeness to which we are called is an accomplished fact; we appropriate that fullness for ourselves by yielding ourselves to the indwelling Christ.

The Secret That Is in the Person of Jesus Christ Is Communicated through Our Person

There is another great truth in this section: we Christians are the channel through which the reality—the presence and power of the indwelling Christ—flows to the life of others and to the world. This happens in two ways.

1. *Our prayer.* Imagine what the Colossians must have felt when they received this letter. Their hearts beat faster within them, a new surge of power flooded their lives, light began to illumine their minds that had been darkened by the confusion of conflicting teaching and deceitful words. The quality of Paul's concern and prayers became a channel of grace.

Get the picture. Paul was in prison far away in Rome. Epaphras had gotten word to him about the crisis of faith and practice with which the Colossians were wrestling. This quickened Paul's mind and his heart ached for them, most of whom he had never seen. Different translations capture the degree of his concern. "For I want you to know how greatly I strive for you" (RSV); "how deep is my anxiety" (Phillips); "how strenuous are my exertions" (NEB). The Greek word used is *agōn,* meaning to have a struggle, and from it we derive our word "agony." Paul agonized in prayer. It is the image of 1:29, *striving according to His working (agōnizomai),* which means to "contend" or "fight." This is no making of conversation, no shallow, "I'm thinking about you," which is as deep as many of us are willing to go in our concern even for family and close friends in need. This is deep intercession, prolonged, penetrating, time and energy-consuming, emotion-draining—the kind of praying that is a channel for the mystery of the fullness of God in Christ to fill the needs of others.

Prayer is the vital vocation of Christians. God has given us the privilege of sharing in His work in the world. Scripture testifies and history confirms that the Lord has ordered His kingdom so that blessings and power for us are to a marked degree dependent upon the prayers of others. What does that say about *our* praying? If the blessings and power of God for others are dependent upon us, who is being cheated?

Paul prays that the Colossians will be *"encouraged,"* that they will be *"knit together in love,"* that they will experience the *"assurance of understanding."* Who needs our intercession to these ends?

There is an awesome challenge in the fact that Paul agonized in prayer "for as many as have not seen my face in the flesh" (2:1). To pray for our loved ones and friends is one thing—and they are in desperate need of our prayers; but to pray for those we do not know—that is something else requiring deeper commitment than most of us have mustered.

But what a residual source of power—people and churches around the world praying for each other, agonizing for the cause of Christ as Paul was *contending* for the Galatians.

2. *Our presence.* Not only are our prayers the channel through which the presence and power flows into the life of others and the world, our personal *presence* is likewise a channel. Because this is so Paul urges the Colossians, *"As you therefore have received Christ Jesus the Lord, so walk in Him"* (v. 6). (See p. 74–75 for a superb example of the presence of the mystery of the indwelling Christ, transparent in a person.)

Through our prayers and in our presence the mystery of the indwelling Christ is communicated.

THE CROSS: GOD'S ANSWER TO OUR DEEPEST NEEDS

[11] In Him you were also circumcised with the circumcision made without hands, by putting off the body of the sins of the flesh, by the circumcision of Christ, [12] buried with Him in baptism, in which you also were raised with Him through faith in the working of God, who raised Him from the dead. [13] And you, being dead in your trespasses and the uncircumcision of your flesh, He has made alive together with Him, having forgiven you all trespasses, [14] having wiped out the handwriting of requirements that was against us, which was contrary to us. And He has taken it out of the way, having nailed it to the Cross. [15] Having disarmed principalities and powers, He made a public spectacle of them, triumphing over them in it.

[16] So let no one judge you in food or in drink, or regarding a festival or a new moon or sabbaths, [17] which are a shadow of things to come, but the substance is of Christ. [18] Let no one cheat you of your reward, taking delight in false humility and worship of angels, intruding into those things which he has not seen, vainly puffed up by his fleshly mind, [19] and not holding fast to the Head, from whom all the body, nourished and knit together by joints and ligaments, grows with the increase that is from God.

—Colossians 2:11–19

A popular monk in the Middle Ages announced that in the cathedral that evening he would preach a sermon on the love of God. The people gathered and stood in silence waiting for the service while the sunlight streamed through the beautiful windows. When the last glint of color had faded from the windows, the old monk took a candle from the altar. Walking to the lifesize figure of Christ on the Cross, he held the light beneath the wounds of the feet, then His hands, then His side. Still without a word, he let the light shine on the thorn-crowned brow.

That was his sermon. The people stood in silence and wept. They knew they were at the center of mystery beyond their knowing, that they were looking at the love of God, the image of the invisible God, giving Himself for us—a love so deep, so inclusive, so expansive, so powerful, so complete that thought of the mind could not comprehend nor measure it, or words express it.

Paul knew that too. He comes back to it again and again: the purpose and power of the Cross. It took the sacrificial love of Jesus, fully expressed on the Cross, to bring the change necessary for persons to "come back" to God. So for Paul, the love of Christ on the Cross had the power to turn man's sin to penitence, rebellion to surrender, enmity against God into love. The very essence of Christianity is the restoration of persons' lost relationship with God. The purpose and power of the Cross was for that restoration.

The Cross as Sacrifice

Three times in the Colossian letter, Paul has spoken of the Cross as the means of redemption. Twice "the blood" of Christ is the image (1:14, 20); the third time he presents the same idea through a different word: *"in the body of His flesh through death"* (1:22). There are other similar passages connecting Christ's work of salvation with sacrifice (cf. Eph. 1:7, 2:15; Rom. 5:9, 10).

Because of the language of such significant passages, it is obvious that Paul looked upon the death of Christ as a sacrifice. We must not allow this, as many have sought to do, to be really cast in the "sacrificial" priestly system of the Old Testament. We must not be driven to work out a "theory" of atonement that is *rational,* and in our efforts to be rational, accredit to God attributes which are clearly inconsistent with the revelation we have in Jesus Christ.

To be sure, the idea of "blood" was a powerful one to the Hebrew; it represented life. Also, the sacrificing of a lamb on the Day of Atonement was a vivid part of the corporate consciousness of Israel, suggesting that shedding of blood was necessary for atonement. No wonder Paul would use that image explicitly in Romans 3:24–25: "they are justified by His grace as a gift, through the redemption which is in Christ Jesus, whom God put forward as an expiation by His blood, to be received by faith" (RSV). The image of Christ as the "Lamb of God who takes away the sins of the world" is more than a powerful symbol; it is a reality. And the connection between the Christian celebration of the Last Supper and the Jewish celebration of the Passover is real and intimate, with the blood of the Passover lamb and the blood of "the Lamb slain from the foundation of the world" poignantly present.

What we must not do, though, is to devise a rational theory that turns God into an angry judge who is appeased only by sacrifice. Nor can we reduce the Cross to a blood covering for sin after the Leviticus pattern (Lev. 27:11), when that pattern found little or no recognition and certainly no support in the prophets. In fact, the prophets critically scorned sacrifices, addressing some of their harshest words to these practices. What is seldom recognized by those who perceive the Cross primarily as a sacrifice in the priest-pattern of the Old Testament—a "blood covering" for sin—is that the sins that were *covered* by the blood sacrifice in Leviticus were sins of ignorance and error. Sins forbidden by the moral law were not "covered" by sacrifices. What was "covered" by sacrifice were the so-called sins of inadvertence.

The scope of the Cross was infinitely greater than the sacrificial system of the Old Testament. So, while we may see in the Cross an extended application of the principle underlying the Levitical sacrifices, it was far more expansive.

What, then, did Paul have in mind when he spoke with such arresting and assured conviction about "the blood of Christ"? Though now we see "through a glass dimly" and "know only in part," it is certain that Paul was speaking of *the outpoured life of Christ on the Cross.* He used the phrase as a distilled expression of all that was involved and demonstrated in the sacrificial death of Christ, in which death, redemption, justification, reconciliation, and new birth were won for all humankind.

The Power and Purpose of the Cross

When we probe to the core depths of our being, when we get down to the base level of our identity, we discover four absolute needs, apart from physical survival needs. There are burning emotional/spiritual/relational needs which, when unmet, leave us less than whole, often crippled, sometimes sick to the point of being cut off from reality. The needs are common to all persons. Even though we may not use the same words to label them, the reality is the same. The needs are *to love and be loved, to receive forgiveness, to experience community,* and *to have a cause for which to live and die.* Other descriptions of our needs—acceptance, affirmation, security, freedom, purposefulness, self-esteem—are rooted in these four.

The Cross meets us at the point of these deepest needs.

1. *Love.* More than anything else, the Cross is love at its deepest and purest. While in the Cross God "pronounced the doom of sin," more startling yet, He revealed in the most persuasive way possible His love, the love of a Holy God for sinful persons.

Charles Denney cast this undeserved, unlimited love of God in the context of its work of reconciliation.

> In the last resort, nothing reconciles but love, and what the soul needs, which has been alienated from God by sin and is suffering under the divine reaction against it, is the manifestation of a love which can assure it that neither the sin itself nor the soul's condemnation of it, nor even the divine reaction against it culminating in death is the last reality in the universe. The last reality is rather love itself, making our sin its own in all its reality, submitting as one with us to all the divine reactions against it, and loving us to the end through it, and in spite of it. Reconciliation is achieved when such a love is manifested, and when, in spite of guilt, distrust and fear, it wins the confidence of the sinful.[1]

Such a love as that demands and awakens an answering love. By the love of God freely poured out on the Cross and received by faith, we are empowered to love others and to receive the love of others.

2. *Forgiveness.* "Pish! He's a good fellow, and 'twill all be well.'" Deep down we know that this idea of Omar Khayyam is far from the reality of the human situation. We are sinners. We may not mean to be, but we are. There is within us the same warring that terrorized Paul—the battle between the "good that I would, and the evil that I would not." In our times of introspection and self-examination, we are often driven to cry with him, "O wretched man that I am!"

Paul's answer to his own cry was an affirmation of confidence in the forgiveness of God through Christ on the Cross. "Christ Jesus set me free from the law of sin and death" (Rom. 8:2). "He who did not spare his own Son but gave him up for us all" (Rom. 8:32, RSV) forgives us, justifies us, makes us as though we were without sin. In this Colossian passage, Paul paints a graphic picture of Christ's work of forgiveness.

He nailed our past sins on the Cross. But not only this: He *"disarmed principalities and powers"* (v. 15), triumphing over them. We do not have to be the puppets or the victims of Satan or any evil spirits working within us or in the world. Nor do we have to achieve our own salvation, or be intimidated by those who seek to impose religious or other rules and regulations. *"Let no one judge you in food or in drink, or regarding a festival or a new moon or sabbaths, which are a shadow of things to come, but the substance is of Christ"* (vv. 16–17). Christ forgives!

3. *Community.* We need to belong. This may be our most desperate need in this twenty-first century. All sorts of forces have combined to destroy family identity and unity. Where in the current American scene is the "local neighborhood"? All the advanced technology that we celebrated as the way to bring us together has driven us apart. We are isolated in our mad thirst for wealth, security, pleasure, success, identity. We need community.

The ground around the Cross is level. We all stand there stripped of pride, knowing that we are impotent to save ourselves, and we are drawn into an experience of love which is the dynamic for community. When we experience belonging to Christ, when lifted up from the earth on the Cross He draws us to Himself, we discover that we belong also to each other.

Paul talked about our mutual identity, our community of belonging, with the image of circumcision (v. 11). The sign of belonging for the Jews was circumcision. This was their badge of identity, the ensign of "sons of Abraham." Paul gave that image a spiritual meaning which forges an unbreakable bond of community:

"In Him you were also circumcised with the circumcision made without hands, by putting off the body of the sins of the flesh, by the circumcision of Christ" (Col. 2:11–12).

Our community is an in-Christ community into which we are initiated by baptism, a death-and-Resurrection community empowered and bound together by Christ (v. 12). That community is the church, though we must never restrict it to the church we know on the corner of Main and Fourth. It is that fellowship, local and visible, but also universal and invisible of which Christ is the Head. He nourishes the community and knits every segment of it together (v. 19).

All our needs to belong are met in Him and the fellowship of His people.

4. *A cause for which to live and die.* Our need for love, for forgiveness and for community are met in the Cross. All these needs focus on ourselves, our identity and enhancement as individual persons. We are so created, however, that we must move out of ourselves to find meaning in a cause—a purpose beyond ourselves for which to live and die. The Cross meets us at the point of this deep need.

Paul's confession of it came earlier in Colossians 1:24: *"I now rejoice in my sufferings for you, and fill up in my flesh what is lacking in the afflictions of Christ, for the sake of His body, which is the church."*

In Philippians Paul stated his purpose, the cause for which he lived and died, even more completely: "that I may know him and the power of his resurrection, and may share his sufferings, becoming like him in his death, that if possible I may attain the resurrection from the dead" (Phil. 3:10, RSV). The more he knew Christ, the more he realized his true self and the more he experienced fulfillment. The more he knew Christ, the more he realized his needs and limitations and the more he had to *press on to the high calling in Christ Jesus.* The more he centered himself in Christ and pursued this high calling, the more he became sensitive to the needs of people around him and the more he realized that Calvary-motivated love had to be the motive dynamic of his life.

So it is with us: cross-centered purpose gives us meaning. Viktor Frankl was a psychiatrist who spent two years in a Nazi concentration camp. Out of that experience he discovered and developed *logotherapy,* a therapeutic approach to healing and health, by discovering *meaning.* Meaning, he says, comes from three sources: love, suffering, and doing a deed. All of these are gathered up in the Cross and in the cross-life to which we are called.

No wonder Paul could sing, *"I rejoice in my sufferings"* (v. 24). Because of the love he had received from the Cross, his purpose was to love, even if that called for suffering. the Cross was the driving force of his life. His burning desire was for all persons to experience the love of Jesus Christ which he had experienced. the Cross gave him meaning for it gave him the cause for which to live and die.

Review now: Christ in you is the secret, the hope of glory. We are the recipients and the communicators of the mystery. Our lives are to be an extension of Calvary, an expression of Christ-life which is a cross-life. A part of the mystery is that the power of Christ works in us and through us. So, the answer is in a person not a philosophy. Christ is the fullness to fill our emptiness. The person of Christ is communicated through our persons, our prayers, and our presence. At the center of it all is the Cross, God's answer to our deepest needs. This is the goal: *"that we may present every man perfect in Christ Jesus"* (1:28).

NOTE

1. Charles Denney, *The Christian Doctrine of Reconciliation,* p. 218.

Chapter Four—The New Life in Christ
Colossians 2:20—3:17

Scripture Outline

Life Hidden with Christ (2:20—3:4)

Put to Death the Old (3:5–11)

Put On the New (3:12–14)

The Fellowship of New Persons in Christ (3:15–17)

To be a Christian is to change, to become new. It is not simply a matter of choosing a new life style, though there is a new style, as we will see in the next chapter; it has to do with being a new person. The new person does not emerge full-blown. Conversion, passing from life to death, may be the miracle of a moment, but the making of a saint—presenting oneself perfect *in Christ*—is the task of a lifetime. The dynamic process of saint-making is to work out in *fact* what is already true in *principle*. In *position*, in our relation to God in Jesus Christ, we are new persons. Now our *condition*, the actual life that we live, must be brought into harmony with our new position.

A man once said to Dwight L. Moody, "Sir, I am a self-made man." Moody replied, "You have saved the Lord from a very great responsibility." It is the Lord who made us and who remakes us. Two things happened in *the fall*, and in our own fall: (1) we became *estranged* from God; (2) His image within us was broken, distorted, defaced. Two things happen in salvation: (1) we are reconciled to God; our estrangement is dissolved by the justifying grace of God in the Cross of Jesus. Our status is changed; we become *friends* of God, accepted by Him as though we were without sin. (2) There is the re-creation of the image of God in the life of the believer. This is the reason John Wesley talked about grace impinging upon us and working in three specific ways: *prevenient* grace, *justifying* grace, *sanctifying* grace. Prevenient grace is the grace of God going before us, pulling us, wooing us, tenderizing our hearts, seeking to open our minds and hearts, and eventually even giving us faith. Even the faith we exercise for our justification is the result of His grace. Justifying faith is our trustful-obedient response to Christ—His life, death, and Resurrection—as our only means of salvation. Sanctifying grace is the work of Christ within us, His Spirit restoring the broken image, completing what has begun in justification.

Nothing less than a new creature *"perfect in Christ Jesus"* (Col. 1:28), "created according to God in true righteousness and holiness" (Eph. 4:24), "renewed in knowledge according to the image of Him who created him" (Col. 3:10) is the aim.

LIFE HIDDEN WITH CHRIST

20 Therefore, if you died with Christ from the basic principles of the world, why, as though living in the world, do you subject yourselves to regulations— 21 "Do not touch, do not taste, do not handle," 22 which all concern things which perish with the using— according to the commandments and doctrines of men? 23 These things indeed have an appearance of wisdom in self-imposed religion, false humility, and neglect of the body, but are of no value against the indulgence of the flesh.

3:1 If then you were raised with Christ, seek those things which are above, where Christ is, sitting at the right hand of God. 2 Set your mind on things above, not on things on the earth. 3 For you died, and your life is hidden with Christ in God. 4 When Christ who is our life appears, then you also will appear with Him in glory.

—Colossians 2:20—3:4

Paul uses a striking word to describe our new life in Christ. "For you have died, and your life is hid with Christ in God" (3:3, RSV). A number of sentences in Colossians 2 and 3 combine to add to the powerful impact of this image. You have *"died"* with Christ and have been *"buried"* with Him in baptism (2:12). You were also *"raised"* with Him through faith in the working of God (2:12). God *"has made you alive together with Him"* (2:13); you have been *"raised with Christ"* (3:1).

Note the emphatic underscoring of accomplished reality. It is a settled fact that we are dead with Christ. There is no question we are risen with Him. We have died to all Christ died to; we are raised to all He was raised to. We now have to live out in practice what has already happened in fact.

Mickey Rooney, the famous American actor, made witness to this in a television interview. Rooney has been crass, crude, often drunk in such appearances, usually angry and insulting. But the interviewer knew something had happened, and questioned Rooney about his recent past when he hit bottom emotionally and financially. Rooney calmly answered, "I don't mean to sound ecclesiastical, but recently I gave my life to the Lord Jesus Christ and now my past is gone."

The Christian is a new person united with Christ. The two overwhelming events through which Jesus passed into the power of an endless life were death and Resurrection. Those who are united with Him must reproduce in their personal spiritual histories these two events. To be *in* and *with* Christ is to be identified with Him in death and Resurrection. What does this mean?

United in Christ's Death

The person whose life is "hid with Christ in God" is dead to sin because He is united with Christ's death which destroyed the power of sin over us. For us, like Paul, there must be a finality about Christ making us victors over sin. There is something bold and defiant and jubilant about the way Paul spoke of death to sin and the old life by our sharing in the death of Christ. Faith in Christ means "being made comfortable unto His death, [having our] nature transformed to die as He died" (Phil. 3:10, Moffatt). Paul "has not spent his life in burying that dead man who died on the road to Damascus, or in celebrating his memory with copious floods of tears. He boldly turned his back upon him once for all in order that the new life that had come to dwell in him might have room for growth and ultimate glory."[1]

The fact is that Christ has destroyed the power of sin. Now, sharing in the death of Christ, we reckon ourselves dead to sin, and are empowered to become what we potentially are.

United in Christ's Resurrection

When Paul refers to *"Christ who is our life"* (3:4), he is making an astounding claim. The new life into which we enter by conversion is nothing else than the life of Christ Himself. If this were his only reference to it we might question it, but this is no sideline thought. Paul speaks of "the life of Jesus" being "made

371

manifest in our body" (2 Cor. 4:10). The "law of the Spirit" which overcomes the "law of sin and death" brings the "life which is in Christ Jesus" (Rom. 8:2).

This new life is not different from the "old" life only in degree; it is a new kind, a new quality of life. Paul makes the radical claim that this new life is nothing less than a new creation (2 Cor. 5:17).

This means at least two things. One, *death has no power over us.* The risen and exalted Lord conquered death. We do not wait for eternal life; it is ours now. Risen with Christ, the glorious privilege of beginning now the life with Christ which will continue eternally is ours.

Sharing Christ's risen life means a second thing: *the power which raised Jesus from the dead is also our power.* We do not have to be the victims of sin. The hampering limitations of the present order need not overcome us. We have moved from the domain of the flesh into the realm of the Spirit. Here is an illustration of it in a letter I received from a woman who with five others had attended a prayer seminar I was leading. These women were a part of a group of twelve who meet every Thursday at 6:30 A.M. for prayer, study, and sharing. Their fellowship has become the true *koinonia* where Christ lives and His Holy Spirit works. The letter confirmed that fact.

> I thought you might be interested in our group of six—obviously thoroughly enjoying the Lord, and each other.
>
> One, an alcoholic, given the simple medicine of love—last drink November, 1973.
>
> One, whose husband left her with two boys—he living here with a "fancy lady"—she, making it alone by the power of Christ.
>
> One, who has just won a battle over cancer.
>
> One, who has just gone through the anguish of placing her mother in a nursing home due to advanced arteriosclerosis.
>
> One whose husband had an affair—now both ladies are in a prayer group, praying hand in hand each week.
>
> One, who was on the verge of a nervous breakdown before coming to Junaluska (N.C.)—now praising the Lord.

She concluded her letter by asking, "How is that to prove that joy and peace are in the Lord while life grinds on?" Those women have made the magnificent discovery that the power which raised Jesus from the dead is available to us who share in His death and Resurrection.

Baptized into Christ

Baptism is Paul's reference point for talking about life *"hidden with Christ in God.* "A Christian's baptism is not unlike Jewish circumcision, Paul says. In baptism we are marked as *Christ*-ians. This is a circumcision made without hands, the circumcision of Christ in which we are *"buried with Him in baptism."*

He then becomes our life. Giacomo Manzu, the artist friend of Pope John XXIII, sculpted the newest doors of St. Peter's in Rome. One door depicts a series of death scenes, "Death by falling," "Death in war," and others. "Death by water" is there, and that is the reason for the sculptor's theme. We are welcomed into the church by *death*. This is the way we enter—the only way. Baptism, our acted out entrance into the church, is by water. So, death by water is a challenging and authentic understanding of baptism. The early church often built its baptismal fonts in the shape of tombs to make the meaning sensually graphic.

With that image clearly in mind we can begin to understand what Paul is talking about when he uses terms like "put off" and "put on" which follow in the next section.

PUT TO DEATH THE OLD

5 Therefore put to death your members which are on the earth: fornication, uncleanness, passion, evil desire, and covetousness, which is idolatry. 6 Because of these things the wrath of God is coming upon the sons of disobedience, 7 in which you yourselves once walked when you lived in them.

8 But now you yourselves are to put off all these: anger, wrath, malice, blasphemy, filthy language out of your mouth. 9 Do not lie to one another, since you have put off the old man with his deeds, 10 and have put on the new man who is renewed in knowledge according to the image of Him who created him, 11 where there is neither Greek nor Jew, circumcised nor uncircumcised, barbarian, Scythian, slave nor free, but Christ is all and in all.

—Colossians 3:5–11

Paul now moves to explain in specific terms what it means to live the new life in Christ. His words are sharp and incisive, leaving no doubt about the dramatic changes that are to be made in our lives.

"Put to death your members which are on the earth" (v. 5). *"Put off"* the evil ways in which you once walked (v. 8). *"Put on the new man"* (v. 10). Together these suggest the radical transformation that comes to those whose lives are hidden with Christ, who have died and are risen with Him.

Don't miss the radical nature of this by looking only on the surface. Paul is not talking about anything so superficial as Cinderella abandoning her servant rags to dress like a princess for the ball. If you want to go to fantasyland for a picture, Paul is talking about something like the prince who has become an ugly frog being kissed by a lovely maiden and becomes a handsome prince again. But this is nothing as peripheral as dress or appearance: it is our *condition,* our nature, that is changed. We are to *"put to death"* the "old man," and *"put on"* the "new man."

Popular talk illumines the image. When a person has been seriously ill and recovers, we say, "She is a new person." A person is depressed, down in the dumps, in despair, moping in self-pity; then something happens—he falls in love, a long-absent friend comes to see him, he has a career change, he experiences some success—and we say, "That made him a new man." At a much, much deeper level, we become new persons as we *put off* the old life and *put on* the new life of Christ.

"Put off the old man" (v. 9). Paul is talking about sin, the reality and ravages of it, its persistent power to delude us and entice us away from the new center of our lives.

You may, at first glance, discount Paul's specific sins that we are to *put off,* as echoes of a puritanism that we have long-since outgrown, as victorian as crinoline. But look again. Phillips translates the list: sexual immorality, dirty-mindedness, uncontrolled passion, evil desire, and the lust for other peoples' goods. Those sins are as modern as McDonald's hamburgers and disco dancing. Sexual immorality is rampant, destroying persons and shattering homes. In the name of self-expression and self-fulfillment we have created a promiscuous society driven by sexual passions. Witness the rampant proliferation of pornography, and the pervasion of sex symbols in advertising. Modern and relevant? Dirty-mindedness and uncontrolled passion?

Paul makes his call to put off the old nature and put on the new even more emphatic as he lists again some of the things that have to go from our lives. "But now you yourselves must lay aside all anger, passion, malice, cursing, filthy talk—have done with them (v. 8, NEB).

This is a vivid demand which is hard to take. Paul is calling for radical surgery. He is saying that we are to put to death every part of our being which is against God, and which prevents us from doing God's will. He said the same thing in Romans 8:13: "For if you live according to the flesh you will die; but if by the Spirit you put to death the deeds of the body, you will live."

The truth is that we can't perform this surgery ourselves. This is where the power of Christ comes into play. The Christian life is no do-it-yourself, make-yourself-right, lift-yourself-by-your-own-bootstraps religion. It is a religion of the heart in which all that we are is yielded to the transforming, healing power of Christ.

Paul is driving home the point that the old life is dead; we must let it die.

The indicative of faith must be matched by the imperative of morality and ethics. The supreme reality for Paul was the union of the believer with his Lord. As indicated earlier, this was a reality of status—of *position,* not yet fully worked out in experience, in *condition.* "Believers were like immigrants to a new country, not yet completely habituated to its ways of life. They had accepted citizenship in a new world and must learn to live in it." So Thomas Aquinas would pray: "Give me, O Lord, a steadfast heart which no unworthy thought can drag downward; an unconquered heart, which no tribulation can wear out; an upright heart, which no unworthy purpose may tempt aside."

That prayer reflects the stance of the person who would seek to *put off* the "old man" and *put on* the new, and leads to the positive expression of Paul's call.

PUT ON THE NEW

12 Therefore, as the elect of God, holy and beloved, put on tender mercies, kindness, humility, meekness, longsuffering; 13 bearing with one another, and forgiving one another, if anyone has a complaint against another; even as Christ forgave you, so you also must do. 14 But above all these things put on love, which is the bond of perfection.

—*Colossians 3:12–14*

As indicated earlier, the *put off—put on* language refers to baptism; and baptism is the outward and visible sign of our dying and rising with Christ. The metaphorical use of putting on new clothing has its parallel in the Old Testament. "Twill greatly rejoice in the Lord . . . for he has clothed me with the garments of salvation" (Is. 61:10, RSV). "I put on righteousness, and it clothed me; my justice was like a robe and a turban" (Job 29:14, RSV). Putting on, then, has to do with a deep and transforming inner experience which reflects itself outwardly. Again, it is not simply a matter of having a new lifestyle; it is being a new person.

Our Identity

Before moving to his positive list—what new persons must put on—Paul addresses the Colossians as *"the elect of God, holy and beloved."* What we do flows out of who we are. Being and doing cannot be separated. "who once were not a people but are now the people of God, who had not obtained mercy but now have obtained mercy" (1 Pet. 2:10). As Christians our identity is certain and clear. We are God's people; once without mercy, now the recipients of His unlimited mercy and grace.

Holy has at least two meanings. It has to do with our character—with how we act, with the attitudes and attributes of our lives. So, Paul urged us to put away the sins of our lives that we may be holy. Holy has also to do with "being set apart," dedicated. God lays His claims upon us, calls us; we respond in dedication. We now have a vocation—to be holy, to be His.

Both meanings of holy help to define our identity. But there is more: *beloved.*

Is there anything more important—to know that I am loved? To get in touch with the meaning of this, think of two or three persons who love you most. Get a picture of them clearly in mind. What do they think about you? How do they feel and act toward you? What do they do for you? Think about the strength you receive from these persons' love.

God's love for you is even greater than any of these persons you have thought about. The witness of Scripture is that God's love is unconditional, not dependent upon our merit. His love is a constant kiss of grace which can keep us going—no matter what.

Tender Mercies

Barclay calls what we are to *put on,* the "garments of Christian grace." This harmonizes with the NEB translation of the first part of verse 12: "put on the garments that suit God's chosen people, his own, his beloved." The first of these is *tender mercies.*

The Greek word is *oiktirmos*. The way this word is rendered in different translations sheds a lot of meaning. What the KJV designates "bowels of mercy," Moffatt calls "tenderness of heart," the ASV "a heart of compassion," Phillips "merciful in action." TEV and RSV translate it "compassion."

This is a great word: "compassion." Mark used it to describe Jesus' feeling toward the people of Galilee. "He has compassion on them, because they were like sheep without a shepherd." Luke used this word to designate the action of the Samaritan for the man on the Jericho road, and the response of the father to his prodigal son.

Compassion begins with pity, but it is more. Compassion is that deep response we have when we do something about our feelings of pity. I can feel sorry for you and do nothing about it. Feeling sorry for you may result in my pitying you. But to be moved by your pain, to feel your situation so deeply that I seek to act in your behalf, is compassion.

Tender mercy, as the NKJV translates the word, suggests the deep feeling of love that has to express itself in action. Mother Teresa of India incarnated this grace and expressed it as vividly as any contemporary person. A conversation with the British journalist Malcolm Muggeridge portrays the meaning clearly.

> Malcolm: Spending a few days with you, I have been immensely struck by the joyfulness of these Sisters who do what an outsider might think to be almost impossibly difficult and painful tasks.
>
> Mother Teresa: That's the spirit of our society, that total surrender, loving trust and cheerfulness. We must be able to radiate the joy of Christ, express it in our actions. If our actions are just useful actions that give no joy to the people, our poor people would never be able to rise up to the call which we want them to hear, the call to come closer to God. We want to make them feel that they are loved. If we went to them with a sad face, we would only make them much more depressed.
>
> Malcolm: Even though you took them things they needed.
>
> Mother Teresa: It is not very often things they need. What they need much more is what we offer them. In these twenty years of work amongst the people, I have come more and more to realize that it is being unwanted

that is the worst disease that any human being can ever experience. Nowadays we have found medicine for leprosy and lepers can be cured. There's medicine for TB and consumptives can be cured. For all kinds of diseases there are medicines and cures. But for being unwanted, except there are willing hands to serve and there's a loving heart to love, I don't think this terrible disease can ever be[2]

That is tender mercy: willing hands to serve because of hearts that go on loving.

Kindness

I had been living in my present home for about six months when the right time came—the time for me to share my faith with a neighbor. She was exasperated when I passed by. Everything had gone wrong during the day, and now her car wouldn't crank.

"You are so kind," she said, after we had gotten the car started. "It's good to know there are still Christians around." The perfect opening for me to respond and share.

In reflection upon that incident I was a bit amazed that she put being kind and being Christian together. Yet kindness is the second "garment of Christian grace" Paul calls us to put on. The Greek word is *chrēstotēs* or *chrēstos*, "good" or "useful." Jesus used it to describe His yoke: "My yoke is *easy.*" Kindness, then is tender goodness, goodness that is for the well-being of the other.

The word "kindness" does not appear often in new translations of the Scripture. Does this mean that the word has lost a good deal of its meaning?

The writers of Scripture defined kindness as the virtue of the person whose neighbor's good is as dear as his own. Maybe that's the reason that in every psalm where the KJV refers to the "kindness" of God, the RSV translates it "steadfast love."

Humility

Paul said the person living a new life is to put on lowliness and humility—*humbleness of mind.* Micah placed humility alongside the great strength of character which enables a person to do goodness, and to love mercy (Mic. 6:8).

There is an earthiness about this word. "Humus" is the root word for earth and out of that root the word "humble" comes. It has the dimension of meaning "of the earth."

The humble know who they are. Humility has nothing to do with self-depreciation, or cowering back, nothing to do with self-disgust at our shabby lives; nor is it a downcast, brow-beaten stance. The humble know who they are in relation to God and other persons. They have perspective, soundly estimating their strengths and weaknesses. They flaunt neither their strength nor weakness, but take their place in God's kingdom without fanfare.

The humble also know their source of power. God's presence and power in their lives gives them certainty and confidence—certainty and confidence not in the power they hold, but in the Power that holds them.

Meekness

The Greek word for meekness is *prautēs,* and the NEB translates it "gentleness." We do well to have such an alternative because "meekness" has lost its meaning in our modern day. We use the word condescendingly most of the time. We do not admire "meek" people, yet Jesus announced that the meek are among the blessed and that it is the meek who will inherit the earth.

Interestingly, and far from the modern image of meek, Aristotle defined *prautēs* as the happy mean between too much and too little anger. With that clue, we may say that the person who has *prautēs* is the person who is self-controlled, because he is God-controlled. With that as a clue, from the Christian perspective, we may say the person who has *prautēs* is a person who knows herself and operates out of the inner realization of God's control of her life. Thus meekness is very close to humility. When Christ is in control of our lives we do not have to control others. We can be gentle with strength.

Patience

(See commentary on Col. 1:11, p. 336 of this volume.)

Forbearing and Forgiving

In a recent copy session, our *Upper Room* staff was working on a very sensitive meditation about abusive parents. The point was made that we can be abusive in our language and attitude, as well as in our action.

I was convicted of my own sin. During the previous couple of days I had been abusive to my wife by silence, by shutting her out, by failing to be responsive to her need to share her life with me. I was going through a rough time, feeling a lot of pressure in some professional relationships and overwhelmed with some immediate tasks. So, I was *down.* She was *up! Some* marvelous things were happening to her, and she was experiencing excitement and joy. She bubbled over, and I allowed my downcast mood to block a positive response. I failed to share in her life. My responses were more like grunts than affirmations. Mostly, I was silent.

It hit me hard as our staff worked on the meditation about abusive parents, that many of us who are not violent in our actions, do violence to persons by our attitudes. Paul urged us to be *forebearing* with one another. To forebear has the negative meaning, "to refrain or abstain," or "to control oneself." But it also has the positive meaning of *bearing* one, or carrying. Thus one translator substitutes "affirming" for fore-bearing in this text. We are forebearing when we affirm, when we value and respect another.

When the copy session to which I referred earlier adjourned for lunch, I was alone with the knowledge that I had been abusive to Jerry by my silence. I could not live with that. I went to the phone, called her and asked her forgiveness. I experienced relief and knew that to a marked degree the tension that had characterized our relationship for the past few days would be relieved.

Forebearing and *forgiving* go together according to Paul: "Be forebearing with one another, and forgiving."

Forgiveness is at the heart of the gospel. At the core of our Christian experience of salvation is our acceptance of God's forgiveness extravagantly provided through Jesus Christ.

Now here is the rub: *forgiven persons must always be forgiving.* As God forgave us, we must forgive others. Only the forgiving can be forgiven.

Charizomai, the Greek word used in this verse, is from the root word *charis,* which means grace; thus to "forgive" is to "give graciously." This forgiveness is gift, not accomplishment. When the gracious giving of our Lord in His suffering and death is real to us, when by faith we accept that *for me,* then we can forgive others. We are not doing it by our own design, or will, or power, but *"even as Christ forgave you"* (v. 13).

When we put on the "new man" all the rules change. Grudges have to go. Revenge is out of the question. We leave judgment to God. We are forbearing and forgiving.

Love

Paul crowns his "garments of Christian grace" consistent with everything he understood and experienced: *"But above all these things put on love, which is the bond of perfection"* (v. 14). In his discussion of the word and gifts of the Holy Spirit, he said, "I show you a more excellent way" (1 Cor. 12:31), and gave the Corinthians the "hymn of love" (1 Cor. 13). He concluded that hymn by naming the great trilogy of Christian graces—faith, hope, and love—and boldly underscored *love* as the greatest of these.

In his list of the fruit of the Spirit in Gal. 5:22, Paul puts love at the top: love, joy, peace, patience, kindness, goodness, faithfulness, gentleness, self-control. Some believe that rather than being *a* fruit of the Spirit, love is *the* fruit of the Spirit, and each fruit of the Spirit which follows in the list is another expression of love (see commentary on Gal. 5:22).

Certainly in Paul's description of the "clothing" of the new person in Christ, love "binds everything together in perfect harmony" (RSV).

THE FELLOWSHIP OF NEW PERSONS IN CHRIST

15 And let the peace of God rule in your hearts, to which also you were called in one body; and be thankful. 16 Let the word of Christ dwell in you richly in all wisdom, teaching and admonishing one another in psalms and hymns and spiritual songs, singing with grace in your hearts to the Lord. 17 And whatever you do in word or deed, do all in the name of the Lord Jesus, giving thanks to God the Father through Him.
—*Colossians 3:15-17*

Paul brings his discussion of the "garments of Christian grace" to a climax by saying, *"Let the peace of God rule in your hearts"* (v. 15). As with love, we must see this as a dynamic of the church as well as personal quality. With the two verses that follow, along with an earlier verse (v. 11), this word describes the fellowship of new persons in Christ.

The NEB renders this, "Let Christ's peace be *arbiter* in your hearts." This is a colorful picture when the literal meaning of the verb is understood. It comes from the athletic arena and Paul is literally saying, "Let the peace of God be the umpire in your heart."

Isn't that vivid? Our hearts are arenas of conflict and competition. All sorts of feelings clash within. Jesus met a man who dwelled among the tombs, bound in chains, who called himself *legion*, "for I am many." Peace ruled in that man's heart as Jesus healed him. He was then seen "clothed in his right mind."

We are a legion of passion and love, of fear and hope, of jealousy and trust, of cynicism and goodwill, of indifference and concern, of distrust and awareness. How are all of these feelings to be arbitrated, to be harmonized? What feelings are to be given reign? What or where or who is the umpire to settle the clashes?

"Let Christ's peace be the umpire." Not only is He the arbiter of all my inner clashings, of the civil war that rages inside me, in my interpersonal relationships, in my family, in the world and especially in the church; in Him we have the key factor for our getting along together—the peace of Christ. To know about the garments of grace is one thing, to wear them gracefully is another. We need to possess without parading these virtues.

Gospel, Grace, and Gifts

The body-life of the Christian congregation is described in verse 16. Here is an exciting rationale to guide us as we plan programs, design curriculum, structure our life, strategize for growth, and engage in worship in our local churches. *"Let the word of Christ dwell in you richly in all wisdom, teaching and admonishing one another in psalms and hymns and spiritual songs, singing with grace in your hearts to the Lord"* (Col. 3:16).

The centrality of the word is crucial. As much as pastor/teachers who are rooted in the word, the entire body needs to be immersed in the word, to the point that it *dwells in us richly in all wisdom*. Wisdom comes from abiding with Christ and allowing His words to abide in us.

Calling forth and affirming the gifts of all our people should be a primary *modus operandi* of the fellowship of new persons in Christ—*teaching and admonishing one another.* In the body of Christ every person is ministered to and is a minister. In Ephesians 4:11–12, Paul says that "His gifts were made that Christians might be properly equipped for their service" (Phillips).

Certainly our gifts are connected with the gospel. The "word of Christ" is a synonym of His living presence within us. We are admonished to let the word of Christ dwell in us richly. The word for dwell is *oikeō; oikos,* a related word means "at home." Christ is to be "at home" in our hearts. Paul carries it even further. He says the word of Christ is to dwell *richly,* abundantly, without limits. The ministry that is given to all Christians, and for which the Holy Spirit gives us gifts, is that of sharing Christ. We are the communicators of our Lord.

That communication is not directed alone to those outside the fellowship, but is the dynamic relationship of persons within the church. We teach and admonish one another, presenting our learnings, sharing our insights, being with, holding responsible, challenging, supporting, questioning, guiding—all for the building up of the body, that we might all be equipped for ministry within and outside the church.

"With grace in your hearts to the Lord" (v. 16). Many translators substitute "thanksgiving" for "grace" in this verse, which may be more accurate. The word is charis, and the truth is the two meanings cannot be separated. In 2 Corinthians 4:15, Paul said, "For it is all for your sake, so that as grace extends to more people it may increase thanksgiving to the glory of God." So grace and thanksgiving go together. Add to that the fact that gifts of the Spirit, as talked about by Paul, charismata, have the same root word as grace and thanksgiving, and you have a rather complete picture of what the church is to be. In the fellowship Christ dwells richly, because of grace (charis). Our response is to be gracious, to be thankful (charis) and to express that in celebration of joy—psalms, hymns, spiritual songs, singing. We are a community of gifts (charisma), equipped by the Spirit to minister to each other and to the world, to share Christ within and outside the church. We are to be then a charis-matic people—grace-filled, grace-equipped, grace-celebrating—in whom Christ dwells richly and through whom grace flows to the world.

Everything about the church is to be Spirit-filled and Spirit-controlled. Our worship is to reflect the centrality of grace.

A Parable of the Kingdom

The church is to be a parable of the kingdom of God when everything is reconciled to Christ. For that reason Paul says within the church, "there is neither Greek nor Jew, circumcised nor uncircumcised, barbarian Scythian, slave nor free, but Christ is all and in all" (v. 11). Barriers are shattered, walls of separation are brought down, and the peaceable kingdom is demonstrated, though in miniature, in the church.

Anyone who is joined to Christ is joined to all others who have a share in the new community. This does not mean that uniqueness and distinctiveness is obliterated; the church is not to be a nameless, faceless fellowship. Christians are not to be carbon copies of another, living a life of cookie-cutter sameness, devoid of individual qualities. The church is made up of all these people Paul named—and his list was not meant to be complete—but the differences personified in these people cannot be grounds for discrimination or division. The Spirit makes us one and in Christ we are of equal worth.

Paul concludes this section by restating the centrality of Christ. *"Whatever you do in word or deed, do all in the name of the Lord Jesus, giving thanks to God the Father through Him"* (v. 17).

NOTES

1. H. Weinel, *St. Paul: The Man and His Work*, p. 97.

2. Malcolm Muggeridge, *Something Beautiful for God* (New York: Harper and Row, 1971), pp. 98–99.

CHAPTER FIVE—A CHRISTIAN STYLE OF RELATIONSHIPS

COLOSSIANS 3:18—4:18

Scripture Outline

Paul turns from a practical description of the new life in Christ to talk very plainly and practically about *a Christian style of relationship.* He spells out the relational gospel for marriage, family, vocation, and our everyday life. Most of the conflict we know is interpersonal conflict. We can trace most of our difficulties to difficult people. We all expect people to perform according to our standard. We need desperately to love and be loved, but often we can't accept expressions of love offered us, and the way we want to express love may be a barrier rather than a blessing in our most intimate relationships.

When we get into the setting in which Paul was writing and understand his message in light of the fact that he was a mid-first century man addressing his contemporaries about applying their new faith to their circumstances and the social conditions of their day, we can get some light and guidance for our own life and times.

THE FAMILY: A PLACE FOR PERSONS

18 Wives, submit to your own husbands, as is fitting in the Lord.

19 Husbands, love your wives and do not be bitter toward them.

20 Children, obey your parents in all things, for this is well pleasing to the Lord.

21 Fathers, do not provoke your children, lest they become discouraged.

—*Colossians 3:18–21*

As in Ephesians 5:22ff, Paul centers his teaching to the Colossians about marriage and family in Christ and family members' mutual commitment to Him: *"As is fitting in the Lord"* (v. 18). (See Ephesians 5:22—6:9 for the fuller testament).

Paul has often been criticized as being down on women. The truth is, he presented a radically new view of marriage and family which elevated women and children to a hitherto unthinkable level of equality. The Hebrew and Greek understanding of marriage reduced women to "things" to be used and enjoyed, not loved and cherished. Women were seen as totally subservient to men, not only in society but in the home. It was a man's world in every way.

Before Paul, Jesus' attitude toward women and marriage was revolutionary. He saw and treated women as persons of worth, not playthings for sexual gratification, or merely agents of procreation. On one occasion the Pharisees sought to entangle Him in a dispute about divorce. Too wise to be trapped, and too compassionate and committed *to* women to let the issue drop, He forced them to look at original and eternal intention for marriage (see Mark 9:2–9).

Paul built on these teachings and spelled out their implications for the early church. Also, he founded his teachings on the fact that the person *in Christ* has a new center of reference, a new Lord of life, and thus operates out of a totally new understanding of reality. People are brothers and sisters, all recipients of grace, and in the eyes of the Lord there is no distinction in worth between male and female.

Verses 18–21 put the emphasis on the value of persons. The family, then, is *a place for persons*—not just a place to eat and sleep, to watch TV, to rest from our work; not just a place where our lunches are fixed and our laundry done; not just a place where we park our cars and husband wife are sexually gratified in an "acceptable" sort of way.

A Center of Caring

To be a place for persons the family must be a center of caring. Paul specifies each person in the family—wives, husbands, children—as he gives specific instruction. We miss the total impact of this if we dissect it and see it only at a particular point. We are usually turned off at the first word, *"Wives, submit to your own husbands, as is fitting in the Lord"* (v. 18).

We will miss a huge part of the meaning of this and dwell on a distorted fragment if we do not see it in context. *Submission* was not a command only for wives in relation to husbands, it was one of the distinct markings of a Christian life style. "Be subject to one another out of reverence to Christ" (Eph. 5:21, RSV) was a general admonition to all Christians. There was the radical nature of the gospel. Wives, children, slaves had been freed from the *stations* to which their culture condemned them. Submission became a matter, not of fitting into the way things were and had always been, but a matter of Christian life style. The instruction Paul gave to husbands about their wives and not being bitter toward them, of not provoking their children, also adds to this radical new understanding of the preciousness of persons and the fact that "stations" had been obliterated in terms of subordinate and superordinate positions in the fellowship of new persons in Christ.

We come back to the point—the family is to be a center for caring, caring for persons who are seen as unique and precious, all the recipients of Christ's love. The family as a center for caring makes it the place we can go and be when all other doors are shut. Because we care, we *notice*. Because we care, we *listen*. Because we care, we are *honest*. Because we care, we *share*. These are the things that enable us to grow. It is in the caring relationship that we are sustained. How desperately we all need it.

Everything said in this passage is centered in Christ. Paul has just finished saying, *"And whatever you do in word or deed, do all in the name of the Lord Jesus"* (v. 17). There is no problem in a husband being the "head" of the household if the husband's life is centered in Christ Jesus, for then he will love his wife and children as Christ loved the church and gave Himself for it.

It is interesting to note that the word used for the attitude of wives in relation to the husband is different from that of children in relation to the father. Wives are to *submit*, children to *obey*. For the wife to respect her husband's position as head of the household does not imply inferiority of status. There is no reservation about "submission" if the quality of love in a relationship prohibits either partner from *using* the other selfishly, if love in the relationship is not only patterned after but is made possible by our response to the love of Jesus for us.

Discipline may become a harsh system which *provokes* and *discourages* children. Paul was aware of this, so he cautioned children and fathers. Obedience is the key word. But we must see obedience in the context of the all-pervading love of God. We trust God and can obey Him because we know He wills our ultimate good. As parents we may be able to demand obedience from our children—but that will be short-lived unless our children can trust us, and what will happen to persons in the process will be detrimental, even destructive, unless they are assured that we are committed to their ultimate well-being. Paul used two strong words here: *erethizō* which means "rouse to anger," *athumeō* which means "to be disheartened, to have one's spirit broken."

Parents' relationships with children shape their personality and especially influence how they relate to themselves and others. Paul was far ahead of his time in his concern about children. He knew that children could be robbed of their self-esteem, have their spirits broken early in life, and have to pay painfully, sometimes for a lifetime, for being emotionally crippled as a child.

When the family is a place for persons, it becomes a center of caring. Where Christ's love is communicated through parents' love, children are affirmed. In that caring context of love, children obey. A persistent style of disobedience on the part of children is usually a lack, or a distortion, or a perversion of love.

Where the family is the center of caring, the wife may be asked to be submissive to her husband—but submissive to his love, not his tyranny; a father has authority over his children, but it must be an authority that is trusted; thus authoritative, not authoritarian. The husband/father is to set the pattern of caring, loving as Jesus loved.

A Cameo of Community

The family is to be a place for persons which becomes a center of caring. That means it is to be a *cameo of community.*

Perceptive observances of the past thirty years of the human scene in the United States contend that there have been two dominant and ostensibly secular quests going on. One is the search for a personal lifestyle, a way of achieving a significant life as an individual. The other is a search for a sustaining community. Persons remain fragmented when the search is divided, for both needs are interrelated, and either is a search for a sustaining community. Persons remain fragmented when the search is divided, for both needs are interrelated, either depending on the other.

While these quests may be ostensibly secular, they are implicitly religious, and have been the major force of the Judeo-Christian tradition. The quest for a personal lifestyle that provides significance and meaning and for a sustaining community are satisfied in authentic Christianity. The family plays a significant role in both quests, especially in the search for sustaining community.

More and more, the pressures of modern living are forcing us to look to a smaller and smaller circle for our fundamental human satisfactions and self-worth. The mobility of our time, the moving in and out, the scattering of our energies, the severing of the larger family ties that has come through the move from a rural to an urban culture—all make us strangers to those around us. The family, often now reduced to a mother and father and children because geographical location excludes grandfathers, aunts, uncles, and cousins—that small family becomes the key to building community. This is the reason we talk about a *cameo of community*. The small family to which we belong is certainly not going to be adequate to sustain us as persons, but this core family should and can be a cameo of community, the place where we learn and practice what community is all about.

This calls for the kind of caring we have already talked about; it also calls for honesty of communication, transparency of character, openness to the necessity of difference, the willingness to risk the pain of conflict which is necessary for growth, the cultivation of freedom which is the key to personhood, and the insistence and commitment to responsibility which is the key to relationship.

Above all it calls for a commitment to Christ, and a willingness to be submissive to one another *in reverence to Christ.*

RELATIONSHIPS OUTSIDE THE FAMILY

[22] Bondservants, obey in all things your masters according to the flesh, not with eyeservice, as men-pleasers, but in sincerity of heart, fearing God. [23] And whatever you do, do it heartily, as to the Lord and not to men, [24] knowing that from the Lord you will receive the reward of the inheritance; for you serve the Lord Christ. [25] But he who does wrong will be repaid for what he has done, and there is no partiality.

4:1 Masters, give your bondservants what is just and fair, knowing that you also have a Master in heaven.

[2] Continue earnestly in prayer, being vigilant in it with thanksgiving; [3] meanwhile praying also for us, that God would open to us a door for the word, to speak the mystery of Christ,

for which I am also in chains, [4] that I may make it manifest, as I ought to speak.

[5] Walk in wisdom toward those who are outside, redeeming the time. [6] Let your speech always be with grace, seasoned with salt, that you may know how you ought to answer each one.

—*Colossians 3:22—4:6*

The Reality above All Realities

Paul's treatment of the family is less full in Colossians than in Ephesians, but the matter of slave/master relationship is treated pretty much the same. Probably the case of Onesimus, the runaway slave from Philemon, was uppermost in his mind. Philemon was a member of the church in Colossae and Paul's letter to him was being delivered at the same time and by the same person delivering the letter to the church.

The reality above all realities is Christ. For masters this means that they are to *"give your bondservants what is just and fair, knowing that you also have a Master in heaven"* (4:1). For slaves it means that what they do, they do *"as to the Lord and not to men, knowing that from the Lord you will receive the reward of the inheritance; for you serve the Lord Christ"* (3:23–24).

There are some differences in the Ephesian and Colossian treatment of master/slave relationships. (1) It is dearer in this passage than in Ephesians that slaves are to serve not out of fear for their masters, but they are to reserve their fear for *the Lord.* (2) The reward of the slave is defined here in a way not mentioned in Ephesians. The *inheritance,* which is life everlasting in the presence of God, is the reward of the Christian, and the only reward worth seeking. (3) In Ephesians the master is reminded that God shows no partiality; in Colossians it is the slave who is addressed with this reminder.

These differences add no significant substance to Paul's teaching about the relationship of slave and master. They do serve to underscore the reality that Christ as the Lord of our lives is the shaper of our relationships. The fact that Paul in one case addresses the master, and in another case the slave, about the non-partiality of God, drives home the point. The master cannot think God is influenced by social position; the slave has no merit, nor can he trade on the fact that men may treat him as irresponsible chattel. The key to our relationship with God is our faith in the Cross of Jesus Christ; the key that is to shape our relationship to others is the indwelling Christ who empowers us to live a *new* life.

Do not criticize Paul for not seeking to change the whole system. Celebrate the fact that his teachings contain the ultimate charter of social equality: *Before their common Master slave and freeman, female and male stand on the same footing.* (See commentary on Eph. 5:22—6:9.)

Be Motivated by Prayer

Paul extends his instructions about relationships outside the family from masters and slaves to all *"those who are outsiders"* (4:5). And his instructions relate to all relationships.

Be motivated by prayer, he says, *"being vigilant in it with thanksgiving"* (4:2). To be bound with persons in prayer secures a relationship, keeps it whole and growing, in a way nothing else can. When I pray *for* another from whom I may be estranged, I cannot remain the same in my feelings and in my separation from that person. When I pray *for* another person about whom I genuinely care, or even *for* a person I may not know, the power of love and caring is so generated within me that it flows out into the life of the other, or is "passed on" to the other in ways I may not even recognize.

When I pray *with* another I am linked with that person in a way no other common experience can bind us. There is no partnership comparable to a prayer partnership.

Walk in Wisdom

"Walk in wisdom toward those who are outside" (4:5). This has special meaning for those who would share the gospel. Paul's sense of urgency is unrivaled in Christian history. Yet he sounds a word of caution concerning our relationship with "outsiders." Phillips translates his word, "Be wise in your behavior towards non-Christians." How much of our "evangelistic witnessing" disregards the feelings and sensitivities of those we seek to win. Neurotically driven to "make our witness" and to save those who are lost, we forget that we do not save, God does. We have no power to convert; that is the work of the Holy Spirit. Our witness is not *ours; it* is our witness of Jesus Christ. If our words, and the way we present those words, do not reflect His love and concern, then we need not be surprised when they fall on stony ground.

Redeem the Time

This word of advice from Paul is connected with how we behave toward outsiders. Among the early Christians, as among those in the present, were persons whose fanatical behavior prejudiced outsiders against them. Paul wanted persons to be attracted to the gospel, not repelled from it. This is the key to understanding his words.

While it is true that the Christian is to use time wisely, there is more here than that. We are *to* live "existentially," alert *to* Christ and *for* Christ in every moment. This has at least two implications. The first is more obvious: We are to be alive to every opportunity to witness in the chance encounter, the unexpected turn in conversation, the opening that comes in the expression of a need or the asking of a question, the signal given by what may appear casual but reflects something deeper, the unplanned incident that brings the "outsider" into our life in a way that mind and heart can meet. We are to seize the critical moment when it comes.

The second implication is more inner-personal than inter-personal. Baths Mills described the critical moment this way: "Halfway through shaving it came. I should have scribbled it on the mirror with a soapy finger or shouted it to my wife in the kitchen, or muttered it to myself until it ran in my head like a tune. But now it's gone, with the whiskers down the drain. Gone forever, like the friends I never knew, the places I never visited, the lost life I never lived."

There are intersections upon which we sometimes come abruptly. We have to choose, and destiny is in the choice. There are flashes of insight that break in upon us, guidance, intuition, discernment, which, if we do not receive, record, and act upon, we lose.

Speak the Word of Grace

Paul's final word to guide us in our relationships was *"Let your speech always be with grace, seasoned with salt, that you may know how you ought to answer each one"* (4:6). Be careful about your conversation, he is saying.

Paul was speaking in the context of how we relate in conversation to outsiders in our efforts to win them for Christ, but his suggestions are relevant to our conversation with all people. Here is a guide for personal evangelism and for the ministry of sharing, which is one of the most available and exciting opportunities we have. With very rare exceptions, all of us have the opportunity of speaking with people every day. How we speak and what we say can bless or curse, create or destroy. The Epistle of James puts it graphically: "The tongue is a little member and boasts of great things. How great a forest is set ablaze by a small fire! And the tongue is a fire" (3:5–6, RSV).

Words can also bless and heal, encourage and give hope. I have among my treasured keepsakes a number of notes and letters which have come to me at the right time, doing what Eliphaz said Job's words had done: "Your words have upheld him who was stumbling, and you have made firm the feeble knees" (Job 4:4, RSV).

The fifties and early sixties were tough days for preachers in Mississippi. For me to function redemptively as a caring pastor and as a faithful prophet kept the inner and outer tension high. I failed often in both roles. I remember vividly one Sunday morning in the early sixties when I had pled the cause of love and of justice. Turmoil and tension, fear and frustration, anger and anxiety dominated the feelings of the people, surfaced above the concern for persons and commitment to the gospel of love, and charged the atmosphere so electrically that persons had difficulty speaking to each other and to me after the worship service. It may have been a sign of kindness that many of those whose anger and opposition was the most pronounced avoided greeting me at the door. I thought that was it. I had lost the cause. Would I have their ear again? Would they listen? Would I even retain my position as pastor?

Wearily I dragged myself across the lawn to my study in another building, to disrobe and debrief what was happening. On my desk was a note which said: "Maxie, I can't even tell you what I'm feeling. I don't know myself. I know that what I'm feeling is deeply wrong and what you were saying today was eternally right. I trust you, Preacher. Don't give up despite what we are saying and thinking and doing to you. You may save us yet!"

That word kept me going—for a long time. I can never think of my five years in that church in Mississippi without a picture of that man coming into my mind, and the memory of his words stirring in my heart. Words stir and sustain and encourage. They create and heal.

Now, a specific word about this verse as a guide to personal evangelism. (1) *"Let your speech always be with grace."* How you speak is vitally important. A loving spirit is essential. Do not take shortcuts, presenting a formula or a plan to win another, without taking the trouble and the time to make friends. Unfeeling invasion of the personal privacy of another will set up a bather for any sharing of Christ. If you want a formula, here is the best one I know: make a friend; be a friend; win the friend for Christ.

(2) *Let your speech be seasoned with salt.* There is a warning against our Christian witness being reduced to "sanctimonious dullness." Salty speech is *earthy. It* is rooted in where we live, and

393

the content of it is personal. My best witness is not in my knowledge of doctrinal propositions, memorized scripture, *or in a well-formulated, flawlessly presented "plan of salvation."* Rather, it is the honest sharing of what Christ has done and is doing in my life.

In ordinary Greek this metaphor, *"seasoned with salt,"* was often used for sparkling conversation. This ingredient should be present in our talk; we need to guard against stodginess or language that makes no sense to an outsider. But Paul is talking about more than *wit* or being a charming conversationalist. Remember Jesus' reference to the Christian as the "salt of the earth"? Though we must not bore our friends with pious platitudes, our talk should always contain that *salty flavor* which Christ gives our lives.

(3) *"Know how you ought to answer each* [one]." Stay centered on the person with whom you are sharing—her needs, concerns, hopes, desires. Remember and affirm the uniqueness of the person. Seek to bring out the *specialness* of the person, as salt brings out the special flavor of food. Give the person your full attention. Her agenda is more important than yours—if you really want to love that person with the love of Christ. If you respect the person, she will respect you and will hear what you have to say when the time is ripe for you to say it.

In all of this guidance there is an overarching ingredient to remember. *Speech with grace* not only suggests the way it should come through to the *ears* of the hearer—pleasant, interesting, charming, earthy—*but also the way it comes through to the heart of the hearer*—helpful, affirming, challenging, calling, inspiring, actually the word of the Lord. Because it is to be a *gracious word,* we can count on God's grace to guide our speaking, even to put the right words on our lips when we need them. We do not have to depend on our own resources for speaking. He who is Lord of our lives can certainly be Lord of our lips.

THE GAME IS FOR A TEAM

7 Tychicus, a beloved brother, faithful minister, and fellow servant in the Lord, will tell you all the news about me. 8 I am sending him to you for this very purpose, that he may know your circumstances and comfort your hearts, 9 with Onesimus, a faithful and beloved brother, who is one of you. They will make known to you all things which are happening here.

[10] Aristarchus my fellow prisoner greets you, with Mark the cousin of Barnabas (about whom you received instructions: if he comes to you, welcome him), [11] and Jesus who is called Justus. These are my only fellow workers for the kingdom of God who are of the circumcision; they have proved to be a comfort to me.

[12] Epaphras, who is one of you, a bondservant of Christ, greets you, always laboring fervently for you in prayers, that you may stand perfect and complete in all the will of God. [13] For I bear him witness that he has a great zeal for you, and those who are in Laodicea, and those in Hierapolis. [14] Luke the beloved physician and Demas greet you. [15] Greet the brethren who are in Laodicea, and Nymphas and the church that is in his house.

[16] Now when this epistle is read among you, see that it is read also in the church of the Laodiceans, and that you like-wise read the epistle from Laodicea. [17] And say to Archippus, "Take heed to the ministry which you have received in the Lord, that you may fulfill it."

[18] This salutation by my own hand—Paul. Remember my chains. Grace be with you. Amen.

—Colossians 4:7–18

Clarence Forsburg tells a story about what it means to be a part of a team. It is a story of Al McGuire and Butch Lee. McGuire was a great basketball coach, who retired from Marquette after winning the NCAA tournament in 1976. Butch Lee was a kind of prima donna player on that team. The story is about McGuire trying to teach Butch Lee about team basketball. This was the coach's word. "Now, Butch, the game is forty minutes long, and if you divide that between the two teams that means there is twenty minutes when one team will have the ball and there's twenty minutes when the other team will have the ball. There are five players on each side. That means each player will have the ball for about four minutes. Now, Butch, I know what you can do with a ball in four minutes. What I want you to show me, is what you can do for the other thirty-six minutes."

There is more than one lesson here and it goes beyond basketball to the whole of life. What do you do when someone else has the ball? When someone else is in the limelight? When you are the supporting member, not star of the game?

In his play "The Cocktail Party," T. S. Eliot spoke to these questions: "Half the harm that is done in this world is due to people

395

who want to feel important. They don't mean to do harm, but the harm does not interest them, or they do not see it, or they justify it because they are absorbed in the endless struggle to think well of themselves." That is the problem—the endless struggle to think well of ourselves, the absorbing quest for significance. Paul's final greeting to the Colossians speaks to this struggle and quest; it also addresses the question about what we do when someone else has the ball. When we read this list of names—Tychicus, Onesimus, Aristarchus, Mark, Justus, Epaphras, Luke, Demas, Nymphas, and Archippus, it is not readily apparent that this is a list of heroes of the faith. Apart from Mark and Luke, how rare it is to hear their names. So it is well that we pause now and then to celebrate the support cast. It is possible for the main character to come through with impact at center stage only if the backup crew are performing well.

The heroes of the faith, mostly unsung and unknown, are celebrated by Paul and we are inspired. On the ship of the church there are no passengers; all are members of the crew. The church is not a trumpet corps, but an orchestra; each member a different instrument playing a unique sound. Added to the sounds of others, the symphony of the gospel is lived and shared with the world.

Pathos and praise are in Paul's final word: *"Remember my chains."* Alford sets fire in our mind by calling our attention to the possibility that when Paul wrote by his own hand his chains moved over the paper; his hand was chained to the soldier who kept him. Whether literally in chains, the image is far more than symbol. Paul is a prisoner for Jesus Christ, literally, in a physical sense—locked up, detained, denied freedom—but far more important in Paul's mind is that he has voluntarily *chained* himself to Christ: *Not I, but Christ lives in me.*

So above the pathos is praise, the singing joy of one who sees in every circumstance the opportunity to preach the gospel and to live Christ. Thus the final note, as always, is grace. What has been sufficient for Paul, even in prison, is sufficient for everyone: *the all-sufficient Christ.*

INTRODUCTION TO PHILEMON

Paul's letter to Philemon is unique for several reasons. It is a private letter, addressed to a very personal concern, and the only complete private letter of Paul's that we have. A vivid witness of the providence of God, it would not be in our Bible today apart from some very surprising circumstances surrounding it. Its charm and beauty make it a notable piece of literature, and though it has nothing of the mark of Paul's doctrinal or theological system, we would be vastly poorer in our understanding of Paul's teaching without it.

The occasion for the letter can be simply stated: Onesimus, a runaway slave, was converted through the influence of Paul and became a trusted, valuable friend and co-worker for Paul during his imprisonment in Rome. Onesimus was a slave of Philemon, who lived in Colossae. Philemon had become a Christian through Paul's influence, and the church in Colossae met in his house. For a time Paul was tempted to keep Onesimus for his own support, but the two of them finally agreed that Onesimus should return to his master, even though they knew masters could do what they wished with runaway slaves brought back to their charge—including having them put to death.

The power of the letter lies in the explosiveness of the issue of slavery and the depths of Paul's understanding and compassion for the master and the slave. Paul has been seen as a supporter of the social structures of his time and thus through history has been called upon as scriptural authority for class discrimination, even the support of a system of slavery. He has been pictured as the champion of structures—family and others—in which women are inferior and do not share equal rights with men. This is not only a distortion of Paul's teaching; it is a self-serving, sinful perversion of those who use it.

It is true that Paul does not challenge the institution of slavery head-on. Nor does he radically contest the family structure which kept women in a second-class position. There is no question, however, that the new order he proclaimed, into which we enter through our new life *in Christ,* leaves no room for class and status. In Christ's kingdom, which is a present experience, "there is neither Jew nor Greek, . . . slave nor free, . . . male nor female; for you are all one in Christ Jesus" (Gal. 3:28). In Colossians and Ephesians he specifically dealt with interpersonal relations and the family structure, which included slaves, calling into question all structures that put any person in a subservient position (see commentary on Col. 3:18—4:5 and Eph. 5:22—6:9).

Lightfoot says, "the word *Emancipation* seems to be trembling on his lips, and yet he does not once utter it," in his letter to Philemon. However, the confidence is there that Philemon "will do even more" than he has been asked (v. 21). That Philemon must have done that "even more" is confirmed by the fact that he kept the letter and passed it on to posterity.

Bishop Lance Webb, author of an inspiring historical novel, *Onesimus,* based on twenty years of research, believes with many others that Onesimus became bishop of the church in Ephesus, serving there at the close of the first and beginning of the second century. This may well have been the reason for the letter to Philemon having been included in the collection of Paul's writings. At the end of his book, Webb quotes from (the) writing of Ignatius to the church at Ephesus, describing the modest but strong character of Onesimus:

> I received the welcome of your congregation in the presence of Onesimus, your bishop in this world, a man whose love is beyond words. My prayer is that you should love him in the spirit of Jesus Christ and all be like him. Blessed is He who let you have such a bishop.

Webb's closing paragraph states:

> Thus, one who once was determined to be his own master instead became a slave of Christ perhaps that he might learn to govern with compassion the people of God under his charge in Ephesus. The words of Paul and John would remain his anthem . . . "Stand fast in the freedom with which Christ has set you free. . . And above all, love one another, for God is love."

AN OUTLINE OF PHILEMON

I. A Letter of Love and Challenge: 1–25
    A. How Do You Measure a Person?: 1–7
    B. The Power of the Gospel: 8–16
    C. The Power of Persuasion: 17–25

CHAPTER ONE—A LETTER OF LOVE AND CHALLENGE

PHILEMON 1–25

Scripture Outline

How Do You Measure a Person? (1–7)

The Power of the Gospel (8–16)

The Power of Persuasion (17–25)

Max Warren in *The Christian Imperative* shared a portion of a note an African headmaster wrote to a friend, thanking him for the talks he had given at the headmaster's school. "We greatly appreciate your helpful talks on the application of the teaching of Jesus in our agricultural work and hygiene, as well as spiritual things. Until now we regarded agriculture and hygiene as secular subjects, without any connection with Christianity." It is amazing that that sort of compartmentalizing of life still goes on, in every corner of the world. What makes it so incredible and amazing is that it persists without any authority of scripture.

Jesus made no such distinctions. Religion, with prayer and worship, was never made one part of life separate from human relationship and daily labor. Some of Jesus' harshest words of condemnation were reserved for "religious" men who vainly thought their worship of God, their "church" life, could be separated from their life in the world. When he talked about judgment he put the measure for it in the realm of human relationship: "inasmuch as you have done it unto the least of these." He promised *life* and life cannot be restricted to a segment of our existence; *life* permeates all life. The leaven of Christ's spirit infuses and shapes the whole loaf of life.

Some have implied that Paul changed the religion of Jesus which throbbed with life into an arid doctrinal system. Having lived with Paul, daily and intensely, for the past two years as I have worked on this commentary, I find no support for that inference. This little letter of Philemon alone refutes such a false view of Paul. He had reflected deeply on the theological implications of the gospel, he did argue vehemently against "false" doctrine, he did feel compelled to state clearly and convincingly what Christians believe—but all this was grounded in his transforming personal experience of Jesus Christ. Also, his writing is shot through with the teaching of Jesus. The letter to Philemon resonates with an understanding of life Jesus set forth in the Sermon on the Mount and gives dynamic witness to the meaning of faith in the marketplace.

HOW DO YOU MEASURE A PERSON?

1:1 Paul, a prisoner of Christ Jesus, and Timothy our brother,
To Philemon our beloved friend and fellow laborer, 2 to the beloved Apphia, Archippus our fellow soldier, and to the church in your house:
3 Grace to you and peace from God our Father and the Lord Jesus Christ.
4 I thank my God, making mention of you always in my prayers, 5 hearing of your love and faith which you have toward the Lord Jesus and toward all the saints, 6 that the sharing of your faith may become effective by the acknowledgment of every good thing which is in you in Christ Jesus. 7 For we have great joy and consolation in your love, because the hearts of the saints have been refreshed by you, brother.
—*Philemon 1–7*

Paul begins his letter with elemental reality. Having long since given up his privileges of birth and personal achievement as "mere rubbish" (Phil. 3:8) to pursue the driving passion of his life, *the knowledge of Christ,* he states bluntly: "I'm a prisoner of Jesus Christ, and I have a brother here, Timothy, who joins me in greeting you." His letter is to Philemon, but he doesn't forget Philemon's wife, Apphia, and his son, Archippus, or the church which meets in their house. He calls Philemon *"our dearly beloved, and fellow laborer"* and Archippus *"our fellow soldier."*

He goes on in verses 5–7 to take the measure of Philemon as a man. He acknowledges Philemon's love for and faith in the Lord, and expresses his joy and consolation in Philemon's love for him.

Can anything be more important than that—who we are in relation to Christ and how we act in relation to others? There is a beautiful expression in verse 7: *"The hearts of the saints have been refreshed by you."* By the strength of his love and the gifts of that love, Philemon has strengthened the entire Christian community. No wonder for the second time Paul calls him "brother."

Modem advertising in the consumer culture of the United States has the freedom to suggest that the car you drive, the clothes you wear, the whiskey or cola you drink, the perfume or deodorant or toothpaste you use can become the measure of persons. Paul, however, tells us you measure persons by their commitment, more specifically the commitment to press on to attain the prize of the high calling of God in Christ Jesus (see Phil. 3:8–14).

Olan Wheelis, a contemporary psychoanalyst and author of a book with the intriguing title *On Not Knowing How to Live,* confesses that he experimented with a lot of ways of finding meaning and of getting his life together: "How to live? Who knows the question knows not how. Who knows not the question cannot tell . . . All my life what I have been searching for is God. That's why I've never been able to enjoy anything. Until a man has found God, he begins at no beginning and works to no end."

Paul knew that, but he would have been clearer and more specific, reversing the statement somewhat. "Until a person has been found by Christ, he or she begins at no beginning and works to no end."

THE POWER OF THE GOSPEL

[8] Therefore, though I might be very bold in Christ to command you what is fitting, [9] yet for love's sake I rather appeal to you—being such a one as Paul, the aged, and now also a prisoner of Jesus Christ— [10] I appeal to you for my son Onesimus, whom I have begotten while in my chains, [11] who once was unprofitable to you, but now is profitable to you and to me.

[12] I am sending him back. You therefore receive him, that is, my own heart, [13] whom I wished to keep with me, that on your behalf he might minister to me in my chains for the gospel. [14] But without your consent I wanted to do nothing, that your good deed might not be by compulsion, as it were, but voluntary.

15 For perhaps he departed for a while for this purpose,
that you might receive him forever, 16 no longer as a slave but
more than a slave—a beloved brother, especially to me but
how much more to you, both in the flesh and in the Lord.
—*Philemon 8–16*

Paul now makes his plea for Onesimus. His words are artful, tender, sensitive, brilliant, understanding, convincing. There is a balance of conviction and compassion—conviction about the worth of
Onesimus, a slave become a Christian; and tender compassion for
Philemon, and the dilemma of a slave-master become a Christian.
To comment on it may detract from the beauty and transparent
expression of deep love. I would beg you to read the passage again
before you continue your consideration of my comments.

The power of the gospel shines through with a rare brilliance.
The markings, faint and obvious, of the redeeming love of Christ
transforming persons, relationships and circumstances, can be noted
throughout the letter. Rehearse the story. Philemon, a wealthy man
of Colossae, hears Paul, probably on one of his business trips to
Ephesus. Captured by the message, he eventually becomes a
Christian, along with his son and wife. He emerges as a leader in the
church that grows up in Colossae and his house becomes one of the
meeting places for this new Christian community.

What about Onesimus? His story is that of the miraculous working of Christ in the life of a person. How did he meet Paul? Had he
heard him personally, in Ephesus perhaps, in the company of his
master Philemon? Or, had he seen such a transformation in his master after Philemon's conversion that curiosity drove him to inquire
about the source of this "new religion" which was making such a difference in Philemon's entire household? We can assume that there
must have been some introduction to Christianity, and perhaps to
Paul, for when Onesimus "hit bottom" as a runaway slave in Rome
and the freedom for which he had risked his life did not give him
the meaning he sought, he turned to Paul in Rome. In that relationship he found the "new life" his master, Philemon, had discovered
in this "new religion" of Jesus. How Onesimus was led to seek Paul
out is not known, but there is no more striking witness to the power
of the gospel radiating from a person's life than this story of a friend-
less slave, seeking a way through a maze of confusion, suffering, and
meaninglessness instinctively turning to Paul who is now in prison
for the sake of the gospel. You would have had great difficulty plant-
ing any doubt about the prevenient grace and providential love of

God in Onesimus' mind. How long a way he had come in his quest for freedom, by how many roads and through how much pain, since he had run away from his master. And here he was—converted through the ministry of the same man through whom his master had been converted, lovingly serving a prisoner of the Lord who was a dear friend of the master from whom he had escaped.

The name Onesimus means *useful* or *profitable*. Paul plays on that meaning and makes a point about the power of Christ to make that which is useless useful (v. 11).

Another witness of the gospel's power is expressed with subtlety in this passage, but with explosive force. Look carefully at verses 15 and 16: *"That you might receive him forever, no longer as a slave but more than a slave—a beloved brother, especially to me but how much more to you, both in the flesh and in the Lord."*

If this is not the outward and complete destruction of an oppressive order, the dynamite is planted, the fuse ignited, and the coming demolition sure. When slaves become brothers, the system has lost its control! To become inwardly free is the first, the giant, and the necessary step from which all that follows in terms of the revolution and change of outward circumstances and social structures come. When Rosa Parks, that tiny black woman in Birmingham, Alabama, refused to move to the back of the bus, an irreversible revolution in civil rights had begun in earnest.

There is no question about the compelling power of the gospel; it is almost irresistible. Those who claim the gospel, however, must be careful how they use and proclaim it. Coercion is out of harmony, even contradictory, to the content and spirit of the gospel. Paul walks a tightwire here, but keeps integrity. No doubt he is tempted to make demands of Philemon who felt deeply his "debt" to Paul. But Paul resists. *Though I might be very bold in Christ to command you what is fitting, yet for love's sake I rather appeal to you* (vv. 8, 9).

Any who would share the good news and live the gospel should note this. Coercion does not validate, but violates the gospel. Was John with the disciples in Jerusalem when Paul visited there? Did he share the teachings of Jesus with Paul? Did Paul remember that word of Jesus quoted by John? "No longer do I call you servants . . . but I have called you friends" (John 15:15). That is the mood of his appeal to Philemon.

Someone defined love as the mood of believing in miracles. Love is much more than that, but it is at least and always that.

Love believes in miracles for love is miracle. That is the reason coercion has no place in sharing the gospel—only love. When we can relate to persons in such a way, and love them to the degree we can call them "my friend," miracles happen.

Paul is willing to risk the working out of love. Love can be invited, but not compelled, so he trusts what Philemon's love will do in relation to Onesimus.

There is one other thing to be noted in this passage. In the fellowship of Christ we cannot take God's grace for granted, nor can we presume upon the grace and generosity of others. One can imagine the debate going on in Paul's mind in verses 13–14. He was trying to persuade himself that it was *right* for him to keep Onesimus, rather than send him back to Philemon. Onesimus was an invaluable helper. Paul needed him. He had become one of Paul's most beloved friends; to send him back was like sending *my own heart* (v. 12), he said. He knew that had Philemon been in Rome he would have spared nothing to be of service to Paul. Was Philemon not there, in the person of his slave? So Paul's mind worked—why should he not keep Onesimus?

But Paul could not be fooled by that rationalization. He would not presume on Philemon's generosity; he would not force an expression of love. Love could work fully only in the context of freedom. Philemon alone could decide what love required of him in relation to Onesimus as well as to Paul.

THE POWER OF PERSUASION

17 If then you count me as a partner, receive him as you would me. 18 But if he has wronged you or owes anything, put that on my account. 19 I, Paul, am writing with my own hand. I will repay—not to mention to you that you owe me even your own self besides. 20 Yes, brother, let me have joy from you in the Lord; refresh my heart in the Lord.

21 Having confidence in your obedience, I write to you, knowing that you will do even more than I say. 22 But, meanwhile, also prepare a guest room for me, for I trust that through your prayers I shall be granted to you.

23 Epaphras, my fellow prisoner in Christ Jesus, greets you, 24 as do Mark, Aristarchus, Demas, Luke, my fellow laborers.

25 The grace of our Lord Jesus Christ be with your spirit. Amen.

—*Philemon 17–25*

This final section includes Paul's last effort to encourage Philemon's obedience to his request, and his final greeting. The winsomeness of Paul's person continues to shine through.

Nothing is more persuasive than self-investment, personal identification with, and involvement in the cause you are championing. In verse 16, Paul reiterated his love for Onesimus, calling him *a beloved brother*. In verse 10, he called Onesimus *"my son,. . . whom I have begotten while in my chains."* It is interesting to note how Paul introduces the whole matter in that verse. He claims the runaway slave as his spiritual son, born while he was in prison, before he even mentions his name, Onesimus, and before he states the fact that he is a slave. That is personal involvement.

Then, in verse 17, he begins to build on his identity and involvement with Philemon, and connects Philemon and Onesimus in his own life: *"If then you count me as a partner, receive him [Onesimus] as you would me."*

"Put your money where your mouth is," is an old saying that is meant to test the seriousness of one's talk and commitment. We are persuasive when we do precisely that—when we are willing to show with our action that we mean what we say. Paul is thus willing. He offers to repay the money Onesimus took from Philemon when he ran away. It was probably a considerable sum since it had carried Onesimus all the way from Colossae to Rome and had sustained him there at least for a time.

It does not matter that Philemon will without doubt refuse such an offer; Paul is serious. He is willing himself to make restitution for his friend.

There is a curious note in verse 19 that would appear a bit coercive if it were not said in the context of the love, tenderness, and compassion Paul has already shared. He makes the statement, almost as an aside, that Philemon owes his own self to Paul. He is under an obligation to Paul that can never be paid. Paul is obviously referring to Philemon's new life in Christ in which Paul has played such a significant role.

Paul cannot resist putting the two facts together—what he has done for Philemon and what he requests Philemon do for Onesimus. Paul can do this, not coercively or in an unjustly demanding way, but because he is asking no more than the discharge of Christian duty. He is not seeking any selfish thing for himself, only something for the sake of Christ. Paul is persuading Philemon to be obedient not to Paul, but to the gospel of love. That must be the end to which we seek to persuade all persons.

Most commentators believe Paul's words about the preparation of a guest room were not a literal request. He probably never gave up hope of recovering his liberty, but it is doubtful that he had any hope of ever getting back to Macedonia. He knew the Colossian Christians, like many others, had been praying for him, and he wanted to affirm them with a cheerful word. E. F. Scott suggests the meaning may have been something like, "Before you know it I may be needing your guest chamber."

Whatever his meaning, we can well believe from his other letters from the Roman prison (Eph., Col., and Phil.) that he was broken in health, had aged prematurely, and longed often for his old friends.

He closed his letter in his typical way, adding the greetings of others to his own. George Buttrick has reminded us that in this list of names is "the gamut from wealth to poverty, from educated to uneducated. If Mark and Luke are the authors respectively of the Gospels that bear their names, they are bracketed with men whose work we hardly know, men who differ in age and nationality at a time when such differences easily became deep cleavages" (The Int. Bible, Vol. 11, p. 572). Buttrick called this the "democracy of the royal Lord," concluding, "Jesus had bridged all the chasms: they were now one in Him. . . . Each man's witness was needed. None was obscure to Paul, let alone to their common Lord."

Paul's benediction was his trademark—sometimes appearing at the beginning as well as the end of his epistles: *The grace of our Lord Jesus Christ be with your spirit.* It is the trademark and signature of all who belong to Jesus Christ.

BIBLIOGRAPHY

Barclay, William. *The All-Sufficient Christ; Studies in Paul's Letter to the Colossians.* Philadelphia: Westminster Press, 1963.

_____. *The Letters to the Galatians and Ephesians.* 2d ed. The Daily Study Bible. Philadelphia: Westminster Press, 1958.

_____. *The Letters to the Philippians, Colossians, and Thessalonians.* The Daily Study Bible. Philadelphia: Westminster Press, 1975.

_____. *The Mind of St. Paul.* New York: Harper, 1958.

Beare, Francis Wright. *A Commentary on the Epistle to the Philippians.* Harper's New Testament Commentaries. New York: Harper, 1959.

Betz, Hans Dieter. *Galatians: A Commentary on Paul's Letter to the Churches in Galatia.* Philadelphia: Fortress Press, 1979.

Caird, George Bradford. *Paul's Letters from Prison: Ephesians, Philippians, Colossians, Philemon, in the Revised Standard Version.* The New Clarendon Bible. Oxford: Oxford University Press, 1976.

Calvin, John. *Commentaries on the Epistles of Paul to the Galatians and Ephesians.* Grand Rapids: Eerdmans, 1957.

_____. *Commentaries on the Epistles of Paul the Apostle to the Philippians, Colossians, and Thessalonians.* Edinburgh: Calvin Translation Society, 1851.

Campbell, John McLeod. *The Nature of Atonement and Its Relation to Remission of Sins and Eternal Life.* New York: Macmillan, reprint 1978.

Dietrich, Suzanne de. *Toward Fullness of Life; Studies in the Letter of Paul to the Philippians.* Philadelphia: Westminster Press, 1966.

Dodd, Charles Harold. *The Meaning of Paul for Today.* London: Swarthmore Press, 1937.

Duncan, George Simpson. *The Epistle of Paul to the Galatians.* The Moffatt New Testament Commentary. London: Hodder and Stoughton, 1934.

Goodspeed, Edgar Johnson. *The Key to Ephesians.* Chicago: University of Chicago Press, 1956.

Hoskyns, E. C., and F. W. Davey. *The Fourth Gospel.* 2d ed. rev. London: Faber and Faber, 1947.

Houlden, James Leslie. *Paul's Letters from Prison: Philippians, Colossians, Philemon and Ephesians.* Pelican New Testament Commentaries. Harmondsworth: Penguin, 1970.

Hunter, Archibald Macbride. *The Gospel According to St. Paul.* Philadelphia: Westminster Press, 1967.

Keck, Leander E. *Paul and His Letters.* Proclamation Commentaries: The New Testament Witnesses for Preaching. Philadelphia: Fortress Press, 1979.

Lightfoot, Joseph Barber. *Dissertation on the Apostolic Age.* Reprinted from editions of St. Paul's Epistles. London: Macmillan, 1892.

_____. *The Epistle of St. Paul to the Galatians.* 3d reprint ed. Classic Commentary Library. Grand Rapids: Zondervan, 1962.

_____. *St. Paul's Epistle to the Ephesians.* Grand Rapids: Zondervan, 1953.

_____. *Saint Paul's Epistle to the Philippians.* New York: Macmillan, 1896.

Mackintosh, Hugh R. *Doctrine of the Person of Christ.* Naperville, Ill.: Allenson, 1912.

Martin, Hugh. *Paul's Letters to His Friends: A Guide to the Epistles.* London: SCM, 1953.

Milton, C. Leslie. *The Formation of the Pauline Corpus of Letters.* London: Epworth Press, 1955.

Moule, C. F. D. *The Epistles of Paul The Apostle to the Colossians and to Philemon.* The Cambridge Greek Testament Commentary. Cambridge: University Press, 1957.

Moule, H. C. G. *The Epistle to the Ephesians.* The Cambridge Bible for Schools and Colleges. Cambridge: University Press, 1895.

_____. *The Epistle to the Philippians.* The Cambridge Bible for Schools and Colleges. Cambridge: University Press, 1890.

Rail, Harris Franklin. *According to Paul.* New York: Scribner, 1944. Robertson, Archibald Thomas. *Paul, The Interpreter of Christ.* New York: George H. Doran, 1921.

Scott, Charles Archibald Anderson. *Christianity According to St. Paul* Cambridge: University Press, 1927.

_____. *Footnotes to St. Paul.* Cambridge: University Press, 1935.

Scott, Ernest Findlay. *The Epistles of Paul to the Colossians, to Philemon and to the Ephesians.* The Moffatt New Testament Commentary. New York: R. R. Smith, 1930.

Stewart, James Stuart. *A Man in Christ; The Vital Elements of Paul's Religion.* New York: Harper, 1935.